Instructor's Solutions Manual

Cindy Trimble & Associates

Basic College Mathematics

SIXTH EDITION

Essentials of Basic College Mathematics

SECOND EDITION

John Tobey   Jeffrey Slater   Jamie Blair

Prentice Hall
is an imprint of

Upper Saddle River, NJ 07458

Editorial Director: Christine Hoag
Editor in Chief: Paul Murphy
Senior Project Editor: Lauren Morse
Assistant Editor: Christine Whitlock
Senior Managing Editor: Linda Mihatov Behrens
Associate Managing Editor: Bayani Mendoza de Leon
Project Manager: Marianne Groth
Art Director: Heather Scott
Supplement Cover Manager: Jim Linehan
Operations Specialist: Ilene Kahn
Senior Operations Supervisor: Diane Peirano

Prentice Hall
is an imprint of

© 2009 Pearson Education, Inc.
Pearson Prentice Hall
Pearson Education, Inc.
Upper Saddle River, NJ 07458

Printed in the United States of America
10 9 8 7 6 5 4

ISBN-13:   978-0-321-56853-3

ISBN-10:   0-321-56853-2

Pearson Education Ltd., London
Pearson Education Singapore, Pte. Ltd.
Pearson Education Canada, Inc.
Pearson Education—Japan
Pearson Education Australia PTY, Limited
Pearson Education North Asia, Ltd., Hong Kong
Pearson Educación de Mexico, S.A. de C.V.
Pearson Education Malaysia, Pte. Ltd.
Pearson Education Upper Saddle River, New Jersey

Contents

Chapter 1

1.1 Exercises

2. $9519 = 9000 + 500 + 10 + 9$

4. $701,285 = 700,000 + 1000 + 200 + 80 + 5$

6. 46,198,253
$= 40,000,000 + 6,000,000 + 100,000 + 90,000$
$+ 8000 + 200 + 50 + 3$

8. 820,310,574
$= 800,000,000 + 20,000,000 + 300,000 + 10,000$
$+ 500 + 70 + 4$

10. $500 + 90 + 6 = 596$

12. $7000 + 600 + 50 + 2 = 7652$

14. $60,000 + 7000 + 200 + 4 = 67,204$

16. $300,000 + 40,000 + 800 = 340,800$

18. a. 0

 b. 800,000

20. a. 9

 b. 9000

22. $376 = $ three hundred seventy-six

24. $7606 = $ seven thousand, six hundred six

26. $55,742 = $ fifty-five thousand, seven hundred forty-two

28. $370,258 = $ three hundred seventy thousand, two hundred fifty-eight

30. $68,089,213 = $ sixty-eight million, eighty-nine thousand, two hundred thirteen

32. $7,436,310,400 = $ seven billion, four hundred thirty-six million, two hundred ten thousand, four hundred

34. 3189

36. 203,374

38. 450,300,249

40. six thousand, three hundred eighty-three

42. 7 million or 7,000,000

44. 8 million or 8,000,000

46. 77,185,000

48. 401,000

50. a. 3

 b. 4

52. a. 9

 b. 7

54. 914,002,052,409,006

56. 6E22 or 60,000,000,000,000,000,000,000

58. 195

Classroom Quiz 1.1

1. $41,127 = 40,000 + 1000 + 100 + 20 + 7$

2. five million, three hundred twenty-seven thousand, eight hundred ninety-six

3. 422,985

1.2 Exercises

2. When zero is added to any number, the sum is identical to that number.

4.

+	1	6	5	3	0	9	4	7	2	8
3	4	9	8	6	3	12	7	10	5	11
9	10	15	14	12	9	18	13	16	11	17
4	5	10	9	7	4	13	8	11	6	12
0	1	6	5	3	0	9	4	7	2	8
2	3	8	7	5	2	11	6	9	4	10
7	8	13	12	10	7	16	11	14	9	15
8	9	14	13	11	8	17	12	15	10	16
1	2	7	6	4	1	10	5	8	3	9
6	7	12	11	9	6	15	10	13	8	14
5	6	11	10	8	5	14	9	12	7	13

6.
$$\begin{array}{r} 4 \\ 6 \\ 2 \\ + 7 \\ \hline 19 \end{array}$$

8.
$$\begin{array}{r} 1 \\ 5 \\ 5 \\ 9 \\ + 9 \\ \hline 29 \end{array}$$

10.
$$\begin{array}{r} 63 \\ 11 \\ + 6 \\ \hline 80 \end{array}$$

12.
$$\begin{array}{r} 54 \\ 21 \\ + 23 \\ \hline 98 \end{array}$$

14.
$$\begin{array}{r} 5773 \\ 425 \\ + 67 \\ \hline 6265 \end{array}$$

16.
$$\begin{array}{r} 5017 \\ 2984 \\ + 1328 \\ \hline 9329 \end{array}$$

18.
$$\begin{array}{r} 6\ 753 \\ + 3\ 265 \\ \hline 10,018 \end{array}$$

20.
$$\begin{array}{r} 83,596 \\ + 56,384 \\ \hline 139,980 \end{array}$$

22.
$$\begin{array}{r} 24 \\ 39 \\ 16 \\ 14 \\ + 9 \\ \hline 102 \end{array} \qquad \begin{array}{r} 9 \\ 14 \\ 16 \\ 39 \\ + 24 \\ \hline 102 \end{array}$$

24.
$$
\begin{array}{r}
426 \\
39 \\
6 \\
52 \\
+\ 802 \\
\hline
1325
\end{array}
\qquad
\begin{array}{r}
802 \\
52 \\
6 \\
39 \\
+\ 426 \\
\hline
1325
\end{array}
$$

26.
$$
\begin{array}{r}
582 \\
1\ 674 \\
336 \\
+\ 8\ 458 \\
\hline
11{,}050
\end{array}
$$

28.
$$
\begin{array}{r}
4{,}002{,}983 \\
2{,}134{,}702 \\
+\ 3{,}592{,}001 \\
\hline
9{,}729{,}686
\end{array}
$$

30.
$$
\begin{array}{r}
982{,}306{,}000 \\
+\ 583{,}215{,}320 \\
\hline
1{,}565{,}521{,}320
\end{array}
$$

32.
$$
\begin{array}{r}
32{,}500 \\
763{,}420 \\
+\ 2{,}837{,}667 \\
\hline
3{,}633{,}587
\end{array}
$$

34. $125 + 60 + 140 + 75 = 400$

36. $20 + 205 + 95 + 42 + 80 = 442$

38.
$$
\begin{array}{r}
235 \\
198 \\
+\ 282 \\
\hline
715
\end{array}
$$
The total amount of money Richy saved is $715.

40.
$$
\begin{array}{r}
2230 \\
2655 \\
+\ 2570 \\
\hline
7455
\end{array}
$$
The total amount for the three months is $7455.

42.
$$
\begin{array}{r}
827 \\
405 \\
631 \\
+\ 472 \\
\hline
2335
\end{array}
$$
2335 feet of fencing are needed.

44.
$$
\begin{array}{r}
5{,}400{,}000 \\
1{,}100{,}000 \\
+\ 1{,}000{,}000 \\
\hline
7{,}500{,}000
\end{array}
$$
The total area is 7,500,000 square miles.

46.
$$
\begin{array}{r}
152{,}239 \\
31{,}820 \\
+\ 26{,}828 \\
\hline
210{,}887
\end{array}
$$
The total area of these three lakes is 210,887 square miles.

48. **a.**
$$
\begin{array}{r}
14{,}311 \\
11{,}077 \\
+\ 12{,}580 \\
\hline
37{,}968
\end{array}
$$
37,968 motorcycles passed inspection

    b.
$$
\begin{array}{r}
37{,}968 \\
56 \\
158 \\
+\ 97 \\
\hline
38{,}279
\end{array}
$$
38,279 motorcycles were assembled.

50.
$$
\begin{array}{r}
21 \\
17 \\
+\ 87 \\
\hline
125
\end{array}
$$
She drove 125 miles.

52. Two sides are 930 feet.
$$\frac{3456}{2} = 1728$$
The other two sides are $1728 - 930 = 798$ feet.

54. $2{,}368{,}521{,}788 + 5{,}721{,}368{,}701 + 4{,}027{,}399{,}206$
$= 12{,}117{,}289{,}695$

56. Answers may vary. A sample is: You could not add the addends in reverse order to check the addition.

Cumulative Review

58. $76{,}208{,}941 =$ seventy-six million, two hundred eight thousand, nine hundred forty-one

59. $121{,}000{,}374 =$ one hundred twenty-one million, three hundred seventy-four

60. eight million, seven hundred twenty-four thousand, three hundred ninety-six $= 8{,}724{,}396$

61. nine million, fifty-one thousand, seven hundred
nineteen = 9,051,719

62. twenty-eight million, three hundred eighty-seven
thousand, eighteen = 28,387,018

Classroom Quiz 1.2

1.
$$\begin{array}{r} 37 \\ 22 \\ 86 \\ 13 \\ + 8 \\ \hline 166 \end{array}$$

2.
$$\begin{array}{r} 982 \\ 531 \\ + 207 \\ \hline 1720 \end{array}$$

3.
$$\begin{array}{r} 721,605 \\ 3,286 \\ 19,125 \\ + 200,290 \\ \hline 944,306 \end{array}$$

1.3 Exercises

2. Since there are not enough ones to subtract 8
ones from 7 ones, we borrow. This means we
change the 1 hundred to an equivalent 10 tens.
From the 10 tens we borrow one, making it 9
tens and 10 ones. Now we have 7 ones and 10
ones or 17 ones. 17 ones subtract 8 ones is 9
ones and 9 tens subtract 8 tens is 1 ten. Thus,
$107 - 88 = 19$.

4. In subtraction, we can subtract numbers
representing the same unit. Thus, we need to
change 7 feet to a number that measures inches.
Since 1 foot equals 12 inches, 7 feet equals
84 inches. Now we subtract:
84 inches − 11 inches = 73 inches.

6.
$$\begin{array}{r} 17 \\ - 8 \\ \hline 9 \end{array}$$

8.
$$\begin{array}{r} 14 \\ - 5 \\ \hline 9 \end{array}$$

10.
$$\begin{array}{r} 17 \\ - 9 \\ \hline 8 \end{array}$$

12.
$$\begin{array}{r} 12 \\ - 7 \\ \hline 5 \end{array}$$

14.
$$\begin{array}{r} 15 \\ - 8 \\ \hline 7 \end{array}$$

16.
$$\begin{array}{r} 16 \\ - 9 \\ \hline 7 \end{array}$$

18.
$$\begin{array}{r} 10 \\ - 7 \\ \hline 3 \end{array}$$

20.
$$\begin{array}{r} 12 \\ - 5 \\ \hline 7 \end{array}$$

22.
$$\begin{array}{r} 96 \\ - 51 \\ \hline 45 \end{array}$$
Check:
$$\begin{array}{r} 51 \\ + 45 \\ \hline 96 \end{array}$$

24.
$$\begin{array}{r} 77 \\ - 36 \\ \hline 41 \end{array}$$
Check:
$$\begin{array}{r} 36 \\ + 41 \\ \hline 77 \end{array}$$

26.
$$\begin{array}{r} 189 \\ - 65 \\ \hline 124 \end{array}$$
Check:
$$\begin{array}{r} 65 \\ + 124 \\ \hline 189 \end{array}$$

28.
$$\begin{array}{r} 659 \\ -\ 247 \\ \hline 412 \end{array}$$
Check: 247
$$\begin{array}{r} +\ 412 \\ \hline 659 \end{array}$$

30.
$$\begin{array}{r} 5780 \\ -\ 530 \\ \hline 5250 \end{array}$$
Check: 530
$$\begin{array}{r} +\ 5250 \\ \hline 5780 \end{array}$$

32.
$$\begin{array}{r} 243,951 \\ -\ 12,400 \\ \hline 231,551 \end{array}$$
Check: 12,400
$$\begin{array}{r} +\ 231,551 \\ \hline 243,951 \end{array}$$

34.
$$\begin{array}{r} 807,965 \\ -\ 304,214 \\ \hline 503,751 \end{array}$$
Check: 304,214
$$\begin{array}{r} +\ 503,751 \\ \hline 807,965 \end{array}$$

36.
$$\begin{array}{r} 45 \\ +\ 141 \\ \hline 186 \end{array}$$
Correct

38.
$$\begin{array}{r} 7254 \\ +\ 2702 \\ \hline 9956 \end{array}$$
Correct

40.
$$\begin{array}{r} 3\ 200 \\ +\ 7\ 670 \\ \hline 10,870 \end{array}$$
Incorrect
$$\begin{array}{r} 7890 \\ -\ 3200 \\ \hline 4690 \end{array}$$

42.
$$\begin{array}{r} 41,181 \\ +\ 58,402 \\ \hline 99,583 \end{array}$$
Correct

44.
$$\begin{array}{r} 86 \\ -\ 33 \\ \hline 53 \end{array}$$

46.
$$\begin{array}{r} 136 \\ -\ 95 \\ \hline 41 \end{array}$$

48.
$$\begin{array}{r} 706 \\ -\ 435 \\ \hline 271 \end{array}$$

50.
$$\begin{array}{r} 861 \\ -\ 345 \\ \hline 516 \end{array}$$

52.
$$\begin{array}{r} 50,000 \\ -\ 7\ 338 \\ \hline 42,662 \end{array}$$

54.
$$\begin{array}{r} 361,000 \\ -\ 121,520 \\ \hline 239,480 \end{array}$$

56.
$$\begin{array}{r} 64,381 \\ -\ 29,997 \\ \hline 34,384 \end{array}$$

58.
$$\begin{array}{r} 3,554,830 \\ -\ 1,710,913 \\ \hline 1,843,917 \end{array}$$

60. $x + 35 = 50$
$15 + 35 = 50$
$x = 15$

62. $25 = x + 18$
$25 = 7 + 18$
$x = 7$

64. $140 + x = 200$
$140 + 60 = 200$
$x = 60$

66.
$$\begin{array}{r} 138,203 \\ -\ 91,951 \\ \hline 46,252 \end{array}$$
Gibson received 46,252 votes.

68. $\begin{array}{r} 22,070,400 \\ -\ 19,018,560 \\ \hline 3,051,840 \end{array}$

The Nile river is 3,051,840 feet longer.

70.   Total received = $3450
Total used = $375 + $2300 = $2675
Down payment = $3450 − $2675 = $775

72. $\begin{array}{r} 9,679,052 \\ -\ 7,823,194 \\ \hline 1,855,858 \end{array}$

1,855,858 people is the population increase.

74.   Illinois = 12,051,683
Indiana + Minnesota = 6,045,521 + 4,830,784
                    = 10,876,305
Difference = 12,057,683 − 10,876,305
           = 1,175,378 people

76. $\begin{array}{r} 9,295,297 \\ -\ 8,881,826 \\ \hline 413,471 \end{array}$

413,471 people is the population increase.

78.   Highest − Lowest = 13,216,340 − 5,263,820
                  = 7,952,520 people

80. $\begin{array}{r} 59 \\ -\ 48 \\ \hline 11 \end{array}$

The increase in the number of homes sold in Irving from 2006 to 2007 was 11 homes.

82. $\begin{array}{r} 190 \\ -\ 157 \\ \hline 33 \end{array}$

The decrease in the number of homes sold in Harvey from 2005 to 2006 was 33 homes.

84. $\begin{array}{r} 279 \\ -\ 261 \\ \hline 18 \end{array}$ $\begin{array}{r} 298 \\ -\ 279 \\ \hline 19 \end{array}$

The greatest change in the number of homes sold in Manchester occurred between 2006 and 2007.

86.   Winchester: 132
Willow Creek: 150
Essex: 72
Manchester: 261
Irving: 47
Harvey: 190
He should select Willow Creek and Harvey.

88.   It is true for all a and b if $c = 0$.
For example: $5 - (3 - 0) = (5 - 3) - 0$
$$5 - 3 = 2 - 0$$
$$2 = 2$$

90. $\begin{array}{r} 300 \\ -\ 228 \\ \hline 72 \end{array}$

Convert 72 feet to the number of 12-foot sections.

Now, $\dfrac{17}{12} = 6$ and each section costs

$80 + $40 = $120.

$\begin{array}{r} \$120 \\ \times\ \ 6 \\ \hline \$720 \end{array}$

Cumulative Review

91.   eight million, four hundred sixty-six thousand, eighty-four = 8,466,084

92.   296,308 = two hundred ninety-six thousand, three hundred eight

93. $\begin{array}{r} 25 \\ 75 \\ 80 \\ 20 \\ +\ 18 \\ \hline 218 \end{array}$

94. $\begin{array}{r} 278,563 \\ +\ 896,187 \\ \hline 1,174,750 \end{array}$

Classroom Quiz 1.3

1. $\begin{array}{r} 7631 \\ -\ 892 \\ \hline 6739 \end{array}$

2. $\begin{array}{r} 706,350 \\ -\ 287,809 \\ \hline 418,541 \end{array}$

3. $\begin{array}{r} 26,300,500 \\ -\ 18,279,156 \\ \hline 8,021,344 \end{array}$

1.4 Exercises

2. You can write 13 as $10 + 3$ and distribute 4 over the addition. $4 \times (10 + 3) = (4 \times 10) + (4 \times 3)$

4.

×	2	7	0	5	3	4	8	12	6	9
1	2	7	0	5	3	4	8	12	6	9
6	12	42	0	30	18	24	48	72	36	54
5	10	35	0	25	15	20	40	60	30	45
3	6	21	0	15	9	12	24	36	18	27
0	0	0	0	0	0	0	0	0	0	0
9	18	63	0	45	27	36	72	108	54	81
4	8	28	0	20	12	16	32	48	24	36
7	14	49	0	35	21	28	56	84	42	63
2	4	14	0	10	6	8	16	24	12	18
8	16	56	0	40	24	32	64	96	48	72

6.
$$\begin{array}{r} 21 \\ \times\ 4 \\ \hline 84 \end{array}$$

8.
$$\begin{array}{r} 15 \\ \times\ 6 \\ \hline 90 \end{array}$$

10.
$$\begin{array}{r} 95 \\ \times\ 7 \\ \hline 665 \end{array}$$

12.
$$\begin{array}{r} 313 \\ \times\ 3 \\ \hline 939 \end{array}$$

14.
$$\begin{array}{r} 538 \\ \times\ 8 \\ \hline 4304 \end{array}$$

16.
$$\begin{array}{r} 5203 \\ \times\ 2 \\ \hline 10,406 \end{array}$$

18.
$$\begin{array}{r} 31,206 \\ \times\ 3 \\ \hline 93,618 \end{array}$$

20.
$$\begin{array}{r} 3\,215 \\ \times\ 6 \\ \hline 19,290 \end{array}$$

22.
$$\begin{array}{r} 48,761 \\ \times\ 7 \\ \hline 341,327 \end{array}$$

24.
$$\begin{array}{r} 257,021 \\ \times\ 9 \\ \hline 2,313,189 \end{array}$$

26.
$$\begin{array}{r} 278 \\ \times\ 10 \\ \hline 2780 \end{array}$$

28.
$$\begin{array}{r} 89,361 \\ \times\ \ \ \ 100 \\ \hline 8,936,100 \end{array}$$

30.
$$\begin{array}{r} 579 \\ \times\ 1000 \\ \hline 579,000 \end{array}$$

32.
$$\begin{array}{r} 614,260 \\ \times\ \ \ \ 10,000 \\ \hline 6,142,600,000 \end{array}$$

34.
$$\begin{array}{r} 332 \\ \times\ 30 \\ \hline 9960 \end{array}$$

36.
$$\begin{array}{r} 4230 \\ \times\ \ 20 \\ \hline 84,600 \end{array}$$

38.
$$\begin{array}{r} 62,000 \\ \times\ \ \ \ 3000 \\ \hline 186,000,000 \end{array}$$

40.
$$\begin{array}{r} 432 \\ \times\ 13 \\ \hline 1296 \\ 432 \\ \hline 5616 \end{array}$$

42.
$$\begin{array}{r} 163 \\ \times\ 35 \\ \hline 815 \\ 489 \\ \hline 5705 \end{array}$$

44.
$$\begin{array}{r} 68 \\ \times\ 49 \\ \hline 612 \\ 272 \\ \hline 3332 \end{array}$$

46.
$$\begin{array}{r} 780 \\ \times\ 24 \\ \hline 3\ 120 \\ 15\ 60 \\ \hline 18,720 \end{array}$$

48.
$$\begin{array}{r} 652 \\ \times\ 92 \\ \hline 1\ 304 \\ 5\ 868 \\ \hline 59,984 \end{array}$$

50.
$$\begin{array}{r} 498 \\ \times\ 39 \\ \hline 4\ 482 \\ 14\ 94 \\ \hline 19,422 \end{array}$$

52.
$$\begin{array}{r} 1268 \\ \times\ 38 \\ \hline 10\ 144 \\ 38\ 04 \\ \hline 48,184 \end{array}$$

54.
$$\begin{array}{r} 3078 \\ \times\ 72 \\ \hline 6\ 156 \\ 215\ 46 \\ \hline 221,616 \end{array}$$

56.
$$\begin{array}{r} 3725 \\ \times\ 546 \\ \hline 22\ 350 \\ 149\ 00 \\ 1\ 862\ 5 \\ \hline 2,033,850 \end{array}$$

58.
$$\begin{array}{r} 392 \\ \times\ 187 \\ \hline 2\ 744 \\ 31\ 36 \\ 39\ 2 \\ \hline 73,304 \end{array}$$

60.
$$\begin{array}{r} 5092 \\ \times\ \ \ \ 302 \\ \hline 10\ 184 \\ 00\ 00 \\ 1\ 527\ 6 \\ \hline 1,537,784 \end{array}$$

62.
$$\begin{array}{r} 2074 \\ \times\ \ \ \ 1003 \\ \hline 6\ 222 \\ 2\ 074 \\ \hline 2,080,222 \end{array}$$

64.
$$\begin{array}{r} 15,200 \\ \times\ \ \ \ \ 30 \\ \hline 456,000 \end{array}$$

66.
$$\begin{array}{r} 302 \\ \times\ \ 30 \\ \hline 9060 \end{array}$$

68.
$$\begin{array}{r} 3000 \\ \times\ \ \ \ 302 \\ \hline 906,000 \end{array}$$

70. $8 \times 3 \times 2 = 24 \times 2 = 48$

72. $15 \times 4 \times 4 = 60 \times 4 = 240$

74.
$$\begin{array}{r} 526 \\ \times\ \ \ \ 21 \\ \hline 526 \\ 10\ 52 \\ \hline 11,046 \end{array}$$

76. $5 \cdot 10 \cdot 18 \cdot 2 = 50 \cdot 36 = 1800$

78. $x = 0$

80.
$$\begin{array}{r} 15 \\ \times\ 60 \\ \hline 900 \end{array}$$
The area is 900 square millimeters.

82. $4 \times 5 + 12 \times 8 = 20 + 96 = 116$
The surveillance area is 116 square miles.

84.
$$\begin{array}{r} 345 \\ \times\ \ \ \ 8 \\ \hline \$2760 \end{array}$$
The total cost of the purchase is $2760.

86.
$$\begin{array}{r} 276 \\ \times\ \ \ 8 \\ \hline \$2208 \end{array}$$
The cost for the car rental is $2208.

88.
$$\begin{array}{r} 48 \\ \times 12 \\ \hline 96 \\ 48 \\ \hline 576 \end{array}$$
576 miles is the distance she can travel.

90.
$$\begin{array}{r} 125 \\ \times\ \ 24 \\ \hline 500 \\ 250 \\ \hline 3000 \end{array}$$
Jorge contributes $3000 to his IRA in one year.

92.
$$\begin{array}{r} 15,800,000 \\ \times\ \ \ \ \ \ \ \ \ \ \ 22,000 \\ \hline 347,600,000,000 \end{array}$$
The approximate total yearly income is
$347,600,000,000.

94.
$$\begin{array}{rrrr} 18 & 26 & 54 & 36 \\ \times\ 2 & \times\ 4 & \times\ 1 & 104 \\ \hline 36 & 104 & 54 & +\ 54 \\ & & & \hline \\ & & & 194 \text{ white paws} \end{array}$$

96.
$$\begin{array}{rrrr} 18 & 26 & 54 & 0 \\ \times\ 0 & \times\ 1 & \times\ 2 & 26 \\ \hline 0 & 26 & 108 & +\ 108 \\ & & & \hline \\ & & & 134 \text{ white ears} \end{array}$$

98. $7(x) = 56$
$7(8) = 56$
$x = 8$

100. $63 = 9(x)$
$63 = 9(7)$
$x = 7$

102. Yes
$5 \times (8 - 3) = 5 \times 8 - 5 \times 3$
$a \times (b - c) = a \times b - a \times c$

Cumulative Review

103.   34,084
          − 27,328
          ‾‾‾‾‾‾‾‾
           6,756

104.   263
             27
            891
              5
          + 63
          ‾‾‾‾‾‾
           1249

105.   1278 − (345 + 128) = 1278 − 473 = $805

106.   1758
           − 1672
          ‾‾‾‾‾‾
            $86

107.   37,125
          − 34,988
          ‾‾‾‾‾‾‾‾
           2 137 people

108.   1,113,539,000,000
          −   720,800,000,000
          ‾‾‾‾‾‾‾‾‾‾‾‾‾‾‾‾‾‾‾‾
              $392,739,000,000

Classroom Quiz 1.4

1.   26,523
         ×   8
         ‾‾‾‾‾‾‾‾‾
         212,184

2.   83
          × 57
          ‾‾‾‾
          581
          415
          ‾‾‾‾
          4731

3.   782
           ×   345
           ‾‾‾‾‾‾
            3 910
           31 28
          234 6
          ‾‾‾‾‾‾
          269,790

1.5 Exercises

2. $5\overline{)35}$ with quotient 7

4. $4\overline{)32}$ with quotient 8

6. $9\overline{)27}$ with quotient 3

8. $7\overline{)49}$ with quotient 7

10. $4\overline{)16}$ with quotient 4

12. $9\overline{)81}$ with quotient 9

14. $6\overline{)54}$ with quotient 9

16. $4\overline{)28}$ with quotient 7

18. $8\overline{)64}$ with quotient 8

20. $9\overline{)72}$ with quotient 8

22. $1\overline{)8}$ with quotient 8

24. $7\overline{)0}$ with quotient 0

26. 12 ÷ 0
         undefined

28. $7\overline{)0}$ with quotient 0

30. $5\overline{)5}$ with quotient 1

32.
$$8)\overline{42} \quad \text{5 R 2}$$
$$\underline{40}$$
$$2$$

Check: 5
$$\underline{\times\, 8}$$
$$40$$
$$\underline{+\, 2}$$
$$42$$

34.
$$9)\overline{75} \quad \text{8 R 3}$$
$$\underline{72}$$
$$3$$

Check: 8
$$\underline{\times\, 9}$$
$$72$$
$$\underline{+\, 3}$$
$$75$$

36.
$$6)\overline{103} \quad \text{17 R 1}$$
$$\underline{6}$$
$$43$$
$$\underline{42}$$
$$1$$

Check: 17
$$\underline{\times\, 6}$$
$$102$$
$$\underline{+\, 1}$$
$$103$$

38.
$$8)\overline{427} \quad \text{53 R 3}$$
$$\underline{40}$$
$$27$$
$$\underline{24}$$
$$3$$

Check: 53
$$\underline{\times\, 8}$$
$$424$$
$$\underline{+\, 3}$$
$$427$$

40.
$$7)\overline{294} \quad \text{42}$$
$$\underline{28}$$
$$14$$
$$\underline{14}$$
$$0$$

Check: 42
$$\underline{\times\, 7}$$
$$294$$

42.
$$8)\overline{224} \quad \text{28}$$
$$\underline{16}$$
$$64$$
$$\underline{64}$$
$$0$$

Check: 28
$$\underline{\times\, 8}$$
$$224$$

44.
$$3)\overline{758} \quad \text{252 R 2}$$
$$\underline{6}$$
$$15$$
$$\underline{15}$$
$$8$$
$$\underline{6}$$
$$2$$

46.
$$7)\overline{403} \quad \text{57 R 4}$$
$$\underline{35}$$
$$53$$
$$\underline{49}$$
$$4$$

48.
$$9)\overline{4095} \quad \text{455}$$
$$\underline{36}$$
$$49$$
$$\underline{45}$$
$$45$$
$$\underline{45}$$
$$0$$

50.
$$
\begin{array}{r}
1347 \text{ R } 4 \\
6\overline{)8086} \\
\underline{6} \\
20 \\
\underline{18} \\
28 \\
\underline{24} \\
46 \\
\underline{42} \\
4
\end{array}
$$

52.
$$
\begin{array}{r}
3021 \text{ R } 1 \\
6\overline{)18,127} \\
\underline{18} \\
1 \\
\underline{0} \\
12 \\
\underline{12} \\
7 \\
\underline{6} \\
1
\end{array}
$$

54.
$$
\begin{array}{r}
4027 \text{ R } 7 \\
8\overline{)32,223} \\
\underline{32} \\
2 \\
\underline{0} \\
22 \\
\underline{16} \\
63 \\
\underline{56} \\
7
\end{array}
$$

56.
$$
\begin{array}{r}
40 \text{ R } 2 \\
5\overline{)202} \\
\underline{20} \\
2 \\
\underline{0} \\
2
\end{array}
$$

58.
$$
\begin{array}{r}
9 \\
36\overline{)324} \\
\underline{324} \\
0
\end{array}
$$

60.
$$
\begin{array}{r}
6 \\
72\overline{)432} \\
\underline{432} \\
0
\end{array}
$$

62.
$$
\begin{array}{r}
523 \text{ R } 11 \\
13\overline{)6810} \\
\underline{65} \\
31 \\
\underline{26} \\
50 \\
\underline{39} \\
11
\end{array}
$$

64.
$$
\begin{array}{r}
28 \text{ R } 5 \\
40\overline{)1125} \\
\underline{80} \\
325 \\
\underline{320} \\
5
\end{array}
$$

66.
$$
\begin{array}{r}
768 \\
8\overline{)6144} \\
\underline{56} \\
54 \\
\underline{48} \\
64 \\
\underline{64} \\
0
\end{array}
$$

68.
$$
\begin{array}{r}
110 \text{ R } 7 \\
32\overline{)3527} \\
\underline{32} \\
32 \\
\underline{32} \\
7 \\
\underline{0} \\
7
\end{array}
$$

70.
$$
\begin{array}{r}
104 \text{ R } 6 \\
19\overline{)1982} \\
\underline{19} \\
82 \\
\underline{76} \\
6
\end{array}
$$

72.
$$
\begin{array}{r}
7 \\
128\overline{)896} \\
\underline{896} \\
0
\end{array}
$$

74.
$$
\begin{array}{r}
134 \\
235\overline{)31,490} \\
\underline{23\ 5} \\
7\ 99 \\
\underline{7\ 05} \\
940. \\
\underline{940} \\
0
\end{array}
$$

76.
$$
\begin{array}{r}
12 \\
131\overline{)1572} \\
\underline{131} \\
262 \\
\underline{262} \\
0
\end{array}
$$
$x = 12$

78.
$$
\begin{array}{r}
730 \\
30\overline{)21,900} \\
\underline{21\ 0} \\
90 \\
\underline{90} \\
0
\end{array}
$$
Each horse eats 730 pounds.

80.
$$
\begin{array}{r}
120,000 \\
76\overline{)9,120,000} \\
\underline{7\ 6} \\
1\ 52 \\
\underline{1\ 52} \\
0
\end{array}
$$
Each snowplow cost $120,000.

82.
$$
\begin{array}{r}
46,179 \\
8\overline{)369,432} \\
\underline{32} \\
49 \\
\underline{48} \\
14 \\
\underline{8} \\
63 \\
\underline{56} \\
72 \\
\underline{72} \\
0
\end{array}
$$
Each person paid $46,179.

84.
$$
\begin{array}{r}
186 \\
70\overline{)13,020} \\
\underline{7\ 0} \\
6\ 02 \\
\underline{5\ 60} \\
420 \\
\underline{420} \\
0
\end{array}
$$
Each bookcase cost $186.

86.
$$
\begin{array}{r}
78 \\
34\overline{)2652} \\
\underline{238} \\
272 \\
\underline{272} \\
0
\end{array}
$$
The length of the lawn is 78 feet.

88.
$$
\begin{array}{r}
82 \\
43\overline{)3526} \\
\underline{344} \\
86 \\
\underline{86} \\
0
\end{array}
$$
The length of the panel is 82 centimeters.

90.
```
    874
  − 138    1st
  ─────
    736
  − 138    2nd
  ─────
    598
  − 138    3rd
  ─────
    460
  − 138    4h
  ─────
    322
  − 138    5th
  ─────
    184
  − 138    6th
  ─────
     46
```

```
           6 R 46
   138)874
       828
       ───
        46
```

Cumulative Review

91.
```
    108
  ×  50
  ─────
   5400
```

92.
```
     7162
  ×   145
  ───────
    35 810
   286 48
   716 2
  ─────────
  1,038,490
```

93.
```
   316,214
  + 89,981
  ────────
   406,195
```

94.
```
   1,360,000
 − 1,293,156
 ──────────
     66,844
```

Classroom Quiz 1.5

1.
```
       368
    8)2944
      24
      ──
      54
      48
      ──
      64
      64
      ──
       0
```

2.
```
          3695 R 4
    7)25,869
      21
      ──
      4 8
      4 2
      ───
       66
       63
       ──
       39
       35
       ──
        4
```

3.
```
            237
   56)13,272
      11 2
      ────
      2 07
      1 68
      ────
       392
       392
       ───
         0
```

How Am I Doing? Sections 1.1–1.5

1. 78,310,436 = seventy-eight million, three hundred ten thousand, four hundred thirty-six

2. 38,247 = 30,000 + 8000 + 200 + 40 + 7

3. 5,064,122

4. 2,747,000 public school graduates were in 1980.

5. 2,802,000 public school graduates are expected in 2010.

6.
```
    13
    31
    88
    43
  + 69
  ────
   244
```

7.
```
   28,318
    5,039
 + 17,213
 ────────
   50,570
```

8.
```
   833,576
 + 517,885
 ─────────
 1,351,461
```

9. $\begin{array}{r} 5728 \\ -\ 1735 \\ \hline 3993 \end{array}$

10. $\begin{array}{r} 100,450 \\ -\ 24,139 \\ \hline 76,311 \end{array}$

11. $\begin{array}{r} 45,861,413 \\ -\ 43,879,761 \\ \hline 1,981,652 \end{array}$

12. $9 \times 6 \times 1 \times 2 = 54 \times 1 \times 2 = 54 \times 2 = 108$

13. $50 \times 10 \times 200 = 500 \times 200 = 100,000$

14. $\begin{array}{r} 2658 \\ \times\quad 7 \\ \hline 18,606 \end{array}$

15. $\begin{array}{r} 68 \\ \times\ 55 \\ \hline 340 \\ 340\ \\ \hline 3740 \end{array}$

16. $\begin{array}{r} 365 \\ \times\quad 908 \\ \hline 2\ 920 \\ 328\ 50\ \ \\ \hline 331,420 \end{array}$

17. $\begin{array}{r} 10,605 \\ 8{\overline{)84,840}} \\ \underline{8}\quad\quad\quad \\ 4\ 8\quad\quad \\ 4\ 8\quad\quad \\ \overline{}\quad\quad \\ 40\quad \\ 40\quad \\ \hline 0\quad \end{array}$

18. $\begin{array}{r} 7,376\ \text{R}\ 1 \\ 7{\overline{)51,633}} \\ \underline{49}\quad\quad\quad \\ 2\ 6\quad\quad \\ 2\ 1\quad\quad \\ \hline 53\quad \\ 49\quad \\ \hline 43 \\ 42 \\ \hline 1 \end{array}$

19. $\begin{array}{r} 26\ \text{R}\ 8 \\ 76{\overline{)1984}} \\ \underline{152}\quad \\ 464 \\ 456 \\ \hline 8 \end{array}$

20. $\begin{array}{r} 139 \\ 42{\overline{)5838}} \\ \underline{42}\quad \\ 163 \\ 126 \\ \hline 378 \\ 378 \\ \hline 0 \end{array}$

1.6 Exercises

2. In exponent notation, the <u>exponent</u> tells how many times to multiply the base.

4. 10^5 is read as <u>10 to the fifth power</u>.

6. $12 \times 5 + 3 \times 5 + 7 \times 5 = 60 + 15 + 35 = 110$
    Yes, because of the distributive property.

8. $2 \times 2 \times 2 \times 2 \times 2 = 2^5$

10. $3 \times 3 \times 3 \times 3 \times 3 \times 3 = 3^6$

12. $1 \times 1 \times 1 \times 1 \times 1 \times 1 \times 1 = 1^7$

14. $27 = 27^1$

16. $3^3 = 3 \times 3 \times 3 = 27$

18. $5^2 = 5 \times 5 = 25$

20. $10^3 = 10 \times 10 \times 10 = 1000$

22. $1^{20} = 1$

24. $2^5 = 2 \times 2 \times 2 \times 2 \times 2 = 32$

26. $4^2 = 4 \times 4 = 16$

28. $12^2 = 12 \times 12 = 144$

30. $3^4 = 3 \times 3 \times 3 \times 3 = 81$

32. $5^4 = 5 \times 5 \times 5 \times 5 = 625$

34. $7^2 = 7 \times 7 = 49$

36. $8^0 = 1$

38. $20^3 = 20 \times 20 \times 20 = 8000$

40. $8^1 = 8$

42. $11^2 = 11 \times 11 = 121$

44. $14^2 = 14 \times 14 = 196$

46. $5^3 = 5 \times 5 \times 5 = 125$

48. $7^0 + 4^3 = 1 + 64 = 65$

50. $7^3 + 4^2 = 343 + 16 = 359$

52. $9^2 + 9 = 81 + 9 = 90$

54. $9 \times 7 + 42 = 63 + 42 = 105$

56. $4 \times 6 - 24 \div 4 = 24 - 24 \div 4 = 24 - 6 = 18$

58. $4^3 \div 4 - 11 = 64 \div 4 - 11 = 16 - 11 = 5$

60. $2 \times 12^2 - 80 = 2 \times 144 - 80 = 288 - 80 = 208$

62. $4^3 - 5 \times (9 + 1) = 4^3 - 5(10)$
$$= 64 - 5(10)$$
$$= 64 - 50$$
$$= 14$$

64. $(600 \div 30) \div 20 = 20 \div 20 = 1$

66. $875 \div (35 \div 7) = 875 \div 5 = 175$

68. $(3)(60) - (60 + 3) = (3)(60) - 63$
$$= 180 - 63$$
$$= 117$$

70. $7^2 + 9^2 \div 3^2 = 49 + 81 \div 9 = 49 + 9 = 58$

72. $(8)(9) - (15 - 5) \div 5 = (8)(9) - 10 \div 5$
$$= 72 - 10 \div 5$$
$$= 72 - 2$$
$$= 70$$

74. $130 - 4^2 \times 5 = 130 - 16 \times 5 = 130 - 80 = 50$

76. $2^3 + 3^2 + 4^3 = 8 + 9 + 64 = 17 + 64 = 81$

78. $120 \div 30 \times 2 \times 5 \div 8 = 4 \times 2 \times 5 \div 8$
$$= 8 \times 5 \div 8$$
$$= 40 \div 8$$
$$= 5$$

80. $8^2 - 4 \times 3 \times 0 \times 7 = 64 - 0 = 64$

82. $7^2 \times 3 \div 3 = 49 \times 3 \div 3 = 147 \div 3 = 49$

84. $75 - 3 \times 5 \times 2 + 15 = 75 - 30 + 15 = 45 + 15 = 60$

86. $5 + 4^3 \times 2 + 7 = 5 + 64 \times 2 + 7$
$$= 5 + 128 + 7$$
$$= 133 + 7$$
$$= 140$$

88. $24 \div 3 \times (5 - 3)^2 = 24 \div 3 \times 2^2$
$$= 24 \div 3 \times 4$$
$$= 8 \times 4$$
$$= 32$$

90. $5^2 \times 3 \div 25 + 7 \times 6 = 25 \times 3 \div 25 + 7 \times 6$
$$= 75 \div 25 + 7 \times 6$$
$$= 3 + 7 \times 6$$
$$= 3 + 42$$
$$= 45$$

92. $8^0 + 7^2 + 3^3 = 1 + 49 + 27 = 77$

94. $2150 - 3^4(2) \div 9 = 2150 - 81(2) \div 9$
$$= 2150 - 162 \div 9$$
$$= 2150 - 18$$
$$= 2132$$

96. $100 - 48 \div (2 \times 3) = 100 - 48 \div 6 = 100 - 8 = 92$

98. $100 - 48 \div 2 \times 3 = 100 - 24 \times 3 = 100 - 72 = 28$

100. $9 \times 8 + 5^0 - (8-4)^3 = 9 \times 8 + 5^0 - 4^3$
$$= 9 \times 8 + 1 - 64$$
$$= 72 + 1 - 64$$
$$= 73 - 64$$
$$= 9$$

102. $10 \times 60 + 12 = 600 + 12 = 612$ minutes
$612 \times 60 = 36{,}720$ seconds

Cumulative Review

103. a.   3

    b.   2,000,000

104. 200,765,909

105. 261,763,002
Two hundred sixty-one million, seven hundred sixty-three thousand, two

106. Perimeter: $2 \times 250 + 2 \times 480 = 500 + 960$
$$= 1460 \text{ feet}$$
1460 feet of fencing is needed to surround field.
Area: $250 \times 480 = 120{,}000$ square feet
120,000 square feet of grass must be planted.

Classroom Quiz 1.6

1. $15 \times 15 \times 15 \times 15 = 15^4$

2. $7^3 = 7 \times 7 \times 7 = 343$

3. $3 + 5^3 - 2 \times (10-4)^2 = 3 + 5^3 - 2 \times 6^2$
$$= 3 + 125 - 2 \times 36$$
$$= 3 + 125 - 72$$
$$= 128 - 72$$
$$= 56$$

1.7 Exercises

2. Since the digit to the right of tens is greater than 5, you round up. When you round up 9 tens, it becomes 10 tens or 100.

4. 4$\underline{5}$ rounds to 50 since 5 is equal to 5.

6. 5$\underline{7}$ rounds to 60 since 7 is greater than 5.

8. 13$\underline{2}$ rounds to 130 since 2 is less than 5.

10. 283$\underline{4}$ rounds to 2830 since 4 is less than 5.

12. 435$\underline{5}$ rounds to 4360 since 5 is equal to 5.

14. 6$\underline{6}$1 rounds to 700 since 6 is greater than 5.

16. 12$\underline{4}$9 rounds to 1200 since 4 is less than 5.

18. 16$\underline{4}$3 rounds to 1600 since 4 is less than 5.

20. 3$\underline{7}$54 rounds to 4000 since 7 is greater than 5.

22. $\underline{5}$15 rounds to 1000 since 5 is equal to 5.

24. 94,$\underline{4}$89 rounds to 94,000 since 4 is less than 5.

26. 5,878,6$\underline{1}$2,843,000 rounds to
5,878,600,000,000 miles since 1 is less than 5.

28. 2$\underline{9}$,028 rounds to 30,000 feet since 9 is greater than 5.

30. a.   363,58$\underline{4}$,435 rounds to 363,580,000 since 4 is less than 5.

    b.   3$\underline{6}$3,584,435 rounds to 400,000,000 since 6 is greater than 5.

32. a.   165,3$\underline{8}$4,000 rounds to 165,400,000 since 8 is greater than 5.

    b.   165,38$\underline{4}$,000 rounds to 165,380,000 since 4 is less than 5.

34.
$$
\begin{array}{r}
200 \\
500 \\
+\ 900 \\
\hline
1600
\end{array}
$$

36.
$$
\begin{array}{r}
60 \\
30 \\
50 \\
+\ 100 \\
\hline
240
\end{array}
$$

38. $200{,}000 + 80{,}000 + 10{,}000 = 290{,}000$

40. $1{,}000{,}000 - 600{,}000 = 400{,}000$

42. $400{,}000 - 60{,}000 = 340{,}000$

44. $90{,}000{,}000 - 50{,}000{,}000 = 40{,}000{,}000$

46. $40 \times 100 = 4000$

48. $6000 \times 3 = 18{,}000$

50. $400,000 \times 200 = 80,000,000$

52. $\begin{array}{r} 400 \\ 20\overline{)8000} \\ \underline{80} \\ 0 \end{array}$

54. $\begin{array}{r} 10,000 \\ 60\overline{)600,000} \\ \underline{60} \\ 0 \end{array}$

56. $10,000,000 \div 500 = 20,000$

58. $\begin{array}{r} 500 \\ 100 \\ 500 \\ + \ 400 \\ \hline 1500 \end{array}$
Correct

60. $\begin{array}{r} 30,000 \\ 50,000 \\ + \ 60,000 \\ \hline 140,000 \end{array}$
Correct

62. $\begin{array}{r} 700,000 \\ - \ 100,000 \\ \hline 600,000 \end{array}$
Incorrect

64. $\begin{array}{r} 40,000,000 \\ - \ 30,000,000 \\ \hline 10,000,000 \end{array}$
Incorrect

66. $\begin{array}{r} 500 \\ \times \quad 50 \\ \hline 25,000 \end{array}$
Incorrect

68. $\begin{array}{r} 8000 \\ \times \quad 90 \\ \hline 720,000 \end{array}$
Correct

70. $\begin{array}{r} 600 \\ 50\overline{)30,000} \end{array}$
Correct

72. $\begin{array}{r} 625 \\ 800\overline{)500,000} \\ \underline{480 \ 0} \\ 20 \ 00 \\ \underline{16 \ 00} \\ 4 \ 000 \\ \underline{4 \ 000} \end{array}$
Correct

74. $40 \times 100 = 4000$
The restaurant is approximately 4000 square yards.

76. $300,000 + 700,000 + 200,000 + 600,000$
$= 1,800,000$
The estimated total is $1,800,000.

78. $70 \times 30 = 2100$
She is estimated to earn $2100.

80. $70,000 - 30,000 = 40,000$
The increase in attendance is estimated at 40,000 people.

82. Sudan: 1,000,000 since 6 is greater than 5.
Brazil: 3,300,000 since 8 is greater than 5.
$3,300,000 - 1,000,000 = 2,300,000$
Brazil is estimated to be 2,300,000 square miles larger than Sudan.

84. a. $9,348,487,000 \div 28,367$
$9,000,000,000 \div 30,000 = 300,000$
It will take the probe 300,000 hours to travel this distance.

b. $300,000 \div 24$
$300,000 \div 20 = 15,000$
It will take the probe 15,000 days to travel this distance.

Cumulative Review

85. $26 \times 3 + 20 \div 4 = 78 + 20 \div 4 = 78 + 5 = 83$

86. $\begin{aligned} 5^2 + 3^2 - (17 - 10) &= 5^2 + 3^2 - 7 \\ &= 25 + 9 - 7 \\ &= 34 - 7 \\ &= 27 \end{aligned}$

87. $\begin{aligned} 3 \times (16 \div 4) + 8 \times 2 &= 3 \times 4 + 8 \times 2 \\ &= 12 + 8 \times 2 \\ &= 12 + 16 \\ &= 28 \end{aligned}$

88. $126 + 4 - (20 \div 5)^3 = 126 + 4 - 4^3$
$$= 126 + 4 - 64$$
$$= 130 - 64$$
$$= 66$$

89.
$$\begin{array}{r} 5489 \\ \times \quad 67 \\ \hline 38\ 423 \\ 329\ 34 \\ \hline 367,763 \end{array}$$

90.
$$\begin{array}{r} 87 \\ 52\overline{)4524} \\ \underline{416} \\ 364 \\ \underline{364} \\ 0 \end{array}$$

Classroom Quiz 1.7

1. 57,6$\underline{2}$1 rounds to 57,600, since 2 is less than 5.

2. 2,34$\underline{2}$,786 rounds to 2,340,000 since 2 is less than 5.

3.
$$\begin{array}{r} 40,000 \\ \times \quad 900,000 \\ \hline 36,000,000,000 \end{array}$$

1.8 Exercises

2.
$$\begin{array}{r} 9,596,960 \\ - \quad 270,550 \\ \hline 9,326,410 \end{array}$$
China has 9,326,410 square kilometers of land.

4.
$$\begin{array}{r} 144 \\ \times \quad 14 \\ \hline 576 \\ 144 \\ \hline 2016 \end{array}$$
Mr. Jim Weston ordered 2016 pencils.

6.
$$\begin{array}{r} 6 \\ 15\overline{)90} \\ \underline{90} \\ 0 \end{array}$$
The pears cost 6¢ per ounce.

8.
$$\begin{array}{r} 50,000 \\ - \quad 103 \\ \hline 49,897 \end{array}$$
49,897 bison live elsewhere.

10.
$$\begin{array}{r} 44,010 \\ \times \quad 26 \\ \hline 264\ 060 \\ 880\ 20 \\ \hline 1,144,260 \end{array}$$
Valleyfair covers 1,144,260 square feet of land.

12.
$$\begin{array}{r} 2,113,000 \\ - \quad 815,100 \\ \hline 1,297,900 \end{array}$$
The difference in population between Paris and Marseille is 1,297,900 people.

14.
$$\begin{array}{r} 4\ 132 \\ 3\ 915 \\ + 3\ 741 \\ \hline 11,788 \end{array} \qquad \begin{array}{r} 4132 \\ - 3741 \\ \hline 391 \end{array}$$
The three rivers have a total run of 11,788 miles. The difference in the lengths of the Nile and Mississippi is 391 miles.

16. $2158 + 156 + 238 + 1119 + 866 + 136 = 4673$
He has \$4673 in the account.

18.
$$\begin{array}{r} 10 \\ \times 5 \\ \hline 50 \end{array} \qquad \begin{array}{r} 6 \\ \times 7 \\ \hline 42 \end{array} \qquad \begin{array}{r} 7 \\ \times 3 \\ \hline 21 \end{array}$$
$50 + 42 + 21 = 113$
The company made \$113.

20.
$$\begin{array}{r} 2746 \\ + 1305 \\ \hline 4051 \end{array} \qquad \begin{array}{r} 4361 \\ - 4051 \\ \hline 310 \end{array}$$
310 launches were completed by other countries.

22. $13 \times 12,350 - 13 \times 7362 = 160,550 - 95,706$
$$= 64,844$$
His profit is \$64,844.

24.　　29,438
　　− 28,862
　　――――――
　　　　576

　　　　　32
　　18)576
　　　　54
　　　　――
　　　　36
　　　　36
　　　　――
　　　　　0

The car achieved 32 miles per gallon.

26.　$27 \times 2 = 54$
　　$94 - 54 = 40$
　　$40 \div 2 = 20$
　　$27 - 20 = 7$
There are 20 tables with 4 chairs and 7 tables with 2 chairs.

28.　　40
　　　29
　　+ 12
　　――――
　　　81

81 students speak Korean, Hindi, or Filipino.

30.　$(8 + 8) - 6 = 16 - 6 = 10$
10 more students speak Indonesian or Romanian than Albanian.

32.　　51,735
　　− 23,900
　　――――――
　　　27,835

$27,835,000,000 more was spent in 2000 than in 1985.

34.　$4 \times 51,735,000,000 = 206,940,000,000$
$206,940,000,000 was spent on highways during that four-year period.

Cumulative Review

35.　$7^3 = 7 \times 7 \times 7 = 343$

36.　$3 \times 2^3 + 15 \div 3 - 4 \times 2 = 3 \times 8 + 15 \div 3 - 4 \times 2$
　　　　　　　　$= 24 + 15 \div 3 - 4 \times 2$
　　　　　　　　$= 24 + 5 - 4 \times 2$
　　　　　　　　$= 24 + 5 - 8$
　　　　　　　　$= 29 - 8$
　　　　　　　　$= 21$

37.　　126
　　× 38
　　――――
　　1008
　　378
　　――――
　　4788

38.　　　　258
　　12)3096
　　　　24
　　　　――
　　　　69
　　　　60
　　　　――
　　　　96
　　　　96
　　　　――
　　　　　0

39.　　 96
　　　123
　　　 57
　　+ 526
　　――――
　　　802

40.　　509,263
　　− 485,978
　　――――――
　　　 23,285

41.　526,195,726 rounds to 526,196,000 because 7 is greater than 5.

42.　3,400,603,025

Classroom Quiz 1.8

1.　Divide the cost of the uniforms by the number of players.

　　　　　657
　　18)11,826
　　　　10 8
　　　　――――
　　　　1 02
　　　　　90
　　　　――――
　　　　　126
　　　　　126
　　　　――――
　　　　　　0

Each team member will pay $657 for a uniform.

2.　Total deposits:　　906
　　　　　　　　　+ 885
　　　　　　　　――――――
　　　　　　　　　1791

Total checks: 29
109
412
+ 683
―――
1233

64
+ 1791
――――
1855
− 1233
――――
622

His new balance will be $622.

3. Senior citizens: 7
× 6
――
42

Age 12 to 64:   8
× 8
――
64

Children under 12:   9
× 3
――
27

42
64
+ 27
―――
133

She needed to collect $133 in fares.

Putting Your Skills to Work

1. Their three credit cards were maxed out at
$8000, there was hospital debt of $12,000, they
still owed $3000 on their car, and they borrowed
$300, $5, $400, and $20.
$5, $20, $300, $400, $3000, $8000, $8000,
$8000, $12,000

2. **a.** Each of the three credit cards will receive
$25, and the hospital will receive $50 and
car debt will receive $200.
$3 \times \$25 + \$50 + \$200 = \$75 + \$50 + \$200$
$= \$125 + \$200$
$= \$325$

    b. The total amount of their minimum payment
is $325.

Chapter 1 Review Problems

1. $892 =$ eight hundred ninety-two

2. $15,802 =$ fifteen thousand, eight hundred two

3. $109,276 =$ one hundred nine thousand, two
hundred seventy-six

4. $423,576,055 =$ four hundred twenty-three
million, five hundred seventy-six thousand, fifty-
five

5. $4364 = 4000 + 300 + 60 + 4$

6. $35,414 = 30,000 + 5000 + 400 + 10 + 4$

7. $42,166,037 = 40,000,000 + 2,000,000 + 100,000$
$+ 60,000 + 6000 + 30 + 7$

8. $1,305,128 = 1,000,000 + 300,000 + 5000 + 100$
$+ 20 + 8$

9. 924

10. 5302

11. 1,328,828

12. 24,705,112

13.   76
+ 39
――
115

14.   148
+ 152
――――
300

15.   235
+ 165
――――
400

16.   12
28
34
+ 76
――
150

17.   123
61
9
84
+ 123
―――
400

21

18.
$$\begin{array}{r} 546 \\ 254 \\ +153 \\ \hline 953 \end{array}$$

19.
$$\begin{array}{r} 226 \\ 134 \\ +647 \\ \hline 1007 \end{array}$$

20.
$$\begin{array}{r} 52{,}134 \\ +7\,966 \\ \hline 60{,}100 \end{array}$$

21.
$$\begin{array}{r} 1\,356 \\ 2\,892 \\ 561 \\ 89 \\ +9\,805 \\ \hline 14{,}703 \end{array}$$

22.
$$\begin{array}{r} 26 \\ 503 \\ 935 \\ 1\,257 \\ +7\,861 \\ \hline 10{,}582 \end{array}$$

23.
$$\begin{array}{r} 36 \\ -19 \\ \hline 17 \end{array}$$

24.
$$\begin{array}{r} 54 \\ -48 \\ \hline 6 \end{array}$$

25.
$$\begin{array}{r} 126 \\ -99 \\ \hline 27 \end{array}$$

26.
$$\begin{array}{r} 543 \\ -372 \\ \hline 171 \end{array}$$

27.
$$\begin{array}{r} 7000 \\ -845 \\ \hline 6155 \end{array}$$

28.
$$\begin{array}{r} 9000 \\ -5833 \\ \hline 3167 \end{array}$$

29.
$$\begin{array}{r} 201{,}340 \\ -120{,}618 \\ \hline 80{,}722 \end{array}$$

30.
$$\begin{array}{r} 320{,}055 \\ -214{,}237 \\ \hline 105{,}818 \end{array}$$

31.
$$\begin{array}{r} 6{,}325{,}034 \\ -89{,}023 \\ \hline 6{,}236{,}011 \end{array}$$

32.
$$\begin{array}{r} 5{,}412{,}022 \\ -79{,}031 \\ \hline 5{,}332{,}991 \end{array}$$

33. $8 \times 1 \times 9 \times 2 = 8 \times 9 \times 2 = 72 \times 2 = 144$

34. $7 \times 6 \times 0 \times 4 = 42 \times 0 \times 4 = 0 \times 4 = 0$

35. $2 \cdot 5 \cdot 10 \cdot 8 = 10 \cdot 10 \cdot 8 = 100 \cdot 8 = 800$

36. $4 \cdot 25 \cdot 1 \cdot 15 = 100 \cdot 1 \cdot 15 = 100 \cdot 15 = 1500$

37. $621 \times 100 = 62{,}100$

38. $84{,}312 \times 1000 = 84{,}312{,}000$

39. $78 \times 10{,}000 = 780{,}000$

40. $563 \times 1{,}000{,}000 = 563{,}000{,}000$

41.
$$\begin{array}{r} 58 \\ \times 32 \\ \hline 1856 \end{array}$$

42.
$$\begin{array}{r} 73 \\ \times 24 \\ \hline 292 \\ 146 \\ \hline 1752 \end{array}$$

43.
$$\begin{array}{r} 150 \\ \times 27 \\ \hline 1050 \\ 300 \\ \hline 4050 \end{array}$$

44.
$$
\begin{array}{r}
360 \\
\times\ 38 \\
\hline
2\ 880 \\
10\ 80 \\
\hline
13,680
\end{array}
$$

45.
$$
\begin{array}{r}
709 \\
\times\ 36 \\
\hline
4\ 254 \\
21\ 27 \\
\hline
25,524
\end{array}
$$

46.
$$
\begin{array}{r}
502 \\
\times\ 48 \\
\hline
4\ 016 \\
20\ 08 \\
\hline
24,096
\end{array}
$$

47.
$$
\begin{array}{r}
123 \\
\times\ 714 \\
\hline
492 \\
1\ 23 \\
86\ 1 \\
\hline
87,822
\end{array}
$$

48.
$$
\begin{array}{r}
431 \\
\times\ 623 \\
\hline
1\ 293 \\
8\ 62 \\
258\ 6 \\
\hline
268,513
\end{array}
$$

49.
$$
\begin{array}{r}
1782 \\
\times\ 305 \\
\hline
8910 \\
534\ 60 \\
\hline
543,510
\end{array}
$$

50.
$$
\begin{array}{r}
2057 \\
\times\ 124 \\
\hline
8\ 228 \\
41\ 14 \\
205\ 7 \\
\hline
255,068
\end{array}
$$

51.
$$
\begin{array}{r}
3182 \\
\times\ 35 \\
\hline
15\ 910 \\
95\ 46 \\
\hline
111,370
\end{array}
$$

52.
$$
\begin{array}{r}
2713 \\
\times\ 42 \\
\hline
5\ 426 \\
108\ 52 \\
\hline
113,946
\end{array}
$$

53.
$$
\begin{array}{r}
1200 \\
\times\ 6000 \\
\hline
7,200,000
\end{array}
$$

54.
$$
\begin{array}{r}
2500 \\
\times\ 3000 \\
\hline
7,500,000
\end{array}
$$

55.
$$
\begin{array}{r}
100,000 \\
\times\ 20,000 \\
\hline
2,000,000,000
\end{array}
$$

56.
$$
\begin{array}{r}
300,000 \\
\times\ 40,000 \\
\hline
12,000,000,000
\end{array}
$$

57. $20 \div 10 = 2$

58. $40 \div 8 = 5$

59. $0 \div 8 = 0$

60. $12 \div 1 = 12$

61. $7 \div 1 = 7$

62. $0 \div 5 = 0$

63. $\dfrac{81}{9} = 9$

64. $\dfrac{42}{6} = 7$

65. $\dfrac{5}{0}$ undefined

66. $\dfrac{24}{6} = 4$

67. $\dfrac{56}{8} = 7$

68. $\dfrac{63}{7} = 9$

69.
$$
\begin{array}{r}
125 \\
6\overline{)750} \\
\underline{6} \\
15 \\
\underline{12} \\
30 \\
\underline{30} \\
0
\end{array}
$$

70.
$$
\begin{array}{r}
125 \\
7\overline{)875} \\
\underline{7} \\
17 \\
\underline{14} \\
35 \\
\underline{35} \\
0
\end{array}
$$

71.
$$
\begin{array}{r}
207 \\
9\overline{)1863} \\
\underline{18} \\
063 \\
\underline{63} \\
0
\end{array}
$$

72.
$$
\begin{array}{r}
309 \\
4\overline{)1236} \\
\underline{12} \\
36 \\
\underline{36} \\
0
\end{array}
$$

73.
$$
\begin{array}{r}
2\,504 \\
6\overline{)15,024} \\
\underline{12} \\
3\,0 \\
\underline{3\,0} \\
024 \\
\underline{24} \\
0
\end{array}
$$

74.
$$
\begin{array}{r}
3\,064 \\
8\overline{)24,512} \\
\underline{24} \\
51 \\
\underline{48} \\
32 \\
\underline{32} \\
0
\end{array}
$$

75.
$$
\begin{array}{r}
36,958 \\
6\overline{)221,748} \\
\underline{18} \\
41 \\
\underline{36} \\
5\,7 \\
\underline{5\,4} \\
34 \\
\underline{30} \\
48 \\
\underline{48} \\
0
\end{array}
$$

76.
$$
\begin{array}{r}
36,921 \\
5\overline{)184,605} \\
\underline{15} \\
34 \\
\underline{30} \\
4\,6 \\
\underline{4\,5} \\
10 \\
\underline{10} \\
5 \\
\underline{5} \\
0
\end{array}
$$

77.
$$
\begin{array}{r}
15,046 \text{ R } 3 \\
8\overline{)120,371} \\
\underline{8} \\
40 \\
\underline{40} \\
0\,37 \\
\underline{32} \\
51 \\
\underline{48} \\
3
\end{array}
$$

78.
$$
\begin{array}{r}
35,783 \text{ R } 4 \\
7{\overline{\smash{\big)}\,250,485}} \\
\underline{21} \\
40 \\
\underline{35} \\
5\,4 \\
4\,9 \\
\underline{} \\
58 \\
\underline{56} \\
25 \\
\underline{21} \\
4
\end{array}
$$

79.
$$
\begin{array}{r}
7 \text{ R } 21 \\
67{\overline{\smash{\big)}\,490}} \\
\underline{469} \\
21
\end{array}
$$

80.
$$
\begin{array}{r}
4 \text{ R } 37 \\
72{\overline{\smash{\big)}\,325}} \\
\underline{288} \\
37
\end{array}
$$

81.
$$
\begin{array}{r}
31 \text{ R } 15 \\
21{\overline{\smash{\big)}\,666}} \\
\underline{63} \\
36 \\
\underline{21} \\
15
\end{array}
$$

82.
$$
\begin{array}{r}
14 \text{ R } 11 \\
22{\overline{\smash{\big)}\,319}} \\
\underline{22} \\
99 \\
\underline{88} \\
11
\end{array}
$$

83.
$$
\begin{array}{r}
38 \text{ R } 30 \\
68{\overline{\smash{\big)}\,2614}} \\
\underline{204} \\
574 \\
\underline{544} \\
30
\end{array}
$$

84.
$$
\begin{array}{r}
60 \text{ R } 22 \\
53{\overline{\smash{\big)}\,3202}} \\
\underline{318} \\
22
\end{array}
$$

85.
$$
\begin{array}{r}
195 \\
45{\overline{\smash{\big)}\,8775}} \\
\underline{45} \\
427 \\
\underline{405} \\
225 \\
\underline{225} \\
0
\end{array}
$$

86.
$$
\begin{array}{r}
258 \\
35{\overline{\smash{\big)}\,9030}} \\
\underline{70} \\
203 \\
\underline{175} \\
280 \\
\underline{280} \\
0
\end{array}
$$

87.
$$
\begin{array}{r}
54 \\
132{\overline{\smash{\big)}\,7128}} \\
\underline{660} \\
528 \\
\underline{528} \\
0
\end{array}
$$

88.
$$
\begin{array}{r}
19 \\
204{\overline{\smash{\big)}\,3876}} \\
\underline{204} \\
1836 \\
\underline{1836} \\
0
\end{array}
$$

89. $13 \times 13 = 13^2$

90. $21 \times 21 \times 21 = 21^3$

91. $8 \times 8 \times 8 \times 8 \times 8 = 8^5$

92. $10 \times 10 \times 10 \times 10 \times 10 \times 10 = 10^6$

93. $2^6 = 2 \times 2 \times 2 \times 2 \times 2 \times 2 = 64$

94. $3^4 = 3 \times 3 \times 3 \times 3 = 81$

95. $2^7 = 2 \times 2 \times 2 \times 2 \times 2 \times 2 \times 2 = 128$

96. $5^3 = 5 \times 5 \times 5 = 125$

97. $7^2 = 7 \times 7 = 49$

98. $9^2 = 9 \times 9 = 81$

99. $6^3 = 6 \times 6 \times 6 = 216$

100. $4^3 = 4 \times 4 \times 4 = 64$

101. $7 + 2 \times 3 - 5 = 7 + 6 - 5 = 13 - 5 = 8$

102. $6 \times 2 - 4 + 3 = 12 - 4 + 3 = 8 + 3 = 11$

103. $2^5 + 4 - (5 + 3^2) = 32 + 4 - (5 + 9)$
$$= 32 + 4 - 14$$
$$= 36 - 14$$
$$= 22$$

104. $4^3 + 20 \div (2 + 2^3) = 64 + 20 \div (2 + 8)$
$$= 64 + 20 \div 10$$
$$= 64 + 2$$
$$= 66$$

105. $34 - 9 \div 9 \times 12 = 34 - 1 \times 12 = 34 - 12 = 22$

106. $2 \times 7^2 - 20 \div 1 = 2 \times 49 - 20 \div 1 = 98 - 20 = 78$

107. $2^3 \times 5 \div 8 + 3 \times 4 = 8 \times 5 \div 8 + 3 \times 4$
$$= 40 \div 8 + 3 \times 4$$
$$= 5 + 3 \times 4$$
$$= 5 + 12$$
$$= 17$$

108. $2^3 + 4 \times 5 - 32 \div (1 + 3)^2 = 2^3 + 4 \times 5 - 32 \div 4^2$
$$= 8 + 4 \times 5 - 32 \div 16$$
$$= 8 + 20 - 2$$
$$= 26$$

109. $6 \times 3 + 3 \times 5^2 - 63 \div (5 - 2)^2$
$$= 6 \times 3 + 3 \times 5^2 - 63 \div 3^2$$
$$= 6 \times 3 + 3 \times 25 - 63 \div 9$$
$$= 18 + 75 - 7$$
$$= 86$$

110. 336<u>4</u> rounds to 3360 since 4 is less than 5.

111. 589<u>5</u> rounds to 5900 since 5 is equal to 5.

112. 15,30<u>5</u> rounds to 15,310 since 5 is equal to 5.

113. 42,64<u>4</u> rounds to 42,640 since 4 is less than 5.

114. 12,<u>3</u>50 rounds to 12,000 since 3 is less than 5.

115. 22,<u>9</u>86 rounds to 23,000 since 9 is greater than 5.

116. 675,<u>8</u>00 rounds to 676,000 since 8 is greater than 5.

117. 202,<u>4</u>98 rounds to 202,000 since 4 is less than 5.

118. 4,6<u>4</u>9,320 rounds to 4,600,000 since 4 is less than 5.

119. 9,99<u>5</u>,312 rounds to 10,000,000 since 5 is equal to 5.

120.
$$\begin{array}{r} 300 \\ 700 \\ 200 \\ +\ 200 \\ \hline 1400 \end{array}$$

121.
$$\begin{array}{r} 20,000 \\ 8\,000 \\ +\ 40,000 \\ \hline 68,000 \end{array}$$

122.
$$\begin{array}{r} 4,000,000 \\ -\ 3,000,000 \\ \hline 1,000,000 \end{array}$$

123.
$$\begin{array}{r} 30,000 \\ -\ 20,000 \\ \hline 10,000 \end{array}$$

124.
$$\begin{array}{r} 1000 \\ \times\quad 6000 \\ \hline 6,000,000 \end{array}$$

125.
$$\begin{array}{r} 3,000,000 \\ \times\qquad\quad 900 \\ \hline 2,700,000,000 \end{array}$$

126.
$$20\overline{)80,000}\ \ 4,000$$
$$\underline{80}$$
$$0$$

127.
$$300\overline{)900,000}\ \ 3\,000$$
$$\underline{900}$$
$$0$$

128.
$$\begin{array}{r} 20 \\ \times\ 12 \\ \hline 40 \\ 20 \\ \hline 240 \end{array}$$
He bought 240 donut holes.

129.
$$\begin{array}{r} 25 \\ \times\ \ 7 \\ \hline 175 \end{array}$$
He typed 175 words.

130.
$$\begin{array}{r} 2462 \\ 1997 \\ +\ 2561 \\ \hline 7020 \end{array}$$
7020 people visited the festival during these three months.

131.
$$\begin{array}{r} 26,300 \\ 14,520 \\ +\ 18,650 \\ \hline 59,470 \end{array}$$
The total purchase price was $59,470.

132.
$$\begin{array}{r} 14,630 \\ -\ 4\ 329 \\ \hline 10,301 \end{array}$$
There was 10,301 feet between them.

133.
$$\begin{array}{rr} 4330 & 4598 \\ +\ 268 & -\ 1250 \\ \hline \$4598 & \$3348 \end{array}$$
Gerardo will have to pay $3348 for tuition and books.

134.
$$\begin{array}{r} 1\ 356 \\ 24\overline{)32,544} \\ \underline{24} \\ 8\ 5 \\ \underline{7\ 2} \\ 1\ 34 \\ \underline{1\ 20} \\ 144 \\ \underline{144} \\ 0 \end{array}$$
Cost per passenger was $1356.

135.
$$\begin{array}{r} 74 \\ 112\overline{)8288} \\ \underline{784} \\ 448 \\ \underline{448} \\ 0 \end{array}$$
The cost was $74 per bed.

136.

Deposits	Withdrawals
24	18
105	145
36	250
+ 177	+ 461
342	874

$810 + 342 - 874 = 278$
Her balance will be $278.

137.
$$\begin{array}{r} 56,720 \\ -\ 56,320 \\ \hline 400\ \text{miles} \end{array}$$

$$\begin{array}{r} 25 \\ 16\overline{)400} \\ \underline{32} \\ 80 \\ \underline{80} \\ 0 \end{array}$$
He got 25 miles per gallon.

138. $3 \times 279 + 4 \times 61 + 2 \times 1980 = 837 + 244 + 3960$
$$= 5041$$
The total price was $5041.

139.
$$\begin{array}{rrrr} 15 & 60 & 42 & 975 \\ \times\ 65 & \times\ 12 & \times\ 8 & 720 \\ \hline 975 & 720 & 336 & +\ 336 \\ & & & \hline \\ & & & 2031 \end{array}$$
The total price is $2031.

140.
$$\begin{array}{r} 55,000,000 \\ -\ 14,500,000 \\ \hline 40,500,000 \end{array}$$
The difference is 40,500,000 tons.

141.
$$\begin{array}{r} 55,000,000 \\ -\ 33,600,000 \\ \hline 21,400,000 \end{array}$$
The greatest increase was 21,400,000 tons between 1990 and 1995.

142.
$$\begin{array}{r} 63,500 \\ -\,33,600 \\ \hline 29,900 \end{array} \qquad \begin{array}{r} 29,900 \\ +\,63,500 \\ \hline 93,400 \end{array}$$

The predicted recovery is 93,400,000 tons in 2010.

143.
$$\begin{array}{r} 205 \\ 36 \\ 1983 \\ +\;\;60 \\ \hline 2284 \end{array}$$

144.
$$\begin{array}{r} 56,793 \\ -\,48,926 \\ \hline 7\,867 \end{array}$$

145.
$$\begin{array}{r} 396 \\ \times\;\;28 \\ \hline 3\,168 \\ 7\,92\;\; \\ \hline 11,088 \end{array}$$

146.
$$\begin{array}{r} 129 \\ 37\overline{)4773} \\ \underline{37}\;\;\;\; \\ 107\;\; \\ \underline{74}\;\; \\ 333 \\ \underline{333} \\ 0 \end{array}$$

147. $4\times12-(12+9)+2^3\div4=4\times12-21+2^3\div4$
$$\begin{aligned} &=4\times12-21+8\div4 \\ &=48-21+8\div4 \\ &=48-21+2 \\ &=29 \end{aligned}$$

148.
$$\begin{array}{cccc} 699 & 78 & 2097 & 3000 \\ \times\;\;3 & \times\;2 & +\,156 & -\,2253 \\ \hline 2097 & 156 & 2253 & 747 \end{array}$$

He has \$747 in his account.

149. a.
$$\begin{array}{r} 22 \\ \times\;15 \\ \hline 110 \\ 22\;\; \\ \hline 330 \end{array}$$

The patio is 330 square feet.

b. $2(22)+2(15)=44+30=74$
He would need 74 feet of fence.

How Am I Doing? Chapter 1 Test

1. 44,007,635 = forty-four million, seven thousand, six hundred thirty-five

2. 26,859 = 20,000 + 6000 + 800 + 50 + 9

3. three million, five hundred eighty-one thousand, seventy-six = 3,581,076

4.
$$\begin{array}{r} 189 \\ 26 \\ 12 \\ 528 \\ +\;\;76 \\ \hline 831 \end{array}$$

5.
$$\begin{array}{r} 763 \\ 220 \\ +\;508 \\ \hline 1491 \end{array}$$

6.
$$\begin{array}{r} 135,484 \\ 2,376 \\ 81,004 \\ +\,100,113 \\ \hline 318,977 \end{array}$$

7.
$$\begin{array}{r} 8961 \\ -\;894 \\ \hline 8067 \end{array}$$

8.
$$\begin{array}{r} 501,760 \\ -\,328,902 \\ \hline 172,858 \end{array}$$

9.
$$\begin{array}{r} 18,400,100 \\ -\,13,174,332 \\ \hline 5,225,768 \end{array}$$

10. $1\times6\times9\times7=6\times9\times7=54\times7=378$

11.
$$\begin{array}{r} 45 \\ \times\;96 \\ \hline 270 \\ 405\;\; \\ \hline 4320 \end{array}$$

12.
$$\begin{array}{r} 326 \\ \times\ 592 \\ \hline 652 \\ 29\ 34 \\ 163\ 0 \\ \hline 192,992 \end{array}$$

13.
$$\begin{array}{r} 18,491 \\ \times\ \ \ \ \ 7 \\ \hline 129,437 \end{array}$$

14.
$$\begin{array}{r} 3\ 014\ \text{R}\ 1 \\ 5\overline{)15,071} \\ \underline{15} \\ 0 \\ \underline{0} \\ 7 \\ \underline{5} \\ 21 \\ \underline{20} \\ 1 \end{array}$$

15.
$$\begin{array}{r} 2\ 358 \\ 6\overline{)14,148} \\ \underline{12} \\ 21 \\ \underline{18} \\ 34 \\ \underline{30} \\ 48 \\ \underline{48} \\ 0 \end{array}$$

16.
$$\begin{array}{r} 352 \\ 37\overline{)13,024} \\ \underline{11\ 1} \\ 1\ 92 \\ \underline{1\ 85} \\ 74 \\ \underline{74} \\ 0 \end{array}$$

17. $14 \times 14 \times 14 = 14^3$

18. $2^6 = 2 \times 2 \times 2 \times 2 \times 2 \times 2 = 64$

19. $\begin{aligned} 5 + 6^2 - 2 \times (9-6)^2 &= 5 + 6^2 - 2 \times 3^2 \\ &= 5 + 36 - 2 \times 9 \\ &= 5 + 36 - 18 \\ &= 41 - 18 \\ &= 23 \end{aligned}$

20. $\begin{aligned} 2^4 + 3^3 + 28 \div 4 &= 16 + 27 + 28 \div 4 \\ &= 16 + 27 + 7 \\ &= 43 + 7 \\ &= 50 \end{aligned}$

21. $\begin{aligned} 4 \times 6 + 3^3 \times 2 + 23 \div 23 &= 4 \times 6 + 27 \times 2 + 23 \div 23 \\ &= 24 + 27 \times 2 + 23 \div 23 \\ &= 24 + 54 + 23 \div 23 \\ &= 24 + 54 + 1 \\ &= 78 + 1 \\ &= 79 \end{aligned}$

22. 94,7$\underline{6}$8 rounds to 94,800 since 6 is greater than 5.

23. 6,46$\underline{2}$,431 rounds to 6,460,000 since 2 is less than 5.

24. 5,2$\underline{7}$8,963 rounds to 5,300,000 since 7 is greater than 5.

25. $5,000,000 \times 30,000 = 150,000,000,000$

26. $1000 + 3000 + 4000 + 8000 = 16,000$

27.
$$\begin{array}{r} 2\ 148 \\ 15\overline{)32,220} \\ \underline{30} \\ 2\ 2 \\ \underline{1\ 5} \\ 72 \\ \underline{60} \\ 120 \\ \underline{120} \\ 0 \end{array}$$

Each person paid $2148.

28.
$$\begin{array}{r} 602 \\ -\ 135 \\ \hline 467 \end{array}$$

The boy is 467 feet from the other side of the river.

29. $3 \times 2 + 1 \times 45 + 2 \times 21 + 2 \times 17 = 6 + 45 + 42 + 34$
$$= 127$$
His total bill was $127.

30.

31	885
902	103
+ 399	26
$1332	17
	+ 9
	$1040

Her balance is $1332 - $1040 = $292.

31.

$$\begin{array}{r} 6800 \\ \times\ \ 110 \\ \hline 0000 \\ 68\ 00 \\ 6800 \\ \hline 748{,}000 \end{array}$$

Area of runway is 748,000 square feet.

32. $2 \times 8 + 2 \times 15 = 16 + 30 = 46$
The perimeter is 46 feet.

Chapter 2

2.1 Exercises

2. In a fraction, the <u>numerator</u> tells the number of parts we are interested in.

4. Answers will vary. An example is: I was late 3 out of 5 times last week. I was late $\frac{3}{5}$ of the time.

6. The number on the top, 9, is the numerator, and the number on the bottom, 11, is the denominator.

8. The number on the top, 9, is the numerator, and the number on the bottom, 10, is the denominator.

10. The number on the top, 1, is the numerator, and the number on the bottom, 15, is the denominator.

12. One out of two equal parts is shaded. The fraction is $\frac{1}{2}$.

14. Three out of ten equal parts are shaded. The fraction is $\frac{3}{10}$.

16. Two out of three equal parts are shaded. The fraction is $\frac{2}{3}$.

18. Three out of eight equal parts are shaded. The fraction is $\frac{3}{8}$.

20. One out of four equal parts is shaded. The fraction is $\frac{1}{4}$.

22. Four out of eleven equal parts are shaded. The fraction is $\frac{4}{11}$.

24. One out of eight equal parts is shaded. The fraction is $\frac{1}{8}$.

26. Five out of nine circles are shaded. The fraction is $\frac{5}{9}$.

28. Seven out of twelve rectangles are shaded. The fraction is $\frac{7}{12}$.

30. Twelve out of fifteen circles are shaded. The fraction is $\frac{12}{15}$.

32. $\frac{3}{7}$; divide a rectangular bar into 7 equal parts. Then shade 3 parts.

34. $\frac{5}{12}$; divide a rectangular bar into 12 equal parts. Then shade 5 parts.

36. $\frac{5}{9}$; divide a rectangular bar into 9 equal parts. Then shade 5 parts.

38. $\dfrac{\text{sales tax}}{\text{total price}} = \dfrac{7}{98}$

40. $\dfrac{\text{amount used to repay}}{\text{total earnings}} = \dfrac{48}{165}$

42. $\dfrac{\text{part time}}{\text{total}} = \dfrac{31}{78+31} = \dfrac{31}{109}$

44. $\dfrac{\text{puppies or adult dogs}}{\text{animals}} = \dfrac{12+25}{12+25+14+31} = \dfrac{37}{82}$

46. $\dfrac{\text{jazz or blues}}{\text{total CDs}} = \dfrac{6+24}{5+6+4+24} = \dfrac{30}{39}$

48. a. $\dfrac{12+19}{25+33} = \dfrac{31}{58}$

b. $\dfrac{8}{25}$

50. We cannot do it. Division by zero is undefined.

Cumulative Review

51.
$$\begin{array}{r} 18 \\ 27 \\ 34 \\ 16 \\ 125 \\ +\ 21 \\ \hline 241 \end{array}$$

52.
$$\begin{array}{r} 56,203 \\ -42,987 \\ \hline 13,216 \end{array}$$

53.
$$\begin{array}{r} 3178 \\ \times\quad 46 \\ \hline 19\ 068 \\ 127\ 12 \\ \hline 146,188 \end{array}$$

54.
$$\begin{array}{r} 1258\ \text{R }4 \\ 24\overline{)30,196} \\ \underline{24} \\ 6\ 1 \\ \underline{4\ 8} \\ 1\ 39 \\ \underline{1\ 20} \\ 196 \\ \underline{192} \\ 4 \end{array}$$

Classroom Quiz 2.1

1. Five out of eight equal parts are shaded. The fraction is $\dfrac{5}{8}$.

2. $\dfrac{\text{number of fixed-rate mortgages}}{\text{total number of mortgages}} = \dfrac{213}{388}$

3. $\dfrac{\text{number who did not drive motorcycles}}{\text{total number of students}}$
$= \dfrac{5+10+17}{3+5+10+17}$
$= \dfrac{32}{35}$

2.2 Exercises

2. A prime number is a whole number greater than 1 that cannot be evenly *divided* except by itself and 1.

4. Every composite number can be written in exactly one way as a *product* of *prime* numbers.

6. $\dfrac{23}{135} = \dfrac{46}{270}$; answers will vary.

8. $9 = 3 \times 3 = 3^2$

10. $8 = 2 \times 4 = 2 \times 2 \times 2 = 2^3$

12. $30 = 2 \times 15 = 2 \times 3 \times 5$

14. $81 = 9 \times 9 = 3 \times 3 \times 3 \times 3 = 3^4$

16. $42 = 6 \times 7 = 2 \times 3 \times 7$

18. $48 = 4 \times 12$
$= 2 \times 2 \times 2 \times 6$
$= 2 \times 2 \times 2 \times 2 \times 3$
$= 2^4 \times 3$

20. $125 = 5 \times 25 = 5 \times 5 \times 5 = 5^3$

22. $99 = 9 \times 11 = 3^2 \times 11$

24. $135 = 27 \times 5 = 3^3 \times 5$

26. $216 = 8 \times 27 = 2^3 \times 3^3$

28. 31 is prime.

30. $51 = 3 \times 17$

32. 71 is prime.

34. $91 = 7 \times 13$

36. 97 is prime.

38. $119 = 7 \times 17$

40. $95 = 5 \times 19$

42. $143 = 11 \times 13$

44. $\dfrac{16}{24} = \dfrac{16 \div 8}{24 \div 8} = \dfrac{2}{3}$

46. $\dfrac{28}{49} = \dfrac{28 \div 7}{49 \div 7} = \dfrac{4}{7}$

48. $\dfrac{45}{75} = \dfrac{45 \div 15}{75 \div 15} = \dfrac{3}{5}$

50. $\dfrac{110}{140} = \dfrac{110 \div 10}{140 \div 10} = \dfrac{11}{14}$

52. $\dfrac{7}{21} = \dfrac{7 \times 1}{7 \times 3} = \dfrac{1}{3}$

54. $\dfrac{42}{56} = \dfrac{2 \times 3 \times 7}{2 \times 2 \times 2 \times 7} = \dfrac{3}{4}$

56. $\dfrac{65}{91} = \dfrac{5 \times 13}{7 \times 13} = \dfrac{5}{7}$

58. $\dfrac{42}{70} = \dfrac{2 \times 3 \times 7}{2 \times 5 \times 7} = \dfrac{3}{5}$

60. $\dfrac{40}{96} = \dfrac{40 \div 8}{96 \div 8} = \dfrac{5}{12}$

62. $\dfrac{72}{132} = \dfrac{72 \div 12}{132 \div 12} = \dfrac{6}{11}$

64. $\dfrac{125}{200} = \dfrac{25 \times 5}{25 \times 8} = \dfrac{5}{8}$

66. $\dfrac{200}{300} = \dfrac{2 \times 100}{3 \times 100} = \dfrac{2}{3}$

68. $\dfrac{210}{390} = \dfrac{30 \times 7}{30 \times 13} = \dfrac{7}{13}$

70. $\dfrac{10}{65} \overset{?}{=} \dfrac{2}{13}$
$10 \times 13 \overset{?}{=} 65 \times 2$
$\qquad 130 = 130$
Yes

72. $\dfrac{24}{72} \overset{?}{=} \dfrac{15}{45}$
$24 \times 45 \overset{?}{=} 72 \times 15$
$\qquad 1080 = 1080$
Yes

74. $\dfrac{70}{120} \overset{?}{=} \dfrac{41}{73}$
$70 \times 73 \overset{?}{=} 120 \times 41$
$\qquad 5110 \neq 4920$
No

76. $\dfrac{18}{24} \overset{?}{=} \dfrac{23}{28}$
$18 \times 28 \overset{?}{=} 24 \times 23$
$\qquad 504 \neq 552$
No

78. $\dfrac{21}{27} \overset{?}{=} \dfrac{112}{144}$
$21 \times 144 \overset{?}{=} 27 \times 112$
$\qquad 3024 = 3024$
Yes

80. $\dfrac{12}{16} = \dfrac{3 \times 4}{4 \times 4} = \dfrac{3}{4}$ in the emergency room.

$\dfrac{4}{16} = \dfrac{4}{4 \times 4} = \dfrac{1}{4}$ in surgery.

82. $\dfrac{315 - 20}{315} = \dfrac{295}{315}$
$\qquad\qquad = \dfrac{5 \times 59}{5 \times 63}$
$\qquad\qquad = \dfrac{59}{63}$

$\dfrac{59}{63}$ of the beepers were not defective.

84. $\dfrac{5,500}{42,500} = \dfrac{11 \times 500}{85 \times 500} = \dfrac{11}{85}$

They have saved $\dfrac{11}{85}$ of the cost of the land.

86. Total number of students is
$1100 + 1700 + 900 + 500 + 300 = 4500.$
$\dfrac{900}{4500} = \dfrac{900 \div 900}{4500 \div 900} = \dfrac{1}{5}$

$\dfrac{1}{5}$ of the students have a medium commute.

88. $\dfrac{1100+1700+900}{4500} = \dfrac{3700}{4500}$

$$= \dfrac{3700 \div 100}{4500 \div 100}$$

$$= \dfrac{37}{45}$$

$\dfrac{37}{45}$ of the students consider their commute less than long.

Cumulative Review

89.
$$
\begin{array}{r}
386 \\
\times\ \ 425 \\
\hline
1\,930 \\
7\,72\ \ \\
154\,4\ \ \ \\
\hline
164,050
\end{array}
$$

90.
$$
\begin{array}{r}
1296 \\
12\overline{)15,552} \\
\underline{12\ \ \ \ \ \ } \\
3\,5 \\
\underline{2\,4} \\
1\,15 \\
\underline{1\,08} \\
72 \\
\underline{72} \\
0
\end{array}
$$

91.
$$
\begin{array}{r}
3200 \\
\times\ \ \ 300 \\
\hline
960,000
\end{array}
$$

92.
$$
\begin{array}{r}
5,130,800,000 \\
-\ 4,559,200,000 \\
\hline
571,600,000
\end{array}
$$

The income of the YMCA was $571,600,000 greater than that of the Salvation Army.

Classroom Quiz 2.2

1. $\dfrac{77}{121} = \dfrac{7 \times 11}{11 \times 11} = \dfrac{7}{11}$

2. $\dfrac{42}{96} = \dfrac{2 \times 3 \times 7}{2 \times 2 \times 2 \times 2 \times 2 \times 3} = \dfrac{7}{16}$

3. $\dfrac{135}{60} = \dfrac{3 \times 3 \times 3 \times 5}{2 \times 2 \times 3 \times 5} = \dfrac{9}{4}$

2.3 Exercises

2. a. Divide the numerator by the denominator.

   b. Write the quotient followed by the fraction with the remainder over the denominator.

4. $2\dfrac{3}{4} = \dfrac{2 \times 4 + 3}{4} = \dfrac{11}{4}$

6. $3\dfrac{3}{8} = \dfrac{3 \times 8 + 3}{8} = \dfrac{27}{8}$

8. $8\dfrac{3}{8} = \dfrac{8 \times 8 + 3}{8} = \dfrac{67}{8}$

10. $15\dfrac{3}{4} = \dfrac{15 \times 4 + 3}{4} = \dfrac{63}{4}$

12. $15\dfrac{4}{5} = \dfrac{15 \times 5 + 4}{5} = \dfrac{79}{5}$

14. $41\dfrac{1}{2} = \dfrac{41 \times 2 + 1}{2} = \dfrac{83}{2}$

16. $6\dfrac{6}{7} = \dfrac{6 \times 7 + 6}{7} = \dfrac{48}{7}$

18. $13\dfrac{5}{7} = \dfrac{13 \times 7 + 5}{7} = \dfrac{96}{7}$

20. $4\dfrac{1}{50} = \dfrac{4 \times 50 + 1}{50} = \dfrac{201}{50}$

22. $12\dfrac{5}{6} = \dfrac{12 \times 6 + 5}{6} = \dfrac{77}{6}$

24. $207\dfrac{2}{3} = \dfrac{207 \times 3 + 2}{3} = \dfrac{623}{3}$

26. $33\dfrac{1}{3} = \dfrac{33 \times 3 + 1}{3} = \dfrac{100}{3}$

28. $5\dfrac{19}{20} = \dfrac{5 \times 20 + 19}{20} = \dfrac{119}{20}$

30. $5\dfrac{17}{20} = \dfrac{5 \times 20 + 17}{20} = \dfrac{117}{20}$

32. $4\overline{)13}$ with quotient 3
$\underline{12}$
1

$$\frac{13}{4} = 3\frac{1}{4}$$

34. $5\overline{)9}$ with quotient 1
$\underline{5}$
4

$$\frac{9}{5} = 1\frac{4}{5}$$

36. $6\overline{)23}$ with quotient 3
$\underline{18}$
5

$$\frac{23}{6} = 3\frac{5}{6}$$

38. $5\overline{)80}$ with quotient 16
$\underline{5}$
30
$\underline{30}$
0

$$\frac{80}{5} = 16$$

40. $13\overline{)42}$ with quotient 3
$\underline{39}$
3

$$\frac{42}{13} = 3\frac{3}{13}$$

42. $2\overline{)47}$ with quotient 23
$\underline{4}$
7
$\underline{6}$
1

$$\frac{47}{2} = 23\frac{1}{2}$$

44. $17\overline{)54}$ with quotient 3
$\underline{51}$
3

$$\frac{54}{17} = 3\frac{3}{17}$$

46. $3\overline{)19}$ with quotient 6
$\underline{18}$
1

$$\frac{19}{3} = 6\frac{1}{3}$$

48. $10\overline{)83}$ with quotient 8
$\underline{80}$
3

$$\frac{83}{10} = 8\frac{3}{10}$$

50. $11\overline{)132}$ with quotient 12
$\underline{11}$
22
$\underline{22}$
0

$$\frac{132}{11} = 12$$

52. $7\overline{)183}$ with quotient 26
$\underline{14}$
43
$\underline{42}$
1

$$\frac{183}{7} = 26\frac{1}{7}$$

54. $9\overline{)196}$ with quotient 21
$\underline{18}$
16
$\underline{9}$
7

$$\frac{196}{9} = 21\frac{7}{9}$$

56. $8\overline{)104}$ quotient 13
$\phantom{8\overline{)}}\underline{8}$
$\phantom{8\overline{)}}24$
$\phantom{8\overline{)}}\underline{24}$
$\phantom{8\overline{)}}0$

$\dfrac{104}{8} = 13$

58. $25\overline{)154}$ quotient 6
$\phantom{25\overline{)}}\underline{150}$
$\phantom{25\overline{)}}4$

$\dfrac{154}{25} = 6\dfrac{4}{25}$

60. $\dfrac{6}{8} = \dfrac{2\times 3}{2\times 4} = \dfrac{3}{4}$

$4\dfrac{6}{8} = 4\dfrac{3}{4}$

62. $\dfrac{15}{90} = \dfrac{1\times 15}{6\times 15} = \dfrac{1}{6}$

$3\dfrac{15}{90} = 3\dfrac{1}{6}$

64. $\dfrac{15}{75} = \dfrac{15\times 1}{15\times 5} = \dfrac{1}{5}$

$10\dfrac{15}{75} = 10\dfrac{1}{5}$

66. $\dfrac{36}{4} = \dfrac{4\times 9}{4} = 9$

68. $\dfrac{63}{45} = \dfrac{9\times 7}{9\times 5} = \dfrac{7}{5}$

70. $\dfrac{112}{21} = \dfrac{7\times 16}{7\times 3} = \dfrac{16}{3}$

72. $360\overline{)390}$ quotient 1
$\phantom{360\overline{)}}\underline{360}$
$\phantom{360\overline{)}}30$

$\dfrac{390}{360} = 1\dfrac{30}{360}$

$\dfrac{30}{360} = \dfrac{1\times 30}{12\times 30} = \dfrac{1}{12}$

$\dfrac{390}{360} = 1\dfrac{30}{360} = 1\dfrac{1}{12}$

74. $328\overline{)764}$ quotient 2
$\phantom{328\overline{)}}\underline{656}$
$\phantom{328\overline{)}}108$

$\dfrac{764}{328} = 2\dfrac{108}{328}$

$\dfrac{108}{328} = \dfrac{4\times 27}{4\times 82} = \dfrac{27}{82}$

$\dfrac{764}{328} = 2\dfrac{108}{328} = 2\dfrac{27}{82}$

76. $1000\overline{)2150}$ quotient 2
$\phantom{1000\overline{)}}\underline{2000}$
$\phantom{1000\overline{)}}150$

$\dfrac{2150}{1000} = 2\dfrac{150}{1000}$

$\dfrac{150}{1000} = \dfrac{3\times 50}{20\times 50} = \dfrac{3}{20}$

$\dfrac{2150}{1000} = 2\dfrac{150}{1000} = 2\dfrac{3}{20}$

78. $244\dfrac{3}{4} = \dfrac{244\times 4 + 3}{4} = \dfrac{979}{4}$

The students used $\dfrac{979}{4}$ pounds of clay.

80. $4\overline{)331}$ quotient 82
$\phantom{4\overline{)}}\underline{32}$
$\phantom{4\overline{)}}11$
$\phantom{4\overline{)}}\underline{8}$
$\phantom{4\overline{)}}3$

$\dfrac{331}{4} = 82\dfrac{3}{4}$

He would need $82\dfrac{3}{4}$ square yards of fabric.

82.

$$\begin{array}{r} 171 \\ 8\overline{)1373} \\ \underline{8} \\ 57 \\ \underline{56} \\ 13 \\ \underline{8} \\ 5 \end{array}$$

$$\frac{1373}{8} = 171\frac{5}{8}$$

A total of $171\frac{5}{8}$ feet of shelving was used.

84. No; 157 is prime and is not a factor of 9810.

Cumulative Review

85.

$$\begin{array}{r} 1,398,210 \\ -1,137,963 \\ \hline 260,247 \end{array}$$

86. $80,000 \times 200,000 = 16,000,000,000$

87. $300,000 \div 1000 = 300$

88.

$$\begin{array}{r} 37 \\ 24\overline{)893} \\ \underline{72} \\ 173 \\ \underline{168} \\ 5 \end{array}$$

37 full cartons are needed. There are 5 books in the carton that is not full.

Classroom Quiz 2.3

1. $3\frac{5}{16} = \frac{3 \times 16 + 5}{16} = \frac{53}{16}$

2.

$$\begin{array}{r} 5 \\ 11\overline{)65} \\ \underline{55} \\ 10 \end{array}$$

$$\frac{65}{11} = 5\frac{10}{11}$$

3. $\frac{68}{17} = \frac{4 \times 17}{1 \times 17} = \frac{4}{1} = 4$

2.4 Exercises

2. $\frac{1}{8} \times \frac{5}{11} = \frac{1 \times 5}{8 \times 11} = \frac{5}{88}$

4. $\frac{4}{7} \times \frac{3}{5} = \frac{4 \times 3}{7 \times 5} = \frac{12}{35}$

6. $\frac{7}{8} \times \frac{16}{21} = \frac{\overset{1}{\cancel{7}}}{\underset{1}{\cancel{8}}} \times \frac{\overset{2}{\cancel{16}}}{\underset{3}{\cancel{21}}} = \frac{2}{3}$

8. $\frac{22}{45} \times \frac{5}{11} = \frac{\overset{2}{\cancel{22}}}{\underset{9}{\cancel{45}}} \times \frac{\overset{1}{\cancel{5}}}{\underset{1}{\cancel{11}}} = \frac{2}{9}$

10. $\frac{9}{4} \times \frac{13}{27} = \frac{\overset{1}{\cancel{9}}}{4} \times \frac{13}{\underset{3}{\cancel{27}}} = \frac{13}{12} \text{ or } 1\frac{1}{12}$

12. $\frac{12}{17} \times \frac{3}{24} = \frac{\overset{1}{\cancel{12}}}{17} \times \frac{3}{\underset{2}{\cancel{24}}} = \frac{3}{34}$

14. $\frac{8}{9} \times 6 = \frac{8}{9} \times \frac{6}{1} = \frac{8 \times 2 \times 3}{3 \times 3} = \frac{8 \times 2}{3} = \frac{16}{3} \text{ or } 5\frac{1}{3}$

16. $5 \times \frac{7}{25} = \frac{5}{1} \times \frac{7}{25} = \frac{\overset{1}{\cancel{5}}}{1} \times \frac{7}{\underset{5}{\cancel{25}}} = \frac{7}{5} \text{ or } 1\frac{2}{5}$

18. $\frac{8}{7} \times \frac{5}{12} \times \frac{3}{10} = \frac{\overset{1}{\cancel{8}}}{7} \times \frac{\overset{1}{\cancel{5}}}{\underset{1}{\cancel{12}}} \times \frac{\overset{1}{\cancel{3}}}{\underset{1}{\cancel{10}}} = \frac{1}{7}$

20. $\frac{5}{7} \times \frac{15}{2} \times \frac{28}{15} = \frac{5 \times 15 \times 7 \times 2 \times 2}{7 \times 2 \times 15} = \frac{5 \times 2}{1} = 10$

22. $\frac{5}{6} \times 3\frac{3}{5} = \frac{5}{6} \times \frac{18}{5} = \frac{3}{1} = 3$

24. $12 \times 5\frac{7}{12} = \frac{12}{1} \times \frac{67}{12} = 67$

26. $0 \times 6\frac{2}{3} = 0$

28. $\frac{5}{5} \times 11\frac{5}{7} = 1 \times \frac{82}{7} = \frac{82}{7}$ or $11\frac{5}{7}$

30. $2\frac{3}{5} \times 1\frac{4}{7} = \frac{13}{5} \times \frac{11}{7} = \frac{143}{35}$ or $4\frac{3}{35}$

32. $4\frac{3}{5} \times \frac{1}{10} = \frac{23}{5} \times \frac{1}{10} = \frac{23}{50}$

34. $5\frac{1}{4} \times 4\frac{4}{7} = \frac{21}{4} \times \frac{32}{7} = \frac{3}{1} \times \frac{8}{1} = 24$

36. $\frac{8}{9} \times 4\frac{1}{11} = \frac{8}{9} \times \frac{45}{11} = \frac{40}{11}$ or $3\frac{7}{11}$

38. $\frac{14}{17} \times \frac{34}{42} = \frac{14 \times 2 \times 17}{17 \times 14 \times 3} = \frac{2}{3}$

40. $4\frac{3}{5} \times 3\frac{3}{4} = \frac{23}{5} \times \frac{15}{4} = \frac{23}{1} \times \frac{3}{4} = \frac{69}{4}$ or $17\frac{1}{4}$

42. $\frac{12}{17} \cdot x = \frac{144}{85}$

    Since $12 \cdot 12 = 144$ and $17 \cdot 5 = 85$,

    $\frac{12}{17} \cdot \frac{12}{5} = \frac{144}{85}$.

    Thus, $x = \frac{12}{5}$.

44. $x \cdot \frac{11}{15} = \frac{77}{225}$

    Since $7 \cdot 11 = 77$ and $15 \cdot 15 = 225$,

    $\frac{7}{15} \cdot \frac{11}{15} = \frac{77}{225}$.

    Therefore, $x = \frac{7}{15}$.

46. $22\frac{5}{8} \times 16\frac{1}{2} = \frac{22 \times 8 + 5}{6} \times \frac{16 \times 2 + 1}{2}$

    $= \frac{181}{8} \times \frac{33}{2}$

    $= \frac{5973}{16}$

    $= 3773\frac{5}{16}$

    The area of the tornado danger zone is

    $373\frac{5}{16}$ square miles.

48. $6\frac{1}{2} \times 56,800 = \frac{13}{2} \times \frac{56,800}{1}$

    $= \frac{13}{1} \times \frac{28,400}{1}$

    $= 359,200$

    The house was worth \$359,200 in 2007.

50. $30 \times 20\frac{1}{2} = \frac{30}{1} \times \frac{41}{2} = \frac{15 \times 2 \times 41}{2} = 15 \times 41 = 615$

    615 square feet of carpet is needed.

52. $\frac{1}{15} \times 225 = \frac{1}{15} \times \frac{225}{1} = \frac{1}{1} \times \frac{15}{1} = 15$

    15 rooms contain surgery patients.

54. $26,500 \times \frac{4}{5} = 21,200$

    The car was worth \$21,200 after one year.

56. $\frac{1340}{1} \times \frac{2}{5} \times \frac{1}{4} = \frac{134 \times 2 \times 5}{1} \times \frac{2}{5} \times \frac{1}{2 \times 2} = 134$

    134 students live in the city and attend classes on Monday, Wednesday, and Friday.

58. There are an infinite number of answers. Any fraction that can be simplified to $\frac{3}{7}$ would be a correct answer. Thus three possible answers to this problem are $\frac{6}{14}, \frac{9}{21}$, or $\frac{12}{28}$.

Cumulative Review

59.
$$31\overline{)16,399}$$
$$\underline{15\ 5}$$
$$89$$
$$\underline{62}$$
$$279$$
$$\underline{279}$$
$$0$$

quotient: 529

The average number of cars using the bridge in one day is 529 cars.

60.
$$42\overline{)15,456}$$
$$\underline{12\ 6}$$
$$2\ 85$$
$$\underline{2\ 52}$$
$$336$$
$$\underline{336}$$
$$0$$

quotient: 368

The average number of calls made per month by one salesperson is 368 calls.

61.
$$\begin{array}{r} 240 \\ \times\ 21 \\ \hline 240 \\ 480 \\ \hline 5040 \end{array}$$

Gerald drives a total of 5040 miles in one year.

62.
$$\begin{array}{r} 12,360 \\ \times\ \ \ 14 \\ \hline 49\ 440 \\ 123\ 60 \\ \hline 173,040 \end{array}$$

In 14 hours, the jet will use 173,040 gallons.

Classroom Quiz 2.4

1. $21 \times \dfrac{5}{7} = \dfrac{21}{1} \times \dfrac{5}{7} = \dfrac{3 \times 7}{1} \times \dfrac{5}{7} = \dfrac{3}{1} \times \dfrac{5}{1} = 15$

2. $\dfrac{13}{15} \times \dfrac{5}{12} = \dfrac{13}{3} \times \dfrac{1}{12} = \dfrac{13}{36}$

3. $7\dfrac{2}{3} \times 1\dfrac{1}{5} = \dfrac{23}{3} \times \dfrac{6}{5} = \dfrac{23}{1} \times \dfrac{2}{5} = \dfrac{46}{5}$ or $9\dfrac{1}{5}$

2.5 Exercises

2. One way to think about it is to imagine how many $\dfrac{1}{3}$-pound rocks could be put in a bag that holds 2 pounds of rocks and then imagine how many $\dfrac{1}{2}$-pound rocks could be put in the same bag. The number of $\dfrac{1}{3}$ pound rocks would be larger. Therefore, $2 \div \dfrac{1}{3}$ is a larger number.

4. $\dfrac{3}{13} \div \dfrac{9}{26} = \dfrac{3}{13} \times \dfrac{26}{9} = \dfrac{2}{3}$

6. $\dfrac{25}{49} \div \dfrac{5}{7} = \dfrac{25}{49} \times \dfrac{7}{5} = \dfrac{5}{7}$

8. $\dfrac{8}{15} \div \dfrac{24}{35} = \dfrac{8}{15} \times \dfrac{35}{24} = \dfrac{7}{9}$

10. $\dfrac{3}{4} \div \dfrac{2}{3} = \dfrac{3}{4} \times \dfrac{3}{2} = \dfrac{9}{8}$ or $1\dfrac{1}{8}$

12. $\dfrac{2}{7} \div \dfrac{2}{7} = \dfrac{2}{7} \times \dfrac{7}{2} = 1$

14. $\dfrac{11}{12} \div \dfrac{1}{5} = \dfrac{11}{12} \times \dfrac{5}{1} = \dfrac{55}{12}$ or $4\dfrac{7}{12}$

16. $1 \div \dfrac{3}{7} = 1 \times \dfrac{7}{3} = \dfrac{7}{3}$ or $2\dfrac{1}{3}$

18. $2 \div \dfrac{7}{8} = \dfrac{2}{1} \times \dfrac{8}{7} = \dfrac{16}{7}$ or $2\dfrac{2}{7}$

20. $\dfrac{9}{16} \div 1 = \dfrac{9}{16} \times 1 = \dfrac{9}{16}$

22. $0 \div \dfrac{5}{16} = 0 \times \dfrac{16}{5} = 0$

24. $\dfrac{24}{29} \div 0$

Division by 0 is undefined.

26. $16 \div \dfrac{8}{11} = \dfrac{16}{1} \times \dfrac{11}{8} = 22$

28. $\dfrac{5}{6} \div \dfrac{12}{1} = \dfrac{5}{6} \times \dfrac{1}{12} = \dfrac{5}{72}$

30. $\dfrac{3}{4} \div \dfrac{9}{16} = \dfrac{3}{4} \times \dfrac{16}{9} = \dfrac{4}{3}$ or $1\dfrac{1}{3}$

32. $2\dfrac{2}{3} \div 4\dfrac{1}{3} = \dfrac{8}{3} \div \dfrac{13}{3} = \dfrac{8}{3} \times \dfrac{3}{13} = \dfrac{8}{13}$

34. $9\dfrac{1}{3} \div 3\dfrac{1}{9} = \dfrac{28}{3} \div \dfrac{28}{9} = \dfrac{28}{3} \times \dfrac{9}{28} = 3$

36. $8000 \div \dfrac{4}{7} = \dfrac{8000}{1} \div \dfrac{4}{7} = \dfrac{8000}{1} \times \dfrac{7}{4} = 14{,}000$

38. $\dfrac{\frac{5}{9}}{100} = \dfrac{5}{9} \div 100 = \dfrac{5}{9} \times \dfrac{1}{100} = \dfrac{1}{180}$

40. $\dfrac{\frac{3}{16}}{\frac{5}{8}} = \dfrac{3}{16} \div \dfrac{5}{8} = \dfrac{3}{16} \times \dfrac{8}{5} = \dfrac{3}{10}$

42. $4\dfrac{3}{4} \div \dfrac{1}{4} = \dfrac{19}{4} \div \dfrac{1}{4} = \dfrac{19}{4} \times \dfrac{4}{1} = 19$

44. $6\dfrac{1}{2} \times \dfrac{1}{3} = \dfrac{13}{2} \times \dfrac{1}{3} = \dfrac{13}{6}$ or $2\dfrac{1}{6}$

46. $1\dfrac{2}{9} \div 4\dfrac{1}{3} = \dfrac{11}{9} \div \dfrac{13}{3} = \dfrac{11}{9} \times \dfrac{3}{13} = \dfrac{11}{39}$

48. $7 \div 1\dfrac{2}{5} = \dfrac{7}{1} \div \dfrac{7}{5} = \dfrac{7}{1} \times \dfrac{5}{7} = \dfrac{5}{1} = 5$

50. $14\dfrac{2}{3} \div 3\dfrac{1}{2} = \dfrac{44}{3} \div \dfrac{7}{2} = \dfrac{44}{3} \times \dfrac{2}{7} = \dfrac{88}{21}$ or $4\dfrac{4}{21}$

52. $\dfrac{16}{3} \div 5\dfrac{1}{3} = \dfrac{16}{3} \div \dfrac{16}{3} = \dfrac{16}{3} \times \dfrac{3}{16} = 1$

54. $\dfrac{11}{20} \times 4\dfrac{1}{2} = \dfrac{11}{20} \times \dfrac{9}{2} = \dfrac{99}{40}$ or $2\dfrac{19}{40}$

56. $5\dfrac{5}{6} \div 7 = \dfrac{35}{6} \div \dfrac{7}{1} = \dfrac{35}{6} \times \dfrac{1}{7} = \dfrac{5}{6}$

58. $\dfrac{8}{2\frac{1}{2}} = 8 \div \dfrac{5}{2} = \dfrac{8}{1} \times \dfrac{2}{5} = \dfrac{16}{5}$ or $3\dfrac{1}{5}$

60. $\dfrac{5\frac{2}{3}}{0}$ is undefined.

62. $\dfrac{\frac{9}{10}}{3\frac{3}{5}} = \dfrac{9}{10} \div 3\dfrac{3}{5} = \dfrac{9}{10} \div \dfrac{18}{5} = \dfrac{9}{10} \times \dfrac{5}{18} = \dfrac{1}{4}$

64. $4\dfrac{2}{3} \times 5\dfrac{1}{7} = \dfrac{14}{3} \times \dfrac{36}{7} = \dfrac{2 \times 7 \times 3 \times 12}{3 \times 7} = 2 \times 12 = 24$

66. $x \div \dfrac{2}{5} = \dfrac{15}{16}$

$x \cdot \dfrac{5}{2} = \dfrac{15}{16}$

$\dfrac{3}{8} \cdot \dfrac{5}{2} = \dfrac{15}{16}$

$x = \dfrac{3}{8}$

68. $x \div \dfrac{11}{6} = \dfrac{54}{121}$

$x \cdot \dfrac{6}{11} = \dfrac{54}{121}$

$\dfrac{9}{11} \cdot \dfrac{6}{11} = \dfrac{54}{121}$

$x = \dfrac{9}{11}$

70. $7\dfrac{1}{2} \div 20 = \dfrac{15}{2} \div \dfrac{20}{1} = \dfrac{15}{2} \times \dfrac{1}{20} = \dfrac{5 \times 3}{2 \times 5 \times 4} = \dfrac{3}{8}$

Each segment of the beach is $\dfrac{3}{8}$ mile.

72. $200 \div 4\dfrac{1}{6} = \dfrac{200}{1} \div \dfrac{25}{6}$

$\phantom{200 \div 4\dfrac{1}{6}} = \dfrac{200}{1} \times \dfrac{6}{25}$

$\phantom{200 \div 4\dfrac{1}{6}} = 8 \times 6$

$\phantom{200 \div 4\dfrac{1}{6}} = 48$

His average speed was 48 miles per hour.

74. $151\dfrac{2}{3} \div 4\dfrac{1}{3} = \dfrac{455}{3} \div \dfrac{13}{3} = \dfrac{455}{3} \times \dfrac{3}{13} = 35$

35 costumes can be made.

76. $16 \div \dfrac{2}{3} = \dfrac{16}{1} \times \dfrac{3}{2} = \dfrac{8 \times 2 \times 3}{2} = 24$

It can be used 24 times.

78. $150 \times \dfrac{4}{5} = 120$

$50 \times \dfrac{5}{8} = \dfrac{125}{4} = 31\dfrac{1}{4}$

Number of pens $= \left(120 + 31\dfrac{1}{4}\right)1200$

$= 151\dfrac{1}{4} \times 1200$

$= \dfrac{605}{4} \times \dfrac{1200}{1}$

$= 181,500$

181,500 pens can be filled.

80. $18 \times 28 = 504$

Exact $= 18\dfrac{1}{4} \times 27\dfrac{1}{2} = \dfrac{73}{4} \times \dfrac{55}{2} = \dfrac{4015}{8} = 501\dfrac{7}{8}$

It is off by only $2\dfrac{1}{8}$.

Cumulative Review

81. $39,576,304 =$ thirty-nine million, five hundred seventy-six thousand, three hundred four

82. $509,270 = 500,000 + 9000 + 200 + 70$

83. $126 + 34 + 9 + 891 + 12 + 27 = 1099$

84. $87,595,631$

85. $\dfrac{9}{10} + \dfrac{3}{5} = \dfrac{9}{10} + \dfrac{3 \times 2}{5 \times 2} = \dfrac{9}{10} + \dfrac{6}{10} = \dfrac{15}{10} = \dfrac{3}{2}$ or $1\dfrac{1}{2}$

86. $\dfrac{17}{20} - \dfrac{3}{4} = \dfrac{17}{20} - \dfrac{3 \times 5}{4 \times 5} = \dfrac{17}{20} - \dfrac{15}{20} = \dfrac{2}{20} = \dfrac{1}{10}$

Classroom Quiz 2.5

1. $\dfrac{16}{27} \div \dfrac{4}{13} = \dfrac{16}{27} \times \dfrac{13}{4} = \dfrac{4}{27} \times \dfrac{13}{1} = \dfrac{52}{27}$ or $1\dfrac{25}{27}$

2. $8\dfrac{1}{4} \div 3\dfrac{5}{6} = \dfrac{33}{4} \div \dfrac{23}{6}$

$= \dfrac{33}{4} \times \dfrac{6}{23}$

$= \dfrac{33}{2} \times \dfrac{3}{23}$

$= \dfrac{99}{46}$ or $2\dfrac{7}{46}$

3. $5\dfrac{1}{8} \div 3 = \dfrac{41}{8} \times \dfrac{1}{3} = \dfrac{41}{24}$ or $1\dfrac{17}{24}$

How Am I Doing? Sections 2.1–2.5

1. Three out of eight equal parts are shaded. The fraction is $\dfrac{3}{8}$.

2. $\dfrac{\text{number from outside the country}}{\text{total number}}$

$= \dfrac{800}{3500 + 2600 + 800}$

$= \dfrac{800}{6900}$

$= \dfrac{8 \times 100}{69 \times 100}$

$= \dfrac{8}{69}$

3. $\dfrac{\text{number defective}}{\text{total number}} = \dfrac{5}{124}$

4. $\dfrac{3}{18} = \dfrac{3 \div 3}{18 \div 3} = \dfrac{1}{6}$

5. $\dfrac{13}{39} = \dfrac{13 \div 13}{39 \div 13} = \dfrac{1}{3}$

6. $\dfrac{16}{112} = \dfrac{16 \div 16}{112 \div 16} = \dfrac{1}{7}$

7. $\dfrac{175}{200} = \dfrac{175 \div 25}{200 \div 25} = \dfrac{7}{8}$

8. $\dfrac{44}{121} = \dfrac{44 \div 11}{121 \div 11} = \dfrac{4}{11}$

9. $3\dfrac{2}{3} = \dfrac{3 \times 3 + 2}{3} = \dfrac{11}{3}$

10. $15\dfrac{1}{3} = \dfrac{15 \times 3 + 1}{3} = \dfrac{46}{3}$

11. $4\overline{)81}$
$\underline{8}$
01

$\underline{0}$
1

$\dfrac{81}{4} = 20\dfrac{1}{4}$

12. $5\overline{)29}$
$\underline{25}$
4

$\dfrac{29}{5} = 5\dfrac{4}{5}$

13. $17\overline{)36}$
$\underline{34}$
2

$\dfrac{36}{17} = 2\dfrac{2}{17}$

14. $\dfrac{5}{11} \times \dfrac{1}{4} = \dfrac{5 \times 1}{11 \times 4} = \dfrac{5}{44}$

15. $\dfrac{3}{7} \times \dfrac{14}{9} = \dfrac{3 \times 2 \times 7}{7 \times 3 \times 3} = \dfrac{2}{3}$

16. $3\dfrac{1}{3} \times 5\dfrac{1}{3} = \dfrac{10}{3} \times \dfrac{16}{3} = \dfrac{160}{9}$ or $17\dfrac{7}{9}$

17. $\dfrac{3}{7} \div \dfrac{3}{7} = \dfrac{3}{7} \times \dfrac{7}{3} = 1$

18. $\dfrac{7}{16} \div \dfrac{7}{8} = \dfrac{7}{16} \times \dfrac{8}{7} = \dfrac{7 \times 8}{2 \times 8 \times 7} = \dfrac{1}{2}$

19. $6\dfrac{4}{7} \div 1\dfrac{5}{21} = \dfrac{46}{7} \div \dfrac{26}{21}$
$\phantom{6\dfrac{4}{7} \div} = \dfrac{46}{7} \times \dfrac{21}{26}$
$\phantom{6\dfrac{4}{7} \div} = \dfrac{2 \times 23 \times 3 \times 7}{7 \times 2 \times 13}$
$\phantom{6\dfrac{4}{7} \div} = \dfrac{69}{13}$ or $5\dfrac{4}{13}$

20. $12 \div \dfrac{4}{7} = \dfrac{12}{1} \times \dfrac{7}{4} = \dfrac{3}{1} \times \dfrac{7}{1} = 21$

Test on Sections 2.1–2.5

1. $\dfrac{\text{number answered correctly}}{\text{total number of questions}} = \dfrac{33}{40}$

2. $\dfrac{\text{number of correct weight}}{\text{total number}} = \dfrac{340}{340 + 112}$
$\phantom{\dfrac{\text{number of correct weight}}{\text{total number}}} = \dfrac{340}{452}$
$\phantom{\dfrac{\text{number of correct weight}}{\text{total number}}} = \dfrac{340 \div 4}{452 \div 4}$
$\phantom{\dfrac{\text{number of correct weight}}{\text{total number}}} = \dfrac{85}{113}$

3. $\dfrac{19}{38} = \dfrac{19 \div 19}{38 \div 19} = \dfrac{1}{2}$

4. $\dfrac{40}{56} = \dfrac{40 \div 8}{56 \div 8} = \dfrac{5}{7}$

5. $\dfrac{24}{66} = \dfrac{24 \div 6}{66 \div 6} = \dfrac{4}{11}$

6. $\dfrac{125}{155} = \dfrac{125 \div 5}{155 \div 5} = \dfrac{25}{31}$

7. $\dfrac{50}{140} = \dfrac{50 \div 10}{140 \div 10} = \dfrac{5}{14}$

8. $\dfrac{84}{36} = \dfrac{84 \div 12}{36 \div 12} = \dfrac{7}{3}$ or $2\dfrac{1}{3}$

9. $12\dfrac{2}{3} = \dfrac{12 \times 3 + 2}{3} = \dfrac{38}{3}$

10. $4\dfrac{1}{8} = \dfrac{4 \times 8 + 1}{8} = \dfrac{33}{8}$

11. $7\overline{)45}$
$\underline{42}$
3

$\dfrac{45}{7} = 6\dfrac{3}{7}$

12. $9\overline{)75}$ with quotient 8, $\underline{72}$, remainder 3

$$\frac{75}{9} = 8\frac{3}{9} = 8\frac{1}{3}$$

13. $\dfrac{3}{8} \times \dfrac{7}{11} = \dfrac{3 \times 7}{8 \times 11} = \dfrac{21}{88}$

14. $\dfrac{35}{16} \times \dfrac{4}{5} = \dfrac{7}{4} \times \dfrac{1}{1} = \dfrac{7}{4}$ or $1\dfrac{3}{4}$

15. $18 \times \dfrac{5}{6} = \dfrac{18}{1} \times \dfrac{5}{6} = \dfrac{3 \times 6 \times 5}{6} = 3 \times 5 = 15$

16. $\dfrac{3}{8} \times 44 = \dfrac{3}{8} \times \dfrac{44}{1} = \dfrac{3 \times 4 \times 11}{2 \times 4} = \dfrac{3 \times 11}{2} = \dfrac{3}{2}$ or $16\dfrac{1}{2}$

17. $2\dfrac{1}{3} \times 5\dfrac{3}{4} = \dfrac{7}{3} \times \dfrac{23}{4} = \dfrac{161}{12}$ or $13\dfrac{5}{12}$

18. $24 \times 3\dfrac{1}{3} = \dfrac{24}{1} \times \dfrac{10}{3} = \dfrac{8}{1} \times \dfrac{10}{1} = 80$

19. $\dfrac{4}{7} \div \dfrac{3}{4} = \dfrac{4}{7} \times \dfrac{4}{3} = \dfrac{4 \times 4}{7 \times 3} = \dfrac{16}{21}$

20. $\dfrac{8}{9} \div \dfrac{1}{6} = \dfrac{8}{9} \times \dfrac{6}{1} = \dfrac{8 \times 3 \times 2}{3 \times 3} = \dfrac{8 \times 2}{3} = \dfrac{16}{3}$ or $5\dfrac{1}{3}$

21. $5\dfrac{1}{4} \div \dfrac{3}{4} = \dfrac{21}{4} \times \dfrac{4}{3} = \dfrac{7 \times 3 \times 4}{4 \times 3} = 7$

22. $5\dfrac{3}{5} \div 2\dfrac{1}{3} = \dfrac{28}{5} \div \dfrac{7}{3} = \dfrac{28}{5} \times \dfrac{3}{7} = \dfrac{4}{5} \times \dfrac{3}{1} = \dfrac{12}{5}$ or $2\dfrac{2}{5}$

23. $2\dfrac{1}{4} \times 3\dfrac{1}{2} = \dfrac{9}{4} \times \dfrac{7}{2} = \dfrac{63}{8}$ or $7\dfrac{7}{8}$

24. $6 \times 2\dfrac{1}{3} = \dfrac{6}{1} \times \dfrac{7}{3} = \dfrac{2 \times 3 \times 7}{3} = 2 \times 7 = 14$

25. $5 \div 1\dfrac{7}{8} = 5 \div \dfrac{15}{8} = \dfrac{5}{1} \times \dfrac{8}{15} = \dfrac{5 \times 8}{5 \times 3} = \dfrac{8}{3}$ or $2\dfrac{2}{3}$

26. $5\dfrac{3}{4} \div 2 = \dfrac{23}{4} \div 2 = \dfrac{23}{4} \times \dfrac{1}{2} = \dfrac{23}{4 \times 2} = \dfrac{23}{8}$ or $2\dfrac{7}{8}$

27. $\dfrac{13}{20} \div \dfrac{4}{5} = \dfrac{13}{20} \times \dfrac{5}{4} = \dfrac{13 \times 5}{5 \times 4 \times 4} = \dfrac{13}{16}$

28. $\dfrac{4}{7} \div 8 = \dfrac{4}{7} \times \dfrac{1}{8} = \dfrac{4}{7 \times 2 \times 4} = \dfrac{1}{14}$

29. $\dfrac{9}{22} \times \dfrac{11}{16} = \dfrac{9 \times 11}{2 \times 11 \times 16} = \dfrac{9}{32}$

30. $\dfrac{14}{25} \times \dfrac{65}{42} = \dfrac{7 \times 2 \times 13 \times 5}{5 \times 5 \times 2 \times 3 \times 7} = \dfrac{13}{5 \times 3} = \dfrac{13}{15}$

31. $5\dfrac{1}{4} \times 8\dfrac{3}{4} = \dfrac{21}{4} \times \dfrac{35}{4} = \dfrac{735}{16} = 45\dfrac{15}{16}$

The area of the garden is $45\dfrac{15}{16}$ square feet.

32. $2\dfrac{2}{3} \times 1\dfrac{1}{2} = \dfrac{8}{3} \times \dfrac{3}{2} = \dfrac{4 \times 2 \times 3}{3 \times 2} = 4$

She will need 4 cups of flour.

33. $62\dfrac{1}{2} \times \dfrac{3}{4} = \dfrac{125}{2} \times \dfrac{3}{4} = \dfrac{375}{8}$ or $46\dfrac{7}{8}$

She drove $46\dfrac{7}{8}$ miles on the highway.

34. $12\dfrac{3}{8} \div \dfrac{3}{4} = \dfrac{99}{8} \times \dfrac{4}{3}$

$$= \dfrac{3 \times 33 \times 4}{4 \times 2 \times 3}$$

$$= \dfrac{33}{2}$$

$$= 16\dfrac{1}{2} \text{ packages}$$

He had 16 full packages with $\dfrac{3}{4} \times \dfrac{1}{2} = \dfrac{3}{8}$ pound left over.

35. $136 \times \dfrac{3}{8} = \dfrac{136}{1} \times \dfrac{3}{8}$

$$= \dfrac{17 \times 8 \times 3}{8}$$

$$= 17 \times 3$$

$$= 51$$

51 computers have Windows XP installed on them.

36. $\dfrac{3}{10} \times 82{,}000 = \dfrac{3}{10} \times \dfrac{82{,}000}{1}$

$\qquad = \dfrac{3}{1} \times \dfrac{8200}{1}$

$\qquad = 24{,}600$

The average household uses 24,600 gallons of water per year for showers and baths.

37. $132 \div 8\dfrac{1}{4} = 132 \div \dfrac{33}{4}$

$\qquad = \dfrac{132}{1} \times \dfrac{4}{33}$

$\qquad = \dfrac{33 \times 4 \times 4}{33}$

$\qquad = 4 \times 4$

$\qquad = 16$

Yung Kim worked 16 hours last week.

38. $56\dfrac{1}{2} \div 8\dfrac{1}{4} = \dfrac{113}{2} \div \dfrac{33}{4}$

$\qquad = \dfrac{113}{2} \times \dfrac{4}{33}$

$\qquad = \dfrac{113 \times 2 \times 2}{2 \times 33}$

$\qquad = \dfrac{226}{33}$

$\qquad = 6\dfrac{28}{33}$

He can make 6 full tents, with

$8\dfrac{1}{4} \times \dfrac{28}{33} = \dfrac{33}{4} \times \dfrac{28}{33} = 7$ yards left over.

39. $32\dfrac{4}{5} \div \dfrac{4}{5} = \dfrac{164}{5} \times \dfrac{5}{4} = 41$

He can use it for 41 days.

2.6 Exercises

2. 6 and 9
Multiples of 6: 6, 12, 18, 24, 30, ...
Multiples of 9: 9, 18, 27, 36, 45, ...
The least common multiple is 18.

4. 22 and 55
Multiples of 22: 22, 44, 66, 88, 110, ...
Multiples of 55: 55, 110, 165, 220, 275, ...
The least common multiple is 110.

6. 18 and 30
Multiples of 18: 18, 36, 54, 72, 90, ...
Multiples of 30: 30, 60, 90, 120, 150, ...
The least common multiple is 90.

8. 8 and 60
Multiples of 8: 8, 16, 24, 32, 40, 48, 56, 64, 72, 80, 88, 96, 104, 112, 120, ...
Multiples of 60: 60, 120, 180, 240, 300, ...
The least common multiple is 120.

10. 25 and 35
Multiples of 25: 25, 50, 75, 100, 125, 150, 175, 200, ...
Multiples of 35: 35, 70, 105, 140, 175, ...
The least common multiple is 175.

12. $8 = 2^3$
$16 = 2^4$
$LCD = 2^4 = 16$

14. $6 = 2 \times 3$
$5 = 5$
$LCD = 2 \times 3 \times 5 = 30$

16. $16 = 2^4$
$3 = 3$
$LCD = 2^4 \times 3 = 48$

18. $4 = 2^2$
$14 = 2 \times 7$
$LCD = 2^2 \times 7 = 28$

20. $15 = 3 \times 5$
$25 = 5^2$
$LCD = 3 \times 5^2 = 75$

22. $11 = 11$
$44 = 2^2 \times 11$
$LCD = 2^2 \times 11 = 44$

24. $20 = 2^2 \times 5$
$30 = 2 \times 3 \times 5$
$LCD = 2^2 \times 3 \times 5 = 60$

26. $6 = 2 \times 3$
$30 = 2 \times 3 \times 5$
$LCD = 2 \times 3 \times 5 = 30$

28. $20 = 2 \times 2 \times 5$
$70 = 2 \times 5 \times 7$
$LCD = 2^2 \times 5 \times 7 = 140$

30. $30 = 2 \times 3 \times 5$
$50 = 2 \times 5 \times 5$
$\text{LCD} = 2 \times 3 \times 5 \times 5 = 150$

32. $5 = 5$
$3 = 3$
$10 = 2 \times 5$
$\text{LCD} = 2 \times 3 \times 5 = 30$

34. $48 = 2 \times 2 \times 2 \times 2 \times 3$
$12 = 2 \times 2 \times 3$
$8 = 2 \times 2 \times 2$
$\text{LCD} = 2^4 \times 3 = 48$

36. $16 = 2^4$
$20 = 2^2 \times 5$
$5 = 5$
$\text{LCD} = 2^4 \times 5 = 80$

38. $30 = 2 \times 3 \times 5$
$40 = 2^3 \times 5$
$8 = 2^3$
$\text{LCD} = 2^3 \times 3 \times 5 = 120$

40. $36 = 2^2 \times 3^2$
$48 = 2^4 \times 3$
$24 = 2^3 \times 3$
$\text{LCD} = 2^4 \times 3^2 = 144$

42. $\dfrac{1}{5} = \dfrac{1}{5} \times \dfrac{7}{7} = \dfrac{7}{35}$
The numerator is 7.

44. $\dfrac{7}{9} = \dfrac{7}{9} \times \dfrac{9}{9} = \dfrac{63}{81}$
The numerator is 63.

46. $\dfrac{2}{13} = \dfrac{2}{13} \times \dfrac{3}{3} = \dfrac{6}{39}$
The numerator is 6.

48. $\dfrac{3}{50} = \dfrac{3}{50} \times \dfrac{2}{2} = \dfrac{6}{100}$
The numerator is 6.

50. $\dfrac{6}{7} = \dfrac{6}{7} \times \dfrac{21}{21} = \dfrac{126}{147}$
The numerator is 126.

52. $\dfrac{3}{25} = \dfrac{3}{25} \times \dfrac{7}{7} = \dfrac{21}{175}$
The numerator is 21.

54. $\dfrac{9}{10} = \dfrac{9 \times 2}{10 \times 2} = \dfrac{18}{20}$
$\dfrac{3}{4} = \dfrac{3 \times 5}{4 \times 5} = \dfrac{15}{20}$

56. $\dfrac{5}{24} = \dfrac{5 \times 3}{24 \times 3} = \dfrac{15}{72}$
$\dfrac{7}{36} = \dfrac{7 \times 2}{36 \times 2} = \dfrac{14}{72}$

58. $\dfrac{13}{30} = \dfrac{13 \times 8}{30 \times 8} = \dfrac{104}{240}$
$\dfrac{41}{80} = \dfrac{41 \times 3}{80 \times 3} = \dfrac{123}{240}$

60. $9 = 3^2$
$54 = 3^3 \times 2$
$\text{LCD} = 2 \times 3^3 = 54$
$\dfrac{7}{9} = \dfrac{7 \times 6}{9 \times 6} = \dfrac{42}{54}$
$\dfrac{42}{54}$ and $\dfrac{35}{54}$

62. $\text{LCD} = 42$
$\dfrac{6}{7} = \dfrac{6 \times 6}{7 \times 6} = \dfrac{36}{42}$
$\dfrac{19}{42}$ and $\dfrac{36}{42}$

64. $20 = 2^2 \times 5$
$8 = 2^3$
$\text{LCD} = 2^3 \times 5 = 40$
$\dfrac{19}{20} = \dfrac{19 \times 2}{20 \times 2} = \dfrac{38}{40}$
$\dfrac{7}{8} = \dfrac{7 \times 5}{8 \times 5} = \dfrac{35}{40}$
$\dfrac{38}{40}$ and $\dfrac{35}{40}$

66. $10 = 2 \times 5$
$25 = 5^2$
$\text{LCD} = 2 \times 5^2 = 50$

$$\frac{9}{10} = \frac{9 \times 5}{10 \times 5} = \frac{45}{50}$$

$$\frac{3}{25} = \frac{3 \times 2}{25 \times 2} = \frac{6}{50}$$

$$\frac{45}{50} \text{ and } \frac{6}{50}$$

68. $30 = 2 \times 3 \times 5$

$15 = 3 \times 5$

$45 = 3^2 \times 5$

$LCD = 2 \times 3^2 \times 5 = 90$

$$\frac{1}{30} = \frac{1 \times 3}{30 \times 3} = \frac{3}{90}$$

$$\frac{7}{15} = \frac{7 \times 6}{15 \times 6} = \frac{42}{90}$$

$$\frac{1}{45} = \frac{1 \times 2}{45 \times 2} = \frac{2}{90}$$

$$\frac{3}{90}, \frac{42}{90}, \frac{2}{90}$$

70. $9 = 3^2$

$6 = 2 \times 3$

$54 = 2 \times 3^3$

$LCD = 2 \times 3^3 = 54$

$$\frac{5}{9} = \frac{5 \times 6}{9 \times 6} = \frac{30}{54}$$

$$\frac{1}{6} = \frac{1 \times 9}{6 \times 9} = \frac{9}{54}$$

$$\frac{3}{54} = \frac{3}{54}$$

$$\frac{30}{54}, \frac{9}{54}, \frac{3}{54}$$

72. $8 = 2^3$

$14 = 2 \times 7$

$16 = 2^4$

$LCD = 2^4 \times 7 = 112$

$$\frac{3}{8} = \frac{3 \times 14}{8 \times 14} = \frac{42}{112}$$

$$\frac{5}{14} = \frac{5 \times 8}{14 \times 8} = \frac{40}{112}$$

$$\frac{13}{16} = \frac{13 \times 7}{16 \times 7} = \frac{91}{112}$$

$$\frac{42}{112}, \frac{40}{112}, \frac{91}{112}$$

74. a. $32 = 2^5$

$6 = 2 \times 3$

$8 = 2^3$

$LCD = 2^5 \times 3 = 96$

b. $\dfrac{5}{32} = \dfrac{5 \times 3}{32 \times 3} = \dfrac{15}{96}$

$$\frac{5}{6} = \frac{5 \times 16}{6 \times 16} = \frac{80}{96}$$

$$\frac{7}{8} = \frac{7 \times 12}{8 \times 12} = \frac{84}{96}$$

$$\frac{15}{96}, \frac{80}{96}, \frac{84}{96}$$

Cumulative Review

75.
$$\begin{array}{r} 208 \text{ R } 13 \\ 35\overline{)7293} \\ \underline{70} \\ 293 \\ \underline{280} \\ 13 \end{array}$$

76.
$$\begin{array}{r} 2566 \\ \times\ \ \ 30 \\ \hline 76,980 \end{array}$$

77. $(5-3)^2 + 4 \times 6 - 3 = 2^2 + 4 \times 6 - 3$
$= 4 + 4 \times 6 - 3$
$= 4 + 24 - 3$
$= 28 - 3$
$= 25$

Classroom Quiz 2.6

1. $14 = 2 \times 7$

$35 = 5 \times 7$

$LCD = 2 \times 5 \times 7 = 70$

2. $5 = 5$

$8 = 2 \times 2 \times 2$

$10 = 2 \times 5$

$LCD = 2 \times 2 \times 2 \times 5 = 40$

3. $\dfrac{11}{18} \times \dfrac{4}{4} = \dfrac{44}{72}$

2.7 Exercises

2. $\dfrac{5}{8} + \dfrac{2}{8} = \dfrac{5+2}{8} = \dfrac{7}{8}$

4. $\dfrac{11}{25} + \dfrac{17}{25} = \dfrac{11+17}{25} = \dfrac{28}{25}$ or $1\dfrac{3}{25}$

6. $\dfrac{17}{30} - \dfrac{7}{30} = \dfrac{17-7}{30} = \dfrac{10}{30} = \dfrac{1}{3}$

8. $\dfrac{103}{110} - \dfrac{3}{110} = \dfrac{103-3}{110} = \dfrac{100}{110} = \dfrac{10}{11}$

10. $\dfrac{1}{4} + \dfrac{1}{3} = \dfrac{3}{12} + \dfrac{4}{12} = \dfrac{3+4}{12} = \dfrac{7}{12}$

12. $\dfrac{4}{9} + \dfrac{1}{6} = \dfrac{8}{18} + \dfrac{3}{18} = \dfrac{8+3}{18} = \dfrac{11}{18}$

14. $\dfrac{5}{16} + \dfrac{1}{2} = \dfrac{5}{16} + \dfrac{8}{16} = \dfrac{5+8}{16} = \dfrac{13}{16}$

16. $\dfrac{2}{3} + \dfrac{4}{7} = \dfrac{14}{21} + \dfrac{12}{21} = \dfrac{26}{21}$ or $1\dfrac{5}{21}$

18. $\dfrac{13}{100} + \dfrac{7}{10} = \dfrac{13}{100} + \dfrac{70}{100} = \dfrac{13+70}{100} = \dfrac{83}{100}$

20. $\dfrac{8}{15} + \dfrac{3}{10} = \dfrac{16}{30} + \dfrac{9}{30} = \dfrac{16+9}{30} = \dfrac{25}{30} = \dfrac{5}{6}$

22. $\dfrac{5}{6} + \dfrac{7}{8} = \dfrac{20}{24} + \dfrac{21}{24} = \dfrac{20+21}{24} = \dfrac{41}{24}$ or $1\dfrac{17}{24}$

24. $\dfrac{12}{35} + \dfrac{1}{10} = \dfrac{24}{70} + \dfrac{7}{70} = \dfrac{24+7}{70} = \dfrac{31}{70}$

26. $\dfrac{37}{20} - \dfrac{2}{5} = \dfrac{37}{20} - \dfrac{8}{20} = \dfrac{37-8}{20} = \dfrac{29}{20}$ or $1\dfrac{9}{20}$

28. $\dfrac{7}{8} - \dfrac{5}{6} = \dfrac{21}{24} - \dfrac{20}{24} = \dfrac{21-20}{24} = \dfrac{1}{24}$

30. $\dfrac{9}{10} - \dfrac{1}{15} = \dfrac{27}{30} - \dfrac{2}{30} = \dfrac{25}{30} = \dfrac{5}{6}$

32. $\dfrac{9}{24} - \dfrac{3}{8} = \dfrac{9}{24} - \dfrac{9}{24} = 0$

34. $\dfrac{7}{10} - \dfrac{2}{5} = \dfrac{7}{10} - \dfrac{4}{10} = \dfrac{7-4}{10} = \dfrac{3}{10}$

36. $\dfrac{20}{25} - \dfrac{4}{5} = \dfrac{20}{25} - \dfrac{20}{25} = 0$

38. $\dfrac{7}{8} - \dfrac{1}{12} = \dfrac{21}{24} - \dfrac{2}{24} = \dfrac{21-2}{24} = \dfrac{19}{24}$

40. $\dfrac{5}{6} - \dfrac{10}{12} = \dfrac{10}{12} - \dfrac{10}{12} = 0$

42. $\dfrac{2}{3} - \dfrac{1}{16} = \dfrac{32}{48} - \dfrac{3}{48} = \dfrac{32-3}{48} = \dfrac{29}{48}$

44. $\dfrac{7}{8} + \dfrac{5}{6} + \dfrac{7}{24} = \dfrac{21}{24} + \dfrac{20}{24} + \dfrac{7}{24}$

$= \dfrac{21+20+7}{24}$

$= \dfrac{48}{24}$

$= 2$

46. $\dfrac{1}{12} + \dfrac{3}{14} + \dfrac{4}{21} = \dfrac{7}{84} + \dfrac{18}{84} + \dfrac{16}{84} = \dfrac{7+18+16}{84} = \dfrac{41}{84}$

48. $\dfrac{1}{12} + \dfrac{5}{36} + \dfrac{32}{36} = \dfrac{3}{36} + \dfrac{5}{36} + \dfrac{32}{36}$

$= \dfrac{3+5+32}{36}$

$= \dfrac{40}{36}$

$= \dfrac{10}{9}$ or $1\dfrac{1}{9}$

50. $x + \dfrac{1}{8} = \dfrac{7}{16}$

$x + \dfrac{2}{16} = \dfrac{7}{16}$

$\dfrac{5}{16} + \dfrac{2}{16} = \dfrac{7}{16}$

$x = \dfrac{5}{16}$

52.
$$x + \frac{3}{4} = \frac{17}{18}$$
$$x + \frac{27}{36} = \frac{34}{36}$$
$$\frac{7}{36} + \frac{27}{36} = \frac{34}{36}$$
$$x = \frac{7}{36}$$

54.
$$x - \frac{3}{14} = \frac{17}{28}$$
$$x - \frac{6}{28} = \frac{17}{28}$$
$$\frac{23}{28} - \frac{6}{28} = \frac{17}{28}$$
$$x = \frac{23}{28}$$

56. $\frac{1}{4} + \frac{1}{2} = \frac{1}{4} + \frac{2}{4} = \frac{3}{4}$

She swam $\frac{3}{4}$ mile.

$\frac{5}{6} + \frac{3}{4} = \frac{10}{12} + \frac{9}{12} = \frac{19}{12}$ or $1\frac{7}{12}$

She ran $1\frac{7}{12}$ miles.

58. $\frac{11}{32} - \frac{1}{8} = \frac{11}{32} - \frac{4}{32} = \frac{7}{32}$

The tread depth will decrease $\frac{7}{32}$ of an inch.

60. $\frac{1}{2} + \frac{1}{3} = \frac{3}{6} + \frac{2}{6} = \frac{5}{6}$

$\frac{5}{6}$ of the bottle is full.

$\frac{5}{6} - \frac{2}{5} = \frac{25}{30} - \frac{12}{30} = \frac{13}{30}$

$\frac{13}{30}$ of a bottle is left.

62. $\frac{1}{8} + \frac{1}{4} = \frac{1}{8} + \frac{2}{8} = \frac{3}{8}$

He needs $\frac{3}{8}$ cup for the two recipes.

$\frac{3}{4} - \frac{3}{8} = \frac{6}{8} - \frac{3}{8} = \frac{3}{8}$

He will have $\frac{3}{8}$ cup left.

Cumulative Review

64. $\frac{15}{85} = \frac{15 \div 5}{85 \div 5} = \frac{3}{17}$

65. $\frac{27}{207} = \frac{27 \div 9}{207 \div 9} = \frac{3}{23}$

66.
$$\begin{array}{r} 8 \\ 14\overline{)125} \\ \underline{112} \\ 13 \end{array}$$
$\qquad \frac{125}{14} = 8\frac{13}{14}$

67. $14\frac{3}{7} = \frac{14 \times 7 + 3}{7} = \frac{101}{7}$

68. $4\frac{1}{3} \div 1\frac{1}{2} = \frac{13}{3} \div \frac{3}{2} = \frac{13}{3} \times \frac{2}{3} = \frac{26}{9}$ or $2\frac{8}{9}$

69. $5\frac{1}{2} \times 1\frac{3}{11} = \frac{11}{2} \times \frac{14}{11} = \frac{1}{1} \times \frac{7}{1} = 7$

Classroom Quiz 2.7

1. $\frac{7}{8} + \frac{7}{10} = \frac{7}{8} \times \frac{5}{5} + \frac{7}{10} \times \frac{4}{4} = \frac{35}{40} + \frac{28}{40} = \frac{63}{40}$ or $1\frac{23}{40}$

2. $\frac{5}{24} + \frac{5}{6} + \frac{3}{8} = \frac{5}{24} + \frac{5}{6} \times \frac{4}{4} + \frac{3}{8} \times \frac{3}{3}$
$\qquad = \frac{5}{24} + \frac{20}{24} + \frac{9}{24}$
$\qquad = \frac{34}{24}$
$\qquad = \frac{17}{12}$ or $1\frac{5}{12}$

3. $\frac{2}{3} - \frac{5}{16} = \frac{2}{3} \times \frac{16}{16} - \frac{5}{16} \times \frac{3}{3} = \frac{32}{48} - \frac{15}{48} = \frac{17}{48}$

2.8 Exercises

2.
$$6\frac{3}{10}$$
$$+\ 4\frac{1}{10}$$
$$10\frac{4}{10} = 10\frac{2}{5}$$

4.
$$8\frac{3}{4}$$
$$-\ 3\frac{1}{4}$$
$$5\frac{2}{4} = 5\frac{1}{2}$$

6.
$$20\frac{1}{4}$$
$$+\ 3\frac{1}{8}$$
　　　　　
$$20\frac{2}{8}$$
$$+\ 3\frac{1}{8}$$
$$23\frac{3}{8}$$

8.
$$8\frac{2}{9}$$
$$+\ 7\frac{7}{9}$$
$$15\frac{9}{9} = 16$$

10.
$$1$$
$$-\ \frac{9}{11}$$
　　　　　
$$\frac{11}{11}$$
$$-\ \frac{9}{11}$$
$$\frac{2}{11}$$

12.
$$1\frac{2}{3}$$
$$+\ \frac{13}{18}$$
　　　　　
$$1\frac{12}{18}$$
$$+\ \frac{13}{18}$$
$$1\frac{25}{18} = 2\frac{7}{18}$$

14.
$$6\frac{2}{5}$$
$$+\ 7\frac{3}{20}$$
　　　　　
$$6\frac{8}{20}$$
$$+\ 7\frac{3}{20}$$
$$13\frac{11}{20}$$

16.
$$8\frac{11}{15}$$
$$-\ 3\frac{3}{10}$$
　　　　　
$$8\frac{22}{30}$$
$$-\ 3\frac{9}{30}$$
$$5\frac{13}{30}$$

18.
$$10\frac{10}{15}$$
$$-\ 10\frac{2}{3}$$
　　　　　
$$10\frac{10}{15}$$
$$-\ 10\frac{10}{15}$$
$$0$$

20.
$$25$$
$$-\ 14\frac{2}{11}$$
　　　　　
$$24\frac{11}{11}$$
$$-\ 14\frac{2}{11}$$
$$10\frac{9}{11}$$

22.
$$8$$
$$+\ 2\frac{3}{4}$$
$$10\frac{3}{4}$$

24.
$$19$$
$$-\ 5\frac{8}{9}$$
　　　　　
$$18\frac{9}{9}$$
$$-\ 5\frac{8}{9}$$
$$13\frac{1}{9}$$

26.
$$22\frac{1}{8}$$
$$+\ 14\frac{3}{8}$$
$$36\frac{4}{8} = 36\frac{1}{2}$$

28.

$$3\frac{2}{3}$$
$$+4\frac{1}{5}$$

$$3\frac{10}{15}$$
$$+4\frac{3}{15}$$
$$7\frac{13}{15}$$

30.

$$11\frac{5}{8}$$
$$+13\frac{1}{2}$$

$$11\frac{5}{8}$$
$$+13\frac{4}{8}$$
$$24\frac{9}{8}=25\frac{1}{8}$$

32.

$$34\frac{1}{20}$$
$$+45\frac{8}{15}$$

$$34\frac{3}{60}$$
$$+45\frac{32}{60}$$
$$79\frac{35}{60}=79\frac{7}{12}$$

34.

$$22\frac{7}{9}$$
$$-16\frac{1}{4}$$

$$22\frac{28}{36}$$
$$-16\frac{9}{36}$$
$$6\frac{19}{36}$$

36.

$$4\frac{1}{12}$$
$$-3\frac{7}{18}$$

$$4\frac{3}{36}$$
$$-3\frac{14}{36}$$

$$3\frac{39}{36}$$
$$-3\frac{14}{36}$$
$$\frac{25}{36}$$

38.

$$8\frac{5}{12}$$
$$-5\frac{9}{10}$$

$$8\frac{25}{60}$$
$$-5\frac{54}{60}$$

$$7\frac{85}{60}$$
$$-5\frac{54}{60}$$
$$2\frac{31}{60}$$

40.

$$40$$
$$-6\frac{3}{7}$$

$$39\frac{7}{7}$$
$$-6\frac{3}{7}$$
$$33\frac{4}{7}$$

42.

$$98$$
$$-89\frac{15}{17}$$

$$97\frac{17}{17}$$
$$-89\frac{15}{17}$$
$$8\frac{2}{17}$$

44.

$$4\frac{2}{3}$$
$$3\frac{4}{5}$$
$$+6\frac{3}{4}$$

$$4\frac{40}{60}$$
$$3\frac{48}{60}$$
$$+6\frac{45}{60}$$
$$13\frac{133}{60}=15\frac{13}{60}$$

46.

$$2\frac{1}{8}$$
$$1\frac{5}{6}$$
$$+1\frac{2}{3}$$

$$2\frac{6}{48}$$
$$1\frac{40}{48}$$
$$+1\frac{32}{48}$$
$$4\frac{78}{48}=5\frac{5}{8}$$

The distance will be $5\frac{5}{8}$ miles.

48.

$$93\frac{5}{8}$$
$$-21\frac{3}{8}$$
$$72\frac{2}{8}=72\frac{1}{4}$$

Shanna made $\$72\frac{1}{4}$ per share.

50.

$$3\frac{3}{4}$$
$$-1\frac{2}{3}$$

$$3\frac{9}{12}$$
$$-1\frac{8}{12}$$
$$2\frac{1}{12}$$

Julio bought $2\frac{1}{12}$ pounds more turkey than salami.

52. a.

$$17\frac{5}{8}$$
$$+13\frac{1}{2}$$

$$17\frac{5}{8}$$
$$+13\frac{4}{8}$$
$$30\frac{9}{8}=31\frac{1}{8}$$

He lost a total of $31\frac{1}{8}$ pounds.

b.

$$46$$
$$-31\frac{1}{8}$$

$$45\frac{8}{8}$$
$$-31\frac{1}{8}$$
$$14\frac{7}{8}$$

He needs to lose another $14\frac{7}{8}$ pounds.

54.
$$\frac{151}{6}-\frac{130}{7}=\frac{1057}{42}-\frac{780}{42}$$
$$=\frac{1057-780}{42}$$
$$=\frac{277}{42}\text{ or }6\frac{25}{42}$$

56. Estimate: $103-87=16$

Exact:

$$102\frac{5}{7}$$
$$-86\frac{2}{3}$$

$$102\frac{15}{21}$$
$$-86\frac{14}{21}$$
$$16\frac{1}{21}$$

Our estimate is very close. We are off by only $\frac{1}{21}$.

58. $\dfrac{3}{5}-\dfrac{1}{3}\times\dfrac{6}{5}=\dfrac{3}{5}-\dfrac{2}{5}=\dfrac{1}{5}$

60.
$$\frac{3}{4}+\frac{1}{4}\div\frac{5}{3}=\frac{3}{4}+\frac{1}{4}\times\frac{3}{5}$$
$$=\frac{3}{4}+\frac{3}{20}$$
$$=\frac{3}{4}\times\frac{5}{5}+\frac{3}{20}$$
$$=\frac{15}{20}+\frac{3}{20}$$
$$=\frac{18}{20}$$
$$=\frac{9}{10}$$

62. $\dfrac{5}{12}\div\dfrac{3}{10}\times\dfrac{9}{5}=\dfrac{5}{12}\times\dfrac{10}{3}\times\dfrac{9}{5}=\dfrac{1}{2}\times\dfrac{5}{1}\times\dfrac{1}{1}=\dfrac{5}{2}\text{ or }2\dfrac{1}{2}$

64.
$$\frac{5}{6}\times\frac{1}{2}+\frac{2}{3}\div\frac{4}{3}=\frac{5}{6}\times\frac{1}{2}+\frac{2}{3}\times\frac{3}{4}$$
$$=\frac{5}{12}+\frac{1}{2}$$
$$=\frac{5}{12}+\frac{1}{2}\times\frac{6}{6}$$
$$=\frac{5}{12}+\frac{6}{12}$$
$$=\frac{11}{12}$$

66.
$$\left(\frac{1}{3}+\frac{1}{6}\right)\times\frac{5}{11}=\left(\frac{1}{3}\times\frac{2}{2}+\frac{1}{6}\right)\times\frac{5}{11}$$
$$=\left(\frac{2}{6}+\frac{1}{6}\right)\times\frac{5}{11}$$
$$=\frac{3}{6}\times\frac{5}{11}$$
$$=\frac{1}{2}\times\frac{5}{11}$$
$$=\frac{5}{22}$$

68. $\left(\dfrac{1}{4}\right)^2\div\dfrac{3}{4}=\dfrac{1}{16}\div\dfrac{3}{4}=\dfrac{1}{16}\times\dfrac{4}{3}=\dfrac{1}{12}$

70. $\dfrac{5}{8}\times\left(\dfrac{2}{5}\right)^2=\dfrac{5}{8}\times\dfrac{4}{25}=\dfrac{1}{2}\times\dfrac{1}{5}=\dfrac{1}{10}$

72. $\dfrac{4}{3} \div \left(\dfrac{3}{5} - \dfrac{3}{10} \right)^2 = \dfrac{4}{3} \div \left(\dfrac{6}{10} - \dfrac{3}{10} \right)^2$

$\qquad\qquad\qquad = \dfrac{4}{3} \div \left(\dfrac{3}{10} \right)^2$

$\qquad\qquad\qquad = \dfrac{4}{3} \div \dfrac{9}{100}$

$\qquad\qquad\qquad = \dfrac{4}{3} \times \dfrac{100}{9}$

$\qquad\qquad\qquad = \dfrac{400}{27}$

$\qquad\qquad\qquad = 14\dfrac{22}{27}$

Cumulative Review

73.
$$
\begin{array}{r}
1200 \\
\times \quad 400 \\
\hline
480,000
\end{array}
$$

74.
$$
\begin{array}{r}
4050 \\
\times \quad 2106 \\
\hline
24\ 300 \\
405\ 00\ \ \\
8\ 100\ \ \ \ \\
\hline
8,529,300
\end{array}
$$

Classroom Quiz 2.8

1.
$$
\begin{array}{r}
7\dfrac{5}{12} \\
+\ 4\dfrac{11}{18} \\
\hline
\end{array}
\qquad
\begin{array}{r}
7\dfrac{15}{36} \\
+\ 4\dfrac{22}{36} \\
\hline
11\dfrac{37}{36} = 12\dfrac{1}{36}
\end{array}
$$

2.
$$
\begin{array}{r}
13\dfrac{2}{9} \\
-\ 7\dfrac{3}{4} \\
\hline
\end{array}
\qquad
\begin{array}{r}
13\dfrac{8}{36} \\
-\ 7\dfrac{27}{36} \\
\hline
\end{array}
\qquad
\begin{array}{r}
12\dfrac{44}{36} \\
-\ 7\dfrac{27}{36} \\
\hline
5\dfrac{17}{36}
\end{array}
$$

3. $\dfrac{3}{7} + \dfrac{5}{8} \div \dfrac{21}{16} = \dfrac{3}{7} + \dfrac{5}{8} \times \dfrac{16}{21} = \dfrac{3}{7} + \dfrac{10}{21} = \dfrac{9}{21} + \dfrac{10}{21} = \dfrac{19}{21}$

2.9 Exercises

2.
$$
\begin{array}{r}
10\dfrac{1}{2} \\
6\dfrac{1}{3} \\
+\ 12\dfrac{1}{4} \\
\hline
\end{array}
\qquad
\begin{array}{r}
10\dfrac{6}{12} \\
6\dfrac{4}{12} \\
+\ 12\dfrac{3}{12} \\
\hline
28\dfrac{13}{12} = 29\dfrac{1}{12}
\end{array}
$$

She drove $29\dfrac{1}{12}$ miles.

4. $\dfrac{4}{5} \times 1190 = \dfrac{4}{5} \times \dfrac{1190}{1}$

$\qquad\qquad = \dfrac{4}{5} \times \dfrac{5 \times 238}{1}$

$\qquad\qquad = 4 \times 238$

$\qquad\qquad = 952$

The average price in 2006 was \$952.

6. $4\dfrac{7}{8} + 1\dfrac{2}{3} = 4\dfrac{21}{24} + 1\dfrac{16}{24} = 5\dfrac{37}{24} = 6\dfrac{13}{24}$

Then $8 - 6\dfrac{13}{24} = 7\dfrac{24}{24} - 6\dfrac{13}{24} = 1\dfrac{11}{24}$

The notch needs to be $1\dfrac{11}{24}$ feet.

8. $14\dfrac{1}{4} \div \dfrac{3}{4} = \dfrac{57}{4} \div \dfrac{3}{4} = \dfrac{57}{4} \times \dfrac{4}{3} = \dfrac{57}{3} = 19$

He will be able to cut 19 floors.

10. $10\dfrac{2}{3} \times 8\dfrac{3}{4} = \dfrac{32}{3} \times \dfrac{35}{4} = \dfrac{280}{3} = 93\dfrac{1}{3}$

The cheese cost $\$93\dfrac{1}{3}$.

12. $7\dfrac{1}{4} \times 62\dfrac{1}{2} = \dfrac{29}{4} \times \dfrac{125}{2} = \dfrac{3625}{8} = 453\dfrac{1}{8}$

The water weighs $453\dfrac{1}{8}$ pounds.

14. $1200 \times \dfrac{1}{10} = 120$

$1200 \times \dfrac{1}{3} = 400$

$+ 1200 \times \dfrac{1}{6} = 200$

$\overline{ 720}$

He had \$480 left.

$$\begin{array}{r} 1200 \\ -\ 720 \\ \hline 480 \end{array}$$

16. $\dfrac{1}{4} \times 960 = 240$

$\dfrac{1}{10} \times 960 = 96$

$\dfrac{1}{3} \times 960 = 320$

$240 + 96 + 320 = 656$

$960 - 656 = 304$

\$304 is left per week.

18. a. $3 \times 7\dfrac{1}{2} \times 11\dfrac{2}{3} = \dfrac{3}{1} \times \dfrac{15}{2} \times \dfrac{35}{3}$

$= \dfrac{1}{1} \times \dfrac{15}{2} \times \dfrac{35}{1}$

$= \dfrac{525}{2}$ or $262\dfrac{1}{2}$

The carpet will cost $262\dfrac{1}{2}$ or \$262.50.

b. $2 \times 7\dfrac{1}{2} + 2 \times 11\dfrac{2}{3} = \dfrac{2}{1} \times \dfrac{15}{2} + \dfrac{2}{1} \times \dfrac{35}{3}$

$= \dfrac{15}{1} + \dfrac{70}{3}$

$= \dfrac{45}{3} + \dfrac{70}{3}$

$= \dfrac{115}{3}$ or $38\dfrac{1}{3}$

They will need $38\dfrac{1}{3}$ feet of moulding.

20. $2 \times 1\dfrac{1}{4} = \dfrac{2}{1} \times \dfrac{5}{4} = \dfrac{5}{2} = 2\dfrac{1}{2}$

$3 \times 2\dfrac{1}{8} = \dfrac{3}{1} \times \dfrac{17}{8} = \dfrac{51}{8} = 6\dfrac{3}{8}$

$$\begin{array}{r} 2\dfrac{1}{2} \\ +\ 6\dfrac{3}{8} \\ \hline \end{array} \qquad \begin{array}{r} 2\dfrac{4}{8} \\ +\ 6\dfrac{3}{8} \\ \hline 8\dfrac{7}{8} \end{array}$$

$$\begin{array}{r} 12\dfrac{1}{2} \\ -\ 8\dfrac{7}{8} \\ \hline \end{array} \qquad \begin{array}{r} 12\dfrac{4}{8} \\ -\ 8\dfrac{7}{8} \\ \hline \end{array} \qquad \begin{array}{r} 11\dfrac{12}{8} \\ -\ 8\dfrac{7}{8} \\ \hline 3\dfrac{5}{8} \end{array}$$

There will be $3\dfrac{5}{8}$ cups left.

22. a. $72\dfrac{7}{8} \div 2\dfrac{3}{4} = \dfrac{583}{8} \div \dfrac{11}{4}$

$= \dfrac{583}{8} \times \dfrac{4}{11}$

$= \dfrac{53}{2}$

$= 26\dfrac{1}{2}$

The boat is traveling at $26\dfrac{1}{2}$ knots.

b. $92\dfrac{3}{4} \div 26\dfrac{1}{2} = \dfrac{371}{4} \div \dfrac{53}{2} = \dfrac{371}{4} \times \dfrac{2}{53} = \dfrac{7}{2} = 3\dfrac{1}{2}$

It will take the boat $3\dfrac{1}{2}$ hours.

24. a. $8693\dfrac{1}{3} \div 1\dfrac{1}{3} = \dfrac{26,080}{3} \div \dfrac{4}{3}$

$= \dfrac{26,080}{3} \times \dfrac{3}{4}$

$= 6520$

It holds 6520 bushels.

b. $8693\dfrac{1}{3} \times 1\dfrac{1}{3} = \dfrac{26,080}{3} \times \dfrac{4}{3}$

$= \dfrac{104,320}{9}$

$= 11,591\dfrac{1}{9}$

The new bin will hold $11,591\dfrac{1}{9}$ cubic feet.

c. $\dfrac{104,320}{9} \div \dfrac{4}{3} = \dfrac{104,320}{9} \times \dfrac{3}{4}$

$= \dfrac{26,080}{3}$

$= 8693\dfrac{1}{3}$

It will hold $8693\dfrac{1}{3}$ bushels.

Cumulative Review

25. $\begin{array}{r} 16{,}846 \\ 19{,}321 \\ + 8{,}078 \\ \hline 44{,}245 \end{array}$

26. $\begin{array}{r} 209{,}364 \\ -\,186{,}927 \\ \hline 22{,}437 \end{array}$

27. $\begin{array}{r} 1683 \\ \times 27 \\ \hline 11\,781 \\ 33\,66 \\ \hline 45{,}441 \end{array}$

28. $\begin{array}{r} 356 \\ 37\overline{)13{,}172} \\ 11\,1 \\ \hline 2\,07 \\ 1\,85 \\ \hline 222 \\ 222 \\ \hline 0 \end{array}$

Classroom Quiz 2.9

1. $4\dfrac{3}{4} \times 2\dfrac{1}{3} = \dfrac{19}{4} \times \dfrac{7}{3} = \dfrac{133}{12}$ or $11\dfrac{1}{12}$

    She ran $11\dfrac{1}{12}$ miles.

2. $\dfrac{75\frac{3}{8}}{2\frac{1}{4}} = \dfrac{603}{8} \div \dfrac{9}{4}$

    $\phantom{\dfrac{75\frac{3}{8}}{2\frac{1}{4}}} = \dfrac{603}{8} \times \dfrac{4}{9}$

    $\phantom{\dfrac{75\frac{3}{8}}{2\frac{1}{4}}} = \dfrac{67}{2}$ or $33\dfrac{1}{2}$

    It can travel $33\dfrac{1}{2}$ miles per hour.

3. $\begin{array}{r} 3\dfrac{1}{5} \\[4pt] 2\dfrac{1}{2} \\[4pt] +\,1\dfrac{3}{4} \\ \hline \end{array}$ $\qquad$ $\begin{array}{r} 3\dfrac{4}{20} \\[4pt] 2\dfrac{10}{20} \\[4pt] +\,1\dfrac{15}{20} \\ \hline 6\dfrac{29}{20} = 7\dfrac{9}{20} \end{array}$

    $7\dfrac{9}{20}$ miles of fence is required to enclose the field.

Putting Your Skills to Work

1. **a.** $6 a pack \times 2$ people $\times 30$ days

    b. $6 \times 2 \times 30 = 360$
    Each month they spent $360.

2. **a.** $360 \times 7 = 2520$

    b. Yes, since $2520 > $2000.

    c. $2520 - $2000 = 520
    Yes, there would be $520 left over for the birthday present.

3. If the vacation only cost $\dfrac{3}{4}$ of $2000, then the total vacation cost would only be
    $\dfrac{3}{4} \times \dfrac{2000}{1} = \$1500.$
    Thus, $2520 - $1500 = $1020 would be left over for the birthday present.

Chapter 2 Review Problems

1. Three out of eight equal parts are shaded. The fraction is $\dfrac{3}{8}$.

2. Five out of twelve equal parts are shaded. The fraction is $\dfrac{5}{12}$.

3. Answers will vary.

4. Answers will vary.

5. $\dfrac{\text{number defective}}{\text{total number}} = \dfrac{9}{80}$

6. $\dfrac{\text{number who would not}}{\text{total number}} = \dfrac{87}{100}$

7. $54 = 2 \times 27 = 2 \times 3 \times 9 = 2 \times 3 \times 3 \times 3 = 2 \times 3^3$

8. $120 = 10 \times 12 = 2 \times 5 \times 2 \times 2 \times 3 = 2^3 \times 3 \times 5$

9. $168 = 8 \times 21 = 2 \times 2 \times 2 \times 3 \times 7 = 2^3 \times 3 \times 7$

10. 59 is prime.

11. $78 = 2 \times 39 = 2 \times 3 \times 13$

12. 167 is prime.

13. $\dfrac{12}{42} = \dfrac{12 \div 6}{42 \div 6} = \dfrac{2}{7}$

14. $\dfrac{13}{52} = \dfrac{13 \div 13}{52 \div 13} = \dfrac{1}{4}$

15. $\dfrac{27}{72} = \dfrac{27 \div 9}{72 \div 9} = \dfrac{3}{8}$

16. $\dfrac{26}{34} = \dfrac{26 \div 2}{34 \div 2} = \dfrac{13}{17}$

17. $\dfrac{168}{192} = \dfrac{168 \div 24}{192 \div 24} = \dfrac{7}{8}$

18. $\dfrac{51}{105} = \dfrac{51 \div 3}{105 \div 3} = \dfrac{17}{35}$

19. $4\dfrac{3}{8} = \dfrac{4 \times 8 + 3}{8} = \dfrac{35}{8}$

20. $15\dfrac{3}{4} = \dfrac{15 \times 4 + 3}{4} = \dfrac{63}{4}$

21. $5\dfrac{2}{7} = \dfrac{5 \times 7 + 2}{7} = \dfrac{37}{7}$

22. $6\dfrac{3}{5} = \dfrac{6 \times 5 + 3}{5} = \dfrac{33}{5}$

23. $\begin{array}{r} 5 \\ 8\overline{)45} \\ \underline{40} \\ 5 \end{array}$

$\dfrac{45}{8} = 5\dfrac{5}{8}$

24. $\begin{array}{r} 4 \\ 21\overline{)100} \\ \underline{84} \\ 16 \end{array}$

$\dfrac{100}{21} = 4\dfrac{16}{21}$

25. $\begin{array}{r} 7 \\ 7\overline{)53} \\ \underline{49} \\ 4 \end{array}$

$\dfrac{53}{7} = 7\dfrac{4}{7}$

26. $\begin{array}{r} 8 \\ 9\overline{)74} \\ \underline{72} \\ 2 \end{array}$

$\dfrac{74}{9} = 8\dfrac{2}{9}$

27. $\dfrac{15}{55} = \dfrac{5 \times 3}{5 \times 11} = \dfrac{3}{11}$

$3\dfrac{15}{55} = 3\dfrac{3}{11}$

28. $\dfrac{234}{16} = \dfrac{117 \times 2}{8 \times 2} = \dfrac{117}{8}$

29. $\begin{array}{r} 4 \\ 32\overline{)132} \\ \underline{128} \\ 4 \end{array}$

$\dfrac{132}{32} = 4\dfrac{4}{32} = 4\dfrac{1}{8}$

30. $\dfrac{4}{7} \times \dfrac{5}{11} = \dfrac{4 \times 5}{7 \times 11} = \dfrac{20}{77}$

31. $\dfrac{7}{9} \times \dfrac{21}{35} = \dfrac{1}{3} \times \dfrac{7}{5} = \dfrac{7}{15}$

32. $12 \times \dfrac{3}{7} \times 0 = 0$

33. $\dfrac{3}{5} \times \dfrac{2}{7} \times \dfrac{10}{27} = \dfrac{1}{1} \times \dfrac{2}{7} \times \dfrac{2}{9} = \dfrac{4}{63}$

34. $12 \times 8\dfrac{1}{5} = \dfrac{12}{1} \times \dfrac{41}{5} = \dfrac{492}{5}$ or $98\dfrac{2}{5}$

35. $5\dfrac{1}{4} \times 4\dfrac{6}{7} = \dfrac{21}{4} \times \dfrac{34}{7} = \dfrac{3}{2} \times \dfrac{17}{1} = \dfrac{51}{2}$ or $25\dfrac{1}{2}$

36. $5\dfrac{1}{8} \times 3\dfrac{1}{5} = \dfrac{41}{8} \times \dfrac{16}{5} = \dfrac{41}{1} \times \dfrac{2}{5} = \dfrac{82}{5}$ or $16\dfrac{2}{5}$

37. $36 \times \dfrac{4}{9} = \dfrac{36}{1} \times \dfrac{4}{9} = \dfrac{4}{1} \times \dfrac{4}{1} = 16$

38. $37\dfrac{5}{8} \times 18 = \dfrac{301}{8} \times \dfrac{18}{1} = \dfrac{301}{4} \times \dfrac{9}{1} = \dfrac{2709}{4} = 677\dfrac{1}{4}$

18 shares cost $\$677\dfrac{1}{4}$.

39. $13\dfrac{1}{2} \times 9\dfrac{2}{3} = \dfrac{27}{2} \times \dfrac{29}{3} = \dfrac{9}{2} \times \dfrac{29}{1} = \dfrac{261}{2}$ or $130\dfrac{1}{2}$

The area is $\dfrac{261}{2}$ or $130\dfrac{1}{2}$ square feet.

40. $\dfrac{3}{7} \div \dfrac{2}{5} = \dfrac{3}{7} \times \dfrac{5}{2} = \dfrac{15}{14}$ or $1\dfrac{1}{14}$

41. $\dfrac{3}{5} \div \dfrac{1}{10} = \dfrac{3}{5} \times \dfrac{10}{1} = 6$

42. $1200 \div \dfrac{5}{8} = \dfrac{1200}{1} \times \dfrac{8}{5} = 1920$

43. $900 \div \dfrac{3}{5} = \dfrac{900}{1} \times \dfrac{5}{3} = 1500$

44. $5\dfrac{3}{4} \div 11\dfrac{1}{2} = \dfrac{23}{4} \div \dfrac{23}{2} = \dfrac{23}{4} \times \dfrac{2}{23} = \dfrac{1}{2}$

45. $20 \div 2\dfrac{1}{2} = \dfrac{20}{1} \div \dfrac{5}{2} = \dfrac{20}{1} \times \dfrac{2}{5} = 8$

46. $0 \div 3\dfrac{7}{5} = 0$

47. $4\dfrac{2}{11} \div 3 = \dfrac{46}{11} \div \dfrac{3}{1} = \dfrac{46}{11} \times \dfrac{1}{3} = \dfrac{46}{33}$ or $1\dfrac{13}{33}$

48. $342 \div 28\dfrac{1}{2} = \dfrac{342}{1} \div \dfrac{57}{2} = \dfrac{342}{1} \times \dfrac{2}{57} = 6 \times 2 = 12$

12 rolls are needed.

49. $420 \div 2\dfrac{1}{4} = \dfrac{420}{1} \div \dfrac{9}{4}$

$\qquad = \dfrac{420}{1} \times \dfrac{4}{9}$

$\qquad = \dfrac{140}{1} \times \dfrac{4}{3}$

$\qquad = \dfrac{560}{3}$ or $186\dfrac{2}{3}$ calories

50. $14 = 2 \times 7$

$49 = 7 \times 7$

$\text{LCD} = 2 \times 7 \times 7 = 98$

51. $20 = 2 \times 2 \times 5$

$25 = 5 \times 5$

$\text{LCD} = 2 \times 2 \times 5 \times 5 = 100$

52. $18 = 2 \times 3 \times 3$

$6 = 2 \times 3$

$45 = 3 \times 3 \times 5$

$\text{LCD} = 2 \times 3 \times 3 \times 5 = 90$

53. $\dfrac{3}{7} = \dfrac{3}{7} \times \dfrac{8}{8} = \dfrac{24}{56}$

54. $\dfrac{11}{24} = \dfrac{11}{24} \times \dfrac{3}{3} = \dfrac{33}{72}$

55. $\dfrac{8}{15} = \dfrac{8}{15} \times \dfrac{10}{10} = \dfrac{80}{150}$

56. $\dfrac{17}{18} = \dfrac{17}{18} \times \dfrac{11}{11} = \dfrac{187}{198}$

57. $\dfrac{9}{14} - \dfrac{5}{14} = \dfrac{4}{14} = \dfrac{2}{7}$

58. $\dfrac{1}{2} + \dfrac{1}{3} + \dfrac{1}{4} = \dfrac{1}{2} \times \dfrac{6}{6} + \dfrac{1}{3} \times \dfrac{4}{4} + \dfrac{1}{4} \times \dfrac{3}{3}$

$\qquad = \dfrac{6}{12} + \dfrac{4}{12} + \dfrac{3}{12}$

$\qquad = \dfrac{13}{12}$ or $1\dfrac{1}{12}$

59. $\dfrac{4}{7}+\dfrac{7}{9}=\dfrac{4}{7}\times\dfrac{9}{9}+\dfrac{7}{9}\times\dfrac{7}{7}=\dfrac{36}{63}+\dfrac{49}{63}=\dfrac{85}{63}$ or $1\dfrac{22}{63}$

60. $\dfrac{7}{8}-\dfrac{3}{5}=\dfrac{7}{8}\times\dfrac{5}{5}-\dfrac{3}{5}\times\dfrac{8}{8}=\dfrac{35}{40}-\dfrac{24}{40}=\dfrac{11}{40}$

61. $\begin{aligned}\dfrac{7}{30}+\dfrac{2}{21}&=\dfrac{7}{30}\times\dfrac{7}{7}+\dfrac{2}{21}\times\dfrac{10}{10}\\[4pt]&=\dfrac{49}{210}+\dfrac{20}{210}\\[4pt]&=\dfrac{69}{210}\\[4pt]&=\dfrac{23}{70}\end{aligned}$

62. $\dfrac{5}{18}+\dfrac{7}{10}=\dfrac{5}{18}\times\dfrac{5}{5}+\dfrac{7}{10}\times\dfrac{9}{9}=\dfrac{25}{90}+\dfrac{63}{90}=\dfrac{88}{90}=\dfrac{44}{45}$

63. $\dfrac{15}{16}-\dfrac{13}{24}=\dfrac{15}{16}\times\dfrac{3}{3}-\dfrac{13}{24}\times\dfrac{2}{2}=\dfrac{45}{48}-\dfrac{26}{48}=\dfrac{19}{48}$

64. $\dfrac{14}{15}-\dfrac{3}{25}=\dfrac{14}{15}\times\dfrac{5}{5}-\dfrac{3}{25}\times\dfrac{3}{3}=\dfrac{70}{75}-\dfrac{9}{75}=\dfrac{61}{75}$

65. $8-2\dfrac{3}{4}=\dfrac{32}{4}-\dfrac{11}{4}=\dfrac{21}{4}$ or $5\dfrac{1}{4}$

66. $6-\dfrac{5}{9}=\dfrac{54}{9}-\dfrac{5}{9}=\dfrac{49}{9}$ or $5\dfrac{4}{9}$

67. $3+5\dfrac{2}{3}=8\dfrac{2}{3}$

68. $9\dfrac{3}{7}+13=22\dfrac{3}{7}$

69.
$\begin{array}{r}3\dfrac{3}{8}\\[4pt]+\,2\dfrac{3}{4}\\\hline\end{array}$ 　　　　$\begin{array}{r}3\dfrac{3}{8}\\[4pt]+\,2\dfrac{6}{8}\\\hline 5\dfrac{9}{8}=6\dfrac{1}{8}\end{array}$

70.
$\begin{array}{r}5\dfrac{11}{16}\\[4pt]-\,2\dfrac{1}{5}\\\hline\end{array}$ 　·　$\begin{array}{r}5\dfrac{55}{80}\\[4pt]-\,2\dfrac{16}{80}\\\hline 3\dfrac{39}{80}\end{array}$

71. $\dfrac{3}{5}\times\dfrac{1}{2}+\dfrac{2}{5}\div\dfrac{2}{3}=\dfrac{3}{5}\times\dfrac{1}{2}+\dfrac{2}{5}\times\dfrac{3}{2}=\dfrac{3}{10}+\dfrac{6}{10}=\dfrac{9}{10}$

72. $\begin{aligned}\left(\dfrac{4}{5}-\dfrac{1}{2}\right)^{2}\times\dfrac{10}{3}&=\left(\dfrac{8}{10}-\dfrac{5}{10}\right)^{2}\times\dfrac{10}{3}\\[4pt]&=\left(\dfrac{3}{10}\right)^{2}\times\dfrac{10}{3}\\[4pt]&=\dfrac{9}{100}\times\dfrac{10}{3}\\[4pt]&=\dfrac{3}{10}\end{aligned}$

73. $\begin{aligned}1\dfrac{7}{8}+2\dfrac{3}{4}+4\dfrac{1}{10}&=1\dfrac{70}{80}+2\dfrac{60}{80}+4\dfrac{8}{80}\\[4pt]&=7\dfrac{138}{80}\\[4pt]&=8\dfrac{58}{80}\\[4pt]&=8\dfrac{29}{40}\end{aligned}$

The total number of miles is $8\dfrac{29}{40}$ miles.

74.
$\begin{array}{r}28\dfrac{1}{6}\\[4pt]-\,1\dfrac{5}{6}\\\hline\end{array}$ 　　　　$\begin{array}{r}27\dfrac{7}{6}\\[4pt]-\,1\dfrac{5}{6}\\\hline 26\dfrac{2}{6}=26\dfrac{1}{3}\end{array}$

Then: $26\dfrac{1}{3}\times10\dfrac{3}{4}=\dfrac{79}{3}\times\dfrac{43}{4}=\dfrac{3397}{12}=283\dfrac{1}{12}$

She can drive $283\dfrac{1}{12}$ miles.

75. $3\dfrac{1}{3}\times2\dfrac{1}{2}=\dfrac{10}{3}\times\dfrac{1}{2}=\dfrac{5}{3}=1\dfrac{2}{3}$ cups sugar

$4\dfrac{1}{4}\times\dfrac{1}{2}=\dfrac{17}{4}\times\dfrac{1}{2}=\dfrac{17}{8}=2\dfrac{1}{8}$ cups flour

76. $24\dfrac{1}{4}\times8\dfrac{1}{2}=\dfrac{97}{4}\times\dfrac{17}{2}=\dfrac{1649}{8}=206\dfrac{1}{8}$

He can drive approximately $206\dfrac{1}{8}$ miles.

77. $48\div3\dfrac{1}{5}=\dfrac{48}{1}\div\dfrac{16}{5}=\dfrac{48}{1}\times\dfrac{5}{16}=\dfrac{3}{1}\times\dfrac{5}{1}=15$

15 lengths can be cut from the pipe.

78. $15\dfrac{3}{4} - 6\dfrac{1}{8} = 15\dfrac{6}{8} - 6\dfrac{1}{8} = 9\dfrac{5}{8}$

It contains $9\dfrac{5}{8}$ liters of water.

79.
$$
\begin{array}{r}
12 \\
9 \\
+\,14 \\
\hline
35
\end{array}
$$

$35 \div 5 = 7$

$7 \times 32\dfrac{1}{2} = \dfrac{7}{1} \times \dfrac{65}{2} = \dfrac{455}{2} = 227\dfrac{1}{2}$

It will take $227\dfrac{1}{2}$ minutes or 3 hours and

$47\dfrac{1}{2}$ minutes.

80. Regular pay: $9\dfrac{1}{2} \times 8 = \dfrac{19}{2} \times \dfrac{8}{1} = 76$

Overtime pay: $1\dfrac{1}{2} \times 9\dfrac{1}{2} = \dfrac{3}{2} \times \dfrac{19}{2} = \dfrac{57}{4}$

Overtime pay: $\dfrac{57}{4} \times 4 = \dfrac{57}{4} \times \dfrac{4}{1} = 57$

Total pay: $76 + 57 = 133$
She earned a total of $133.

81. $70 \times 15\dfrac{3}{4} = \dfrac{70}{1} \times \dfrac{63}{4} = \dfrac{2205}{2}$ or $1102\dfrac{1}{2}$

$70 \times 24 = 1680$

$$
\begin{array}{r}
1680 \\
-\,1102\dfrac{1}{2} \\
\hline
\end{array}
\qquad
\begin{array}{r}
1679\dfrac{2}{2} \\
-\,1102\dfrac{1}{2} \\
\hline
577\dfrac{1}{2}
\end{array}
$$

He made $577\dfrac{1}{2}$ or $577.50.

82. $1\dfrac{1}{2} + \dfrac{1}{16} + \dfrac{1}{8} + \dfrac{1}{4} = 1\dfrac{8}{16} + \dfrac{1}{16} + \dfrac{2}{16} + \dfrac{4}{16} = 1\dfrac{15}{16}$

$3 - 1\dfrac{15}{16} = 2\dfrac{16}{16} - 1\dfrac{15}{16} = 1\dfrac{1}{16}$

The bolt extends $1\dfrac{1}{16}$ inches.

83.
$$
\begin{array}{r}
\dfrac{1}{10} \times 880 = \quad 88 \\[4pt]
\dfrac{1}{2} \times 880 = \quad 440 \\[4pt]
+\,\dfrac{1}{8} \times 880 = +110 \\
\hline
638
\end{array}
$$

Left over:
$$
\begin{array}{r}
880 \\
-\,638 \\
\hline
242
\end{array}
$$

She has $242 left over.

84. a. $460 \div 18\dfrac{2}{5} = \dfrac{460}{1} \div \dfrac{92}{5} = \dfrac{460}{1} \times \dfrac{5}{92} = 25$

His car gets 25 miles per gallon.

b. $18\dfrac{2}{5} \times 3\dfrac{1}{5} = \dfrac{92}{5} \times \dfrac{16}{5} = \dfrac{1472}{25} = 58\dfrac{22}{25}$

His trip cost $58\dfrac{22}{25}$.

85. $\dfrac{27}{63} = \dfrac{27 \div 9}{63 \div 9} = \dfrac{3}{7}$

86. $\dfrac{7}{5} + \dfrac{11}{25} = \dfrac{35}{75} + \dfrac{33}{75} = \dfrac{68}{75}$

87.
$$
\begin{array}{ccc}
4\dfrac{1}{3} & 4\dfrac{4}{12} & 3\dfrac{16}{12} \\[6pt]
-\,2\dfrac{11}{12} & -\,2\dfrac{11}{12} & -\,2\dfrac{11}{12} \\
\hline
& & 1\dfrac{5}{12}
\end{array}
$$

88. $\dfrac{36}{49} \times \dfrac{14}{33} = \dfrac{3 \times 12 \times 2 \times 7}{3 \times 11 \times 7 \times 7} = \dfrac{24}{77}$

89. $4\dfrac{1}{4} \div \dfrac{3}{2} = \dfrac{17}{4} \div \dfrac{3}{2} = \dfrac{17}{4} \times \dfrac{2}{3} = \dfrac{17}{2} \times \dfrac{1}{3} = \dfrac{17}{6}$ or $2\dfrac{5}{6}$

90. $\left(\dfrac{4}{7}\right)^3 = \dfrac{4}{7} \times \dfrac{4}{7} \times \dfrac{4}{7} = \dfrac{64}{343}$

91. $\dfrac{3}{8} \div \dfrac{1}{10} = \dfrac{3}{8} \times \dfrac{10}{1} = \dfrac{3}{4} \times \dfrac{5}{1} = \dfrac{15}{4}$ or $3\dfrac{3}{4}$

92. $5\dfrac{1}{2} \times 18 = \dfrac{11}{2} \times \dfrac{18}{1} = \dfrac{11}{1} \times \dfrac{9}{1} = 99$

93. $150 \div 3\frac{1}{8} = \frac{150}{1} \div \frac{25}{8} = \frac{150}{1} \times \frac{8}{25} = \frac{6}{1} \times \frac{8}{1} = 48$

How Am I Doing? Chapter 2 Test

1. $\frac{3}{5}$; 3 of the 5 parts are shaded.

2. $\frac{\text{number that went in}}{\text{total number}} = \frac{311}{388}$

3. $\frac{18}{42} = \frac{18 \div 6}{42 \div 6} = \frac{3}{7}$

4. $\frac{15}{70} = \frac{15 \div 5}{70 \div 5} = \frac{3}{14}$

5. $\frac{225}{50} = \frac{225 \div 25}{50 \div 25} = \frac{9}{2}$

6. $6\frac{4}{5} = \frac{6 \times 5 + 4}{5} = \frac{34}{5}$

7. $14\overline{)145}$ $\frac{145}{14} = 10\frac{5}{14}$
$\begin{array}{r}10\\ 145 \\ \underline{14} \\ 5\end{array}$

8. $42 \times \frac{2}{7} = \frac{42}{1} \times \frac{2}{7} = \frac{6 \times 7 \times 2}{1 \times 7} = \frac{12}{1} = 12$

9. $\frac{7}{9} \times \frac{2}{5} = \frac{7 \times 2}{9 \times 5} = \frac{14}{45}$

10. $2\frac{2}{3} \times 5\frac{1}{4} = \frac{8}{3} \times \frac{21}{4} = \frac{2 \times 4 \times 3 \times 7}{3 \times 4} = 14$

11. $\frac{7}{8} \div \frac{5}{11} = \frac{7}{8} \times \frac{11}{5} = \frac{7 \times 11}{8 \times 5} = \frac{77}{40}$ or $1\frac{37}{40}$

12. $\frac{12}{31} \div \frac{8}{13} = \frac{12}{31} \times \frac{13}{8} = \frac{3 \times 4 \times 13}{31 \times 2 \times 4} = \frac{39}{62}$

13. $7\frac{1}{5} \div 1\frac{1}{25} = \frac{36}{5} \div \frac{26}{25}$
$= \frac{36}{5} \times \frac{25}{26}$
$= \frac{2 \times 18 \times 5 \times 5}{5 \times 2 \times 13}$
$= \frac{18 \times 5}{13}$
$= \frac{90}{13}$ or $6\frac{12}{13}$

14. $5\frac{1}{7} \div 3 = \frac{36}{7} \div \frac{3}{1} = \frac{36}{7} \times \frac{1}{3} = \frac{3 \times 12 \times 1}{7 \times 3} = \frac{12}{7}$ or $1\frac{5}{7}$

15. $12 = 2 \times 2 \times 3$
$18 = 2 \times 3 \times 3$
$\text{LCD} = 2^2 \times 3^2 = 36$

16. $16 = 2 \times 2 \times 2 \times 2$
$24 = 2 \times 2 \times 2 \times 3$
$\text{LCD} = 2 \times 2 \times 2 \times 2 \times 3 = 48$

17. $4 = 2 \times 2$
$8 = 2 \times 2 \times 2$
$6 = 2 \times 3$
$\text{LCD} = 2 \times 2 \times 2 \times 3 = 24$

18. $\frac{5}{12} = \frac{5}{12} \times \frac{6}{6} = \frac{30}{72}$

19. $\frac{7}{9} - \frac{5}{12} = \frac{28}{36} - \frac{15}{36} = \frac{13}{36}$

20. $\frac{2}{15} + \frac{5}{12} = \frac{8}{60} + \frac{25}{60} = \frac{33}{60} = \frac{11}{20}$

21. $\frac{1}{4} + \frac{3}{7} + \frac{3}{14} = \frac{7}{28} + \frac{12}{28} + \frac{6}{28} = \frac{25}{28}$

22. $8\frac{3}{5} + 5\frac{4}{7} = 8\frac{21}{35} + 5\frac{20}{35} = 13\frac{41}{35} = 14\frac{6}{35}$

23. $18\frac{6}{7} - 13\frac{13}{14} = 18\frac{12}{14} - 13\frac{13}{14} = 17\frac{26}{14} - 13\frac{13}{14} = 4\frac{13}{14}$

24. $\frac{2}{9} \div \frac{8}{3} \times \frac{1}{4} = \frac{2}{9} \times \frac{3}{8} \times \frac{1}{4} = \frac{1}{48}$

25. $\left(\frac{1}{2} + \frac{1}{3}\right) \times \frac{7}{5} = \left(\frac{3}{6} + \frac{2}{6}\right) \times \frac{7}{5} = \frac{5}{6} \times \frac{7}{5} = \frac{7}{6}$ or $1\frac{1}{6}$

26. $16\dfrac{1}{2} \times 9\dfrac{1}{3} = \dfrac{33}{2} \times \dfrac{28}{3} = 11 \times 14 = 154$

    The kitchen is 154 square feet.

27. $18\dfrac{2}{3} \div 2\dfrac{1}{3} = \dfrac{56}{3} \div \dfrac{7}{3} = \dfrac{56}{3} \times \dfrac{3}{7} = \dfrac{8 \times 7 \times 3}{3 \times 7} = 8$

    He can make 8 packages.

28. $\dfrac{9}{10} - \dfrac{1}{5} = \dfrac{9}{10} - \dfrac{2}{10} = \dfrac{7}{10}$

    He has $\dfrac{7}{10}$ of a mile left to walk.

29. $4\dfrac{1}{8} + 3\dfrac{1}{6} + 6\dfrac{3}{4} = 4\dfrac{3}{24} + 3\dfrac{4}{24} + 6\dfrac{18}{24}$
    $$= 13\dfrac{25}{24}$$
    $$= 14\dfrac{1}{24}$$

    She jogged $14\dfrac{1}{24}$ miles.

30. **a.** $\dfrac{1}{4} \times 120 = \dfrac{1}{4} \times \dfrac{120}{1} = 30$

    $\dfrac{1}{12} \times 120 = \dfrac{1}{12} \times \dfrac{120}{1} = 10$

    $\dfrac{1}{3} \times 120 = \dfrac{1}{3} \times \dfrac{120}{1} = 40$

    $120 - 30 - 10 - 40 = 40$
    They shipped 40 oranges.

    b. $\dfrac{24}{100} \times \dfrac{40}{1} = \dfrac{48}{5}$ or $9\dfrac{3}{5}$

    It cost $\$9\dfrac{3}{5}$ or $\$9.60$.

31. **a.** $48\dfrac{1}{8} \div \dfrac{5}{8} = \dfrac{385}{8} \times \dfrac{8}{5} = \dfrac{385}{5} = 77$

    They can make 77 candles.

    b. Cost is $48\dfrac{1}{8} \times 2 \div 77 = \dfrac{385}{8} \times \dfrac{2}{1} \times \dfrac{1}{77}$
    $$= \dfrac{385}{308}$$
    $$= 1\dfrac{77}{308}$$
    $$= \$1\dfrac{1}{4}.$$

c. Profit per candle: $12 - 1\dfrac{1}{4} = 11\dfrac{4}{4} - 1\dfrac{1}{4} = 10\dfrac{3}{4}$

Profit is

$$10\dfrac{3}{4} \times 77 = \dfrac{43}{4} \times \dfrac{77}{1} = \dfrac{3311}{4} = \$827\dfrac{3}{4}.$$

Cumulative Test for Chapters 1–2

1. eighty-four million, three hundred sixty-one thousand, two hundred eight

2.
   $$\begin{array}{r} 235 \\ 152 \\ 95 \\ +\ 78 \\ \hline 560 \end{array}$$

3.
   $$\begin{array}{r} 156,200 \\ 364,700 \\ +\ 198,320 \\ \hline 719,220 \end{array}$$

4.
   $$\begin{array}{r} 5718 \\ -\ 3643 \\ \hline 2075 \end{array}$$

5.
   $$\begin{array}{r} 1,000,361 \\ -\ \ 983,145 \\ \hline 17,216 \end{array}$$

6.
   $$\begin{array}{r} 126 \\ \times\ 38 \\ \hline 1008 \\ 378 \\ \hline 4788 \end{array}$$

7.
   $$\begin{array}{r} 70,000 \\ \times\ \ \ \ 12 \\ \hline 140\ 000 \\ 700\ 00 \\ \hline 840,000 \end{array}$$

8.

$$
\begin{array}{r}
4658 \\
7\overline{)32,606} \\
\underline{28} \\
4\ 6 \\
\underline{4\ 2} \\
40 \\
\underline{35} \\
56 \\
\underline{56} \\
0
\end{array}
$$

9.

$$
\begin{array}{r}
308\ \text{R}\ 11 \\
15\overline{)4631} \\
\underline{45} \\
131 \\
\underline{120} \\
11
\end{array}
$$

10. $7^2 = 7 \times 7 = 49$

11. 6,037,452 rounds to 6,037,000 since 4 is less than 5.

12. $6 \times 2^3 + 12 \div (4+2) = 6 \times 2^3 + 12 \div 6$
$$= 6 \times 8 + 12 \div 6$$
$$= 48 + 2$$
$$= 50$$

13. $4 \times \$25 + 2 \times \$36 + \$65 = \$100 + \$72 + \$65$
$$= \$237$$
His total bill was \$237.

14. $516 + 199 + 203 = 918$ for checks
$64 + 1160 - 918 = 1224 - 918 = 306$
Her balance will be \$306.

15. Women: $\dfrac{83}{112}$

Men: $\dfrac{112-83}{112} = \dfrac{29}{112}$

16. $\dfrac{28}{52} = \dfrac{28 \div 4}{52 \div 4} = \dfrac{7}{13}$

17. $18\dfrac{3}{4} = \dfrac{18 \times 4 + 3}{4} = \dfrac{75}{4}$

18.

$$
\begin{array}{r}
14 \\
7\overline{)100} \\
\underline{7} \\
30 \\
\underline{28} \\
2
\end{array}
$$

$\dfrac{100}{7} = 14\dfrac{2}{7}$

19. $3\dfrac{1}{2} \times 4\dfrac{2}{3} = \dfrac{7}{2} \times \dfrac{14}{3} = \dfrac{7}{1} \times \dfrac{7}{3} = \dfrac{49}{3}$ or $16\dfrac{1}{3}$

20. $\dfrac{44}{49} \div 2\dfrac{13}{21} = \dfrac{44}{49} \div \dfrac{55}{21}$
$$= \dfrac{44}{49} \times \dfrac{21}{55}$$
$$= \dfrac{4 \times 11 \times 3 \times 7}{7 \times 7 \times 5 \times 11}$$
$$= \dfrac{12}{35}$$

21. $8 = 2 \times 2 \times 2$
$10 = 2 \times 5$
$\text{LCD} = 2^3 \times 5 = 40$

22. $\dfrac{7}{18} + \dfrac{20}{27} = \dfrac{21}{54} + \dfrac{40}{54} = \dfrac{61}{54}$ or $1\dfrac{7}{54}$

23. $2\dfrac{1}{8} + 6\dfrac{3}{4} = 2\dfrac{1}{8} + 6\dfrac{6}{8} = 8\dfrac{7}{8}$

24. $12\dfrac{1}{5} - 4\dfrac{2}{3} = 12\dfrac{3}{15} - 4\dfrac{10}{15} = 11\dfrac{18}{15} - 4\dfrac{10}{15} = 7\dfrac{8}{15}$

25. $\dfrac{1}{2} \times \dfrac{2}{3} + \dfrac{1}{4} \div \dfrac{3}{2} = \dfrac{1}{3} + \dfrac{1}{4} \div \dfrac{3}{2}$
$$= \dfrac{1}{3} + \dfrac{1}{4} \times \dfrac{2}{3}$$
$$= \dfrac{1}{3} + \dfrac{1}{6}$$
$$= \dfrac{2}{6} + \dfrac{1}{6}$$
$$= \dfrac{3}{6}$$
$$= \dfrac{1}{2}$$

26.

$$5\frac{1}{2}$$
$$+\,6\frac{3}{4}$$

$$5\frac{2}{4}$$
$$+\,6\frac{3}{4}$$
$$11\frac{5}{4} = 12\frac{1}{4}$$

$$15$$
$$-\,12\frac{1}{4}$$

$$14\frac{4}{4}$$
$$-\,12\frac{1}{4}$$
$$2\frac{3}{4}$$

He must lose $2\frac{3}{4}$ pounds.

27. $221\frac{2}{5} \div 9 = \dfrac{1107}{5} \div \dfrac{9}{1}$

$$= \frac{1107}{5} \times \frac{1}{9}$$

$$= \frac{123}{5}$$

$$= 24\frac{3}{5}$$

The car achieved $24\frac{3}{5}$ miles per gallon.

28. $2\frac{1}{2} \times 1\frac{3}{4} = \dfrac{5}{2} \times \dfrac{7}{4} = \dfrac{35}{8}$ or $4\frac{3}{8}$

She needs $4\frac{3}{8}$ cups of flour.

$$12 - 4\frac{3}{8} = \frac{12}{1} - \frac{35}{8} = \frac{96}{8} - \frac{35}{8} = \frac{61}{8} \text{ or } 7\frac{5}{8}$$

$7\frac{5}{8}$ cups will be left.

29.

$$30,000$$
$$\times \quad\;\; 2,000$$
$$\overline{60,000,000} \text{ miles}$$

30. $960 \times \dfrac{1}{6} = \dfrac{960}{1} \times \dfrac{1}{6} = \dfrac{960}{6} = 160$

The cost $160.

Chapter 3

3.1 Exercises

2. The word that describes the decimal point is *and*.

4. When writing $82.75 on a check, we write 75¢ as $\dfrac{75}{100}$.

6. 0.78 = seventy-eight hundredths

8. 12.4 = twelve and four tenths

10. 2.056 = two and fifty-six thousandths

12. 54.0013 = fifty-four and thirteen ten-thousandths

14. $510.31 = five hundred ten and $\dfrac{31}{100}$ dollars

16. $5304.05 = five thousand three hundred four and $\dfrac{5}{100}$ dollars

18. $20,000.67 = twenty thousand and $\dfrac{67}{100}$ dollars

20. six tenths = 0.6

22. eighteen hundredths = 0.18

24. twenty-two thousandths = 0.022

26. one thousand three hundred eighteen millionths = 0.001318

28. $\dfrac{3}{10} = 0.3$

30. $\dfrac{84}{100} = 0.84$

32. $\dfrac{6}{100} = 0.06$

34. $\dfrac{328}{1000} = 0.328$

36. $\dfrac{7794}{10,000} = 0.7794$

38. $5\dfrac{3}{10} = 5.3$

40. $52\dfrac{77}{100} = 52.77$

42. $2\dfrac{23}{1000} = 2.023$

44. $116\dfrac{312}{10,000} = 116.0312$

46. $0.05 = \dfrac{5}{100} = \dfrac{1}{20}$

48. $8.9 = 8\dfrac{9}{10}$

50. $15.75 = 15\dfrac{75}{100} = 15\dfrac{3}{4}$

52. $29.875 = 29\dfrac{875}{1000} = 29\dfrac{7}{8}$

54. $4.0016 = 4\dfrac{16}{10,000} = 4\dfrac{1}{625}$

56. $7.0605 = 7\dfrac{605}{10,000} = 7\dfrac{121}{2000}$

58. $581.2406 = 581\dfrac{2406}{10,000} = 581\dfrac{1203}{5000}$

60. $0.3375 = \dfrac{3375}{10,000} = \dfrac{27}{80}$

62. a. $\dfrac{13,700}{100,000} = \dfrac{137}{1000}$

$\dfrac{137}{1000}$ of the male population of Utah were smokers in 2005.

b. $\dfrac{9300}{100,000} = \dfrac{93}{1000}$

$\dfrac{93}{1000}$ of the female population of Utah were smokers in 2005.

64. $\dfrac{2}{100,000,000} = \dfrac{1}{50,000,000}$

Cumulative Review

65.
$$
\begin{array}{r}
207 \\
54 \\
123 \\
86 \\
+\ 55 \\
\hline
525
\end{array}
$$

66.
$$
\begin{array}{r}
12,843 \\
-11,905 \\
\hline
938
\end{array}
$$

67. 56,7$\underline{5}$8 rounds to 56,800 since 5 is equal to 5.

68. 8,069,$\underline{4}$82 rounds to 8,069,000 since 4 is less than 5.

Classroom Quiz 3.1

1. 9.158 = nine and one hundred fifty-eight thousandths

2. $\dfrac{692}{10,000} = 0.0692$

3. $26.85 = 26\dfrac{85}{100} = 26\dfrac{17}{20}$

3.2 Exercises

2. 2.6 > 2.58
The numbers to the left of the decimals are the same. The number in tenths place of 2.6 is 6, which is greater than 5, the number in the tenths place of 2.58. Thus, 2.6 is the greater number.

4. 72.54 < 72.56
The numbers to the left of the decimals and in the tenths place are the same. The number in hundredths place of 72.54 is 4, which is less than 6, the number in the hundredths place of 72.56. Thus, 72.54 is the smaller number.

6. 0.460 = 0.46
Adding a zero in the thousandths place of 0.46 on the right, we get 0.460. The two numbers are equal.

8. 0.0037 < 0.036
The hundredths place is the first digit where the numbers differ. Since 0 < 3, 0.0037 is the smaller number.

10. 2.0056 < 2.006
The thousandths place is the first digit where the numbers differ. Since 5 < 6, 2.0056 is the smaller number.

12. 406.78 < 407.75
406 < 407, so 406.78 is the smaller number.

14. 0.666 < 0.6666
Adding a zero in the ten-thousandths place of 0.666, we get 0.6660. The ten-thousandths place is the first digit where the numbers differ. Since 0 < 6, 0.6660 is the smaller number.

16. 0.555 > 0.5505
The thousandths place is the first digit where the numbers differ. Since 5 > 0, 0.555 is the greater number.

18. $\dfrac{54}{1000} = 0.054$

Written in decimal form, $\dfrac{54}{1000}$ is 0.054.

20. $\dfrac{5}{100} > 0.005$

Written in decimal form, $\dfrac{5}{100}$ is 0.05. The hundredths place is the first place that 0.05 and 0.005 differ. Since 5 > 0, 0.05 is the greater number.

22. 18.038, 18.04, 18.32

24. 0.002, 0.0025, 0.0052

26. 5.01, 5.02, 5.1, 5.23

28. 33.02, 33.079, 33.082, 33.088

30. 15.001, 15.0019, 15.002, 15.018, 15.020

32. 8.35 rounds to 8.4.
Find the tenths place: 8.3̲5. The digit to the right of the tenths place is equal to 5. We round up to 8.4 and drop the digit to the right.

34. 47.94 rounds to 47.9.
Find the tenths place: 47.9̲4. The digit to the right of the tenths place is less than 5. We round down to 47.9 and drop the digit to the right.

36. 454.99 rounds to 455.0.
Find the tenths place: 454.9̲9. The digit to the right of the tenths place is greater than 5. We round up to 455.0 and drop the digit to the right.

38. 4082.74 rounds to 4082.7.
Find the tenths place: 4082.7̲4. The digit to the right of the tenths place is less than 5. We round down to 4082.7 and drop the digit to the right.

40. 47.071 rounds to 47.07.
Find the hundredths place: 47.07̲1. The digit to the right of the hundredths place is less than 5. We round down to 47.07 and drop the digit to the right.

42. 24.999 rounds to 25.00.
Find the hundredths place: 24.99̲9. The digit to the right of the hundredths place is greater than 5. We round up to 25.00 and drop the digit to the right.

44. 283.8441 rounds to 283.84.
Find the hundredths place: 283.84̲41. The digit to the right of the hundredths place is less than 5. We round down to 283.84 and drop the digits to the right.

46. 4609.285 rounds to 4609.29.
Find the hundredths place: 4609.28̲5. The digit to the right of the hundredths place is equal to 5. We round up to 4609.29 and drop the digit to the right.

48. 8.10263 rounds to 8.103.
Find the thousandths place: 8.102̲63. The digit to the right of the thousandths place is greater than 5. We round up to 8.103 and drop the digits to the right.

50. 0.063148 rounds to 0.0631.
Find the ten-thousandths place: 0.0631̲48. The digit to the right of the ten-thousandths place is less than 5. We round down to 0.0631 and drop the digits to the right.

52. 15.4159266 rounds to 15.41593.
Find the hundred-thousandths place: 15.41592̲66. The digit to the right of the hundred-thousandths place is greater than 5. We round up to 15.41593 and drop the digits to the right.

54. 389.645 rounds to 390.
The digit to the right of the decimal is greater than 5. We round up to 390 and drop the digits to the right.

56. $912.75 rounds to $913.

58. $20,159.48 rounds to $20,159.

60. $42.9261 rounds to $42.93.

62. $3928.649 rounds to $3928.65.

64. CD: $1.2593 rounds to $1.26.
Toy: $1.7143 rounds to $1.71.

66. $\pi \approx 3.14159$: The digit to the right of the hundredths place, 1, is less than 5. We round down to 3.14.
$e \approx 2.71828$: The digit to the right of the hundredths place, 8, is greater than 5. We round up to 2.72.

68. 1.05, 1.512, $\frac{15}{10}$, 1.0513, 0.049, $\frac{151}{100}$, 0.0515, 0.052, 1.051
1.0500, 1.5120, 1.5000, 1.0513, 0.0490, 1.5100, 0.0515, 0.0520, 1.0510
0.0490, 0.0515, 0.0520, 1.0500, 1.0510, 1.0513, 1.5000, 1.5100, 1.5120
0.049, 0.0515, 0.052, 1.05, 1.051, 1.0513, $\frac{15}{10}$, $\frac{151}{100}$, 1.512

70. The bank rounds up for any fractional part of a cent.

Cumulative Review

71. $3\frac{1}{4}$ $3\frac{2}{8}$
$2\frac{1}{2}$ $2\frac{4}{8}$
$+6\frac{3}{8}$ $+6\frac{3}{8}$
                $11\frac{9}{8}=12\frac{1}{8}$

72. $27\dfrac{1}{5}-16\dfrac{3}{4}=27\dfrac{4}{20}-16\dfrac{15}{20}$

$\qquad\qquad\;\; =26\dfrac{24}{20}-16\dfrac{15}{20}$

$\qquad\qquad\;\; =10\dfrac{9}{20}$

73.
$$\begin{array}{r} 47,073 \\ -\,46,381 \\ \hline 692 \end{array}$$
The trip was 692 miles long.

74.
$$\begin{array}{r} 18,700 \\ 2,500 \\ 800 \\ +\;9,800 \\ \hline 31,800 \end{array}$$
The cost was \$31,800.

Classroom Quiz 3.2

1. 7.7, 7.67, 7.76, 7.067
Add zeros to make the comparison easier.
7.700, 7.670, 7.760, 7.067
Rearrange with the smallest first.
7.067, 7.67, 7.7, 7.76

2. 58.2637 rounds to 58.26.
Find the hundredths place: 58.2637. The digit to the right of the hundredths place is less than 5. We round down to 58.26 and drop the digits to the right.

3. 122.78658 rounds to 122.787.
Find the thousandths place: 122.78658. The digit to the right of the thousandths place is equal to 5. We round up to 122.787 and drop the digits to the right.

3.3 Exercises

2.
$$\begin{array}{r} 78.3 \\ +\;29.4 \\ \hline 107.7 \end{array}$$

4.
$$\begin{array}{r} 193.42 \\ +\,768.78 \\ \hline 962.20 \end{array}$$

6.
$$\begin{array}{r} 176.5 \\ 8.4 \\ +\;22.5 \\ \hline 207.4 \end{array}$$

8.
$$\begin{array}{r} 9.284 \\ +\;5.770 \\ \hline 15.054 \end{array}$$

10.
$$\begin{array}{r} 7.0276 \\ 3.4510 \\ +\,16.9800 \\ \hline 27.4586 \end{array}$$

12.
$$\begin{array}{r} 13.00 \\ 4.52 \\ +\,63.70 \\ \hline 81.22 \end{array}$$

14.
$$\begin{array}{r} 215.45 \\ 48.00 \\ 30.77 \\ +\;15.80 \\ \hline 310.02 \end{array}$$

16.
$$\begin{array}{r} 432.51 \\ 16.08 \\ 892.10 \\ 301.20 \\ +\;84.00 \\ \hline 1725.89 \end{array}$$

18.
$$\begin{array}{r} 5.09 \\ 6.70 \\ +\;9.28 \\ \hline 21.07 \end{array}$$
The perimeter is 21.07 meters.

20.
$$\begin{array}{r} 7.15 \\ 12.45 \\ +\,10.75 \\ \hline 30.35 \end{array}$$
She drank a total of 30.35 ounces.

22.
$$\begin{array}{r} 37.25 \\ 5.89 \\ 13.95 \\ 10.49 \\ +\;4.05 \\ \hline 71.63 \end{array}$$
Anika's bill was \$71.63.

24.
$$\begin{array}{r} 23,195.0 \\ +\;1,723.1 \\ \hline 24,918.1 \end{array}$$
The final reading was 24,918.1 miles.

26.   52.89
     105.37
      76.04
      25.00
  + 167.82
     427.12
The total deposit was $427.12.

28.   15.8
  − 6.7
    9.1

30.   84.33
  − 8.09
  76.24

32.   209.00
  − 81.54
  127.46

34.   243.967
  − 84.200
  159.767

36.   181.90
  − 62.23
  119.67

38.   52.0708
  − 41.9312
  10.1396

40.   12.000
  − 7.981
    4.019

42.   4986.71
  − 3615.93
  1370.78

44.   2.80000
  − 0.07763
  2.72237

46.   241.983
  + 75.48
  317.463

48.   79.20
  − 45.93
  33.27

50.   18.00
  − 2.75
  15.25

52.   382.700
  − 291.927
  90.773

54.   7.675
  − 3.700
  3.975
Grace gained 3.975 kilograms.

56.   14,537.9
  − 12,265.4
  2,272.5
They drove 2272.5 miles.

58.   65.49   200.00
  27.75   − 112.19
 + 18.95   87.81
 112.19
Nathan has $87.81 left.

60.   9.39
  − 7.93
  1.46
The thickness of the pipe is 146 centimeters.

62.   39.70
  − 4.64
  35.06
Mexico had 35.06 million hectares of rainforest in 2006.

64.   0.023
  − 0.015
  0.008
The difference is 0.008 milligram. No, it is not safe to drink.

66.   298.3
  − 126.6
  171.7
$171.7 billion or $171,700,000,000 more dollars were earned in construction in 2000 than 1980.

68.
$$
\begin{array}{r}
96.4 \\
-\ 38.1 \\
\hline
58.3
\end{array}
$$
$58.3 billion or $58,300,000,000 dollars more were earned in communications than in mining in 1990.

70. $3.80 + 1.70 + 2.20 + 2.30 + 0.70 + 1.00 = \$11.70$
$3.79 + 1.65 + 2.19 + 2.29 + 0.68 + 0.99 = \$11.59$
The estimate is very close to the actual amount. Difference is 11 cents.

72. $x + 4.8 = 23.1$
$$
\begin{array}{r}
23.1 \\
-\ 4.8 \\
\hline
18.3
\end{array}
$$
$x = 18.3$

74. $210.3 + x = 301.2$
$$
\begin{array}{r}
301.2 \\
-\ 210.3 \\
\hline
90.9
\end{array}
$$
$x = 90.9$

76. $7.076 = x + 5.602$
$$
\begin{array}{r}
7.076 \\
-\ 5.602 \\
\hline
1.474
\end{array}
$$
$1.474 = x$

Cumulative Review

77.
$$
\begin{array}{r}
2536 \\
\times\ \ \ \ 8 \\
\hline
20,288
\end{array}
$$

78.
$$
\begin{array}{r}
827 \\
\times\ \ \ 59 \\
\hline
7\ 443 \\
41\ 35 \\
\hline
48,793
\end{array}
$$

79. $\dfrac{1}{4} \times 100 = \dfrac{1}{4} \times \dfrac{100}{1} = \dfrac{1}{1} \times \dfrac{25}{1} = 25$

80. $800 \times \dfrac{1}{2} = \dfrac{800}{1} \times \dfrac{1}{2} = \dfrac{400}{1} \times \dfrac{1}{1} = 400$

Classroom Quiz 3.3

1.
$$
\begin{array}{r}
9.800 \\
71.562 \\
+\ 19.390 \\
\hline
100.752
\end{array}
$$

2.
$$
\begin{array}{r}
9.0702 \\
-\ 4.9631 \\
\hline
4.1071
\end{array}
$$

3.
$$
\begin{array}{r}
68.200 \\
-\ 5.793 \\
\hline
62.407
\end{array}
$$

3.4 Exercises

2. The first factor has two decimals places. The second factor has one. You add the number of decimal places to get three decimal places. You multiply 345×9 to obtain 3105. Now you must place the decimal three places to the left in your answer. The result is 3.105.

4. When you multiply a number by 1000, you move the decimal point three places to the right. The answer would be 5080.7.

6.
$$
\begin{array}{r}
0.9 \\
\times\ 0.3 \\
\hline
0.27
\end{array}
$$

8.
$$
\begin{array}{r}
0.17 \\
\times\ 0.4 \\
\hline
0.068
\end{array}
$$

10.
$$
\begin{array}{r}
0.067 \\
\times\ 0.07 \\
\hline
0.00469
\end{array}
$$

12.
$$
\begin{array}{r}
316 \\
\times\ 0.24 \\
\hline
12\ 64 \\
63\ 2 \\
\hline
75.84
\end{array}
$$

14.
$$
\begin{array}{r}
0.037 \\
\times\ 0.011 \\
\hline
0037 \\
037 \\
\hline
0.000407
\end{array}
$$

16.   18.07
    ×   0.05
      0.9035

18.   5119
    ×   0.7
     3583.3

20.   1.892
    ×   0.007
    0.013244

22.   0.6178
    ×   5004
     2 4712
   308 900
  3091.4712

24.   3720
    ×   8.1
     372 0
   29 760
  30,132.0 or 30,132

26.   73.2
    ×   2.45
     3 660
    29 28
  146 4
  179.340 or 179.34

28.   826.75
    ×   0.01
     8.2675

30.   1.89
    ×   25
     945
    378
   47.25
He bought 47.25 liters.

32.   14.75
    ×   40
   590.00
He earns $590 in one week.

34.   17.5
    ×   8.6
    10 50
   1400
  150.50
The driveway is 150.5 square yards.

36.   230.50
    ×   16
   1383 00
   2305 0
   3688.00
She will pay a total of $3688.

38.   18.6   514.8
    × 19.5   − 362.7
     9 30   152.1 miles
   167 4
   186
  362.70 miles
Steve can travel 152.1 miles further than Jim on a tank of gas.

40. Move the decimal one place to the right.
$1.98 \times 10 = 19.8$

42. Move the decimal two places to the right.
$86.375 \times 100 = 8637.5$

44. Move the decimal three places to the right.
$34.105 \times 1000 = 34,105$

46. Move the decimal four places to the right.
$1.27986 \times 10,000 = 12,798.6$

48. Move the decimal two places to the right.
$7163.241 \times 10^2 = 716,324.1$

50. Move the decimal four places to the right.
$763.49 \times 10^4 = 7,634,900$

52. $39.36 \times 100 = 3936$
There are about 3936 inches in 100 meters.

54. $1.45 \times 1000 = 1450$
He spent $1450.

56. a.   15.75
    − 0.95
    14.80
Tomba gained 14.8 pounds.

b.
$$\begin{array}{r} 15.75 \\ -\,13.50 \\ \hline 2.25 \end{array}$$

$0.25 + 0.25 + 0.25 + 0.25 + 0.25 + 0.25$
$+ 0.25 + 0.25 + 0.25 = 9(0.25) = 2.25$
It will take 9 weeks to lose the weight.

58. a.
$$\begin{array}{r} 3220 \\ \times \quad 3.5 \\ \hline 11270.0 \end{array}$$
The jewelry store spent \$11,270.

b. $17.75 - 3.5 = 14.25$
$$\begin{array}{r} 14.25 \\ \times \quad 28 \\ \hline 399.00 \end{array}$$
They will make a \$399 profit.

60. To multiply by numbers such as 0.2, 0.02, 0.002, and 0.0002, first double the second number. Then move the decimal point to the left using the rule stated in exercise 59.

Cumulative Review

61.
$$\begin{array}{r} 204 \\ 20\overline{)4080} \\ \underline{40} \\ 080 \\ \underline{80} \\ 0 \end{array}$$
The answer is 204.

62.
$$\begin{array}{r} 201 \\ 35\overline{)7035} \\ \underline{70} \\ 035 \\ \underline{35} \\ 0 \end{array}$$
The answer is 201.

63.
$$\begin{array}{r} 127 \\ 48\overline{)6099} \\ \underline{48} \\ 129 \\ \underline{96} \\ 339 \\ \underline{336} \\ 3 \end{array}$$
The answer is 127 R 3.

64.
$$\begin{array}{r} 451 \\ 124\overline{)56,024} \\ \underline{49\ 6} \\ 6\ 42 \\ \underline{6\ 20} \\ 224 \\ \underline{124} \\ 100 \end{array}$$
The answer is 451 R 100.

65.
$$\begin{array}{r} 90.5 \\ -\,73.9 \\ \hline 16.6 \end{array}$$
There are 16.6 million or 16,600,000 more pet cats than pet dogs.

66.
$$\begin{array}{r} 73.9 \\ -\,16.6 \\ \hline 57.3 \end{array}$$
There are 57.3 million or 57,300,000 more pet dogs than pet birds.

67.
$$\begin{array}{r} 73.9 \\ 18.2 \\ 16.6 \\ +\,11.0 \\ \hline 119.7 \end{array} \qquad \begin{array}{r} 148.6 \\ -\,119.7 \\ \hline 28.9 \end{array}$$
There are 28.9 million or 28,900,000 more pet fish than pet dogs, small animals, birds, and reptiles combined.

68.
$$\begin{array}{r} 73.9 \\ +\,90.5 \\ \hline 164.4 \end{array} \qquad \begin{array}{r} 164.4 \\ -\,148.6 \\ \hline 15.8 \end{array}$$
There are 15.8 million or 15,800,000 more pet cats and dogs combined than pet fish.

Classroom Quiz 3.4

1.
$$\begin{array}{r} 0.93 \\ \times \quad 0.05 \\ \hline 0.0465 \end{array}$$

2.
$$\begin{array}{r} 0.198 \\ \times \quad 15.7 \\ \hline 1386 \\ 990 \\ 1\ 98 \\ \hline 3.1086 \end{array}$$

3. Move the decimal two places the right.

$$9.186 \times 10^2 = 918.6$$

How Am I Doing? Sections 3.1–3.4

1. 47.813 = forty-seven and eight hundred thirteen thousandths

2. $\dfrac{567}{10,000} = 0.0567$

3. $4.09 = 4\dfrac{9}{100}$

4. $0.525 = \dfrac{525}{1000} = \dfrac{525 \div 25}{1000 \div 25} = \dfrac{21}{40}$

5. 1.6, 1.59, 1.61, 1.601
Add zeros to make the comparison easier.
1.600, 1.590, 1.610, 1.601
Rearrange with the smallest first.
1.59, 1.6, 1.601, 1.61

6. 123.49268 rounds to 123.5.
Find the tenths place: 123.49268. The digit to the right of the tenths place is greater than 5. We round up to 123.5 and drop the digits to the right.

7. 8.065447 rounds to 8.0654.
Find the ten-thousandths place: 8.065447.
The digit to the right of the ten-thousandths place is less than 5. We round down to 8.0654 and drop the digits to the right.

8. 17.98523 rounds to 17.99.
Find the hundredths place; 17.98523. The digit to the right of the hundredths place is equal to 5. We round up to 17.99 and drop the digits to the right.

9.
$$
\begin{array}{r}
5.12 \\
4.70 \\
8.03 \\
+\ 1.60 \\
\hline
19.45
\end{array}
$$

10.
$$
\begin{array}{r}
24.613 \\
0.273 \\
+\ 2.305 \\
\hline
27.191
\end{array}
$$

11.
$$
\begin{array}{r}
42.16 \\
-\ 31.57 \\
\hline
10.59
\end{array}
$$

12.
$$
\begin{array}{r}
26.000 \\
-\ 18.329 \\
\hline
7.671
\end{array}
$$

13.
$$
\begin{array}{r}
11.67 \\
\times\ 0.03 \\
\hline
0.3501
\end{array}
$$

14. Move the decimal three places to the right.
$4.7805 \times 1000 = 4780.5$

15. Move the decimal five places to the right.
$0.0003796 \times 10^5 = 37.96$

16.
$$
\begin{array}{r}
3.14 \\
\times\ 2.5 \\
\hline
1\ 570 \\
6\ 28 \\
\hline
7.850
\end{array}
$$

17.
$$
\begin{array}{r}
982 \\
\times\ 0.007 \\
\hline
6.874
\end{array}
$$

18.
$$
\begin{array}{r}
0.00052 \\
\times\ \ \ \ 0.006 \\
\hline
0.00000312
\end{array}
$$

3.5 Exercises

2.
$$
\begin{array}{r}
2.16 \\
8\overline{)17.28} \\
\underline{16} \\
12 \\
\underline{\ 8} \\
48 \\
\underline{48} \\
0
\end{array}
$$

4.
$$
\begin{array}{r}
13.86 \\
6\,)\overline{83.16} \\
\underline{6} \\
23 \\
\underline{18} \\
5\;1 \\
\underline{4\;8} \\
3\,6 \\
\underline{3\,6} \\
0
\end{array}
$$

6.
$$
\begin{array}{r}
21.06 \\
8\,)\overline{168.48} \\
\underline{16} \\
8 \\
\underline{8} \\
48 \\
\underline{48} \\
0
\end{array}
$$

8.
$$
\begin{array}{r}
64.3 \\
0.5_\wedge\,)\overline{32.1_\wedge5} \\
\underline{30} \\
2\;1 \\
\underline{2\;0} \\
1\;5 \\
\underline{1\;5} \\
0
\end{array}
$$

10.
$$
\begin{array}{r}
7.615 \\
0.08_\wedge\,)\overline{0.60_\wedge920} \\
\underline{56} \\
4\;9 \\
\underline{4\;8} \\
12 \\
\underline{8} \\
40 \\
\underline{40} \\
0
\end{array}
$$

12.
$$
\begin{array}{r}
2\;1 \\
3.6_\wedge\,)\overline{75.6_\wedge} \\
\underline{72} \\
3\;6 \\
\underline{3\;6} \\
0
\end{array}
$$

14.
$$
\begin{array}{r}
130 \\
5.6_\wedge\,)\overline{7280_\wedge} \\
\underline{56} \\
168 \\
\underline{168} \\
0
\end{array}
$$

16.
$$
\begin{array}{r}
5.50 \\
8\,)\overline{44.00} \\
\underline{40} \\
4\;0 \\
\underline{4\;0} \\
0
\end{array}
$$

The answer is 5.5.

18.
$$
\begin{array}{r}
2.31 \\
1.8_\wedge\,)\overline{4.1_\wedge60} \\
\underline{3\;6} \\
5\;6 \\
\underline{5\;4} \\
20 \\
\underline{18} \\
2
\end{array}
$$

The answer is 2.3.

20.
$$
\begin{array}{r}
33.75 \\
0.95_\wedge\,)\overline{32.06_\wedge70} \\
\underline{28\;5} \\
356 \\
\underline{285} \\
71\;7 \\
\underline{66\;5} \\
5\;20 \\
\underline{4\;75} \\
45
\end{array}
$$

The answer is 33.8.

22.
$$
\begin{array}{r}
65.955 \\
4\overline{)263.820} \\
\underline{24} \\
23 \\
\underline{20} \\
3\,8 \\
\underline{3\,6} \\
22 \\
\underline{20} \\
20 \\
\underline{20} \\
20 \\
\underline{20} \\
0
\end{array}
$$

The answer is 65.96.

24.
$$
\begin{array}{r}
12.235 \\
1.7_\wedge\overline{)20.8_\wedge000} \\
\underline{17} \\
38 \\
\underline{34} \\
4\,0 \\
\underline{3\,4} \\
60 \\
\underline{51} \\
90 \\
\underline{85} \\
5
\end{array}
$$

The answer is 12.24.

26.
$$
\begin{array}{r}
0.130 \\
24\overline{)3.126} \\
\underline{2\,4} \\
72 \\
\underline{72} \\
06
\end{array}
$$

The answer is 0.13.

28.
$$
\begin{array}{r}
0.0252 \\
8\overline{)0.2019} \\
\underline{16} \\
41 \\
\underline{40} \\
19
\end{array}
$$

The answer is 0.025.

30.
$$
\begin{array}{r}
12.2463 \\
0.69_\wedge\overline{)8.45_\wedge0000} \\
\underline{69} \\
1\,55 \\
\underline{1\,38} \\
17\,0 \\
\underline{13\,8} \\
3\,20 \\
\underline{2\,76} \\
440 \\
\underline{414} \\
260 \\
\underline{207} \\
53
\end{array}
$$

The answer is 12.246.

32.
$$
\begin{array}{r}
116.3 \\
12\overline{)1396_\wedge0} \\
\underline{12} \\
19 \\
\underline{12} \\
76 \\
\underline{72} \\
4\,0 \\
\underline{3\,6} \\
4
\end{array}
$$

The answer is 116.

34.
$$
\begin{array}{r}
90.3 \\
0.0024_\wedge\overline{)0.2168_\wedge0} \\
\underline{216} \\
8\,0 \\
\underline{7\,2} \\
8
\end{array}
$$

The answer is 90.

36.

$$
\begin{array}{r}
213.75 \\
1.6_\wedge\overline{)342.0_\wedge00} \\
\underline{32}\ \ \ \ \ \ \\
22\ \ \ \ \ \ \\
\underline{16}\ \ \ \ \ \\
6\ 0\ \ \ \\
\underline{4\ 8}\ \ \ \\
1\ 2\ \ 0\ \\
\underline{1\ 1\ \ 2}\ \\
80 \\
\underline{80} \\
0
\end{array}
$$

It is 213.75 miles.

38. a.

$$
\begin{array}{r}
67.6 \\
+\ 33.6 \\
\hline
101.2
\end{array}
\qquad
\begin{array}{r}
25.3 \\
4\overline{)101.2} \\
\underline{8}\ \ \ \ \\
21\ \ \\
\underline{20}\ \ \\
1\ 2 \\
\underline{1\ 2} \\
0
\end{array}
$$

They each drink 25.3 ounces.

b.

$$
\begin{array}{r}
20.24 \\
5\overline{)101.20} \\
\underline{10}\ \ \ \ \ \\
1\ 2\ \ \\
\underline{1\ 0}\ \ \\
20\ \\
\underline{20}\ \\
0
\end{array}
$$

They each drink 20.24 ounces.

40.

$$
\begin{array}{r}
37.5 \\
32\overline{)1200.0} \\
\underline{96}\ \ \ \ \ \\
240\ \ \\
\underline{224}\ \ \\
16\ 0 \\
\underline{16\ 0} \\
0
\end{array}
$$

Each ticket was $37.50.

42.

$$
\begin{array}{r}
9 \\
125.75_\wedge\overline{)1131.75_\wedge} \\
\underline{1131.75} \\
0
\end{array}
$$

He must make 9 payments.

44. a.

$$
\begin{array}{r}
47.75 \\
28.34 \\
+\ 30.65 \\
\hline
106.74
\end{array}
\qquad
\begin{array}{r}
35.58 \\
3\overline{)106.74} \\
\underline{9}\ \ \ \ \ \ \\
16\ \ \ \\
\underline{15}\ \ \ \\
1\ 7 \\
\underline{1\ 5} \\
24 \\
\underline{24} \\
0
\end{array}
$$

The average precipitation is 35.58 inches.

b.

$$
\begin{array}{r}
47.75 \\
-\ 27.24 \\
\hline
20.51
\end{array}
\qquad
\begin{array}{r}
0.6836 \\
30\overline{)20.5100} \\
\underline{18\ 0}\ \ \ \ \\
2\ 51\ \ \\
\underline{2\ 40}\ \ \\
110\ \\
\underline{90}\ \\
200 \\
\underline{180} \\
20
\end{array}
$$

The average daily precipitation is about
0.684 inch greater in April.

46. $0.5 \times n = 3.55$

$$
\begin{array}{r}
7.1 \\
0.5_\wedge\overline{)3.5_\wedge5} \\
\underline{3\ 5}\ \ \\
0\ 5 \\
\underline{5} \\
0
\end{array}
$$

$n = 7.1$

48. $1.7 \times n = 129.2$

$$
\begin{array}{r}
76 \\
1.7_\wedge\overline{)129.2_\wedge} \\
\underline{119}\ \ \\
10\ 2 \\
\underline{10\ 2} \\
0
\end{array}
$$

$n = 76$

50. $n \times 0.063 = 2.835$

$$
\begin{array}{r}
45 \\
0.063_\wedge\overline{)2.835_\wedge} \\
2\,52 \\
\hline
315 \\
315 \\
\hline
0
\end{array}
$$

$n = 45$

52. $\dfrac{3.8702}{0.0523} \times \dfrac{10,000}{10,000} = \dfrac{38,702}{523}$

$$
\begin{array}{r}
74 \\
523\overline{)38,702} \\
36\,61 \\
\hline
2\,092 \\
2\,092 \\
\hline
0
\end{array}
$$

Yes; multiplying and dividing the numerator and denominator by 10,000 is the same as multiplying by $\dfrac{10,000}{10,000}$, which is 1.

Cumulative Review

54. $\dfrac{3}{8} + 2\dfrac{4}{5} = \dfrac{15}{40} + 2\dfrac{32}{40} = 2\dfrac{47}{40} = 3\dfrac{7}{40}$

55. $2\dfrac{13}{16} - 1\dfrac{7}{8} = 2\dfrac{13}{16} - 1\dfrac{14}{16} = 1\dfrac{29}{16} - 1\dfrac{14}{16} = \dfrac{15}{16} \cdot$

56. $3\dfrac{1}{2} \times 2\dfrac{1}{6} = \dfrac{7}{2} \times \dfrac{13}{6} = \dfrac{91}{12}$ or $7\dfrac{7}{12}$

57. $7\dfrac{1}{2} \div \dfrac{1}{2} = \dfrac{15}{2} \div \dfrac{1}{2} = \dfrac{15}{2} \times \dfrac{2}{1} = \dfrac{15}{1} \times \dfrac{1}{1} = 15$

58.
$$
\begin{array}{r}
34.95 \\
-\ 9.74 \\
\hline
25.21
\end{array}
$$
There was $25.21 billion or $25,210,000,000 more property damage during Hurricane Andrew than Hugo.

59.
$$
\begin{array}{r}
9.74 \\
-\ 8.52 \\
\hline
1.22
\end{array}
$$
There was $1.22 billion or $1,220,000,000 more property damage during Hurricane Hugo than Betsy.

60.
$$
\begin{array}{r}
3.60 \\
34.95_\wedge\overline{)12600_\wedge 00} \\
10485 \\
\hline
2115\ 0 \\
2097\ 0 \\
\hline
18\ 00
\end{array}
$$
There was about 3.6 times more property damage during Hurricane Katrina than Andrew.

61.
$$
\begin{array}{r}
14.78 \\
8.52\overline{)12600_\wedge 00} \\
852 \\
\hline
4080 \\
3408 \\
\hline
672\ 0 \\
596\ 4 \\
\hline
75\ 60 \\
68\ 16 \\
\hline
7\ 44
\end{array}
$$
There was about 14.8 times more property damage during Hurricane Katrina than Betsy.

Classroom Quiz 3.5

1.
$$
\begin{array}{r}
6.25 \\
0.09_\wedge\overline{)0.56_\wedge 25} \\
54 \\
\hline
2\ 2 \\
1\ 8 \\
\hline
45 \\
45 \\
\hline
0
\end{array}
$$

2.
$$
\begin{array}{r}
1\ 72 \\
0.48_\wedge\overline{)82.56_\wedge} \\
48 \\
\hline
34\ 5 \\
33\ 6 \\
\hline
96 \\
96 \\
\hline
0
\end{array}
$$

3.
$$\begin{array}{r} 2.527 \\ 7\overline{)17.690} \\ \underline{14} \\ 3\,6 \\ \underline{3\,5} \\ 19 \\ \underline{14} \\ 50 \\ \underline{49} \\ 1 \end{array}$$

The answer is 2.53.

3.6 Exercises

2. To convert a fraction to an equivalent decimal, divide the <u>denominator</u> into the numerator.

4. 1. Perform operations inside parentheses.

    2. Simplify any expressions with exponents.

    3. Multiply or divide from left to right.

    4. Add or subtract from left to right.

6.
$$\begin{array}{r} 0.75 \\ 4\overline{)3.00} \\ \underline{2\,8} \\ 20 \\ \underline{20} \\ 0 \end{array}$$

$$\frac{3}{4} = 0.75$$

8.
$$\begin{array}{r} 0.4 \\ 5\overline{)2.0} \\ \underline{2\,0} \\ 0 \end{array}$$

$$\frac{2}{5} = 0.4$$

10.
$$\begin{array}{r} 0.375 \\ 8\overline{)3.000} \\ \underline{2\,4} \\ 60 \\ \underline{56} \\ 40 \\ \underline{40} \\ 0 \end{array}$$

$$\frac{3}{8} = 0.375$$

12.
$$\begin{array}{r} 0.075 \\ 40\overline{)3.000} \\ \underline{3\,00} \\ 2\,80 \\ \underline{200} \\ 200 \\ \underline{200} \\ 0 \end{array}$$

$$\frac{3}{40} = 0.075$$

14.
$$\begin{array}{r} 0.92 \\ 25\overline{)23.00} \\ \underline{22\,5} \\ 50 \\ \underline{50} \\ 0 \end{array}$$

$$\frac{23}{25} = 0.92$$

16.
$$\begin{array}{r} 2.8 \\ 5\overline{)14.0} \\ \underline{10} \\ 4\,0 \\ \underline{4\,0} \\ 0 \end{array}$$

$$\frac{14}{5} = 2.8$$

18. $3\dfrac{13}{16}$ means $3+\dfrac{13}{16}$.

$$
\begin{array}{r}
0.8125 \\
16\overline{)13.0000} \\
12\ 8 \\ \hline
20 \\
16 \\ \hline
40 \\
32 \\ \hline
80 \\
80 \\ \hline
0
\end{array}
$$

$\dfrac{13}{16}=0.8125$ and $3\dfrac{13}{16}=3.8125$

20. $2\dfrac{5}{12}$ means $2+\dfrac{5}{12}$.

$$
\begin{array}{r}
0.41666 \\
12\overline{)5.00000} \\
4\ 8 \\ \hline
20 \\
12 \\ \hline
80 \\
72 \\ \hline
80 \\
72 \\ \hline
80 \\
72 \\ \hline
8
\end{array}
$$

$\dfrac{5}{12}=0.41\overline{6}$ and $2\dfrac{5}{12}=2.41\overline{6}$

22.
$$
\begin{array}{r}
0.833 \\
6\overline{)5.0000} \\
4\ 8 \\ \hline
20 \\
18 \\ \hline
20 \\
18 \\ \hline
20 \\
18 \\ \hline
20
\end{array}
$$

$\dfrac{5}{6}=0.8\overline{3}$

24.
$$
\begin{array}{r}
0.63 \\
11\overline{)7.00} \\
6\ 6 \\ \hline
40 \\
33 \\ \hline
7
\end{array}
$$

$\dfrac{7}{11}=0.\overline{63}$

26. $7\dfrac{1}{3}$ means $7+\dfrac{1}{3}$.

$$
\begin{array}{r}
0.333 \\
3\overline{)1.0} \\
9 \\ \hline
10 \\
9 \\ \hline
10 \\
9 \\ \hline
1
\end{array}
$$

$\dfrac{1}{3}=0.\overline{3}$ and $7\dfrac{1}{3}=7.\overline{3}$

28. $8\dfrac{7}{9}$ means $8+\dfrac{7}{9}$.

$$
\begin{array}{r}
0.777 \\
9\overline{)7.000} \\
6\ 3 \\ \hline
70 \\
63 \\ \hline
70 \\
63 \\ \hline
7
\end{array}
$$

$\dfrac{7}{9}=0.\overline{7}$ and $8\dfrac{7}{9}=8.\overline{7}$

30.
$$
\begin{array}{r}
0.4705 \\
17\overline{)8.0000} \\
6\ 8 \\ \hline
1\ 20 \\
1\ 19 \\ \hline
100 \\
85 \\ \hline
15
\end{array}
$$

$\dfrac{8}{17}$ rounds to 0.471.

32.

$$
\begin{array}{r}
0.9523 \\
21\overline{)20.0000} \\
\underline{18\ 9} \\
1\ 10 \\
\underline{1\ 05} \\
50 \\
\underline{42} \\
80 \\
\underline{63} \\
17
\end{array}
$$

$\dfrac{20}{21}$ rounds to 0.952.

34.

$$
\begin{array}{r}
0.1041 \\
48\overline{)5.000} \\
\underline{4\ 8} \\
20 \\
\underline{0} \\
200 \\
\underline{192} \\
80 \\
\underline{48} \\
32
\end{array}
$$

$\dfrac{5}{48}$ rounds to 0.104.

36.

$$
\begin{array}{r}
2.1428 \\
7\overline{)15.0000} \\
\underline{14} \\
1\ 0 \\
\underline{7} \\
30 \\
\underline{28} \\
20 \\
\underline{14} \\
60 \\
\underline{56} \\
4
\end{array}
$$

$\dfrac{15}{7}$ rounds to 2.143.

38.

$$
\begin{array}{r}
0.0263 \\
38\overline{)1.0000} \\
\underline{76} \\
240 \\
\underline{228} \\
120 \\
\underline{114} \\
6
\end{array}
$$

$\dfrac{1}{38}$ rounds to 0.026.

40.

$$
\begin{array}{r}
0.3846 \\
13\overline{)5.0000} \\
\underline{3\ 9} \\
1\ 10 \\
\underline{1\ 04} \\
60 \\
\underline{52} \\
80 \\
\underline{78} \\
2
\end{array}
$$

$\dfrac{5}{13}$ rounds to 0.385.

42.

$$
\begin{array}{r}
1.2142 \\
14\overline{)17.0000} \\
\underline{14} \\
3\ 0 \\
\underline{2\ 8} \\
20 \\
\underline{14} \\
60 \\
\underline{56} \\
40 \\
\underline{28} \\
12
\end{array}
$$

$\dfrac{17}{14}$ rounds to 1.214.

44. $4\dfrac{11}{17}$ means $4 + \dfrac{11}{17}$.

$$
\begin{array}{r}
0.6470 \\
17\overline{)11.000} \\
\underline{10\ 2} \\
80 \\
\underline{68} \\
120 \\
\underline{119} \\
10
\end{array}
$$

$\dfrac{11}{17}$ rounds to 0.647, and $4\dfrac{11}{17}$ round to 6.647.

46.
$$
\begin{array}{r}
0.9090 \\
11\overline{)10.0000} \\
\underline{9\ 9} \\
100 \\
\underline{99} \\
10
\end{array}
$$

$\dfrac{10}{11} = 0.\overline{90} > 0.9$

48.
$$
\begin{array}{r}
0.9375 \\
16\overline{)15.0000} \\
\underline{14\ 4} \\
60 \\
\underline{48} \\
120 \\
\underline{112} \\
80 \\
\underline{80} \\
0
\end{array}
$$

$0.9 < 0.9375 = \dfrac{15}{16}$

50.
$$
\begin{array}{r}
0.38 \\
50\overline{)19.00} \\
\underline{15\ 0} \\
4\ 00 \\
\underline{4\ 00} \\
0
\end{array}
$$

$\dfrac{19}{50} = 0.38$

The decrease was \$0.38.

52. $10\dfrac{1}{2}$ means $10 + \dfrac{1}{2}$.

$$
\begin{array}{r}
0.5 \\
2\overline{)1.0} \\
\underline{1.0} \\
0
\end{array}
$$

$10\dfrac{1}{2} = 10.5$

$$
\begin{array}{r}
10.69 \\
-10\ \dfrac{1}{2} \\
\end{array}
\qquad
\begin{array}{r}
10.69 \\
-10.50 \\
\hline
0.19
\end{array}
$$

The difference is 0.19 inch.

54.
$$
\begin{array}{r}
0.0625 \\
16\overline{)1.0000} \\
\underline{96} \\
40 \\
\underline{32} \\
80 \\
\underline{80} \\
0
\end{array}
$$

$0.0625 - 0.055 = 0.0075$
It is too small by 0.0075 inch.

56. $9.6 + 3.6 - (0.4)^2 = 9.6 + 3.6 - 0.16$
$ = 13.2 - 0.16$
$ = 13.04$

58. $9.6 \div 3 + 0.21 \times 6 = 3.2 + 1.26 = 4.46$

60. $61.95 \div 1.05 - 2 \times (1.7 + 1.3)^3$
$ = 61.95 \div 1.05 - 2 \times 3^3$
$ = 61.95 \div 1.05 - 2 \times 27$
$ = 59 - 54$
$ = 5$

62. $(1.1)^3 + 8.6 \div 2.15 - 0.086$
$ = 1.331 + 8.6 \div 2.15 - 0.086$
$ = 1.331 + 4 - 0.086$
$ = 5.331 - 0.086$
$ = 5.245$

64. $(32.16 - 32.02)^2 \div (2.24 + 1.76) = (0.14)^2 \div 4$
$ = 0.0196 \div 4$
$ = 0.0049$

66. $(0.6)^3 + (7 - 6.3) \times 0.07 = 0.216 + 0.7 \times 0.07$
$ = 0.216 + 0.049$
$ = 0.265$

68. $(2.4)^2 + 3.6 \div (1.2 - 0.7) = 5.76 + 3.6 \div 0.5$
$$= 5.76 + 7.2$$
$$= 12.96$$

70. $5.9 \times 3.6 \times 2.4 - 0.1 \times 0.2 \times 0.3 \times 0.4$
$$= 50.976 - 0.0024$$
$$= 50.9736$$

72. From the calculator, $\dfrac{17,359}{19,826} = 0.875567$.

74. a. $1.89\overline{89}$
$$\underline{-\ 0.01\overline{89}}$$
$$1.88$$

b. 1.89898989
$$\underline{-\ 0.18999999}$$
$$1.70898989$$

c.   (b) is a repeating and (a) is a nonrepeating.

Cumulative Review

75. $\dfrac{25}{2} = 12\dfrac{1}{2}$

$$12\dfrac{1}{2} \qquad 12\dfrac{2}{4} \qquad 11\dfrac{6}{4}$$
$$\underline{-\ 6\dfrac{3}{4}} \qquad \underline{-\ 6\dfrac{3}{4}} \qquad \underline{-\ 6\dfrac{3}{4}}$$
$$5\dfrac{3}{4}$$

The water is $5\dfrac{3}{4}$ feet deep.

76. $6\dfrac{1}{2} \qquad\qquad 6\dfrac{5}{10}$
$$\underline{+\ 25\dfrac{4}{5}} \qquad\qquad \underline{+\ 25\dfrac{8}{10}}$$
$$31\dfrac{13}{10} = 32\dfrac{3}{10}$$

The depth of the water is $32\dfrac{3}{10}$ feet.

Classroom Quiz 3.6

1. $4\dfrac{7}{16}$ means $4 + \dfrac{7}{16}$.

$$\begin{array}{r} 0.4375 \\ 16\overline{)7.0000} \\ \underline{6\ 4} \\ 60 \\ \underline{48} \\ 120 \\ \underline{112} \\ 80 \\ \underline{80} \\ 0 \end{array}$$

$\dfrac{7}{16} = 0.4375$ and $4\dfrac{7}{16} = 4.4375$

2. $$\begin{array}{r} 0.7222 \\ 18\overline{)13.0000} \\ \underline{12\ 6} \\ 40 \\ \underline{36} \\ 40 \\ \underline{36} \\ 40 \\ \underline{36} \\ 4 \end{array}$$

$\dfrac{13}{18}$ rounds to 0.722.

3. $(0.6)^2 + 0.82 \div 0.2 - 1.93$
$$= 0.36 + 0.82 \div 0.2 - 1.93$$
$$= 0.36 + 4.1 - 1.93$$
$$= 4.46 - 1.93$$
$$= 2.53$$

3.7 Exercises

2. $5,927,000 + 9,983,000$
$$\approx 6,000,000 + 10,000,000$$
$$= 16,000,000$$

4. $6949.45 - 1432.88 \approx 7000 - 1000 = 6000$

6. $47,225 \times 0.463 \approx 50,000 \times 0.5 = 25,000$

8. $34.5684 \div 0.55 \approx 30 \div 0.6 = 50$

10. $865,987,273.45 \div 55,872$
$\approx 900,000,000 \div 60,000$
$= 15,000$
The average price was about $15,000.

12. Estimate:
$$\begin{array}{r} 100 \\ \times\ 50 \\ \hline 5000 \end{array}$$

$$\begin{array}{r} 109.7 \\ \times\ \ 48.8 \\ \hline 87\ 76 \\ 877\ 6\ \ \\ 4388\ \ \ \ \\ \hline 5353.36 \end{array}$$
The area is 5353.36 square meters.

14. Estimate:
$$\begin{array}{r} 20\ \ \\ 40\overline{)800} \\ 80\ \ \\ \hline 00 \end{array}$$

$$\begin{array}{r} 22.9 \\ 35.2_\wedge\overline{)808.0_\wedge} \\ 704\ \ \ \ \\ \hline 104\ 0\ \\ 70\ 4\ \\ \hline 33\ 6\ \ 0 \\ 31\ 6\ \ 8 \\ \hline 19\ \ 2 \end{array}$$
About 23 bottles can be prepared.

16. Estimate:
$3 \times 1 = \$3$
$2 \times 2 = \$4$
$3 + 4 = \$7$

$$\begin{array}{r} 2.7 \\ \times 1.29 \\ \hline 243 \\ 54\ \ \\ 2\ 7\ \ \ \\ \hline 3.483 \end{array} \qquad \begin{array}{r} 1.8 \\ \times 1.49 \\ \hline 162 \\ 72\ \ \\ 1\ 8\ \ \ \\ \hline 2.682 \end{array}$$

Sum is $3.483 + 2.682 = 6.165$ which rounds to $6.17.

18. Estimate:
$$\begin{array}{r} 55,000 \\ -\ 54,000 \\ \hline 1\ 000 \end{array}$$

$$\begin{array}{r} 14.2 \\ 70\overline{)1000.0} \\ 70\ \ \ \ \ \\ \hline 300\ \ \ \\ 280\ \ \ \\ \hline 20\ 0\ \\ 14\ 0\ \\ \hline 2\ 0 \end{array}$$

$$\begin{array}{r} 55,401 \\ -\ 54,089 \\ \hline 1\ 312 \end{array}$$

$$\begin{array}{r} 20 \\ 65.6_\wedge\overline{)1312.0_\wedge} \\ 1312\ \ \ \\ \hline 0\ 0 \\ 0\ 0 \\ \hline 0 \end{array}$$
They got 20 miles per gallon.

20. Estimate:
$$\begin{array}{r} 30 \\ \times 0.2 \\ \hline 6.0 \end{array}$$

$$\begin{array}{r} 28.5 \\ \times 0.23 \\ \hline 855 \\ 5\ 70\ \ \\ \hline 6.555 \end{array}$$
6.555 which rounds to 6.56
It will cost $6.56.

22. Estimate:
$3 + 3 + 2 = 8$
$8 \times 8 = 64$

$$\begin{array}{r} 2.7 \\ 3.3 \\ +\ 1.8 \\ \hline 7.8\ \text{gallons} \end{array} \qquad \begin{array}{r} 7.40 \\ \times\ \ 7.8 \\ \hline 5\ 290 \\ 51\ 80\ \ \\ \hline 57.720\ \text{or}\ 57.72 \end{array}$$

The total cost is $57.72.

24. Estimate:
$40 + 8 \times 2 = 40 + 16 = 56$
$60 \times 10 = 600$
Time $= 40 + 8 \times 1.5 = 40 + 12 = 52$
Earnings $= 52 \times \$14.30 = \$743.60$
Her total earnings for that week were $743.60.

26. Estimate:
$20 + 40 + 20 = 80$
$100 - 80 = 20$

total spent:		Difference:
18.50		100.00
42.75		− 82.50
+ 21.25		17.50
82.50		

Raul had $17.50 left.

28. Estimate:
$10 \times 30 = 300$
$800 \times 300 = 240,000$
$240,000 - 140,000 = 100,000$

$$\begin{array}{r} 12 \\ \times\, 30 \\ \hline 360 \text{ months} \end{array}$$

Total of payments:
$$\begin{array}{r} 764.35 \\ \times\qquad 360 \\ \hline 458\ 610\ 0 \\ 229\ 305 \\ \hline 275{,}166.00 \end{array}$$

Difference:
$$\begin{array}{r} 275{,}166 \\ -\ 140{,}000 \\ \hline 135{,}166 \end{array}$$

They will pay $275,166 which is $135,166 more than they borrowed.

30. Estimate:
$0.08 \div 6 = 0.013$
$0.015 - 0.013 = 0.002$

$$\begin{array}{r} 0.01325 \\ 6\overline{)0.07950} \\ \underline{6} \\ 19 \\ \underline{18} \\ 15 \\ \underline{12} \\ 30 \\ \underline{30} \\ 0 \end{array}$$

$$\begin{array}{r} 0.01500 \\ -\ 0.01325 \\ \hline 0.00175 \end{array}$$

Yes, it is safe by 0.00175 milligram per liter.

32. Estimate: $25,000,000 \div 10 = 2,500,000$

$$\frac{25,000,000}{11.50} = 2,173,913$$

You could purchase 2,173,913 games.

34. Estimate: $70 - 40 = 30$

$$\begin{array}{r} 66.4 \\ -\ 43.8 \\ \hline 22.6 \end{array}$$

It increased by 22.6 quadrillion Btu; from 1960 to 1970.

36. Estimate:
$80 + 90 + 100 = 270$
$300 \div 3 = 100$

$$\begin{array}{r} 84.1 \\ 89.3 \\ +\ 96.8 \\ \hline 270.2 \end{array}$$

$$\begin{array}{r} 90.06 \\ 3\overline{)270.20} \\ \underline{27} \\ 20 \\ \underline{18} \\ 2 \end{array}$$

The average consumption for 1990, 2000, and 2010 was ≈ 90.1 quadrillion Btu; 90,100,000,000,000,000 Btu

Cumulative Review

37. $\dfrac{4}{7} + \dfrac{1}{2} \times \dfrac{2}{3} = \dfrac{4}{7} + \dfrac{1}{3} = \dfrac{12}{21} + \dfrac{7}{21} = \dfrac{19}{21}$

38. $\dfrac{3}{19} + \dfrac{5}{38} - \dfrac{2}{19} = \dfrac{6}{38} + \dfrac{5}{38} - \dfrac{4}{38} = \dfrac{6+5-4}{38} = \dfrac{7}{38}$

39. $\dfrac{7}{25} \times \dfrac{15}{42} = \dfrac{7 \times 3 \times 5}{5 \times 5 \times 2 \times 3 \times 7} = \dfrac{1}{10}$

40. $2\dfrac{2}{3} \div \dfrac{1}{3} = \dfrac{8}{3} \times \dfrac{3}{1} = 8$

Classroom Quiz 3.7

1. Total snowfall:

Total snowfall:	Difference:
22.5	90.5
32.7	− 82.1
+ 26.9	8.4 inches
82.1 inches	

Pine City received 8.4 inches less than normal.

2. Distance traveled:

$$46,228.2$$
$$- 45,678.2$$
$$\overline{550.0 \text{ miles}}$$

$$
\begin{array}{r}
22.91 \\
24\overline{)550.00} \\
\underline{48} \\
70 \\
\underline{48} \\
22\,0 \\
\underline{21\,6} \\
40 \\
\underline{24} \\
16
\end{array}
$$

They used 22.9 gallons.

3. overtime rate:

$$
\begin{array}{r}
9.50 \\
\times \;\; 1.5 \\
\hline
4\,750 \\
9\,50 \\
\hline
14.250 = \$14.25
\end{array}
$$

$$
\begin{array}{r}
9.50 \\
\times \;\;\; 40 \\
\hline
380.00
\end{array}
\qquad
\begin{array}{r}
14.25 \\
\times \;\;\; 17 \\
\hline
99\,75 \\
142\,5 \\
\hline
242.25
\end{array}
$$

$$
\begin{array}{r}
380.00 \\
+\;242.25 \\
\hline
622.25
\end{array}
$$

Joel earned $622.25 last week.

Putting Your Skills to Work

1. SHELL: $3.55
ARCO: $3.43 + $0.45 = $3.88
She should choose SHELL.

2. SHELL: 3($3.55) = $10.65
ARCO: 3($3.43) + $0.45 = $10.74
She should choose SHELL.

3. SHELL: 4($3.55) = $14.20
ARCO: 4($3.43) + $0.45 = $14.17
She should choose ARCO.

4. SHELL: 10($3.55) = $35.50
ARCO: 10($3.43) + $0.45 = $34.75
She should choose ARCO.

5. $3.55x = 3.43x + 0.45$
$0.12x = 0.45$
$x = 3.75$
She needs to buy 3.75 gallons for the price to be the same.

6. Answers may vary.

7. Answers may vary.

Chapter 3 Review Problems

1. 13.672 = thirteen and six hundred seventy-two thousandths

2. 0.00084 = eighty-four hundred-thousandths

3. $\dfrac{7}{10} = 0.7$

4. $\dfrac{81}{100} = 0.81$

5. $1\dfrac{523}{1000} = 1.523$

6. $\dfrac{79}{10,000} = 0.0079$

7. $0.17 = \dfrac{17}{100}$

8. $0.036 = \dfrac{36}{1000} = \dfrac{9}{250}$

9. $34.24 = 34\dfrac{24}{100} = 34\dfrac{6}{25}$

10. $1.00025 = 1\dfrac{25}{100,000} = 1\dfrac{1}{4000}$

11. Since $\dfrac{9}{100} = 0.09,\;\; 2\dfrac{9}{100} = 2 + 0.09 = 2.09.$

$2\dfrac{9}{100} = 2.09$

12. $0.716 > 0.706$
The hundredths place is the first digit where the numbers differ. Since $1 > 0$, 0.716 is the greater number.

13. $\dfrac{65}{100} < 0.655$

This is true because $\dfrac{65}{100} = 0.65$ and $0.65 < 0.655.$

14. 0.824 > 0.804
The hundredths place is the first digit where the numbers differ. Since 2 > 0, 0.824 is the greater number.

15. 0.981, 0.918, 0.98, 0.901
Add zeros to make the comparison easier.
0.981, 0.918, 0.980, 0.901
Rearrange with the smallest first.
0.901, 0.918, 0.98, 0.981

16. 5.62, 5.2, 5.6, 5.26, 5.59
Add zeros to make the comparison easier.
5.62, 5.20, 5.60, 5.26, 5.59
Rearrange with the smallest first.
5.2, 5.26, 5.59, 5.6, 5.62

17. 0.419, 0.49, 0.409, 0.491
Add zeros to make the comparison easier.
0.419, 0.490, 0.409, 0.491
Rearrange with the smallest first.
0.409, 0.419, 0.49, 0.491

18. 2.36, 2.3, 2.362, 2.302
Add zeros to make the comparison easier.
2.360, 2.300, 2.362, 2.302
Rearrange with the smallest first.
2.3, 2.302, 2.36, 2.362

19. 0.613 rounds to 0.6
Find the tenths place: 0.$\underline{6}$13. The digit to the right of the tenths place is less than 5. We round down to 0.6 and drop the digits to the right.

20. 19.2076 rounds to 19.21.
Find the hundredths place: 19.2$\underline{0}$76. The digit to the right of the hundredths place is greater than 5. We round up to 19.21 and drop the digits to the right.

21. 9.85215 rounds to 9.8522.
Find the ten-thousandths place: 9.852$\underline{1}$5. The digit to the right of the ten-thousandths place is equal to 5. We round up to 9.8522 and drop the digit to the right.

22. $156.48 rounds to $156.

23.
$$\begin{array}{r} 9.6 \\ 11.5 \\ 21.8 \\ +\ 34.7 \\ \hline 77.6 \end{array}$$

24.
$$\begin{array}{r} 2.50 \\ 32.70 \\ 116.94 \\ +\ 0.67 \\ \hline 152.81 \end{array}$$

25.
$$\begin{array}{r} 17.030 \\ -\ 2.448 \\ \hline 14.582 \end{array}$$

26.
$$\begin{array}{r} 182.422 \\ -\ 68.550 \\ \hline 113.872 \end{array}$$

27.
$$\begin{array}{r} 0.098 \\ \times\ 0.032 \\ \hline 0196 \\ 0294 \\ \hline 0.003136 \end{array}$$

28.
$$\begin{array}{r} 126.83 \\ \times\ \ \ \ \ 7 \\ \hline 887.81 \end{array}$$

29.
$$\begin{array}{r} 7.8 \\ \times\ 5.2 \\ \hline 15\ 6 \\ 390 \\ \hline 405.6 \end{array}$$

30.
$$\begin{array}{r} 7053 \\ \times\ 0.34 \\ \hline 282\ 12 \\ 2115\ 9 \\ \hline 2398.02 \end{array}$$

31. Move the decimal three places to the right.
$0.000613 \times 10^3 = 0.613$

32. Move the decimal five places to the right.
$1.2354 \times 10^5 = 123,540$

33.
$$\begin{array}{r} 3.49 \\ \times\ 2.5 \\ \hline 1\ 745 \\ 6\ 98 \\ \hline 8.725 \end{array}$$
The cost is $8.73.

34.
$$
\begin{array}{r}
0.00258 \\
0.07_\wedge\overline{)0.00_\wedge01806} \\
\underline{14} \\
40 \\
\underline{35} \\
56 \\
\underline{56} \\
0
\end{array}
$$

35.
$$
\begin{array}{r}
36.8 \\
5.2_\wedge\overline{)191.3_\wedge6} \\
\underline{156} \\
35\,3 \\
\underline{31\,2} \\
4\,1\,6 \\
\underline{4\,1\,6} \\
0
\end{array}
$$

36.
$$
\begin{array}{r}
232.9 \\
8\overline{)1863.2} \\
\underline{16} \\
26 \\
\underline{24} \\
23 \\
\underline{16} \\
7\,2 \\
\underline{7\,2} \\
0
\end{array}
$$

37.
$$
\begin{array}{r}
574.42 \\
1.3_\wedge\overline{)746.7_\wedge50} \\
\underline{65} \\
96 \\
\underline{91} \\
57 \\
\underline{52} \\
5\,5 \\
\underline{5\,2} \\
30 \\
\underline{26} \\
4
\end{array}
$$

574.42 rounds to 574.4.

38.
$$
\begin{array}{r}
0.0589 \\
0.06_\wedge\overline{)0.00_\wedge3539} \\
\underline{30} \\
53 \\
\underline{48} \\
59 \\
\underline{54} \\
5
\end{array}
$$

0.0589 rounds to 0.059.

39.
$$
\begin{array}{r}
0.9166 \\
12\overline{)11.0000} \\
\underline{10\,8} \\
20 \\
\underline{12} \\
80 \\
\underline{72} \\
80 \\
\underline{72} \\
8
\end{array}
$$

$$\frac{11}{12} = 0.91\overline{6}$$

40.
$$
\begin{array}{r}
0.85 \\
20\overline{)17.00} \\
\underline{160} \\
1\,00 \\
\underline{1\,00} \\
0
\end{array}
$$

$$\frac{17}{20} = 0.85$$

41. $1\dfrac{5}{6}$ means $1+\dfrac{5}{6}$.

$$
\begin{array}{r}
0.833 \\
6\overline{)5.000} \\
\underline{4\,8} \\
20 \\
\underline{18} \\
20 \\
\underline{18} \\
2
\end{array}
$$

$$\frac{5}{6} = 0.8\overline{3} \text{ and } 1\frac{5}{6} = 1.8\overline{3}$$

42.

$$16 \overline{)\begin{array}{l} 1.1875 \\ 19.0000 \end{array}}$$

$$\begin{array}{r} \underline{16} \\ 3\,0 \\ \underline{1\,6} \\ 1\,40 \\ \underline{1\,28} \\ 120 \\ \underline{112} \\ 80 \\ \underline{80} \\ 0 \end{array}$$

$$\frac{19}{16} = 1.1875$$

43.

$$14 \overline{)\begin{array}{l} 0.7857 \\ 11.0000 \end{array}}$$

$$\begin{array}{r} \underline{9\,8} \\ 1\,20 \\ \underline{1\,12} \\ 80 \\ \underline{70} \\ 100 \\ \underline{98} \\ 2 \end{array}$$

$$\frac{11}{14} \text{ rounds to } 0.786.$$

44.

$$29 \overline{)\begin{array}{l} 0.3448 \\ 10.0000 \end{array}}$$

$$\begin{array}{r} \underline{8\,7} \\ 1\,30 \\ \underline{1\,16} \\ 140 \\ \underline{116} \\ 240 \\ \underline{232} \\ 8 \end{array}$$

$$\frac{10}{29} \text{ rounds to } 0.345.$$

45.

$$17 \overline{)\begin{array}{l} 0.2941 \\ 5.0000 \end{array}}$$

$$\begin{array}{r} \underline{3\,4} \\ 1\,60 \\ \underline{1\,53} \\ 70 \\ \underline{68} \\ 20 \\ \underline{17} \\ 3 \end{array}$$

$$\frac{5}{17} \text{ rounds to } 0.294, \text{ and } 2\frac{5}{17} \text{ rounds to } 2.294.$$

46.

$$23 \overline{)\begin{array}{l} 0.3913 \\ 9.0000 \end{array}}$$

$$\begin{array}{r} \underline{6\,9} \\ 2\,10 \\ \underline{207} \\ 30 \\ \underline{23} \\ 70 \\ \underline{69} \\ 1 \end{array}$$

$$\frac{9}{23} \text{ rounds to } 0.391, \text{ and } 3\frac{9}{23} \text{ rounds to } 3.391.$$

47. $2.3 \times 1.82 + 3 \times 5.12 = 4.186 + 15.36 = 19.546$

48. $2.175 \div 0.15 \times 10 + 27.32 = 14.5 \times 10 + 27.32$
$$= 145 + 27.32$$
$$= 172.32$$

49. $3.57 - (0.4)^3 \times 2.5 \div 5 = 3.57 - 0.064 \times 2.5 \div 5$
$$= 3.57 - 0.16 \div 5$$
$$= 3.57 - 0.032$$
$$= 3.538$$

50. $2.4 \div (2 - 1.6)^2 + 8.13 = 2.4 \div (0.4)^2 + 8.13$
$$= 2.4 \div 0.16 + 8.13$$
$$= 15 + 8.13$$
$$= 23.13$$

51.
$$\begin{array}{r} 2398.26 \\ -\ 1959.07 \\ \hline 439.19 \end{array}$$

52. $32.15 \times 0.02 \times 10^2 = 32.15 \times 0.02 \times 100$
$= 0.643 \times 100$
$= 64.3$

53. $1.809 - 0.62 + 3.27 = 1.189 + 3.27 = 4.459$

54.

$$
\begin{array}{r}
.904 \\
2.3_{\wedge}\overline{)2.0_{\wedge}792} \\
\underline{2\ 0\ 7} \\
92 \\
\underline{92} \\
0
\end{array}
$$

0.904

55. $8 \div 0.4 + 0.1 \times (0.2)^2 = 20 + 0.1 \times 0.04$
$= 20 + 0.004$
$= 20.004$

56. $(3.8 - 2.8)^3 \div (0.5 + 0.3) = 1^3 \div 0.8 = 1 \div 0.8 = 1.25$

57. Tickets $= 228 + 2.5 \times 388 + 3 \times 430$
$= 228 + 970 + 1290$
$= 2488$
Not tickets $= 2600 - 2488 = 112$
112 people still have not received their tickets.

58.

$$
\begin{array}{r}
26325.8 \\
-\ 26005.8 \\
\hline
320.0
\end{array}
$$

$$
\begin{array}{r}
24.80 \\
12.9_{\wedge}\overline{)320.0_{\wedge}00} \\
\underline{258} \\
62\ 0 \\
\underline{51\ 6} \\
10\ 4\ 0 \\
\underline{10\ 3\ 2} \\
80 \\
\underline{0} \\
80
\end{array}
$$

His car got 24.8 miles per gallon.

59.

$$
\begin{array}{r}
189.60 \\
\times\ \ \ \ \ \ 48 \\
\hline
1516\ 80 \\
7584\ 0 \\
\hline
\$9100.80
\end{array}
$$

$$
\begin{array}{r}
9100.80 \\
-\ 6930.50 \\
\hline
\$2170.30
\end{array}
$$

He pays $2170.30 extra.

60.

$$
\begin{array}{r}
8.26 \\
\times\ \ \ \ \ 38 \\
\hline
66\ 08 \\
247\ 8 \\
\hline
\$313.88
\end{array}
$$

He will earn more at the ABC Company.

61.

$$
\begin{array}{r}
0.0025 \\
12\overline{)0.0300} \\
\underline{24} \\
60 \\
\underline{60} \\
0
\end{array}
$$

$$
\begin{array}{r}
0.0025 \\
-\ 0.0020 \\
\hline
0.0005
\end{array}
$$

No; it is not safe by 0.0005 milligram per liter.

62.

$$
\begin{array}{r}
15.748 \\
2.54\overline{)40.00000} \\
\underline{25\ 4} \\
14\ 60 \\
\underline{12\ 70} \\
1\ 900 \\
\underline{1\ 778} \\
1220 \\
\underline{1016} \\
2040 \\
\underline{2032} \\
8
\end{array}
$$

This measurement was 15.75 inches.

63. a. Fence $= 2 \times 18.3 + 2 \times 9.6$
$= 36.6 + 19.2$
$= 55.8$
He needs 55.8 feet.

b.

$$
\begin{array}{r}
18.3 \\
\times\ \ \ 9.6 \\
\hline
10\ 98 \\
164\ 7 \\
\hline
175.68
\end{array}
$$

The area is 175.68 square feet.

64.

$$
\begin{array}{r}
75.5 \\
\times\ 18.5 \\
\hline
37\ 75 \\
604\ 0 \\
755 \\
\hline
1396.75
\end{array}
$$

The area is 1396.75 square feet.

65. Galeton to Wellsboro
$5.7 + 18.4 = 24.1$ miles
Coudersport to Gaines
$16.3 + 8.2 + 5.7 = 30.2$ miles
Difference
$30.2 - 24.1 = 6.1$
The distance is 6.1 miles longer.

66.

$$
\begin{array}{r}
118.9 \\
25.6 \\
18.9 \\
43.9 \\
22.6 \\
13.8 \\
+\ 16.2 \\
\hline
259.9
\end{array}
$$

It is 259.9 feet around the field.

67.

$$
\begin{array}{r}
212.50 \\
\times\ \ \ \ \ 60 \\
\hline
\$12,750.00
\end{array}
$$

$$
\begin{array}{r}
199.50 \\
\times\ \ \ \ \ 60 \\
\hline
11,970.00 \\
+\ \ \ \ 285.00 \\
\hline
\$12,255.00
\end{array}
$$

They should change to the new loan.

68.

$$
\begin{array}{r}
720.00 \\
-\ 479.00 \\
\hline
241.00
\end{array}
$$

The average monthly benefit increased $241.00 from 1985 to 1995.

69.

$$
\begin{array}{r}
950 \\
-\ 720 \\
\hline
230
\end{array}
$$

The average monthly benefit increased $230 from 1995 to 2005.

70.

$$
\begin{array}{r}
11.366 \\
30\overline{)341.000} \\
\underline{30} \\
41 \\
\underline{30} \\
11\ 0 \\
\underline{9\ 0} \\
2\ 00 \\
\underline{1\ 80} \\
200 \\
\underline{180} \\
20
\end{array}
$$

$\dfrac{341}{30}$ rounds to 11.37.

The average daily benefit was $11.37 in 1980.

71.

$$
\begin{array}{r}
31.666 \\
30\overline{)950.000} \\
\underline{90} \\
50 \\
\underline{30} \\
20\ 0 \\
\underline{18\ 0} \\
2\ 00 \\
\underline{1\ 80} \\
200 \\
\underline{180} \\
20
\end{array}
$$

$\dfrac{950}{30}$ rounds to 31.67.

The average daily benefit was $31.67 in 2005.

72.

$$
\begin{array}{r}
950 \\
-\ 603 \\
\hline
347
\end{array}
$$

The average monthly benefit increased $347 from 1990 to 2005.
$950 + 347 = 1297$

$$\begin{array}{r} 43.233 \\ 30\overline{)1297.000} \\ \underline{120} \\ 97 \\ \underline{90} \\ 7\,0 \\ \underline{6\,0} \\ 1\,00 \\ \underline{90} \\ 100 \\ \underline{90} \\ 0 \end{array}$$

The average daily benefit will be $43.23 in 2020.

73.
$$\begin{array}{r} 950 \\ -\,720 \\ \hline 230 \end{array}$$

The average monthly benefit increased $230 from 1995 to 2005.
$950 + 230 = 1180$

$$\begin{array}{r} 39.333 \\ 30\overline{)1180.000} \\ \underline{90} \\ 280 \\ \underline{270} \\ 10\,0 \\ \underline{9\,0} \\ 1\,00 \\ \underline{90} \\ 100 \\ \underline{90} \\ 10 \end{array}$$

The average daily benefit will be $39.33 in 2015.

How Am I Doing? Chapter 3 Test

1. 12.043 – twelve and forty-three thousandths

2. $\dfrac{3977}{10,000} = 0.3977$

3. $7.15 = 7\dfrac{15}{100} = 7\dfrac{3}{20}$

4. $0.261 = \dfrac{261}{1000}$

5. 2.19, 2.91, 2.9, 2.907
Add zeros to make the comparison easier.
2.190, 2.910, 2.900, 2.907
Rearrange with the smallest first.
2.19, 2.9, 2.907, 2.91

6. 78.6562 rounds to 78.66.
Find the hundredths place: 78.6562. The digit to the right of the hundredths place is greater than 5. We round up to 78.66 and drop the digits to the right.

7. 0.0341752 rounds to 0.0342.
Find the ten-thousandths place: 0.0341752. The digit to the right of the ten-thousandths place is greater than 5. We round up to 0.0342 and drop the digits to the right.

8.
$$\begin{array}{r} 96.200 \\ 1.348 \\ +\ 2.150 \\ \hline 99.698 \end{array}$$

9.
$$\begin{array}{r} 17.00 \\ 2.10 \\ 16.80 \\ 0.04 \\ +\ 1.59 \\ \hline 37.53 \end{array}$$

10.
$$\begin{array}{r} 1.0075 \\ -\ 0.9096 \\ \hline 0.0979 \end{array}$$

11.
$$\begin{array}{r} 72.300 \\ -\ 1.145 \\ \hline 71.155 \end{array}$$

12.
$$\begin{array}{r} 8.31 \\ \times\ 0.07 \\ \hline 0.5817 \end{array}$$

13. Move the decimal three places to the right.
$2.189 \times 10^3 = 2189$

14.

$$
\begin{array}{r}
0.1285 \\
0.08_\wedge\overline{)0.01_\wedge0280} \\
\underline{8} \\
22 \\
\underline{16} \\
68 \\
\underline{64} \\
40 \\
\underline{40} \\
0
\end{array}
$$

15.

$$
\begin{array}{r}
47 \\
0.69_\wedge\overline{)32.43_\wedge} \\
\underline{27\ 6} \\
4\ 83 \\
\underline{4\ 83} \\
0
\end{array}
$$

16.

$$
\begin{array}{r}
1.2 \\
9\overline{)11.0} \\
\underline{9} \\
2\ 0 \\
\underline{1\ 8} \\
2
\end{array}
$$

$$\frac{11}{9} = 1.\overline{2}$$

17.

$$
\begin{array}{r}
0.875 \\
8\overline{)7.000} \\
\underline{6\ 4} \\
60 \\
\underline{56} \\
40 \\
\underline{40} \\
0
\end{array}
$$

$$\frac{7}{8} = 0.875$$

18. $(0.3)^3 + 1.02 \div 0.5 - 0.58$

$= 0.027 + 1.02 \div 0.5 - 0.58$

$= 0.027 + 2.04 - 0.58$

$= 2.067 - 0.58$

$= 1.487$

19. $19.36 \div (0.24 + 0.26) \times (0.4)^2 = 19.36 \div 0.5 \times 0.16$

$\qquad\qquad\qquad\qquad\qquad\qquad\qquad\quad = 19.36 \div 0.5 \times 0.16$

$\qquad\qquad\qquad\qquad\qquad\qquad\qquad\quad = 38.72 \times 0.16$

$\qquad\qquad\qquad\qquad\qquad\qquad\qquad\quad = 6.1952$

20.

$$
\begin{array}{r}
3.17 \\
\times\ \ 8.5 \\
\hline
1\ 585 \\
25\ 36 \\
\hline
26.945
\end{array}
$$

Peter spent $26.95.

21.

$$
\begin{array}{r}
42780.5 \\
-\ 42620.5 \\
\hline
160.0
\end{array}
$$

$$
\begin{array}{r}
18.82 \\
8.5\overline{)160.000} \\
\underline{85} \\
75\ 0 \\
\underline{68\ 0} \\
7\ 00 \\
\underline{6\ 80} \\
200 \\
\underline{170} \\
30
\end{array}
$$

His car achieved 18.8 miles per gallon.

22.

$$
\begin{array}{r}
8.01 \\
5.03 \\
+\ \ 8.53 \\
\hline
21.57
\end{array}
$$

$$
\begin{array}{r}
25.00 \\
-\ 21.57 \\
\hline
3.43
\end{array}
$$

It is 3.43 centimeters less.

23. Time = $40 + 1.5 \times 9 = 40 + 13.5 = 53.5$ hours

Salary = $7.30 \times 53.5 = $390.55

She earned $390.55.

Cumulative Test for Chapters 1–3

1. 38,056,954 = thirty-eight million, fifty-six thousand, nine hundred fifty-four

2.

$$
\begin{array}{r}
156,028 \\
301,579 \\
+\ \ 21,980 \\
\hline
479,587
\end{array}
$$

3.

$$
\begin{array}{r}
1,091,000 \\
-\ 1,036,520 \\
\hline
54,480
\end{array}
$$

4.
$$\begin{array}{r} 589 \\ \times\ \ 67 \\ \hline 4\ 123 \\ 35\ 34 \\ \hline 39,463 \end{array}$$

5.
$$\begin{array}{r} 316 \\ 15\overline{)4740} \\ \underline{45} \\ 24 \\ \underline{15} \\ 90 \\ \underline{90} \\ 0 \end{array}$$

6. $20 \div 4 + 2^5 - 7 \times 3 = 20 \div 4 + 32 - 7 \times 3$
$$= 5 + 32 - 21$$
$$= 37 - 21$$
$$= 16$$

7. $\dfrac{18}{45} = \dfrac{18 \div 9}{45 \div 9} = \dfrac{2}{5}$

8.
$$\begin{array}{r} 5\dfrac{3}{8} \\ + 2\dfrac{11}{12} \\ \hline \end{array} \qquad \begin{array}{r} 5\dfrac{9}{24} \\ + 2\dfrac{22}{24} \\ \hline 9\dfrac{31}{24} = 8\dfrac{7}{24} \end{array}$$

9. $\dfrac{23}{35} - \dfrac{2}{5} = \dfrac{23}{35} - \dfrac{2}{5} \times \dfrac{7}{7} = \dfrac{23}{35} - \dfrac{14}{35} = \dfrac{9}{35}$

10. $\dfrac{5}{16} \times \dfrac{4}{5} + \dfrac{9}{10} \times \dfrac{2}{3} = \dfrac{1}{4} + \dfrac{3}{5} = \dfrac{5}{20} + \dfrac{12}{20} = \dfrac{17}{20}$

11. $52 \div 3\dfrac{1}{4} = 52 \div \dfrac{13}{4} = \dfrac{52}{1} \times \dfrac{4}{13} = 16$

12. $1\dfrac{3}{8} \div \dfrac{5}{12} = \dfrac{11}{8} \div \dfrac{5}{12}$
$$= \dfrac{11}{8} \times \dfrac{12}{5}$$
$$= \dfrac{11 \times 4 \times 3}{4 \times 2 \times 5}$$
$$= \dfrac{33}{10}$$
$$= 3\dfrac{3}{10}$$

13. $58,216 \times 438,207 \approx 60,000 \times 400,000$
$$= 24,000,000,000$$

14. $\dfrac{39}{1000} = 0.039$

15. 2.1, 20.1, 2.01, 2.12, 2.11
Add zeros to make the comparison easier.
2.10, 20.10, 2.01, 2.12, 2.11
Rearrange with the smallest first.
2.01, 2.1, 2.11, 2.12, 20.1

16. 26.07984 rounds to 26.080.
Find the thousandths place: 26.07<u>9</u>84. The digit to the right of the thousandths place is greater than 5. We round up to 26.080 and drop the digits to the right.

17.
$$\begin{array}{r} 3.126 \\ 8.400 \\ 10.330 \\ + \ \ 0.090 \\ \hline 21.946 \end{array}$$

18.
$$\begin{array}{r} 28.100 \\ - 14.982 \\ \hline 13.118 \end{array}$$

19.
$$\begin{array}{r} 28.7 \\ \times 0.05 \\ \hline 1.435 \end{array}$$

20. Move the decimal three places to the right.
$0.1823 \times 1000 = 182.3$

21.
$$\begin{array}{r} 1.058 \\ 0.06_{\wedge}\overline{)0.06_{\wedge}348} \\ \underline{6} \\ 3 \\ \underline{0} \\ 34 \\ \underline{30} \\ 48 \\ \underline{48} \\ 0 \end{array}$$

22.

$$
\begin{array}{r}
0.8125 \\
16\overline{)13.0000} \\
\underline{12\ 8} \\
20 \\
\underline{16} \\
40 \\
\underline{32} \\
80 \\
\underline{80} \\
0
\end{array}
$$

$$\frac{13}{16} = 0.8125$$

23. $1.44 \div 0.12 + (0.3)^3 + 1.57$
$= 1.44 \div 0.12 + 0.027 + 1.57$
$= 12 + 0.027 + 1.57$
$= 12.027 + 1.57$
$= 13.597$

24. a.

$$
\begin{array}{r}
10.5 \\
\times\ 10.5 \\
\hline
5\ 25 \\
105\ 0 \\
\hline
110.25
\end{array}
$$

The area is 110.25 square feet.

b.

$$
\begin{array}{r}
10.5 \\
\times\ 4 \\
\hline
42.0
\end{array}
$$

The perimeter is 42 feet.

25.

$$
\begin{array}{r}
199.36 \\
1.03 \\
166.35 \\
+\ 93.50 \\
\hline
460.24
\end{array}
$$

$$
\begin{array}{r}
90.00 \\
37.49 \\
+\ 137.18 \\
\hline
264.67
\end{array}
$$

$$
\begin{array}{r}
460.24 \\
-\ 264.67 \\
\hline
195.57
\end{array}
$$

Her balance will be $195.57.

26.

$$
\begin{array}{r}
60 \\
320.50_\wedge\overline{)19,230.00_\wedge} \\
\underline{19,230.0} \\
0
\end{array}
$$

It will take 60 months.

Chapter 4

4.1 Exercises

2. A rate is a comparison of two quantities that have <u>different</u> units.

4. This is a rate because it compares different units: loaves of bread to pounds of flour.

6. $8:20 = \dfrac{8}{20} = \dfrac{8 \div 4}{20 \div 4} = \dfrac{2}{5}$

8. $50:35 = \dfrac{50}{35} = \dfrac{50 \div 5}{35 \div 5} = \dfrac{10}{7}$

10. $360:480 = \dfrac{360}{480} = \dfrac{360 \div 120}{480 \div 120} = \dfrac{3}{4}$

12. $135 \text{ to } 120 = \dfrac{135}{120} = \dfrac{135 \div 15}{120 \div 15} = \dfrac{9}{8}$

14. $55 \text{ to } 77 = \dfrac{55}{77} = \dfrac{55 \div 11}{77 \div 11} = \dfrac{5}{7}$

16. $21 \text{ to } 98 = \dfrac{21}{98} = \dfrac{21 \div 7}{98 \div 7} = \dfrac{3}{14}$

18. $90 \text{ to } 54 = \dfrac{90}{54} = \dfrac{90 \div 18}{54 \div 18} = \dfrac{5}{3}$

20. $50 \text{ years to } 85 \text{ years} = \dfrac{50}{85} = \dfrac{50 \div 5}{85 \div 5} = \dfrac{10}{17}$

22. $255 \text{ meters to } 15 \text{ meters} = \dfrac{255}{15} = \dfrac{255 \div 15}{15 \div 15} = \dfrac{17}{1}$

24. $\$54 \text{ to } \$78 = \dfrac{54}{78} = \dfrac{54 \div 6}{78 \div 6} = \dfrac{9}{13}$

26. $91 \text{ tons to } 133 \text{ tons} = \dfrac{91}{133} = \dfrac{91 \div 7}{133 \div 7} = \dfrac{13}{19}$

28. $4\dfrac{1}{3} \text{ feet to } 5\dfrac{2}{3} \text{ feet} = \dfrac{4\frac{1}{3}}{5\frac{2}{3}}$

$= 4\dfrac{1}{3} \div 5\dfrac{2}{3}$

$= \dfrac{13}{3} \div \dfrac{17}{3}$

$= \dfrac{13}{3} \times \dfrac{3}{17}$

$= \dfrac{13}{17}$

30. $\dfrac{28}{16} = \dfrac{28 \div 4}{16 \div 4} = \dfrac{7}{4}$

32. $\dfrac{28}{285}$

34. $\dfrac{315}{1225} = \dfrac{315 \div 35}{1225 \div 35} = \dfrac{9}{35}$

36. $\dfrac{315}{255} = \dfrac{315 \div 15}{255 \div 15} = \dfrac{21}{17}$

38. $\dfrac{34}{714} = \dfrac{34 \div 34}{714 \div 34} = \dfrac{1}{21}$

40. $\dfrac{\$50}{15 \text{ sandwiches}} = \dfrac{\$50 \div 5}{15 \text{ sandwiches} \div 5}$
$= \dfrac{\$10}{3 \text{ sandwiches}}$

42. $\dfrac{98 \text{ pounds}}{22 \text{ people}} = \dfrac{98 \text{ pounds} \div 2}{22 \text{ people} \div 2} = \dfrac{49 \text{ pounds}}{11 \text{ people}}$

44. $\dfrac{\$150}{12 \text{ plants}} = \dfrac{\$150 \div 6}{12 \text{ plants} \div 6} = \dfrac{\$25}{2 \text{ plants}}$

46. $\dfrac{9540 \text{ rev}}{18 \text{ miles}} = \dfrac{9540 \text{ rev} \div 18}{18 \text{ miles} \div 18}$
$= \dfrac{530 \text{ rev}}{1 \text{ mile}}$
$= 530 \text{ rev/mile}$

48. $\dfrac{\$156,000}{24 \text{ people}} = \dfrac{\$156,000 \div 24}{24 \text{ people} \div 24}$

$\qquad\qquad = \dfrac{\$6500}{1 \text{ person}}$ or $\$6500$/person

50. $\dfrac{\$315}{35 \text{ hours}} = \dfrac{\$315 \div 35}{35 \text{ hours} \div 35} = \$9$/hr

52. $\dfrac{322 \text{ miles}}{14 \text{ gal}} = \dfrac{322 \text{ miles} \div 14}{14 \text{ gal} \div 14} = 23$ miles/gal

54. $\dfrac{3600 \text{ people}}{24 \text{ square miles}} = \dfrac{3600 \text{ people} \div 24}{24 \text{ sq mi} \div 24}$

$\qquad\qquad = 150$ people/sq mi

56. $\dfrac{930 \text{ points}}{15 \text{ games}} = \dfrac{930 \text{ points} \div 15}{15 \text{ games} \div 15} = 62$ points/game

58. $\dfrac{374 \text{ miles}}{5.5 \text{ hours}} = \dfrac{374 \text{ miles} \div 5.5}{5.5 \text{ hours} \div 5.5} = 68$ mi/hour

60. $\dfrac{375 \text{ trees}}{15 \text{ acres}} = \dfrac{375 \text{ trees} \div 15}{15 \text{ acres} \div 15} = 25$ trees/acre

62. $\dfrac{78 \text{ children}}{26 \text{ families}} = \dfrac{78 \text{ children} \div 26}{26 \text{ families} \div 26}$

$\qquad\qquad = 3$ children/family

64. $\dfrac{\$6150}{150 \text{ shares}} = \dfrac{\$6150}{150 \text{ shares} \div 150} = \$41$/share

The cost is $\$41$/share.

66. Profit total: $\begin{array}{r} \$3560 \\ - \$2400 \\ \hline \$1160 \end{array}$

$\dfrac{\$1160}{40 \text{ pairs}} = \$29$ profit per pair

The store made a profit of $\$29$ per pair.

68. a. 16-ounce can: $\dfrac{\$2.88}{16 \text{ oz}} = \$0.18$/oz

26-ounce can: $\dfrac{\$4.16}{26 \text{ oz}} = \$0.16$/oz

b. $0.18 - 0.16 = 0.02$

2 cents per ounce or $\$0.02$/oz is saved.

70. a. $\dfrac{27,900}{6500} \approx 4.3$ people/acre

There are 4.3 people/acre in St. Kilda.

b. $\dfrac{38,700}{9200} \approx 4.2$ people/acre

There are 4.2 people/acre in Caulfield.

c. St. Kilda is more crowded.

72. a.

$$\begin{array}{r} 10.01 \\ 58\overline{)581.00} \\ \underline{58} \\ 01\,00 \\ \underline{58} \\ 42 \end{array} \qquad \begin{array}{r} 10.33 \\ 54\overline{)558.00} \\ \underline{54} \\ 180 \\ \underline{162} \\ 1\,80 \end{array}$$

The rates of at-bats per home run are:
Ryan Howard, 10.0; David Ortiz, 10.3

b. Ryan Howard hit home runs more often.

74. $\dfrac{1960}{330} \approx$ Mach 5.9

$\dfrac{1920}{330} \approx$ Mach 5.8

$5.9 - 5.8 = 0.1$
It was decreased by Mach 0.1.

Cumulative Review

75. $\begin{array}{r} 2\frac{1}{4} \\ + \frac{3}{8} \\ \hline \end{array} \qquad \begin{array}{r} 2\frac{2}{8} \\ + \frac{3}{8} \\ \hline 2\frac{5}{8} \end{array}$

76. $\dfrac{5}{7} \div \dfrac{3}{21} = \dfrac{5}{7} \times \dfrac{21}{3} = \dfrac{5 \times 21}{7 \times 3} = 5$

77. $\dfrac{3}{5} \times \dfrac{5}{8} - \dfrac{2}{3} \times \dfrac{1}{4} = \dfrac{3}{8} - \dfrac{2}{12} = \dfrac{9}{24} - \dfrac{4}{24} = \dfrac{5}{24}$

78. $3\dfrac{1}{16} - 2\dfrac{1}{24} = 3\dfrac{3}{48} - 2\dfrac{2}{48} = 1\dfrac{1}{48}$

79. $12 \times 5.2 = 62.4$ sq yd

$\dfrac{\$764.40}{62.4 \text{ sq yd}} = \$12.25$/sq yd

The cost of the carpet is $\$12.25$/square yard.

80. $1050 \times \$23 = \$24{,}150$ total
$1050 \times (39 - 23) = 1050 \times 16 = \$16{,}800$ profit
The store paid \$24,150 and the profit was
\$16,800.

Classroom Quiz 4.1

1. $26 \text{ to } 96 = \dfrac{26}{96} = \dfrac{26 \div 2}{96 \div 2} = \dfrac{13}{48}$

2. $\dfrac{128 \text{ pounds}}{36 \text{ people}} = \dfrac{128 \text{ pounds} \div 4}{36 \text{ people} \div 4} = \dfrac{32 \text{ pounds}}{9 \text{ people}}$

3. $\dfrac{592 \text{ patients}}{27 \text{ doctors}} = 21.93 \text{ patients/doctor}$

4.2 Exercises

2. Answers may vary. One possible answer: Cross multiply and if the products are equal then the statement is a proportion.

$$\frac{3}{4} = \frac{6}{8}$$
$$3 \times 8 \overset{?}{=} 4 \times 6$$
$$24 = 24 \quad \text{True}$$

Therefore, $\dfrac{3}{4} = \dfrac{6}{8}$ is a proportion.

4. 12 is to 10 as 6 is to 5.
$$\frac{12}{10} = \frac{6}{5}$$

6. 120 is to 15 as 160 is to 20.
$$\frac{120}{15} = \frac{160}{20}$$

8. $2\frac{1}{2}$ is to 10 as $7\frac{1}{2}$ is to 30.
$$\frac{2\frac{1}{2}}{10} = \frac{7\frac{1}{2}}{30}$$

10. 5.5 is to 10 as 11 is to 20.
$$\frac{5.5}{10} = \frac{11}{20}$$

12. $\dfrac{2 \text{ cups rice}}{3 \text{ cups water}} = \dfrac{8 \text{ cups rice}}{12 \text{ cups water}}$

14. $\dfrac{32 \text{ pages}}{2 \text{ hours}} = \dfrac{80 \text{ pages}}{5 \text{ hours}}$

16. $\dfrac{20 \text{ pounds}}{\$75} = \dfrac{30 \text{ pounds}}{\$112.50}$

18. $\dfrac{1200 \text{ students}}{24 \text{ sections}} = \dfrac{1450 \text{ students}}{29 \text{ sections}}$

20. $\dfrac{16 \text{ pounds}}{1520 \text{ square feet}} = \dfrac{19 \text{ pounds}}{1805 \text{ square feet}}$

22. $\dfrac{8}{6} \overset{?}{=} \dfrac{20}{15}$
$8 \times 15 \overset{?}{=} 6 \times 20$
$120 = 120$
It is a proportion.

24. $\dfrac{14}{11} \overset{?}{=} \dfrac{12}{10}$
$14 \times 10 \overset{?}{=} 11 \times 12$
$140 \neq 132$
It is not a proportion.

26. $\dfrac{99}{100} \overset{?}{=} \dfrac{49}{50}$
$99 \times 50 \overset{?}{=} 100 \times 49$
$4950 \neq 4900$
It is not a proportion.

28. $\dfrac{315}{2100} \overset{?}{=} \dfrac{15}{100}$
$315 \times 100 \overset{?}{=} 2100 \times 15$
$31{,}500 = 31{,}500$
It is a proportion.

30. $\dfrac{6}{14} \overset{?}{=} \dfrac{4.5}{10.5}$
$6 \times 10.5 \overset{?}{=} 14 \times 4.5$
$63 = 63$
It is a proportion.

32. $\dfrac{11}{12} \overset{?}{=} \dfrac{9.5}{10}$
$11 \times 10 \overset{?}{=} 12 \times 9.5$
$110 \neq 114$
It is not a proportion.

34. $\dfrac{7}{1\frac{1}{2}} \overset{?}{=} \dfrac{14}{3}$
$7 \times 3 \overset{?}{=} 1\frac{1}{2} \times 14$
$21 = 21$
It is a proportion.

36. $\dfrac{2\frac{1}{3}}{3} \overset{?}{=} \dfrac{7}{15}$

$\dfrac{\frac{7}{3}}{3} \overset{?}{=} \dfrac{7}{15}$

$15 \times \dfrac{7}{3} \overset{?}{=} 3 \times 7$

$35 \neq 21$

It is not a proportion.

38. $\dfrac{2.5}{\frac{1}{2}} \overset{?}{=} \dfrac{21}{5}$

$5 \times 2.5 \overset{?}{=} \dfrac{1}{2} \times 21$

$12.5 \neq 10.5$

It is not a proportion.

40. $\dfrac{75 \text{ miles}}{5 \text{ hours}} \overset{?}{=} \dfrac{105 \text{ miles}}{7 \text{ hours}}$

$75 \times 7 \overset{?}{=} 5 \times 105$

$525 = 525$

It is a proportion.

42. $\dfrac{286 \text{ gallons}}{12 \text{ acres}} \overset{?}{=} \dfrac{429 \text{ gallons}}{18 \text{ acres}}$

$286 \times 18 \overset{?}{=} 12 \times 429$

$5148 = 5148$

It is a proportion.

44. $\dfrac{52 \text{ free throws}}{80 \text{ attempts}} \overset{?}{=} \dfrac{60 \text{ free throws}}{95 \text{ attempts}}$

$52 \times 95 \overset{?}{=} 80 \times 60$

$4940 \neq 4800$

It is not a proportion.

46. $\dfrac{9600 \text{ female}}{8200 \text{ male}} \overset{?}{=} \dfrac{12,480 \text{ female}}{10,660 \text{ male}}$

$9600 \times 10,660 \overset{?}{=} 8200 \times 12,480$

$102,336,000 = 102,336,000$ Yes

The ratio is the same for both nights.

48. a. $\dfrac{650}{5} \overset{?}{=} \dfrac{580}{4}$

$650 \times 4 \overset{?}{=} 5 \times 580$

$2600 \neq 2900$

no

The boxes do not fold at the same rate.

b. The machine that folds 580 boxes in four hours will fold more.

50. $\dfrac{22 \text{ inches}}{16 \text{ inches}} \overset{?}{=} \dfrac{11 \text{ inches}}{8.5 \text{ inches}}$

$22 \times 8.5 \overset{?}{=} 16 \times 11$

$187 \neq 176$

No, the ratio is not the same.

52. a. $\dfrac{63}{161} \overset{?}{=} \dfrac{171}{437}$

$\dfrac{63}{161} \overset{?}{=} \dfrac{63 \div 7}{161 \div 7} = \dfrac{9}{23}$

$\dfrac{171}{437} = \dfrac{171 \div 19}{437 \div 19} = \dfrac{9}{23}$

Yes, the fractions are equal.

b. $\dfrac{63}{121} \overset{?}{=} \dfrac{171}{437}$

$63 \times 437 \overset{?}{=} 161 \times 171$

$27,531 = 27,531$ True

c. The equality test for fractions; for most students it is faster to multiply than to reduce fractions.

Cumulative Review

54. $9.6 + 7.8 + 2.56 + 3.004 + 0.1765 = 23.1405$

55.
$$\begin{array}{r} 3.04 \\ \times \ 5.92 \\ \hline 608 \\ 2\ 736 \\ 15\ 20 \\ \hline 17.9968 \end{array}$$

56.
$$\begin{array}{r} 29,366,215 \\ -\ 28,963,807 \\ \hline 402,408 \end{array}$$

57.
$$\begin{array}{r} 25.8 \\ 7.03_\wedge \overline{)181.37_\wedge 4} \\ \underline{140\ 6} \\ 40\,77 \\ \underline{35\,15} \\ 5\,62\ 4 \\ \underline{5\,62\ 4} \\ 0 \end{array}$$

58.

$$3\frac{1}{4}$$
$$+\;4\frac{3}{8}$$

$$3\frac{2}{8}$$
$$+\;4\frac{3}{8}$$
$$7\frac{5}{8}$$

$$20$$
$$-\;7\frac{5}{8}$$

$$19\frac{8}{8}$$
$$-\;7\frac{5}{8}$$
$$12\frac{3}{8}$$

She needs to walk $12\frac{3}{8}$ miles.

Classroom Quiz 4.2

1. 9 is to 15 as 6 is to 10.

$$\frac{9}{15}=\frac{6}{10}$$

2. $2\frac{1}{3}$ is to 7 as 7 is to 21.

$$\frac{2\frac{1}{3}}{7}=\frac{7}{21}$$

3. $\dfrac{16\text{ home runs}}{94\text{ games}}\overset{?}{=}\dfrac{14\text{ home runs}}{88\text{ games}}$

$$16\times88\overset{?}{=}94\times14$$
$$1408\neq1316$$

It is not a proportion.

How Am I Doing? Sections 4.1–4.2

1. 13 to 18 $=\dfrac{13}{18}$

2. 44 to 220 $=\dfrac{44}{220}=\dfrac{1}{5}$

3. \$72 to \$16 $=\dfrac{72}{16}=\dfrac{9}{2}$

4. 135 meters to 165 meters $=\dfrac{135}{165}=\dfrac{9}{11}$

5. a. $\dfrac{70}{240}=\dfrac{7}{24}$

b. $\dfrac{22}{240}=\dfrac{11}{120}$

6. $\dfrac{9}{300}=\dfrac{3\text{ flight attendants}}{100\text{ passengers}}$

7. $\dfrac{620}{840}=\dfrac{31\text{ gallons}}{42\text{ square feet}}$

8. $\dfrac{65}{4}=16.25$ miles/hour

9. $\dfrac{435}{15}=\$29$ per CD player

10. $\dfrac{2400}{15}=160$ cookies/pound of cookie dough

11. 13 is to 40 as 39 is to 120.

$$\frac{13}{40}=\frac{39}{120}$$

12. 116 is to 148 as 29 is to 37.

$$\frac{116}{148}=\frac{29}{37}$$

13. $\dfrac{33\text{ nautical miles}}{2\text{ hours}}=\dfrac{49.5\text{ nautical miles}}{3\text{ hours}}$

14. $\dfrac{3000\text{ shoes}}{\$370}=\dfrac{7500\text{ shoes}}{\$925}$

15. $\dfrac{14}{31}\overset{?}{=}\dfrac{42}{93}$

$$14(93)\overset{?}{=}31(42)$$
$$1302=1302$$

It is a proportion.

16. $\dfrac{17}{33}\overset{?}{=}\dfrac{19}{45}$

$$45(17)\overset{?}{=}33(19)$$
$$765\neq627$$

It is not a proportion.

17. $\dfrac{6.5}{4.8}\overset{?}{=}\dfrac{120}{96}$

$$6.5\times96\overset{?}{=}4.8\times120$$
$$624\neq576$$

It is not a proportion.

18. $\dfrac{15}{24} \stackrel{?}{=} \dfrac{1\frac{5}{8}}{2\frac{3}{5}}$

$15 \times 2\dfrac{3}{5} \stackrel{?}{=} 24 \times 1\dfrac{5}{8}$

$39 = 39$

It is a proportion.

19. $\dfrac{670}{1541} \stackrel{?}{=} \dfrac{820}{1886}$

$670(1886) \stackrel{?}{=} 1541(820)$

$1,263,620 = 1,263,620$

It is a proportion.

20. $\dfrac{30}{4} \stackrel{?}{=} \dfrac{3000}{400}$

$30(400) \stackrel{?}{=} 4(3000)$

$12,000 = 12,000$

It is a proportion.

4.3 Exercises

2. Form the cross product $c \times n = a \times b$. Multiply $a \times b$. Then use the steps explained in exercise 1.

4. $6 \times n = 72$

$\dfrac{6 \times n}{6} = \dfrac{72}{6}$

$n = 12$

6. $2 \times n = 19.6$

$\dfrac{2 \times n}{2} = \dfrac{19.6}{2}$

$n = 9.8$

8. $n \times 3.8 = 95$

$\dfrac{n \times 3.8}{3.8} = \dfrac{95}{3.8}$

$n = 25$

10. $40.6 = 5.8 \times n$

$\dfrac{40.6}{5.8} = \dfrac{5.8 \times n}{5.8}$

$7 = n$

12. $\dfrac{6}{7} \times n = 26$

$\dfrac{\frac{6}{7} \times n}{\frac{6}{7}} = \dfrac{26}{\frac{6}{7}}$

$n = 26 \div \dfrac{6}{7}$

$n = 26 \times \dfrac{7}{6}$

$n = \dfrac{182}{6}$

$n = 30\dfrac{1}{3}$

14. $\dfrac{n}{28} = \dfrac{3}{7}$

$n \times 7 = 28 \times 3$

$\dfrac{n \times 7}{7} = \dfrac{84}{7}$

$n = 12$

Check: $\dfrac{12}{28} \stackrel{?}{=} \dfrac{3}{7}$

$12 \times 7 \stackrel{?}{=} 28 \times 3$

$84 = 84$

16. $\dfrac{4}{n} = \dfrac{2}{7}$

$4 \times 7 = n \times 2$

$\dfrac{28}{2} = \dfrac{n \times 2}{2}$

$14 = n$

Check: $\dfrac{4}{14} \stackrel{?}{=} \dfrac{2}{7}$

$4 \times 7 \stackrel{?}{=} 14 \times 2$

$28 = 28$

18. $\dfrac{13}{30} = \dfrac{n}{15}$

$13 \times 15 = 30 \times n$

$\dfrac{195}{30} = \dfrac{30 \times n}{30}$

$6.5 = n$

Check: $\dfrac{13}{30} \stackrel{?}{=} \dfrac{6.5}{15}$

$13 \times 15 \stackrel{?}{=} 30 \times 6.5$

$195 = 195$

20.

$$\frac{40}{160} = \frac{1.5}{n}$$
$$40 \times n = 1.5 \times 160$$
$$\frac{40 \times n}{40} = \frac{240}{40}$$
$$n = 6$$

Check:
$$\frac{40}{160} \overset{?}{=} \frac{1.5}{6}$$
$$40 \times 6 \overset{?}{=} 160 \times 1.5$$
$$240 = 240$$

22.

$$\frac{n}{22} = \frac{25}{11}$$
$$n \times 11 = 22 \times 25$$
$$\frac{n \times 11}{11} = \frac{550}{11}$$
$$n = 50$$

Check:
$$\frac{50}{22} \overset{?}{=} \frac{25}{11}$$
$$50 \times 11 \overset{?}{=} 22 \times 25$$
$$550 = 550$$

24.

$$\frac{16}{10} = \frac{n}{9}$$
$$16 \times 9 = 10 \times n$$
$$\frac{144}{10} = \frac{10 \times n}{10}$$
$$14.4 = n$$

Check:
$$\frac{16}{10} \overset{?}{=} \frac{14.4}{9}$$
$$16 \times 9 \overset{?}{=} 10 \times 14.4$$
$$144 = 144$$

26.

$$\frac{180}{n} = \frac{4}{3}$$
$$180 \times 3 = n \times 4$$
$$\frac{540}{4} = \frac{n \times 4}{4}$$
$$n = 135$$

Check:
$$\frac{180}{135} \overset{?}{=} \frac{4}{3}$$
$$180 \times 3 \overset{?}{=} 135 \times 4$$
$$540 = 540$$

28.

$$\frac{62}{n} = \frac{5}{4}$$
$$4 \times 62 = 5 \times n$$
$$\frac{248}{5} = \frac{5 \times n}{5}$$
$$49.6 = n$$

30.

$$\frac{12}{8} = \frac{21}{n}$$
$$12 \times n = 8 \times 21$$
$$\frac{12 \times n}{12} = \frac{168}{12}$$
$$n = 14$$

32.

$$\frac{n}{18} = \frac{3.5}{1}$$
$$1 \times n = 18 \times 3.5$$
$$n = 63$$

34.

$$\frac{2.5}{n} = \frac{0.5}{10}$$
$$2.5 \times 10 = 0.5 \times n$$
$$\frac{25}{0.5} = \frac{0.5 \times n}{0.5}$$
$$50 = n$$

36.

$$\frac{7}{16} = \frac{n}{26.2}$$
$$7 \times 26.2 = 16 \times n$$
$$\frac{183.4}{16} = \frac{16 \times n}{16}$$
$$n \approx 11.5$$

38.

$$\frac{12.5}{16} = \frac{n}{12}$$
$$12 \times 12.5 = 16 \times n$$
$$\frac{150}{16} = \frac{16 \times n}{16}$$
$$9.4 \approx n$$

40.

$$\frac{5}{n} = \frac{12\frac{1}{2}}{100}$$
$$100 \times 5 = 12\frac{1}{2} \times n$$
$$\frac{500}{12\frac{1}{2}} = \frac{12\frac{1}{2} \times n}{12\frac{1}{2}}$$
$$40 = n$$

42.

$$\frac{n \text{ grams}}{10 \text{ liters}} = \frac{7 \text{ grams}}{25 \text{ liters}}$$
$$n \times 25 = 10 \times 7$$
$$\frac{n \times 25}{25} = \frac{70}{25}$$
$$n = 2.8$$

44. $\dfrac{190 \text{ kilometers}}{3 \text{ hours}} = \dfrac{n \text{ kilometers}}{5 \text{ hours}}$

$190 \times 5 = 3 \times n$

$\dfrac{950}{3} = \dfrac{3 \times n}{3}$

$n \approx 316.67$

46. $\dfrac{50 \text{ gallons}}{12 \text{ acres}} = \dfrac{36 \text{ gallons}}{n \text{ acres}}$

$50 \times n = 12 \times 36$

$\dfrac{50 \times n}{50} = \dfrac{432}{50}$

$n = 8.64$

48. $\dfrac{3 \text{ kilograms}}{6.6 \text{ pounds}} = \dfrac{n \text{ kilograms}}{10 \text{ pounds}}$

$3 \times 10 = 6.6 \times n$

$\dfrac{30}{6.6} = \dfrac{6.6 \times n}{6.6}$

$n \approx 4.55$

50. $\dfrac{12 \text{ quarters}}{3 \text{ dollars}} = \dfrac{87 \text{ quarters}}{n \text{ dollars}}$

$12 \times n = 3 \times 87$

$\dfrac{12 \times n}{12} = \dfrac{261}{12}$

$n = 21.75$

52. $\dfrac{2\frac{1}{2} \text{ acres}}{3 \text{ people}} = \dfrac{n \text{ acres}}{5 \text{ people}}$

$2\dfrac{1}{2} \times 5 = 3 \times n$

$\dfrac{\frac{25}{2}}{3} = \dfrac{3 \times n}{3}$

$\dfrac{25}{2} \div 3 = n$

$\dfrac{25}{2} \times \dfrac{1}{3} = n$

$\dfrac{25}{6} = n$

$4\dfrac{1}{6} = n$

54. $\dfrac{3.5 \text{ centimeters}}{2.5 \text{ centimeters}} = \dfrac{n \text{ centimeters}}{6 \text{ centimeters}}$

$3.5 \times 6 = 2.5 \times n$

$\dfrac{21}{2.5} = \dfrac{2.5 \times n}{2.5}$

$8.4 = n$

The print will be 8.4 centimeters wide.

56. $\dfrac{n}{7\frac{1}{4}} = \dfrac{2\frac{1}{5}}{4\frac{1}{8}}$

$4\dfrac{1}{8} \times n = 7\dfrac{1}{4} \times 2\dfrac{1}{5}$

$\dfrac{33}{8} \times n = \dfrac{29}{4} \times \dfrac{11}{5}$

$\dfrac{\frac{33}{8} \times n}{\frac{33}{8}} = \dfrac{\frac{319}{20}}{\frac{33}{8}}$

$n = \dfrac{319}{20} \times \dfrac{8}{33}$

$n = \dfrac{58}{15} \text{ or } 3\dfrac{13}{15}$

58. $\dfrac{9\frac{3}{4}}{n} = \dfrac{8\frac{1}{2}}{4\frac{1}{3}}$

$4\dfrac{1}{3} \times 9\dfrac{3}{4} = 8\dfrac{1}{2} \times n$

$\dfrac{13}{3} \times \dfrac{39}{4} = \dfrac{17}{2} \times n$

$\dfrac{\frac{169}{4}}{\frac{17}{2}} = \dfrac{\frac{17}{2} \times n}{\frac{17}{2}}$

$\dfrac{169}{34} = n$

$4\dfrac{33}{34} = n$

Cumulative Review

60. $4^3 + 20 \div 5 + 6 \times 3 - 5 \times 2$

$= 64 + 20 \div 5 + 6 \times 3 - 5 \times 2$

$= 64 + 4 + 18 - 10$

$= 76$

61. $(3+1)^3 - 30 \div 6 - 144 \div 12$

$= 4^3 - 30 \div 6 - 144 \div 12$

$= 64 - 30 \div 6 - 144 \div 12$

$= 64 - 5 - 12$

$= 47$

62. $0.563 =$ five hundred sixty-three thousandths

63. thirty-four ten-thousandths $= 0.0034$

64. Purchase:

$$
\begin{array}{r}
156 \\
\times\ 32 \\
\hline
312 \\
468 \\
\hline
4992
\end{array}
$$

Sales:

$$
\begin{array}{r}
78 \\
\times\ 45 \\
\hline
390 \\
312 \\
\hline
3510
\end{array}
\qquad
\begin{array}{r}
78 \\
\times\ 39 \\
\hline
702 \\
234 \\
\hline
3042
\end{array}
$$

Profit $= 3510 + 3042 - 4992 = 1560$
He will make a profit of \$1560.

65. Team 1 will play each of the other 7 teams 2 times = 14. Team 2 will play each of the remaining 6 teams 2 times = 12. Team 3 will play each of the remaining 5 teams = 10.
$14 + 12 + 10 + 8 + 6 + 4 + 2 = 56$
A total of 56 games will have been played.

Classroom Quiz 4.3

1.
$$
\frac{n}{33} = \frac{28}{132}
$$
$$
n \times 132 = 33 \times 28
$$
$$
\frac{n \times 132}{132} = \frac{924}{132}
$$
$$
n = 7
$$

2.
$$
\frac{3\frac{1}{4}}{2} = \frac{13}{n}
$$
$$
3\frac{1}{4} \times n = 2 \times 13
$$
$$
\frac{3\frac{1}{4} \times n}{3\frac{1}{4}} = \frac{26}{3\frac{1}{4}}
$$
$$
n = 8
$$

3.
$$
\frac{7 \text{ inches of snow}}{56 \text{ inches of rain}} = \frac{n \text{ inches of snow}}{35 \text{ inches of rain}}
$$
$$
7 \times 35 = 56 \times n
$$
$$
\frac{245}{56} = \frac{56 \times n}{56}
$$
$$
n \approx 4.4
$$

4.4 Exercises

2. She should continue with the number of cars observed on her trip down the mountain on the top of the fraction. That would be 60. She does not know the number of people, so this would be n. The proportion would be
$$
\frac{15 \text{ cars}}{17 \text{ people}} = \frac{60 \text{ cars}}{n \text{ people}}.
$$

4.
$$
\frac{n \text{ desserts}}{320 \text{ people}} = \frac{19 \text{ desserts}}{16 \text{ people}}
$$
$$
16 \times n = 19 \times 320
$$
$$
\frac{16 \times n}{16} = \frac{19 \times 320}{16}
$$
$$
n = 380
$$
380 desserts must be available.

6.
$$
\frac{n \text{ tablespoons}}{12 \text{ ounces}} = \frac{1\frac{1}{2} \text{ tablespoons}}{8 \text{ ounces}}
$$
$$
8 \times n = 12 \times 1\frac{1}{2}
$$
$$
\frac{8 \times n}{8} = \frac{18}{8}
$$
$$
n = \frac{18}{8} \text{ or } 2\frac{2}{8} = 2\frac{1}{4}
$$
$2\frac{1}{4}$ tablespoons of cocoa is needed.

8.
$$
\frac{n \text{ centimeters}}{12 \text{ inches}} = \frac{2\frac{1}{2} \text{ centimeters}}{1 \text{ inch}}
$$
$$
1 \times n = 12 \times 2\frac{1}{2}
$$
$$
n = 30
$$
Approximately 30 centimeters are in one foot.

10.
$$
\frac{0.511 \text{ British pounds}}{1 \text{ U.S. dollar}} = \frac{n \text{ British pounds}}{220 \text{ U.S. dollars}}
$$
$$
0.511 \times 220 = 1 \times n
$$
$$
112.42 = n
$$
He received 112.42 British pounds.

12.
$$
\frac{n \text{ feet}}{22 \text{ feet}} = \frac{11 \text{ feet}}{7 \text{ feet}}
$$
$$
7 \times n = 22 \times 11
$$
$$
\frac{7 \times n}{7} = \frac{242}{7}
$$
$$
n = 346
$$
The width of the river is 34.6 feet.

14. $\dfrac{n \text{ miles}}{5.7 \text{ inches}} = \dfrac{250 \text{ miles}}{4 \text{ inches}}$

$4 \times n = 5.7 \times 250$

$\dfrac{4 \times n}{4} = \dfrac{1425}{4}$

$n \approx 356$

The approximate distance between the two mountains is 356 miles.

16. $\dfrac{4 \text{ cups of chocolate chips}}{6 \text{ people}} = \dfrac{n \text{ cups of chocolate chips}}{26 \text{ people}}$

$4 \times 26 = 6 \times n$

$\dfrac{104}{6} = \dfrac{6 \times n}{6}$

$n = 17\dfrac{1}{3}$

$17\dfrac{1}{3}$ cups of chocolate chips are needed.

18. $\dfrac{52 \text{ runs}}{260 \text{ innings}} = \dfrac{n \text{ runs}}{9 \text{ innings}}$

$52 \times 9 = 260 \times n$

$\dfrac{468}{260} = \dfrac{260 \times n}{260}$

$1.8 = n$

He would give up 1.8 runs.

20. $\dfrac{n \text{ gallons}}{318 \text{ miles}} = \dfrac{5 \text{ gallons}}{75 \text{ miles}}$

$75 \times n = 318 \times 5$

$\dfrac{75 \times n}{75} = \dfrac{1590}{75}$

$n = 21.2$

She used 21.2 gallons.

22. $\dfrac{n \text{ total}}{26 \text{ tagged}} = \dfrac{18 \text{ total}}{6 \text{ tagged}}$

$6 \times n = 26 \times 18$

$\dfrac{6 \times n}{6} = \dfrac{468}{6}$

$n = 78$

The estimate is 78 giraffes.

24. $\dfrac{2 \text{ gallons}}{750 \text{ sq ft}} = \dfrac{n \text{ gallons}}{7875 \text{ sq ft}}$

$2 \times 7875 = 750 \times n$

$\dfrac{15,750}{750} = \dfrac{750 \times n}{750}$

$21 = n$

$\text{Cost} = 21 \text{ gallons} \times \dfrac{\$8.50}{1 \text{ gallon}} = \$178.50$

The painter will spend \$178.50.

26. $\dfrac{100 \text{ people}}{88 \text{ satisfied}} = \dfrac{1700 \text{ people}}{n \text{ satisfied}}$

$100 \times n = 88 \times 1700$

$\dfrac{100 \times n}{100} = \dfrac{149,600}{100}$

$n = 1496$

There are 1496 satisfied customers.

28. Water: $\dfrac{n \text{ cups}}{5 \text{ servings}} = \dfrac{2 \text{ cups}}{6 \text{ servings}}$

$n \times 6 = 5 \times 2$

$\dfrac{n \times 6}{6} = \dfrac{10}{6}$

$n = \dfrac{10}{6} = \dfrac{5}{3} = 1\dfrac{2}{3}$

$1\dfrac{2}{3}$ cups of water

Milk: $\dfrac{n \text{ cups}}{5 \text{ servings}} = \dfrac{\frac{3}{4} \text{ cup}}{6 \text{ servings}}$

$n \times 6 = 5 \times \dfrac{3}{4}$

$n \times 6 = \dfrac{15}{4}$

$\dfrac{n \times 6}{6} = \dfrac{\frac{15}{4}}{6}$

$n = \dfrac{15}{4} \div 6 = \dfrac{15}{4} \times \dfrac{1}{6} = \dfrac{5}{8}$

$\dfrac{5}{8}$ cup of milk

You need $1\dfrac{2}{3}$ cups of water and $\dfrac{5}{8}$ cup of milk.

30. a. water: $\dfrac{3}{4} \times 5 = \dfrac{15}{4}$ milk: $2 \times 2\dfrac{1}{2} = 5$

$2 \times \dfrac{15}{4} = \dfrac{15}{2}$

You need $7\dfrac{1}{2}$ cups of water and 5 cups of milk.

b. $\dfrac{n \text{ servings}}{5 \text{ cups}} = \dfrac{6 \text{ servings}}{2 \text{ cups}}$

$2 \times n = 5 \times 6$

$\dfrac{2 \times n}{2} = \dfrac{5 \times 6}{2}$

$n = 15$

15 servings to 1 box

You obtain 30 servings to 2 boxes.

32. Alfonso Soriano hit more home runs per dollar.

34. Ray Allen made more three-point shots per dollar.

Cumulative Review

35. 56,179 rounds to 56,200

36. 196,379,910 rounds to 196,380,000

37. 56.148 rounds to 56.1

38. 2.74895 rounds to 2.7490

39. a. $1\dfrac{3}{16} \times \dfrac{4}{5} = \dfrac{19}{16} \times \dfrac{4}{5} = \dfrac{76}{80} = \dfrac{19}{20}$

One frame requires $\dfrac{19}{20}$ of a square foot.

b. $\dfrac{19}{20} \times 1500 = 19 \times 75 = 1452$

A total of 1452 square feet are needed.

Classroom Quiz 4.4

1. $\dfrac{4 \text{ eggs}}{13 \text{ people}} = \dfrac{n \text{ eggs}}{39 \text{ people}}$

$4 \times 39 = 13 \times n$

$\dfrac{156}{13} = \dfrac{13 \times n}{13}$

$n = 12$

He will need 12 eggs.

2.
$$\frac{\$320}{3000 \text{ square feet}} = \frac{\$n}{5000 \text{ square feet}}$$
$$320 \times 5000 = 3000 \times n$$
$$\frac{1,600,000}{3000} = \frac{3000 \times n}{3000}$$
$$n = 533.33$$

It would cost \$533.33 to fertilize 5000 square feet.

3.
$$\frac{5 \text{ hits}}{31 \text{ at bats}} = \frac{n \text{ hits}}{120 \text{ at bats}}$$
$$5 \times 120 = 31 \times n$$
$$\frac{600}{31} = \frac{31 \times n}{31}$$
$$n \approx 19.35$$

We expect she got 19 hits.

Putting Your Skills to Work

1. All plans include 100 minutes.
Plan A: \$39.99
Plan B: \$39.99
Plan C: \$49.99
Plan D: \$59.99
He should choose either plan A or B.

2. Plan A: 300 min = \$39.99
50 min = \$0.20×50 = \$10
Total = \$49.99
Plans B, C, and D include 350 minutes.
Plan B: \$39.99
Plan C: \$49.99
Plan D: \$59.99
He should choose plan B.

3. Plan A: 300 min = \$39.99
250 min = \$0.20×250 = \$50
Total = \$89.99
Plan B: 450 min = \$39.99
100 min = \$0.45×100 = \$45
Total = \$84.99
He should choose plan B.

4. 10 hours = 60 × 10 = 600 min
Plan A: 300 min = \$39.99
300 min = \$0.20×300 = \$60
Total = \$99.99
Plan B: 450 min = \$39.99
150 min = \$0.45×150 = \$67.50
Total = \$107.49
He should choose plan A.

5. 16 hours + 40 min = 16 × 60 + 40 = 1000 min
Plan A: 300 min = \$39.99
700 min = \$0.20×700 = \$140
Total = \$179.99
Plan B: 450 min = \$39.99
550 min = \$0.45×550 = \$247.50
Total = \$251.49
Plan C: 600 min = \$49.99
400 min = \$0.20×400 = \$80
Total = \$129.99
Plan D: 900 min = \$59.99
100 min = \$0.40×100 = \$40
Total = \$99.99
He should choose plan D.

6. See the totals in exercise 5. He should choose plan C.

7. Plan C: 600 min = \$49.99
300 min = \$0.20×300 = \$60
Total = \$109.99
$$\text{Average} = \frac{109.99}{900} \approx 0.12$$
His average rate is \$0.12 per minute.

8. Plan A: 13 hours, 20 minutes = 800 minutes
300 minutes: \$39.99
500 minutes: \$0.20×500 = \$100
Total = \$139.99
$$\text{Average} = \frac{139.99}{800} \approx 0.17$$
His average rate is \$0.17 per minute.

9. Answers will vary.

10. Answers will vary.

Chapter 4 Review Problems

1. $88:40 = \frac{88}{40} = \frac{88 \div 8}{40 \div 8} = \frac{11}{5}$

2. $65:39 = \frac{65}{39} = \frac{65 \div 13}{39 \div 13} = \frac{5}{3}$

3. $28:35 = \frac{28}{35} = \frac{28 \div 7}{35 \div 7} = \frac{4}{5}$

4. $250:475 = \frac{250}{475} = \frac{250 \div 25}{475 \div 25} = \frac{10}{19}$

5. $2\frac{1}{3}$ to $4\frac{1}{4} = \dfrac{2\frac{1}{3}}{4\frac{1}{4}}$

$$= 2\frac{1}{3} \div 4\frac{1}{4}$$

$$= \frac{7}{3} \div \frac{17}{4}$$

$$= \frac{7}{3} \times \frac{4}{17}$$

$$= \frac{28}{51}$$

6. $\dfrac{27}{81} = \dfrac{27 \div 27}{81 \div 27} = \dfrac{1}{3}$

7. $\dfrac{180}{531} = \dfrac{180 \div 9}{531 \div 9} = \dfrac{20}{59}$

8. $\dfrac{168}{300} = \dfrac{168 \div 12}{300 \div 12} = \dfrac{14}{25}$

9. $\dfrac{26 \text{ tons}}{65 \text{ tons}} = \dfrac{26 \div 13}{65 \div 13} = \dfrac{2}{5}$

10. $\dfrac{\$60}{\$480} = \dfrac{60 \div 60}{480 \div 60} = \dfrac{1}{8}$

11.
$$\begin{array}{r} 60 \\ +\ 45 \\ \hline 105 \end{array}$$
$\dfrac{\$105}{\$480} = \dfrac{105 \div 15}{480 \div 15} = \dfrac{7}{32}$

12. $\dfrac{\$75}{6 \text{ people}} = \dfrac{\$25}{2 \text{ people}}$

13. $\dfrac{44 \text{ revolutions}}{121 \text{ minutes}} = \dfrac{4 \text{ revolusions}}{11 \text{ minutes}}$

14. $\dfrac{75 \text{ heartbeats}}{60 \text{ seconds}} = \dfrac{5 \text{ heartbeats}}{4 \text{ seconds}}$

15. $\dfrac{12 \text{ cups}}{27 \text{ cakes}} = \dfrac{4 \text{ cups}}{9 \text{ cakes}}$

16. $\dfrac{\$2125}{125 \text{ shares}} = \dfrac{\$17}{1 \text{ share}} = \$17/\text{share}$

17. $\dfrac{\$1344}{12 \text{ credit-hours}} = \$112/\text{credit-hour}$

18. $\dfrac{\$742.50}{55 \text{ sq yd}} = \dfrac{\$13.50}{1 \text{ yd}} = \$13.50/\text{square yard}$

19. $\dfrac{\$600}{48 \text{ DVDs}} = \$12.50/\text{DVD}$

20. a. $\dfrac{\$2.96}{4 \text{ oz}} = \dfrac{\$2.96 \div 4}{4 \text{ oz} \div 4} = \$0.74/\text{oz}$
The cost of the small jar is $0.74/oz.

    b. $\dfrac{\$5.22}{9 \text{ oz}} = \dfrac{\$5.22 \div 9}{9 \text{ oz} \div 9} = \$0.58/\text{oz}$
The cost of the large jar is $0.58/oz.

    c. $\begin{array}{r} \$0.74 \\ -\ 0.58 \\ \hline \$0.16/\text{oz} \end{array}$
The savings is $0.16/oz.

21. a. $\dfrac{\$2.75}{12.5 \text{ oz}} = \dfrac{\$2.75 \div 12.5}{12.5 \text{ oz} \div 12.5} = \$0.22/\text{oz}$
The cost of the large can is $0.22/oz.

    b. $\dfrac{\$1.75}{7.0 \text{ oz}} = \dfrac{\$1.75 \div 7.0}{7.0 \text{ oz} \div 7.0} = \$0.25/\text{oz}$
The cost of the small can is $0.25/oz.

    c. $0.25 - 0.22 = 0.03 = \$0.03/\text{oz}$
The savings is $0.03/oz.

22. $\dfrac{12}{48} = \dfrac{7}{28}$

23. $\dfrac{1\frac{1}{2}}{5} = \dfrac{4}{13\frac{1}{3}}$

24. $\dfrac{7.5}{45} = \dfrac{22.5}{135}$

25. $\dfrac{3 \text{ buses}}{138 \text{ passengers}} = \dfrac{5 \text{ buses}}{230 \text{ passengers}}$

26. $\dfrac{15 \text{ pounds}}{\$4.50} = \dfrac{27 \text{ pounds}}{\$8.10}$

27. $\dfrac{16}{48} \overset{?}{=} \dfrac{2}{12}$

$16 \times 12 \overset{?}{=} 48 \times 2$

$192 \ne 96$

It is not a proportion.

28. $\dfrac{20}{25} \overset{?}{=} \dfrac{8}{10}$

$20 \times 10 \overset{?}{=} 25 \times 8$

$200 = 200$

It is a proportion.

29. $\dfrac{36}{30} \overset{?}{=} \dfrac{60}{50}$

$36 \times 50 \overset{?}{=} 30 \times 60$

$1800 = 1800$

It is a proportion.

30. $\dfrac{28}{12} \overset{?}{=} \dfrac{84}{36}$

$28 \times 36 \overset{?}{=} 12 \times 84$

$1008 = 1008$

It is a proportion.

31. $\dfrac{37}{33} \overset{?}{=} \dfrac{22}{19}$

$37 \times 19 \overset{?}{=} 33 \times 22$

$703 \ne 726$

It is not a proportion.

32. $\dfrac{15}{18} \overset{?}{=} \dfrac{18}{22}$

$15 \times 22 \overset{?}{=} 18 \times 18$

$330 \ne 324$

It is not a proportion.

33. $\dfrac{84 \text{ miles}}{7 \text{ gallons}} \overset{?}{=} \dfrac{108 \text{ miles}}{9 \text{ gallons}}$

$84 \times 9 \overset{?}{=} 7 \times 108$

$756 = 756$

It is a proportion.

34. $\dfrac{156 \text{ rev}}{6 \text{ min}} \overset{?}{=} \dfrac{181 \text{ rev}}{7 \text{ min}}$

$156 \times 7 \overset{?}{=} 6 \times 181$

$1092 \ne 1086$

It is not a proportion.

35. $9 \times n = 162$

$\dfrac{9 \times n}{9} = \dfrac{162}{9}$

$n = 18$

36. $5 \times n = 38$

$\dfrac{5 \times n}{5} = \dfrac{38}{5}$

$n = 7\dfrac{3}{5} \text{ or } 7.6$

37. $442 = 20 \times n$

$\dfrac{442}{20} = \dfrac{20 \times n}{20}$

$22.1 = n \text{ or } n = 22\dfrac{1}{10}$

38. $663 = 39 \times n$

$\dfrac{663}{39} = \dfrac{39 \times n}{39}$

$17 = n$

39. $\dfrac{3}{11} = \dfrac{9}{n}$

$3 \times n = 11 \times 9$

$\dfrac{3 \times n}{3} = \dfrac{99}{3}$

$n = 33$

40. $\dfrac{2}{7} = \dfrac{12}{n}$

$2 \times n = 7 \times 12$

$\dfrac{2 \times n}{2} = \dfrac{84}{2}$

$n = 42$

41. $\dfrac{n}{28} = \dfrac{6}{24}$

$24 \times n = 28 \times 6$

$\dfrac{24 \times n}{24} = \dfrac{168}{24}$

$n = 7$

42. $\dfrac{n}{32} = \dfrac{15}{20}$

$n \times 20 = 32 \times 15$

$\dfrac{n \times 20}{20} = \dfrac{480}{20}$

$n = 24$

43.
$$\frac{2\frac{1}{4}}{9} = \frac{4\frac{3}{4}}{n}$$

$$2\frac{1}{4} \times n = 9 \times 4\frac{3}{4}$$

$$\frac{9}{4} \times n = 9 \times \frac{19}{4}$$

$$\frac{\frac{9}{4} \times n}{\frac{9}{4}} = \frac{\frac{171}{4}}{\frac{9}{4}}$$

$$n = \frac{171}{4} \div \frac{9}{4} = \frac{171}{4} \times \frac{4}{9} = \frac{171}{9} = 19$$

44.
$$\frac{3\frac{1}{3}}{2\frac{2}{3}} = \frac{7}{n}$$

$$3\frac{1}{3} \times n = 2\frac{2}{3} \times 7$$

$$\frac{10}{3} \times n = \frac{8}{3} \times 7$$

$$\frac{\frac{10}{3} \times n}{\frac{10}{3}} = \frac{\frac{56}{3}}{\frac{10}{3}}$$

$$n = \frac{56}{3} \div \frac{10}{3} = \frac{56}{3} \times \frac{3}{10} = \frac{56}{10} = \frac{28}{5} = 5\frac{3}{5} \text{ or } 5.6$$

45.
$$\frac{42}{50} = \frac{n}{6}$$

$$6 \times 42 = 50 \times n$$

$$\frac{252}{50} = \frac{50 \times n}{50}$$

$$5.0 \approx n$$

46.
$$\frac{38}{45} = \frac{n}{8}$$

$$8 \times 38 = 45 \times n$$

$$\frac{304}{45} = \frac{45 \times n}{45}$$

$$6.8 \sim n$$

47.
$$\frac{2.25}{9} = \frac{4.75}{n}$$

$$2.25 \times n = 9 \times 4.75$$

$$\frac{2.25 \times n}{2.25} = \frac{42.75}{2.25}$$

$$n = 19$$

48.
$$\frac{3.5}{5} = \frac{10.5}{n}$$

$$3.5 \times n = 5 \times 10.5$$

$$\frac{3.5 \times n}{3.5} = \frac{52.5}{3.5}$$

$$n = 15$$

49.
$$\frac{20}{n} = \frac{43}{16}$$

$$20 \times 16 = n \times 43$$

$$\frac{320}{43} = \frac{n \times 43}{43}$$

$$n \approx 7.4$$

50.
$$\frac{36}{n} = \frac{109}{18}$$

$$36 \times 18 = n \times 109$$

$$\frac{648}{109} = \frac{n \times 109}{109}$$

$$n \approx 5.9$$

51.
$$\frac{35 \text{ miles}}{28 \text{ gallons}} = \frac{15 \text{ miles}}{n \text{ gallons}}$$

$$35 \times n = 28 \times 15$$

$$\frac{35 \times n}{35} = \frac{420}{35}$$

$$n = 12$$

52.
$$\frac{8 \text{ defective}}{100 \text{ perfect}} = \frac{44 \text{ defective}}{n \text{ perfect}}$$

$$8 \times n = 100 \times 44$$

$$\frac{8 \times n}{8} = \frac{4400}{8}$$

$$n = 550$$

53.
$$\frac{3 \text{ gallons}}{2 \text{ rooms}} = \frac{n \text{ gallons}}{10 \text{ rooms}}$$

$$3 \times 10 = 2 \times n$$

$$\frac{30}{2} = \frac{2 \times n}{2}$$

$$15 = n$$

They need 15 gallons.

54.
$$\frac{49 \text{ coffee}}{100 \text{ adults}} = \frac{n \text{ coffee}}{3450 \text{ adults}}$$

$$49 \times 3450 = 100 \times n$$

$$\frac{169,050}{100} = \frac{100 \times n}{100}$$

$$1691 \approx n$$

1691 employees drink coffee.

55. $\dfrac{24 \text{ francs}}{5 \text{ dollars}} = \dfrac{n \text{ francs}}{420 \text{ dollars}}$

$24 \times 420 = 5 \times n$

$\dfrac{10,080}{5} = \dfrac{5 \times n}{5}$

$2016 = n$

She received 2016 francs.

56. $\dfrac{6 \text{ francs}}{4.8 \text{ dollars}} = \dfrac{n \text{ francs}}{125 \text{ dollars}}$

$6 \times 125 = 4.8 \times n$

$\dfrac{750}{4.8} = \dfrac{4.8 \times n}{4.8}$

$n = 156.25$

They received 156.25 Swiss francs.

57. $\dfrac{225 \text{ miles}}{3 \text{ inches}} = \dfrac{n \text{ miles}}{8 \text{ inches}}$

$225 \times 8 = 3 \times n$

$\dfrac{1800}{3} = \dfrac{3 \times n}{3}$

$600 = n$

The cities are 600 miles apart.

58. $\dfrac{8 \text{ rebounds}}{3 \text{ games}} = \dfrac{n \text{ rebounds}}{15 \text{ games}}$

$8 \times 15 = 3 \times n$

$\dfrac{120}{3} = \dfrac{3 \times n}{3}$

$n = 40$

You would expect Kyle to make 40 rebounds.

59. $\dfrac{6 \text{ feet}}{16 \text{ feet}} = \dfrac{n \text{ feet}}{320 \text{ feet}}$

$6 \times 320 = 16 \times n$

$\dfrac{1920}{16} = \dfrac{16 \times n}{16}$

$120 = n$

The height of the building is 120 feet.

60. a. $\dfrac{680 \text{ miles}}{26 \text{ gallons}} = \dfrac{200 \text{ miles}}{n \text{ gallons}}$

$680 \times n = 26 \times 200$

$\dfrac{680 \times n}{680} = \dfrac{5200}{680}$

$n \approx 7.65$

They will need an additional 7.65 gallons.

b.　　$\begin{array}{r} 7.65 \\ \times\ \ 3.20 \\ \hline 1\ 5300 \\ 22\ 95 \\ \hline 24.4800 \end{array}$

The additional fuel will cost $24.48.

61. $\dfrac{3.5 \text{ cm}}{2.5 \text{ cm}} = \dfrac{8 \text{ cm}}{n \text{ cm}}$

$3.5 \times n = 2.5 \times 8$

$\dfrac{3.5 \times n}{3.5} = \dfrac{20}{3.5}$

$n \approx 5.71$

The print will be 5.71 centimeters tall.

62. $\dfrac{3 \text{ grams}}{50 \text{ pounds}} = \dfrac{n \text{ grams}}{125 \text{ pounds}}$

$3 \times 125 = 50 \times n$

$\dfrac{375}{50} = \dfrac{50 \times n}{50}$

$7.5 = n$

She should take 7.5 grams.

63. $\dfrac{22 \text{ pavers}}{3 \text{ feet}} = \dfrac{n \text{ pavers}}{65 \text{ feet}}$

$22 \times 65 = 3 \times n$

$\dfrac{1430}{3} = \dfrac{3 \times n}{3}$

$n = 476.67$

Technically, 476.67 pavers, but in real life, 477 pavers will be needed.

64. $\dfrac{21 \text{ eat at cafeteria}}{35 \text{ students}} = \dfrac{n \text{ eat at cafeteria}}{2800 \text{ students}}$

$21 \times 2800 = 35 \times n$

$\dfrac{58,800}{35} = \dfrac{35 \times n}{35}$

$n = 1680$

1680 students eat at least once a week in the cafeteria.

65. $\dfrac{3 \text{ gallons}}{500 \text{ sq ft}} = \dfrac{n \text{ gallons}}{1400 \text{ sq ft}}$

$3 \times 1400 = 500 \times n$

$\dfrac{4200}{500} = \dfrac{500 \times n}{500}$

$8.4 = n$

He needs 8.4 gallons which equals 9 gallons in real life.

66.
$$\frac{n \text{ liters}}{1250 \text{ runners}} = \frac{2 \text{ liters}}{3 \text{ runners}}$$
$$3 \times n = 1250 \times 2$$
$$\frac{3 \times n}{3} = \frac{2500}{3}$$
$$n \approx 833.33$$

Technically, they need 833.33 liters, but in real life, 834 liters will be needed.

67.
$$\frac{14 \text{ cm}}{145 \text{ feet}} = \frac{11 \text{ cm}}{n \text{ feet}}$$
$$14 \times n = 145 \times 11$$
$$\frac{14 \times n}{14} = \frac{1595}{14}$$
$$n \approx 113.93$$

Width is approximately 113.93 feet.

68.
$$\frac{40 \text{ days}}{3 \text{ minutes}} = \frac{365 \text{ days}}{n \text{ minutes}}$$
$$40 \times n = 3 \times 365$$
$$\frac{40 \times n}{40} = \frac{1095}{40}$$
$$n \approx 27.38$$

27.38 minutes will be gained in one year.

69.
$$\frac{68 \text{ goals}}{27 \text{ games}} = \frac{n \text{ goals}}{34 \text{ games}}$$
$$68 \times 34 = 27 \times n$$
$$\frac{2312}{27} = \frac{27 \times n}{27}$$
$$86 \approx n$$

She is expected to score 86 goals.

70.
$$\frac{345 \text{ calories}}{10 \text{ ounces}} = \frac{n \text{ calories}}{16 \text{ ounces}}$$
$$345 \times 16 = 10 \times n$$
$$\frac{5520}{10} = \frac{10 \times n}{10}$$
$$552 = n$$

You would expect 552 calories in the 16-ounce milkshake.

71.
$$\frac{n \text{ people}}{45,600 \text{ residents}} = \frac{3 \text{ people}}{10 \text{ residents}}$$
$$10 \times n = 45,600 \times 3$$
$$\frac{10 \times n}{10} = \frac{136,800}{10}$$
$$n \approx 13,680$$

You would expect 13,680 people to read the *Boston Globe*.

72.
$$\frac{n \text{ trips}}{240 \text{ trips}} = \frac{13 \text{ trips}}{16 \text{ trips}}$$
$$16 \times n = 240 \times 13$$
$$\frac{16 \times n}{16} = \frac{3120}{16}$$
$$n = 195$$

195 trips will have the passengers spotting at least one whale.

How Am I Doing? Chapter 4 Test

1. $\dfrac{18}{52} = \dfrac{18 \div 2}{52 \div 2} = \dfrac{9}{26}$

2. $\dfrac{70}{185} = \dfrac{70 \div 5}{185 \div 5} = \dfrac{14}{37}$

3. $\dfrac{784 \text{ miles}}{24 \text{ gallons}} = \dfrac{784 \text{ miles} \div 8}{24 \text{ gallons} \div 8} = \dfrac{98 \text{ miles}}{3 \text{ gallons}}$

4. $\dfrac{2100 \text{ square feet}}{45 \text{ pounds}} = \dfrac{2100 \text{ square feet} \div 15}{45 \text{ pounds} \div 15}$
$$= \dfrac{140 \text{ square feet}}{3 \text{ pounds}}$$

5. $\dfrac{19 \text{ tons}}{5 \text{ days}} = \dfrac{19 \text{ tons} \div 5}{5 \text{ days} \div 5} = 3.8 \text{ tons/day}$

6. $\dfrac{\$57.96}{7 \text{ hours}} = \dfrac{\$57.96 \div 7}{7 \text{ hours} \div 7} = \$8.28/\text{hour}$

7. $\dfrac{5400 \text{ feet}}{22 \text{ poles}} = \dfrac{5400 \text{ feet} \div 22}{22 \text{ poles} \div 22} = 245.45 \text{ feet/pole}$

8. $\dfrac{\$9373}{110 \text{ shares}} = \dfrac{\$9373 \div 110}{110 \text{ shares} \div 110} = \$85.21/\text{share}$

9. $\dfrac{17}{29} = \dfrac{51}{87}$

10. $\dfrac{2\frac{1}{2}}{10} = \dfrac{6}{24}$

11. $\dfrac{490 \text{ miles}}{21 \text{ gallons}} = \dfrac{280 \text{ miles}}{12 \text{ gallons}}$

12. $\dfrac{3 \text{ hours}}{180 \text{ miles}} = \dfrac{5 \text{ hours}}{300 \text{ miles}}$

13. $\dfrac{50}{24} \overset{?}{=} \dfrac{34}{16}$

$50 \times 16 \overset{?}{=} 24 \times 34$

$800 \neq 816$

It is not a proportion.

14. $\dfrac{3\frac{1}{2}}{14} = \dfrac{5}{20}$

$3\dfrac{1}{2} \times 20 \overset{?}{=} 14 \times 5$

$\dfrac{7}{2} \times \dfrac{20}{1} \overset{?}{=} 70$

$70 = 70$

It is a proportion.

15. $\dfrac{32 \text{ smokers}}{46 \text{ nonsmokers}} \overset{?}{=} \dfrac{160 \text{ smokers}}{230 \text{ nonsmokers}}$

$32 \times 230 \overset{?}{=} 46 \times 160$

$7360 \neq 7360$

It is not a proportion.

16. $\dfrac{\$0.74}{16 \text{ ounces}} \overset{?}{=} \dfrac{\$1.84}{40 \text{ ounces}}$

$0.74 \times 40 \overset{?}{=} 16 \times 1.84$

$29.6 \neq 29.44$

It is not a proportion.

17. $\dfrac{n}{20} = \dfrac{4}{5}$

$n \times 5 = 20 \times 4$

$\dfrac{n \times 5}{5} = \dfrac{80}{5}$

$n = 16$

18. $\dfrac{8}{3} = \dfrac{60}{n}$

$8 \times n = 3 \times 60$

$\dfrac{8 \times n}{8} = \dfrac{180}{8}$

$n = 22.5$

19. $\dfrac{2\frac{2}{3}}{8} = \dfrac{6\frac{1}{3}}{n}$

$2\dfrac{2}{3} \times n = 8 \times 6\dfrac{1}{3}$

$\dfrac{8}{3} \times n = 8 \times \dfrac{19}{3}$

$\dfrac{\frac{8}{3} \times n}{\frac{8}{3}} = \dfrac{\frac{152}{3}}{\frac{8}{3}}$

$n = \dfrac{152}{3} \div \dfrac{8}{3} = \dfrac{152}{3} \times \dfrac{3}{8} = 19$

20. $\dfrac{4.2}{11} = \dfrac{n}{77}$

$4.2 \times 77 = 11 \times n$

$\dfrac{323.4}{11} = \dfrac{11 \times n}{11}$

$29.4 = n$

21. $\dfrac{45 \text{ women}}{15 \text{ men}} = \dfrac{n \text{ women}}{40 \text{ men}}$

$45 \times 40 = 15 \times n$

$\dfrac{1800}{15} = \dfrac{15 \times n}{15}$

$120 = n$

22. $\dfrac{5 \text{ kg}}{11 \text{ pounds}} = \dfrac{32 \text{ kg}}{n \text{ pounds}}$

$5 \times n = 11 \times 32$

$\dfrac{5 \times n}{5} = \dfrac{352}{5}$

$n = 70.4$

23. $\dfrac{n \text{ inches of snow}}{14 \text{ inches of rain}} = \dfrac{12 \text{ inches of snow}}{1.4 \text{ inches of rain}}$

$n \times 1.4 = 14 \times 12$

$\dfrac{n \times 1.4}{1.4} = \dfrac{168}{1.4}$

$n = 120$

24. $\dfrac{5 \text{ pounds of coffee}}{\$n} = \dfrac{\frac{1}{2} \text{ pound of coffee}}{\$5.20}$

$5 \times 5.20 = \dfrac{1}{2} \times n$

$\dfrac{26}{\frac{1}{2}} = \dfrac{\frac{1}{2} \times n}{\frac{1}{2}}$

$52 = n$

25. $\dfrac{3 \text{ eggs}}{11 \text{ people}} = \dfrac{n \text{ eggs}}{22 \text{ people}}$

$3 \times 22 = 11 \times n$

$\dfrac{66}{11} = \dfrac{11 \times n}{11}$

$6 = n$

He will need 6 eggs.

26. $\dfrac{42 \text{ ft}}{170 \text{ lb}} = \dfrac{20 \text{ ft}}{n \text{ lb}}$

$42 \times n = 170 \times 20$

$\dfrac{42 \times n}{42} = \dfrac{3400}{42}$

$n \approx 80.95$

This cable will weigh 80.95 pounds.

27. $\dfrac{9 \text{ inches}}{57 \text{ miles}} = \dfrac{3 \text{ inches}}{n \text{ miles}}$

$9 \times n = 57 \times 3$

$\dfrac{9 \times n}{9} = \dfrac{171}{9}$

$n = 19$

3 inches represents 19 miles.

28. $\dfrac{\$240}{4000 \text{ sq ft}} = \dfrac{\$n}{6000 \text{ sq ft}}$

$240 \times 6000 = 4000 \times n$

$\dfrac{1{,}440{,}000}{4000} = \dfrac{4000 \times n}{4000}$

$360 = n$

It will cost $360.

29. $\dfrac{n \text{ miles}}{220 \text{ km}} = \dfrac{1 \text{ mile}}{1.61 \text{ km}}$

$1.61 \times n = 220 \times 1$

$\dfrac{1.61 \times n}{1.61} = \dfrac{220}{1.61}$

$n \approx 136.646$

The distance is about 136.6 miles.

30. $\dfrac{570 \text{ km}}{9 \text{ hr}} = \dfrac{n \text{ km}}{11 \text{ hr}}$

$570 \times 11 = 9 \times n$

$6270 = 9 \times n$

$\dfrac{6270}{9} = \dfrac{9 \times n}{9}$

$696.67 \approx n$

He could go 696.67 kilometers.

31. $\dfrac{n \text{ free throws made}}{120 \text{ free throws}} = \dfrac{11 \text{ free throws made}}{15 \text{ free throws}}$

$15 \times n = 120 \times 11$

$\dfrac{15 \times n}{15} = \dfrac{1320}{15}$

$n = 88$

You would expect 88 more free throws made.

32. $\dfrac{7 \text{ hits}}{34 \text{ bats}} = \dfrac{n \text{ hits}}{155 \text{ bats}}$

$7 \times 155 = 34 \times n$

$\dfrac{1085}{34} = \dfrac{34 \times n}{34}$

$32 \approx n$

She would have 32 hits.

Cumulative Test for Chapters 1–4

1. $26{,}597{,}089 =$ Twenty-six million, five hundred ninety-seven thousand, eighty-nine

2.
$$\begin{array}{r} 68 \\ 23\overline{)1564} \\ \underline{138} \\ 184 \\ \underline{184} \\ 0 \end{array}$$

3. $\dfrac{1}{4} + \dfrac{1}{8} \times \dfrac{3}{4} = \dfrac{1}{4} + \dfrac{3}{32} = \dfrac{1}{4} \times \dfrac{8}{8} + \dfrac{3}{32} = \dfrac{8}{32} + \dfrac{3}{32} = \dfrac{11}{32}$

4. $8\dfrac{1}{3} - 5\dfrac{3}{4} = 8\dfrac{4}{12} - 5\dfrac{9}{12} = 7\dfrac{16}{12} - 5\dfrac{9}{12} = 2\dfrac{7}{12}$

5. $\dfrac{20}{1} \times 3\dfrac{1}{4} = \dfrac{20}{1} \times \dfrac{13}{4} = 65$

6.
$$\begin{array}{r} 12.100 \\ - \ 3.8416 \\ \hline 8.2584 \end{array}$$

7.
$$\begin{array}{r} 2.55 \\ \times \ 1.08 \\ \hline 2040 \\ 2\,550 \\ \hline 2.7540 \end{array}$$

8. $\dfrac{18}{25} \div \dfrac{14}{5} = \dfrac{18}{25} \times \dfrac{5}{14} = \dfrac{90}{350} = \dfrac{9}{35}$

9. $16.1455 \times 10^3 = 16.1455 \times 1000 = 16{,}145.5$

10. 56.8918 rounds to 56.9

11.
$$\begin{array}{r} 258.920 \\ +67.358 \\ \hline 326.278 \end{array}$$

12.
$$0.15_{\wedge}\overline{)0.55_{\wedge}20}$$
$$\begin{array}{r} 3.68 \\ \underline{45} \\ 102 \\ 90 \\ \hline 120 \\ 120 \\ \hline 0 \end{array}$$

13.
$$32\overline{)5.0000}$$
$$\begin{array}{r} .15625 \\ \underline{32} \\ 180 \\ \underline{160} \\ 200 \\ \underline{192} \\ 80 \\ \underline{64} \\ 160 \\ \underline{160} \\ 0 \end{array}$$
$$\frac{5}{12} = 0.15625$$

14.
$$\frac{12}{17} \overset{?}{=} \frac{30}{42.5}$$
$$12 \times 42.5 \overset{?}{=} 17 \times 30$$
$$510 = 510$$
It is a proportion.

15.
$$\frac{4\frac{1}{3}}{13} \overset{?}{=} \frac{2\frac{2}{3}}{8}$$
$$4\frac{1}{3} \times 8 \overset{?}{=} 13 \times 2\frac{2}{3}$$
$$\frac{13}{3} \times 8 \overset{?}{=} 13 \times \frac{8}{3}$$
$$\frac{104}{3} = \frac{104}{3}$$
It is a proportion.

16.
$$\frac{9}{2.1} = \frac{n}{0.7}$$
$$9 \times 0.7 = 2.1 \times n$$
$$\frac{6.3}{2.1} = \frac{2.1 \times n}{2.1}$$
$$3 = n$$

17.
$$\frac{50}{20} = \frac{5}{n}$$
$$50 \times n = 20 \times 5$$
$$\frac{50 \times n}{50} = \frac{100}{50}$$
$$n = 2$$

18.
$$\frac{n}{70} = \frac{32}{51}$$
$$n \times 51 = 70 \times 32$$
$$\frac{n \times 51}{51} = \frac{2240}{51}$$
$$n \approx 43.9$$

19.
$$\frac{7}{n} = \frac{28}{36}$$
$$7 \times 36 = n \times 28$$
$$\frac{252}{28} = \frac{n \times 28}{28}$$
$$n = 9$$

20.
$$\frac{n}{11} = \frac{5}{16}$$
$$n \times 16 = 11 \times 5$$
$$\frac{n \times 16}{16} = \frac{55}{16}$$
$$n \approx 3.4$$

21.
$$\frac{3\frac{1}{3}}{7} = \frac{10}{n}$$
$$3\frac{1}{3} \times n = 7 \times 10$$
$$\frac{\frac{10}{3} \times n}{\frac{10}{3}} = \frac{70}{\frac{10}{3}}$$
$$n = 70 \times \frac{3}{10}$$
$$n = 21$$

22. $\dfrac{300 \text{ miles}}{4 \text{ inches}} = \dfrac{625 \text{ miles}}{n \text{ inches}}$

$$300 \times n = 4 \times 625$$
$$\frac{300 \times n}{300} = \frac{2500}{300}$$
$$n \approx 8.33$$

They will appear to be apart by 8.33 inches.

23. $\dfrac{26 \text{ haircuts}}{\$117 \text{ tips}} = \dfrac{31 \text{ haircuts}}{n \text{ tips}}$

$$26 \times n = 117 \times 31$$
$$\frac{26 \times n}{26} = \frac{3627}{26}$$
$$n = 139.5$$

She will earn \$139.50 in tips.

24. $\dfrac{14 \text{ people}}{3.5 \text{ lb}} = \dfrac{20 \text{ people}}{n \text{ lb}}$

$$14 \times n = 3.5 \times 20$$
$$\frac{14 \times n}{14} = \frac{70}{14}$$
$$n = 5$$

She will need 5 pounds.

25. $\dfrac{39 \text{ gallons sap}}{2 \text{ gallons syrup}} = \dfrac{n \text{ gallons sap}}{11 \text{ gallons syrup}}$

$$39 \times 11 = 2 \times n$$
$$\frac{429}{2} = \frac{2 \times n}{2}$$
$$214.5 = n$$

214.5 gallons of maple sap is needed.

Chapter 5

5.1 Exercises

2. The number 1 written as a percent is 100%.

4. Move the decimal point two places to the right. Write the % symbol at the end of the number.

6. $\dfrac{67}{100} = 67\%$

8. $\dfrac{7}{100} = 7\%$

10. $\dfrac{90}{100} = 90\%$

12. $\dfrac{110}{100} = 110\%$

14. $\dfrac{15.8}{100} = 15.8\%$

16. $\dfrac{0.019}{100} = 0.019\%$

18. $\dfrac{54}{100} = 54\%$

20. 7 out of 100 students majored in exercise science.
$\dfrac{7}{100} = 7\%$

22. $42\% = 0.42$

24. $6\% = 0.06$

26. $40\% = 0.40 = 0.4$

28. $81.5\% = 0.815$

30. $0.09\% = 0.0009$

32. $0.61\% = 0.0061$

34. $9.6\% = 0.096$

36. $189\% = 1.89$

38. $0.66 = 66\%$

40. $0.40 = 40\%$

42. $0.03 = 3\%$

44. $0.408 = 40.8\%$

46. $0.009 = 0.9\%$

48. $0.0026 = 0.26\%$

50. $1.86 = 186\%$

52. $4.32 = 432\%$

54. $0.37 = 37\%$

56. $0.8 = 80\%$

58. $0.25 = 25\%$

60. $1.48 = 148\%$

62. $\dfrac{40}{100} = 40\%$

64. $0.055 = 5.5\%$

66. $49\% = 0.49$

68. $210\% = 2.10 = 2.1$

70. $\dfrac{0.8}{100} = 0.008$

72. $\dfrac{35}{100} = 0.35$

74. $\dfrac{59}{100} = 59\%$
59% voted for George W. Bush.

76. $1\% = 0.01$
0.01 plan to donate the money.

78. $30\% = 0.3$
0.3 get their vitamin A from carrots.

80. $3.7\% = 0.037$; $13.4\% = 0.134$
General Motors increased by 0.037, while Ford decreased by 0.134.

82. $10.65 = \dfrac{1065}{100}$

$= 1065 \times \dfrac{1}{100}$

$= 1065$ "per one hundred"

$= 1065$ percent

$= 1065\%$

We change 10.65 to $10.65 \times \dfrac{1}{100}$ and use the

idea that percent means "per one hundred."

84. a. $3724\% = 37.24$

    b. $3724\% = \dfrac{3724}{100}$

    c. $3724\% = \dfrac{3724}{100} = \dfrac{3724 \div 4}{100 \div 4} = \dfrac{931}{25}$

Cumulative Review

85. $0.56 = \dfrac{56}{100} = \dfrac{56 \div 4}{100 \div 4} = \dfrac{14}{25}$

86. $0.78 = \dfrac{78}{100} = \dfrac{78 \div 2}{100 \div 2} = \dfrac{39}{50}$

87.

$$\begin{array}{r} 0.6875 \\ 16\overline{)11.000} \\ \underline{9\ 6} \\ 1\ 40 \\ \underline{1\ 28} \\ 120 \\ \underline{112} \\ 80 \\ \underline{80} \\ 0 \end{array}$$

$\dfrac{11}{16} = 0.6875$

88.

$$\begin{array}{r} 0.875 \\ 8\overline{)7.000} \\ \underline{6\ 4} \\ 60 \\ \underline{56} \\ 40 \\ \underline{40} \\ 0 \end{array}$$

$\dfrac{7}{8} = 0.875$

89. $3 \times 246 + 7 \times 380 + 5 \times 168 + 9 \times 122$

$= 738 + 2660 + 840 + 1098$

$= 5336$

There are a total of 5336 vases.

Classroom Quiz 5.1

  1. $0.026 = 2.6\%$

  2. $\dfrac{3.7}{100} = 3.7\%$

  3. $0.09\% = 0.0009$

5.2 Exercises

  2. Change the fraction to a decimal by dividing the denominator into the numerator. Change the decimal to a percent by moving the decimal point two places to the right and add % symbol.

  4. $8\% = \dfrac{8}{100} = \dfrac{2}{25}$

  6. $47\% = \dfrac{47}{100}$

  8. $35\% = \dfrac{35}{100} = \dfrac{7}{20}$

 10. $25\% = \dfrac{25}{100} = \dfrac{1}{4}$

 12. $40\% = \dfrac{40}{100} = \dfrac{2}{5}$

 14. $6.5\% = 0.065 = \dfrac{65}{1000} = \dfrac{13}{200}$

16. $92.5\% = 0.925 = \dfrac{925}{1000} = \dfrac{37}{40}$

18. $12.2\% = 0.122 = \dfrac{122}{1000} = \dfrac{61}{500}$

20. $38.75\% = 0.3875 = \dfrac{3975}{10,000} = \dfrac{31}{80}$

22. $256\% = \dfrac{256}{100} = \dfrac{64}{25} = 2\dfrac{14}{25}$

24. $420\% = \dfrac{420}{100} = 4\dfrac{20}{100} = 4\dfrac{1}{5}$

26. $3600\% = \dfrac{3600}{100} = 36$

28. $4\dfrac{3}{5}\% = \dfrac{\frac{23}{5}}{100} = \dfrac{23}{500}$

30. $37\dfrac{1}{2}\% = \dfrac{\frac{75}{2}}{100} = \dfrac{75}{200} = \dfrac{3}{8}$

32. $9\dfrac{3}{5}\% = \dfrac{\frac{48}{5}}{100} = \dfrac{48}{500} = \dfrac{12}{125}$

34. $22.9\% = \dfrac{22.9}{100} = \dfrac{22.9 \times 10}{100 \times 10} = \dfrac{229}{1000}$

The number of crimes decreased by $\dfrac{229}{1000}$.

36. $5\dfrac{2}{25}\% = \dfrac{\frac{127}{25}}{100} = \dfrac{127}{2500}$

This was an increase of $\dfrac{127}{2500}$.

38. $\dfrac{1}{4} = 0.25 = 25\%$

40. $\dfrac{9}{10} = 0.9 = 90\%$

42. $\dfrac{11}{20} = 0.55 = 55\%$

44. $\dfrac{22}{25} = 0.88 = 88\%$

46. $\dfrac{13}{40} = 0.325 = 32.5\%$

48. $\dfrac{7}{4} = 1.75 = 175\%$

50. $3\dfrac{3}{4} = 3.75 = 375\%$

52. $2\dfrac{5}{8} = 2.625 = 262.5\%$

54. $\dfrac{2}{3} \approx 0.6667 = 66.67\%$

56. $\dfrac{8}{15} \approx 0.5333 = 53.33\%$

58. $\dfrac{12}{5} = 2.4 = 240\%$

60. $\dfrac{43}{50} = 0.86 = 86\%$

62.
$$\begin{array}{r} 0.28 \\ 25\overline{)7.00} \\ \underline{5\ 0} \\ 2\ 00 \\ \underline{2\ 00} \\ 0 \end{array}$$

$\dfrac{7}{25} = 0.28 = 28\%$

This represents 28% of your income.

64.
$$\begin{array}{r} 0.0275 \\ 400\overline{)11.0000} \\ \underline{8\ 00} \\ 3\ 000 \\ \underline{2\ 800} \\ 2000 \\ \underline{2000} \\ 0 \end{array}$$

$\dfrac{11}{400} = 0.0275 = 2.75\%$

This represents 2.75% of the earth's total surface area.

66.
$$8\overline{)5.00} \quad \begin{array}{r} 0.62 \\ \hline \end{array}$$
$$\underline{4\,8}$$
$$20$$
$$\underline{16}$$
$$4$$

$$\frac{5}{8} = 0.62\frac{4}{8} = 0.62\frac{1}{2} = 62\frac{1}{2}\%$$

68.
$$90\overline{)11.00} \quad \begin{array}{r} 0.12 \\ \hline \end{array}$$
$$\underline{90}$$
$$2\,00$$
$$\underline{1\,80}$$
$$20$$

$$\frac{11}{90} = 0.12\frac{20}{90} = 0.12\frac{2}{9} = 12\frac{2}{9}\%$$

70.
$$15\overline{)11.00} \quad \begin{array}{r} 0.73 \\ \hline \end{array}$$
$$\underline{10\,5}$$
$$50$$
$$\underline{45}$$
$$5$$

$$\frac{11}{15} = 0.73\frac{5}{15} = 0.73\frac{1}{3} = 73\frac{1}{3}\%$$

72.
$$9\overline{)8.00} \quad \begin{array}{r} 0.88 \\ \hline \end{array}$$
$$\underline{7\,2}$$
$$80$$
$$\underline{72}$$
$$8$$

$$\frac{8}{9} = 0.88\frac{8}{9} = 88\frac{8}{9}\%$$

74.
$$12\overline{)1.00000} \quad \begin{array}{r} 0.08333 \\ \hline \end{array}$$
$$\underline{96}$$
$$40$$
$$\underline{36}$$
$$40$$
$$\underline{36}$$
$$40$$
$$\underline{36}$$
$$4$$

$$\frac{1}{12} \approx 0.0833 = 8.33\%$$

76. $0.85 = 85\%$
$$0.85 = \frac{85}{100} = \frac{17}{20}$$
$$\frac{17}{20}; \; 0.85; \; 85\%$$

78. $0.085 = 8.5\%$
$$0.085 = \frac{85}{1000} = \frac{85 \div 5}{1000 \div 5} = \frac{17}{200}$$
$$\frac{17}{200}; \; 0.085; \; 8.5\%$$

80.
$$9\overline{)7.00000} \quad \begin{array}{r} 0.77777 \\ \hline \end{array}$$
$$\underline{6\,3}$$
$$70$$
$$\underline{63}$$
$$70$$
$$\underline{63}$$
$$70$$
$$\underline{63}$$
$$70$$
$$\underline{63}$$
$$7$$

$$\frac{7}{9} \approx 0.7778 = 77.78\%$$

$$\frac{7}{9}; \; 0.7778; \; 77.78\%$$

82. $\dfrac{5}{8} = 0.625$

$2\dfrac{5}{8} = 2.625$

$2\dfrac{5}{8}\% = 0.02625$ or 0.0263

$0.02625 = \dfrac{2625}{100,000} = \dfrac{21}{800}$

$\dfrac{21}{800}$; 0.0263; $2\dfrac{5}{8}\%$

84. $18\dfrac{7}{12}\% = \dfrac{18\frac{7}{12}}{100}$

$\qquad = 18\dfrac{7}{12} \div 100$

$\qquad = \dfrac{223}{12} \times \dfrac{1}{100}$

$\qquad = \dfrac{223}{1200}$

86. $\dfrac{417}{600} = \dfrac{n}{100}$

$417 \times 100 = 600 \times n$

$41,700 = 600 \times n$

$\dfrac{41,700}{600} = \dfrac{600 \times n}{600}$

$69.5 = n$

69.5%

Cumulative Review

87. $\dfrac{15}{n} = \dfrac{8}{3}$

$15 \times 3 = n \times 8$

$\dfrac{45}{8} = \dfrac{n \times 8}{8}$

$n = 5.625$

88. $\dfrac{32}{24} = \dfrac{n}{3}$

$32 \times 3 = 24 \times n$

$96 = 24 \times n$

$\dfrac{96}{24} = \dfrac{24 \times n}{24}$

$4 = n$

89.
$$\begin{array}{r} 10,041 \\ 986 \\ 4,283 \\ + 533,855 \\ \hline 549,165 \end{array}$$

There were a total of 549,165 documents.

90. $2\dfrac{1}{2} \times 1800 = \dfrac{5}{2} \times \dfrac{1800}{1} = 4500$

The new steak house has an area of 4500 square feet.

Classroom Quiz 5.2

1. $62\% = \dfrac{62}{100} = \dfrac{31}{50}$

2. $8\dfrac{3}{4}\% = \dfrac{\frac{35}{4}}{100} = \dfrac{35}{400} = \dfrac{7}{80}$

3. $\dfrac{17}{40} = 0.425 = 42.5\%$

5.3A Exercises

2. $500 is 30% of what number?

4. This type is called "a percent problem when we do not know the amount." We can translate this into an equation.

$n = 65\% \times 600$

$n = 0.65 \times 600$

$n = 390$

6. This is a type called "a percent problem when we do not know the percent." We can translate this into an equation.

$n \times 35 = 14$

$35n = 14$

$n = 0.4$

The answer is 40%.

8. What is 9% of 65?

$n = 9\% \times 65$

10. 65% of what is 28?

$65\% \times n = 28$

12. 24 is what percent of 144?

$24 = n \times 144$

14. What is 30% of 210?

$n = 30\% \times 210$

$n = 0.30 \times 210$

$n = 63$

16. Find 60% of 210.

$n = 60\% \times 210$

$n = 0.6 \times 210$

$n = 126$

18. What is 8% of $215?

$n = 8\% \times 215$

$n = 0.8 \times 215$

$n = 17.20$

The service fee would be $17.20.

20. 3% of what is 18?

$3\% \times n = 18$

$0.03n = 18$

$\dfrac{0.03n}{0.03} = \dfrac{18}{0.03}$

$n = 600$

22. 36 is 6% of what?

$36 = 6\% \times n$

$36 = 0.06 \times n$

$\dfrac{36}{0.06} = \dfrac{0.06n}{0.06}$

$600 = n$

24. $12\% \times n = 522$

$0.12 \times n = 522$

$\dfrac{0.12n}{0.12} = \dfrac{522}{0.12}$

$n = 4350$

The population is 4350.

26. What percent of 300 is 135?

$n \times 300 = 135$

$\dfrac{300n}{300} = \dfrac{135}{300}$

$n = 0.45$

$n = 45\%$

28. 78 is what percent of 200?

$78 = n \times 200$

$\dfrac{78}{200} = \dfrac{n \times 200}{200}$

$0.39 = n$

$39\% = n$

30. 28 is what percent of 140?

$28 = n \times 140$

$\dfrac{28}{140} = \dfrac{n \times 140}{140}$

$0.20 = n$

$20\% = n$

20% of the bill was for labor.

32. 60% of 215 is what?

$60\% \times 215 = n$

$0.60 \times 215 = n$

$129 = n$

34. 160% of what is 152?

$160\% \times n = 152$

$1.60 \times n = 152$

$\dfrac{1.60 \times n}{1.60} = \dfrac{152}{1.60}$

$n = 95$

36. 72 is what percent of 900?

$72 = n \times 900$

$\dfrac{72}{900} = \dfrac{n \times 900}{900}$

$0.08 = n$

$8\% = n$

38. Find 0.3% of 540.

$n = 0.3\% \times 540$

$n = 0.003 \times 540$

$n = 1.62$

40. What percent of 45 is 16.2?

$n \times 45 = 16.2$

$\dfrac{n \times 45}{45} = \dfrac{16.2}{45}$

$n = 0.36$

$n = 36\%$

42. 10 is 25% of what?

$10 = 25\% \times n$

$10 = 0.25 \times n$

$\dfrac{10}{0.25} = \dfrac{0.25 \times n}{0.25}$

$40 = n$

44. 6 is what percent of 800?

$6 = n \times 800$

$\dfrac{6}{800} = \dfrac{800n}{800}$

$0.0075 = n$

$0.75\% = n$

46. What is 17.5% of 260?
$n = 17.5\% \times 260$
$n = 0.175 \times 260$
$n = 45.5$

48. 27 is what percent of 45?
$27 = n \times 45$
$$\frac{27}{45} = \frac{n \times 45}{45}$$
$0.6 = n$
$60\% = n$

50. 15 is what percent of 400?
$15 = n \times 400$
$$\frac{15}{400} = \frac{n \times 400}{400}$$
$0.0375 = n$
$3.75\% = n$
3.75% were not perfect.

52. What is 15% of 420?
$n = 15\% \times 420$
$n = 0.15 \times 420$
$n = 63$
63 students do not eat a proper breakfast.

54. 570 = 60% of what?
$570 = 60\% \times n$
$570 = 0.6 \times n$
$$\frac{570}{0.6} = \frac{0.6 \times n}{0.6}$$
$950 = n$
950 students graduated from college last year.

56. Find 90% of 15% of 2700.
$n = 90\% \times 15\% \times 2700$
$n = 0.90 \times 0.15 \times 2700$
$n = 364.5$

Cumulative Review

57.
$$\begin{array}{r} 1.36 \\ \times\ 1.8 \\ \hline 1\,088 \\ 1\,36 \\ \hline 2.448 \end{array}$$

58.
$$\begin{array}{r} 5.06 \\ \times\ 0.82 \\ \hline 1012 \\ 4\,048 \\ \hline 4.1492 \end{array}$$

59.
$$\begin{array}{r} 2834 \\ 0.06_\wedge \overline{)170.04_\wedge} \\ \underline{12} \\ 50 \\ \underline{48} \\ 2\,0 \\ \underline{1\,8} \\ 24 \\ \underline{24} \\ 0 \end{array}$$

60.
$$\begin{array}{r} 2.36 \\ 0.9_\wedge \overline{)2.1_\wedge 24} \\ \underline{1\,8} \\ 3\,2 \\ \underline{2\,7} \\ 54 \\ \underline{54} \\ 0 \end{array}$$

Classroom Quiz 5.3A

1. What is 0.06% of 27,000?
$n = 0.06\% \times 27,000$
$n = 0.0006 \times 27,000$
$n = 16.2$

2. 115.2 is 72% of what number?
$115.2 = 72\% \times n$
$115.2 = 0.72 \times n$
$$\frac{115.2}{0.72} = \frac{0.72 \times n}{0.72}$$
$160 = n$

3. 39 is what percent of 300?
$39 = n \times 300$
$$\frac{39}{300} = \frac{n \times 300}{300}$$
$0.13 = n$
13%

5.3B Exercises

		p	b	a
2.	65% of 820 is 532.	65	820	532
4.	What is 35% of 95?	35	95	a
6.	38% of what is 2280?	38	b	2280
8.	50 is what percent of 250?	p	250	50

10. 80% of 90 is what?
$$\frac{a}{90} = \frac{80}{100}$$
$$100 \times a = 80 \times 90$$
$$\frac{100a}{100} = \frac{7200}{100}$$
$$a = 72$$

12. Find 150% of 80.
$$\frac{a}{80} = \frac{150}{100}$$
$$100a = 80 \times 150$$
$$\frac{100a}{100} = \frac{12,000}{100}$$
$$a = 120$$

14. 0.8% of 9000 is what?
$$\frac{a}{9000} = \frac{0.8}{100}$$
$$100a = 9000 \times 0.8$$
$$\frac{100a}{100} = \frac{7200}{100}$$
$$a = 72$$

16. 45 is 60% of what?
$$\frac{45}{b} = \frac{60}{100}$$
$$45 \times 100 = 60b$$
$$\frac{4500}{60} = \frac{60b}{60}$$
$$75 = b$$

18. 120% of what is 90?
$$\frac{90}{b} = \frac{120}{100}$$
$$90 \times 100 = 120b$$
$$\frac{9000}{120} = \frac{120b}{120}$$
$$75 = b$$

20. 6000 is 0.4% of what?
$$\frac{6000}{b} = \frac{0.4}{100}$$
$$6000 \times 100 = 0.4b$$
$$\frac{600,000}{0.4} = \frac{0.4b}{0.4}$$
$$1,500,000 = b$$

22. 70 is what percent of 1400?
$$\frac{p}{100} = \frac{70}{1400}$$
$$1400p = 100 \times 70$$
$$\frac{1400p}{1400} = \frac{7000}{1400}$$
$$p = 5$$
5%

24. What percent of 120 is 18?
$$\frac{18}{120} = \frac{p}{100}$$
$$120p = 18 \times 100$$
$$\frac{120p}{120} = \frac{1800}{120}$$
$$p = 15$$

26. 20% of 75 is what?
$$\frac{a}{75} = \frac{20}{100}$$
$$100a = 20 \times 75$$
$$\frac{100a}{100} = \frac{1500}{100}$$
$$a = 15$$

28. 200% of what is 120?
$$\frac{120}{b} = \frac{200}{100}$$
$$120 \times 100 = 200b$$
$$\frac{12,000}{200} = \frac{200b}{200}$$
$$60 = b$$

30. 75 is what percent of 600?
$$\frac{p}{100} = \frac{75}{600}$$
$$600p = 100 \times 75$$
$$\frac{600p}{600} = \frac{7500}{600}$$
$$p = 12.5$$
12.5%

32. Find 0.4% of 650.

$$\frac{a}{650} = \frac{0.4}{100}$$
$$100a = 650 \times 0.4$$
$$\frac{100a}{100} = \frac{260}{100}$$
$$a = 2.6$$

34. What percent of 49 is 34.3?

$$\frac{p}{100} = \frac{34.3}{49}$$
$$49p = 100 \times 34.3$$
$$\frac{49p}{49} = \frac{3430}{49}$$
$$p = 70$$
70%

36. 52 is 40% of what?

$$\frac{52}{b} = \frac{40}{100}$$
$$52 \times 100 = 40b$$
$$\frac{5200}{40} = \frac{40b}{40}$$
$$130 = b$$

38. 24% of what is $6300?

$$\frac{6300}{b} = \frac{24}{100}$$
$$6300 \times 100 = 24b$$
$$\frac{630,000}{24} = \frac{24b}{24}$$
$$26,250 = b$$

Rachel's annual salary was $26,250.

40. What percent of 60 is 12?

$$\frac{p}{100} = \frac{12}{60}$$
$$60p = 100 \times 12$$
$$\frac{60p}{60} = \frac{1200}{60}$$
$$p = 20$$

20% resulted in a home run.

42. What is 8% of 250?

$$\frac{a}{250} = \frac{8}{100}$$
$$100a = 250 \times 8$$
$$\frac{100a}{100} = \frac{2000}{100}$$
$$a = 20$$

20 people had outstanding warrants for their arrest.

44. 8 is what percent of 40?

$$\frac{p}{100} = \frac{8}{40}$$
$$40p = 100 \times 8$$
$$\frac{40p}{40} = \frac{800}{40}$$
$$p = 20$$

20% of the problems she did incorrectly.

46.
```
   3 540
   1 986
   1 520
     583
     833
     904
 + 1 190
  10,556
```

583 is what percent of 10,556?

$$\frac{p}{100} = \frac{583}{10,556}$$
$$10,556p = 100 \times 583$$
$$\frac{10,556p}{10,556} = \frac{58,300}{10,556}$$
$$p \approx 5.5$$

About 5.5% was spent on clothing.

48.
$$125\% \times 833 = n$$
$$1.25 \times 833 = n$$
$$1041.25 = n$$
$$115\% \times 1986 = n$$
$$1.15 \times 1986 = n$$
$$2283.9 = n$$

```
New total:    3540.00
              2283.90
              1520.00
               583.00
              1041.25
               904.00
          +   1190.00
             11,062.15
```

1190 is what percent of 11,062.15?

$$\frac{p}{100} = \frac{1190}{11,062.15}$$
$$p \approx 10.76$$

About 10.8% was used for miscellaneous items.

Cumulative Review

49. $\dfrac{4}{5}+\dfrac{8}{9}=\dfrac{4}{5}\times\dfrac{9}{9}+\dfrac{8}{9}\times\dfrac{5}{5}$

$\qquad\quad=\dfrac{36}{45}+\dfrac{40}{45}$

$\qquad\quad=\dfrac{76}{45}$

$\qquad\quad=1\dfrac{31}{45}$

50. $\dfrac{7}{13}-\dfrac{1}{2}=\dfrac{14}{26}-\dfrac{13}{26}=\dfrac{1}{26}$

51. $\left(2\dfrac{4}{5}\right)\left(1\dfrac{1}{2}\right)=\dfrac{14}{5}\times\dfrac{3}{2}=\dfrac{42}{10}=\dfrac{21}{5}=4\dfrac{1}{5}$

52. $1\dfrac{2}{5}\div\dfrac{3}{4}=\dfrac{7}{5}\div\dfrac{3}{4}=\dfrac{7}{5}\times\dfrac{4}{3}=\dfrac{28}{15}=1\dfrac{13}{15}$

Classroom Quiz 5.3B

1. What is 145% of 96?

$\dfrac{a}{96}=\dfrac{145}{100}$

$100a=96\times145$

$\dfrac{100a}{100}=\dfrac{13,920}{100}$

$a=139.2$

2. 88 is 0.4% of what number?

$\dfrac{88}{b}=\dfrac{0.4}{100}$

$88\times100=0.4b$

$\dfrac{8800}{0.4}=\dfrac{0.4b}{0.4}$

$22,000=b$

3. 126 is what percent of 800?

$\dfrac{p}{100}=\dfrac{126}{800}$

$800p=100\times126$

$\dfrac{800p}{800}=\dfrac{12,600}{800}$

$p=15.75$

15.75%

How Am I Doing? Sections 5.1–5.3

1. $0.17=17\%$

2. $0.387=38.7\%$

3. $7.95=795\%$

4. $5.18=518\%$

5. $0.006=0.6\%$

6. $0.0004=0.04\%$

7. $\dfrac{17}{100}=17\%$

8. $\dfrac{89}{100}=89\%$

9. $\dfrac{13.4}{100}=13.4\%$

10. $\dfrac{19.8}{100}=19.8\%$

11. $\dfrac{6\frac{1}{2}}{100}=6\dfrac{1}{2}\%$

12. $\dfrac{1\frac{3}{8}}{100}=1\dfrac{3}{8}\%$

13. $10\overline{)8.0}$ with quotient 0.8

$\dfrac{8}{10}=0.8=80\%$

14. $30\overline{)15.00}$ with quotient $.50$

$\quad\underline{15\ 0}$

$\qquad 00$

$\dfrac{15}{30}=0.50=50\%$

15. $20\overline{)52.0}$ with quotient 2.6

$\quad\underline{40}$

$\quad 12\ 0$

$\quad\underline{12\ 0}$

$\qquad 0$

$\dfrac{52}{20}=2.6=260\%$

16.
$$16\overline{)17.0000}$$
has quotient 1.0625

$$\begin{array}{r} \underline{16} \\ 1\ 00 \\ \underline{96} \\ 40 \\ \underline{32} \\ 80 \\ \underline{80} \\ 0 \end{array}$$

$$\frac{17}{16} = 1.0625 = 106.25\%$$

17.
$$7\overline{)5.000}$$
has quotient $.71428$

$$\begin{array}{r} \underline{4\ 9} \\ 10 \\ \underline{7} \\ 30 \\ \underline{28} \\ 20 \\ \underline{14} \\ 60 \\ \underline{56} \\ 4 \end{array}$$

$$\frac{5}{7} \approx 0.7143 = 71.43\%$$

18.
$$7\overline{)2.00000}$$
has quotient $.28571$

$$\begin{array}{r} \underline{1\ 4} \\ 60 \\ \underline{56} \\ 40 \\ \underline{35} \\ 50 \\ \underline{49} \\ 10 \end{array}$$

$$\frac{2}{7} \approx 0.2857 = 28.57\%$$

19.
$$24\overline{)18.00}$$
has quotient $.75$

$$\begin{array}{r} \underline{16\ 8} \\ 1\ 20 \\ \underline{1\ 20} \\ 0 \end{array}$$

$$\frac{18}{24} = 0.75 = 75\%$$

20.
$$36\overline{)9.00}$$
has quotient $.25$

$$\begin{array}{r} \underline{7\ 2} \\ 1\ 80 \\ \underline{1\ 80} \\ 0 \end{array}$$

$$\frac{9}{36} = 0.25 = 25\%$$

21. $4\dfrac{2}{5} = \dfrac{22}{5} = 4.4 = 440\%$

22. $2\dfrac{3}{4} = \dfrac{11}{4} = 2.75 = 275\%$

23. $\dfrac{1}{300} = \dfrac{1}{3}\left(\dfrac{1}{100}\right) = \dfrac{1}{3}\% \approx 0.33\%$

24. $\dfrac{1}{400} = \dfrac{1}{4}\left(\dfrac{1}{100}\right) = \dfrac{1}{4}\% = 0.25\%$

25. $22\% = \dfrac{22}{100} = \dfrac{11}{50}$

26. $53\% = \dfrac{53}{100}$

27. $150\% = \dfrac{150}{100} = \dfrac{3}{2}$ or $1\dfrac{1}{2}$

28. $160\% = \dfrac{160}{100} = \dfrac{8}{5}$ or $1\dfrac{3}{5}$

29. $6\dfrac{1}{3}\% = \dfrac{6\frac{1}{3}}{100} = \dfrac{\frac{19}{3}}{100} = \dfrac{19}{300}$

30. $3\dfrac{1}{8}\% = \dfrac{3\frac{1}{8}}{100} = \dfrac{\frac{25}{8}}{100} = \dfrac{25}{800} = \dfrac{1}{32}$

31. $51\dfrac{1}{4}\% = \dfrac{\frac{205}{4}}{100} = \dfrac{205}{400} = \dfrac{41}{80}$

32. $43\dfrac{3}{4}\% = \dfrac{\frac{175}{4}}{100} = \dfrac{175}{400} = \dfrac{7}{16}$

33. What is 70% of 60?
$n = 70\% \times 60$
$n = 0.70(60)$
$n = 42$

34. Find 12% of 200.
$n = 12\% \times 200$
$n = 0.12(200)$
$n = 24$

35. 68 is what percent of 72?
$\dfrac{p}{100} = \dfrac{68}{72}$
$72p = 68 \times 100$
$\dfrac{72p}{72} = \dfrac{6800}{72}$
$p \approx 94.44$
94.44%

36. What percent of 76 is 34?
$\dfrac{p}{100} = \dfrac{34}{76}$
$76p = 34 \times 100$
$\dfrac{76p}{76} = \dfrac{3400}{76}$
$p \approx 44.74$
44.74%

37. 8% of what number is 240?
$\dfrac{8}{100} = \dfrac{240}{b}$
$8b = 240 \times 100$
$\dfrac{8b}{8} = \dfrac{24,000}{8}$
$b = 3000$

38. 354 is 40% of what number?
$\dfrac{40}{100} = \dfrac{354}{b}$
$40b = 354 \times 100$
$\dfrac{40b}{40} = \dfrac{35,400}{40}$
$b = 885$

5.4 Exercises

2. $n \times 29\% = 58$
$\dfrac{0.29n}{0.29} = \dfrac{58}{0.29}$
$n = 200$
He made 200 attempts.

4. $n \times 125\% = 9.50$
$1.25n = 9.50$
$\dfrac{1.25n}{1.25} = \dfrac{9.50}{1.25}$
$n = 7.6$
Last year she earned \$7.60/hour.

6. $85 + 280 = 365$
$365 \times n = 85$
$\dfrac{365 \times n}{365} = \dfrac{85}{365}$
$n \approx 0.2329$
23.39% of the coffees were espressos.

8. $n = 5\%$ of $180 = 0.05 \times 180 = 9$
\$9 is the tax he paid.

10. $5\% \times n = 10.75$
$0.05n = 10.75$
$\dfrac{0.05n}{0.05} = \dfrac{10.75}{0.05}$
$n = 215$
The price of the artwork was \$215.

12. $350 \times n = 52.50$
$\dfrac{350 \times n}{350} = \dfrac{52.50}{350}$
$n = 0.15$
15% is set aside for car payments.

14. $n \times 28\% = 8400$
$\dfrac{0.28n}{0.28} = \dfrac{8400}{0.28}$
$n = 30,000$
Her income last year was \$30,000.

16. $469 \times n = 20$
$\dfrac{469 \times n}{469} = \dfrac{20}{469}$
$n \approx 0.0426$
4.26% of his at-bats resulted in a home run.

18. $n = 0.8\% \times 28{,}000$
$n = 0.008 \times 28{,}000$
$n = 224$
224 children were under age 12.

20. $n \times 115\% = 47.50$
$\dfrac{1.15n}{1.15} = \dfrac{47.50}{1.15}$
$n \approx 41.30$
She can afford to spend $41.30.

22. $106\% \times n = 25{,}440$
$1.06n = 25{,}440$
$\dfrac{1.06n}{1.06} = \dfrac{25{,}440}{1.06}$
$n = 24{,}000$
The price was $24,000.

24. $12\% + 7\% = 19\%$
$n = 19\% \times 9000$
$n = 0.19 \times 9000$
$n = 1710$
1710 flights are delayed less than two hours.

26. a. $20\% + 16\% = 36\%$
$n = 36\% \times 6{,}000{,}000$
$n = 0.36 \times 6{,}000{,}000$
$n = 2{,}160{,}000$
$2,160,000 was paid to cover staff and rental.

   b. $\begin{array}{r} 6{,}000{,}000 \\ -\ 2{,}160{,}000 \\ \hline 3{,}840{,}000 \end{array}$
$3,840,000 was left over for research.

28. $n = 30\% \times 130$
$n = 0.3 \times 130$
$n = 39$
Discount is $39. Cost is $130 − $39 = $91.

30. a. $n = 25\% \times 1150$
$n = 0.25 \times 1150$
$n = 287.5$
Discount was $287.50.

   b. Cost of refrigerator and stove is
$1150 − $287.50 = $862.50.

Cumulative Review

31. 1,698,481 rounds to 1,698,000.

32. 2,452,399 rounds to 2,452,400.

33. 1.63474 rounds to 1.63.

34. 0.7995 rounds to 0.800.

35. 0.055613 rounds to 0.0556.

36. 0.079152 rounds to 0.0792.

Classroom Quiz 5.4

1. a. $n = 20\% \times \$633$
$n = 0.20 \times 633$
$n = 126.6$
The discount was $126.60.

   b. $\$633 - \$126.60 = \$506.40$
She paid $506.40.

2. $\dfrac{p}{100} = \dfrac{19}{28}$
$28p = 100 \times 19$
$\dfrac{28p}{28} = \dfrac{1900}{28}$
$p \approx 67.85$
67.9% of the students drove to school.

3. $3380 = 26\% \times n$
$3380 = 0.26 \times n$
$\dfrac{3380}{0.26} = \dfrac{0.26 \times n}{0.26}$
$13{,}000 = n$
13,000 people live in that city.

5.5 Exercises

2. $\begin{aligned} \text{Commission} &= 3\% \times 230{,}000 \\ &= 0.03 \times 230{,}000 \\ &= 6900 \end{aligned}$
In commission, she earned $6900.

4. $\begin{aligned} \text{Total income} &= 500 + 0.5\% \times 340{,}000 \\ &= 500 + 0.005 \times 340{,}000 \\ &= 500 + 1700 \\ &= 2200 \end{aligned}$
His total income was $2200.

6. $\text{Decrease} = 267 - 183 = 84$
$\text{Percent} = \dfrac{84}{267} \approx 0.3146 \approx 31.5\%$
This was a decrease of 31.5%.

8. Decrease $= 807 - 635 = 172$

Percent $= \dfrac{172}{807} \approx 0.2131 \approx 21.3\%$

This was a decrease of 21.3%.

10. $I = P \times R \times T$
$= 450 \times 1.2\% \times 1$
$= 450 \times 0.012 \times 1$
$= 5.4$
She earned \$5.40.

12. $I = P \times R \times T$
$= 3000 \times 7\% \times 1$
$= 3000 \times 0.07 \times 1$
$= 210$
He will need to pay \$210.

14. $3 \text{ months} = \dfrac{3}{12} = \dfrac{1}{4} \text{ year}$

$I = P \times R \times T$

$= 9200 \times 15\% \times \dfrac{1}{4}$

$= 9200 \times 0.15 \times \dfrac{1}{4}$

$= 1380 \times \dfrac{1}{4}$

$= 345$

She needs to pay \$345.

16. Rate $= \dfrac{63,000}{9,000,000} = 0.007 = 0.7\%$

Her commission rate was 0.7%.

18. Total sales $= \dfrac{42,000}{6\%} = \dfrac{42,000}{0.06} = 700,000$

The sales total was \$700,000.

20. Breathe $= 12\% \times 4.58 = 0.12 \times 4.58 = 0.5496$
You breathe about 0.55 liter.

22. Red hair $= 11\%$ of $5,600,000$
$= 0.11 \times 5,600,000$
$= 616,000$
616,000 people have red hair.

24. Decrease $= 5955 - 5877 = 78$

Percent $= \dfrac{78}{5955} \approx 0.01309 = 1.31\%$

1.31% is the percent of decrease.

26. Increase $= 29 - 20 = 9$

$\dfrac{p}{100} = \dfrac{9}{20}$

$20p = 9 \times 100$

$\dfrac{20p}{20} = \dfrac{900}{20}$

$p = 45$

45% is the percent of increase.

28. a. $I = P \times R \times T$
$= 1258 \times 2\% \times 1$
$= 1258 \times 0.02 \times 1$
$= 25.16$
\$25.16 is the interest Nikki paid.

b. Cost to pay off $= \$1258 + 25.16$
$= \$1283.16.$

30. a. Sales tax $= 7\% \times 12,600$
$= 0.07 \times 12,600$
$= 882$
The sales tax is \$882.

b. Final price $= \$12,600 + \$882.$

32. Interest $= 12\% \times 1600 = 0.12 \times 1600 = 192$
Payoff $= 1600 + 192 = 1792$
The total amount they need to pay off is \$1792.

34. a. Down payment $= 11\% \times 188,000$
$= 0.11 \times 188,000$
$= 20,680$
Their down payment was \$20,680.

b. Mortgage $= 188,000 - 20,680 = 167,320$
Their mortgage was \$167,320.

36. $\dfrac{p}{100} = \dfrac{917}{960}$

$960p = 100 \times 917$

$\dfrac{960p}{960} = \dfrac{91,700}{960}$

$p \approx 95.5$

95.5% is used to pay off the interest charge.

38. Discount $= 29\% \times 1249.95$
$= 0.29 \times 1249.95$
≈ 362.49
The discount was \$362.49.
Sale price $= \$1249.95 - \$362.49 = \$887.46.$

Cumulative Review

39. $3(12-6)-4(12\div3)=3(6)-4(4)=18-16=2$

40. $\begin{aligned}7+4^3\times2-15&=7+64\times2-15\\&=7+128-15\\&=135-15\\&=120\end{aligned}$

41. $\begin{aligned}\left(\frac{5}{2}\right)\left(\frac{1}{3}\right)-\left(\frac{2}{3}-\frac{1}{3}\right)^2&=\left(\frac{5}{2}\right)\left(\frac{1}{3}\right)-\left(\frac{1}{3}\right)^2\\&=\left(\frac{5}{2}\right)\left(\frac{1}{3}\right)-\frac{1}{9}\\&=\frac{5}{6}-\frac{1}{9}\\&=\frac{15}{18}-\frac{2}{18}\\&=\frac{13}{18}\end{aligned}$

42. $\begin{aligned}(6.8-6.6)^2+2(1.8)&=(0.2)^2+2(1.8)\\&=0.04+3.6\\&=3.64\end{aligned}$

Classroom Quiz 5.5

1. $n=3\%\times316{,}200$
$n=0.03\times316{,}200$
$n=9486$
Her commission is \$9486.

2. Decrease $=400-225=175$
Percentage $=\dfrac{175}{400}=0.4375$
The percent of decrease is 43.75%.

3. Six months $=\dfrac{6}{12}=\dfrac{1}{2}$ year
$\begin{aligned}I&=P\times R\times T\\&=8500\times12\%\times\frac{1}{2}\\&=8500\times0.12\times\frac{1}{2}\\&=1020\times\frac{1}{2}\\&=510\end{aligned}$
The simple interest is \$510.

Putting Your Skills to Work

1. $\begin{aligned}1000+36\times669.28&=1000+24{,}094.08\\&=25{,}094.08\end{aligned}$
Louvy would pay \$25,094.08 over the entire length of the loan.

2. $\begin{aligned}1000+36\times388.06&=1000+13{,}970.16\\&=14{,}970.16\end{aligned}$
Louvy would pay \$14,970.16 over the entire length of the lease.

3. $14{,}970.16+11{,}000.00=25{,}970.16$
This would bring the total cost up to \$25,970.16.

4. Answers will vary.

5. Answers will vary.

6. Answers will vary.

Chapter 5 Review Problems

1. $0.62=62\%$

2. $0.43=43\%$

3. $0.372=37.2\%$

4. $0.529=52.9\%$

5. $2.2=220\%$

6. $1.8=180\%$

7. $2.52=252\%$

8. $4.37=437\%$

9. $1.036=103.6\%$

10. $1.052=105.2\%$

11. $0.006=0.6\%$

12. $0.002=0.2\%$

13. $\dfrac{62.5}{100}=62.5\%$

14. $\dfrac{37.5}{100}=37.5\%$

15. $\dfrac{4\frac{1}{12}}{100}=4\frac{1}{12}\%$

16. $\dfrac{3\frac{5}{12}}{100} = 3\dfrac{5}{12}\%$

17. $\dfrac{317}{100} = 317\%$

18. $\dfrac{225}{100} = 225\%$

19. $\dfrac{19}{25} = 0.76 = 76\%$

20. $\dfrac{13}{25} = 0.52 = 52\%$

21. $\dfrac{11}{20} = 0.55 = 55\%$

22. $\dfrac{9}{40} = 0.225 = 22.5\%$

23. $\dfrac{7}{12} \approx 0.5833 = 58.33\%$

24. $\dfrac{14}{15} \approx 0.9333 = 93.33\%$

25. $2\dfrac{1}{4} = 2.25 = 225\%$

26. $3\dfrac{3}{4} = 3.75 = 375\%$

27. $2\dfrac{7}{9} \approx 2.7778 = 277.78\%$

28. $5\dfrac{5}{9} \approx 5.5556 = 555.56\%$

29. $\dfrac{152}{80} = 1.9 = 190\%$

30. $\dfrac{200}{80} = 2.5 = 250\%$

31. $\dfrac{3}{800} = 0.00375 \approx 0.38\%$

32. $\dfrac{5}{800} = 0.00625 \approx 0.63\%$

33. $32\% = 0.32$

34. $68\% = 0.68$

35. $15.75\% = 0.1575$

36. $12.35\% = 0.1235$

37. $236\% = 2.36$

38. $177\% = 1.77$

39. $32\dfrac{1}{8} = 32.125\% = 0.32125$

40. $26\dfrac{3}{8}\% = 26.375\% = 0.26375$

41. $72\% = \dfrac{72}{100} = \dfrac{72 \div 4}{100 \div 4} = \dfrac{18}{25}$

42. $92\% = \dfrac{92}{100} = \dfrac{92 \div 4}{100 \div 4} = \dfrac{23}{25}$

43. $175\% = \dfrac{175}{100} = \dfrac{175 \div 25}{100 \div 25} = \dfrac{7}{4}$

44. $260\% = \dfrac{260}{100} = \dfrac{260 \div 20}{100 \div 20} = \dfrac{13}{5}$

45. $16.4\% = 0.164 = \dfrac{164}{1000} = \dfrac{164 \div 4}{1000 \div 4} = \dfrac{41}{250}$

46. $30.5\% = 0.305 = \dfrac{305}{1000} = \dfrac{305 \div 5}{1000 \div 5} = \dfrac{61}{200}$

47. $13\dfrac{1}{4}\% = \dfrac{31\frac{1}{4}}{100}$
$$= 31\dfrac{1}{4} \div 100$$
$$= \dfrac{125}{4} \times \dfrac{1}{100}$$
$$= \dfrac{125}{400}$$
$$= \dfrac{125 \div 25}{400 \div 25}$$
$$= \dfrac{5}{16}$$

48. $43\frac{3}{4}\% = \dfrac{43\frac{3}{4}}{100}$

$\phantom{43\frac{3}{4}\%} = 43\frac{3}{4} \div 100$

$\phantom{43\frac{3}{4}\%} = \dfrac{175}{4} \times \dfrac{1}{100}$

$\phantom{43\frac{3}{4}\%} = \dfrac{175}{400}$

$\phantom{43\frac{3}{4}\%} = \dfrac{175 \div 25}{400 \div 25}$

$\phantom{43\frac{3}{4}\%} = \dfrac{7}{16}$

49. $0.08\% = 0.0008 = \dfrac{8}{10,000} = \dfrac{8 \div 8}{10,000 \div 8} = \dfrac{1}{1250}$

50. $0.04\% = 0.0004 = \dfrac{4}{10,000} = \dfrac{4 \div 4}{10,000 \div 4} = \dfrac{1}{2500}$

51. $5)\overline{\begin{array}{l}0.6\\3.0\end{array}}$

$\underline{3\,0}$

0

$0.6 = 60\%$

$\dfrac{3}{5}$; 0.6; 60%

52. $\dfrac{7}{10} = 0.7 = 70\%$

$\dfrac{7}{10}$; 0.7; 70%

53. $37.5\% = 0.375 = \dfrac{375}{1000} = \dfrac{3}{8}$

$\dfrac{3}{8}$; 0.375; 37.5%

54. $56.25\% = 0.5625 = \dfrac{5625}{10,000} = \dfrac{9}{16}$

$\dfrac{9}{16}$; 0.5625; 56.25%

55. $0.008 = 0.8\%$

$0.008 = \dfrac{8}{1000} = \dfrac{1}{125}$

$\dfrac{1}{125}$; 0.008; 0.8%

56. $0.45 = 45\%$

$0.45 = \dfrac{45}{100} = \dfrac{9}{20}$

$\dfrac{9}{20}$; 0.45; 45%

57. What is 20% of 85?

$n = 20\% \times 85$

$n = 0.2 \times 85$

$n = 17$

58. What is 25% of 92?

$n = 25\% \times 92$

$n = 0.25 \times 92$

$n = 23$

59. 15 is 25% of what number?

$25\% \times n = 15$

$0.25n = 15$

$\dfrac{0.25n}{0.25} = \dfrac{15}{0.25}$

$n = 60$

60. 30 is 75% of what number?

$75\% \times n = 30$

$0.75n = 30$

$\dfrac{0.75n}{0.75} = \dfrac{30}{0.75}$

$n = 40$

61. 50 is what percent of 130?

$50 = n \times 130$

$\dfrac{50}{130} = \dfrac{n \times 130}{130}$

$0.3846 \approx n$

38.46%

62. 70 is what percent of 180?

$70 = n \times 180$

$\dfrac{70}{180} = \dfrac{n \times 180}{180}$

$0.3889 \approx n$

38.89%

63. Find 162% of 60.

$n = 162\% \times 60$

$n = 162 \times 60$

$n = 97.2$

64. Find 124% of 80.

$n = 124\% \times 80$

$n = 1.24 \times 80$

$n = 99.2$

65. 92% of what number is 147.2?

$$92\% \times n = 147.2$$
$$0.92n = 147.2$$
$$\frac{0.92n}{0.92} = \frac{147.2}{0.92}$$
$$n = 160$$

66. 68% of what number is 95.2?

$$68\% \times n = 95.2$$
$$0.68n = 95.2$$
$$\frac{0.68n}{0.68} = \frac{95.2}{0.68}$$
$$n = 140$$

67. What percent of 70 is 14?

$$n \times 70 = 14$$
$$\frac{n \times 70}{70} = \frac{14}{70}$$
$$n = 0.2$$
20%

68. What percent of 60 is 6?

$$n \times 60 = 6$$
$$\frac{n \times 60}{60} = \frac{6}{60}$$
$$n = 0.1$$
10%

69. $n = 35\% \times 140$
$n = 0.35 \times 140$
$n = 49$
49 students are sophomores.

70. $n = 64\% \times 150$
$n = 0.64 \times 150$
$n = 96$
96 trucks had four-wheel drive.

71. $n \times 61\% = 6832$
$$0.61n = 6832$$
$$\frac{0.61n}{0.61} = \frac{6832}{0.61}$$
$$n = 11,200$$
Two years ago, it was worth $11,200.

72. $n \times 12\% = 9624$
$$0.12n = 9624$$
$$\frac{0.12n}{0.12} = \frac{9624}{0.12}$$
$$n = 80,200$$
The total budget was $80,200.

73. Days = 29 + 31 + 30 = 90
Rain days = 20 + 18 + 16 = 54
$$90 \times n = 54$$
$$\frac{90 \times n}{90} = \frac{54}{90}$$
$$n = 0.6$$
It rained 60% of the time.

74. $600 \times n = 45$
$$\frac{600 \times n}{600} = \frac{45}{600}$$
$$n = 0.075$$
7.5% of the applicants obtained a job.

75. What is 5% of 3670?
$n = 5\% \times 3670$
$n = 0.05 \times 3670$
$n = 183.5$
He paid $183.50.

76. What is 6% of 12,600?
$n = 6\% \times 12,600$
$n = 0.06 \times 12,600$
$n = 756$
They paid $756.

77. $38\% \times n = 684$
$$0.38n = 684$$
$$\frac{0.38n}{0.38} = \frac{684}{0.38}$$
$$n = 1800$$
Their monthly income is $1800.

78. Rate $= \dfrac{26,000}{650,500} = 0.04 = 4\%$
Her commission rate was 4%.

79. Rate $= \dfrac{5010}{83,500} = 0.06 = 6\%$
His commission rate was 6%.

80. Commission $= 7.5\% \times 16,000$
$= 0.075 \times 16,000$
$= 1200$
She earned $1200.

81. a. Discount $= 25\% \times \$1450$
$= 0.25 \times 1450$
$= 362.5$
$362.50 was the discount.

b. Total pay $= \$1450 - \$362.50 = 1087.5$
$1087.50 was the price for the set.

82. a. Rebate = 12% × 2125 = 0.12 × 2125 = 255
The rebate was $255.

b. Computer costs = $2125 − $255 = $1870.

83. Increase = 39,109 − 33,625 = 5484

$$\frac{p}{100} = \frac{5484}{33,625}$$

$$33,625p = 100 \times 5484$$

$$\frac{33,625p}{33,625} = \frac{548,400}{33,625}$$

$$p \approx 16.309$$

16.31% was the percent of increase.

84. Increase = $12,796 − $9258 = $3538

$$\frac{p}{100} = \frac{3538}{9258}$$

$$9258p = 100 \times 3538$$

$$\frac{9258p}{9258} = \frac{353,800}{9258}$$

$$p \approx 38.215$$

38.22% was the percent of increase.

85. a. Discount = 14% of 24,000
= 0.14 × 24,000
= $3360
The discount is $3360.

b. Cost = 24,000 − 3360 = $20,640.

86. $I = PRT$

a. $I = 6000(0.11)(0.5) = \$330$
In six months, she will earn $330.

b. $I = 6000(0.11)(2) = \$1320$
In two years, she will earn $1320.

87. a. $3 \text{ months} = \frac{3}{12} = \frac{1}{4} \text{ year}$

$$I = P \times R \times T$$

$$= 3000 \times 8\% \times \frac{1}{4}$$

$$= 3000 \times 0.08 \times \frac{1}{4}$$

$$= 240 \times \frac{1}{4}$$

$$= 60$$

In three months $60 will be due.

b. $I = P \times R \times T$
$= 3000 \times 8\% \times 3$
$= 3000 \times 0.08 \times 3$
$= 240 \times 3$
$= 720$
In three years $720 will be due.

How Am I Doing? Chapter 5 Test

1. 0.57 = 57%

2. 0.01 = 1%

3. 0.008 = 0.8%

4. 12.8 = 1280%

5. 3.56 = 356%

6. $\frac{71}{100} = 71\%$

7. $\frac{1.8}{100} = 1.8\%$

8. $\frac{3\frac{1}{7}}{100} = 3\frac{1}{7}\%$

9.
$$\begin{array}{r} 0.475 \\ 40\overline{)19.000} \\ \underline{16\ 0} \\ 3\ 00 \\ \underline{2\ 80} \\ 200 \\ \underline{200} \\ 0 \end{array}$$

$$\frac{19}{40} = 0.475 = 47.5\%$$

10.
$$\begin{array}{r} 0.75 \\ 36\overline{)27.00} \\ \underline{25\ 2} \\ 1\ 80 \\ \underline{1\ 80} \\ 0 \end{array}$$

$$\frac{27}{36} = 75\%$$

11.
$$75\overline{)225}$$
$$\underline{225}$$
$$0$$

$$\frac{225}{75} = 3 = 300\%$$

12.
$$4\overline{)3.00}$$ (quotient 0.75)
$$\underline{2\ 8}$$
$$20$$
$$\underline{20}$$
$$0$$

$$1\frac{3}{4} = 1.75 = 175\%$$

13. $0.0825 = 8.25\%$

14. $3.024 = 302.4\%$

15. $152\% = \dfrac{152}{100} = \dfrac{38}{25} = 1\dfrac{13}{25}$

16. $7\dfrac{3}{4}\% = \dfrac{7\frac{3}{4}}{100} = 7\dfrac{3}{4} \div 100 = \dfrac{31}{4} \times \dfrac{1}{100} = \dfrac{31}{400}$

17. $n = 40\% \times 50$
$n = 0.4 \times 50$
$n = 20$

18. $33.8 = 26\% \times n$
$33.8 = 0.26n$
$\dfrac{33.8}{0.26} = \dfrac{0.26n}{0.26}$
$130 = n$

19. $n \times 72 = 40$
$\dfrac{n \times 72}{72} = \dfrac{40}{72}$
$n \approx 0.5556 = 55.56\%$

20. $n = 0.8\% \times 25{,}000$
$n = 0.008 \times 25{,}000$
$n = 200$

21. $16\% \times n = 800$
$0.16n = 800$
$\dfrac{0.16n}{0.16} = \dfrac{800}{0.16}$
$n = 5000$

22. $92 = n \times 200$
$\dfrac{92}{200} = \dfrac{n \times 200}{200}$
$n = 0.46$
$n = 46\%$

23. $132\% \times 530 = n$
$1.32 \times 530 = n$
$699.6 = n$

24. $p \times 75 = 15$
$\dfrac{75p}{75} = \dfrac{15}{75}$
$p = 0.2 = 20\%$

25. $n = 4\% \times 152{,}300$
$n = 0.04 \times 152{,}300$
$n = 6092$
6092 is her commission.

26. a. $33\% \times 457 = n$
$0.33 \times 457 = n$
$150.81 = n$
150.81 is the discount.

    b. $457 - 150.81 = 306.19$
306.19 is the amount they paid.

27. $75 = n \times 84$
$\dfrac{75}{84} = \dfrac{n \times 84}{84}$
$n \approx 0.8929$
89.29% of the parts were not defective.

28. Increase $= 228 - 185 = 43$
$\dfrac{p}{100} = \dfrac{43}{185}$
$185p = 100 \times 43$
$\dfrac{185p}{185} = \dfrac{4300}{185}$
$p \approx 23.24$
23.24% is the percent of increase.

29. $5160 = 43\% \times n$
$5160 = 0.43n$
$\dfrac{5160}{0.43} = \dfrac{0.43n}{0.43}$
$12{,}000 = n$
There are $12{,}000$ registered voters.

30. a. $I = P \times R \times T = 3000 \times 0.16 \times \dfrac{6}{12} = 240$

In six months she paid $240.

b. $I = P \times R \times T = 3000 \times 0.16 \times 2 = 960$

In two years she paid $960.

Cumulative Test for Chapters 1–5

1.
$$\begin{array}{r} 38 \\ 196 \\ + \ 2007 \\ \hline 2241 \end{array}$$

2.
$$\begin{array}{r} 23,007 \\ - \ 14,563 \\ \hline 8,444 \end{array}$$

3.
$$\begin{array}{r} 126 \\ \times \ 42 \\ \hline 252 \\ 504 \ \ \\ \hline 5292 \end{array}$$

4.
$$\begin{array}{r} 89 \\ 36 \overline{)3204} \\ \underline{288} \\ 324 \\ \underline{324} \\ 0 \end{array}$$

5.

$\begin{array}{r} 2\dfrac{1}{4} \\ + \ 3\dfrac{1}{3} \\ \hline \end{array}$ $\begin{array}{r} 2\dfrac{3}{12} \\ + \ 3\dfrac{4}{12} \\ \hline 5\dfrac{7}{12} \ \text{or} \ \dfrac{67}{12} \end{array}$

6.

$\begin{array}{r} 5\dfrac{2}{5} \\ - \ 2\dfrac{7}{10} \\ \hline \end{array}$ $\begin{array}{r} 5\dfrac{4}{10} \\ - \ 2\dfrac{7}{10} \\ \hline \end{array}$ $\begin{array}{r} 4\dfrac{14}{10} \\ - \ 2\dfrac{7}{10} \\ \hline 2\dfrac{7}{10} \end{array}$

7. $3\dfrac{1}{8} \times \dfrac{12}{5} = \dfrac{25}{8} \times \dfrac{12}{5} = \dfrac{5 \times 3}{2} = \dfrac{15}{2} \text{ or } 7\dfrac{1}{2}$

8. $\dfrac{21}{4} \div 1\dfrac{3}{4} = \dfrac{21}{4} \div \dfrac{7}{4} = \dfrac{21}{4} \times \dfrac{4}{7} = 3$

9. 77.18$\underline{3}$2 rounds to 77.183

10.
$$\begin{array}{r} 5.600 \\ 3.210 \\ 18.300 \\ + \ 7.008 \\ \hline 34.118 \end{array}$$

11.
$$\begin{array}{r} 3.16 \\ \times \ 2.8 \\ \hline 2\,528 \\ 6\,32 \ \ \\ \hline 8.848 \end{array}$$

12.
$$\begin{array}{r} 0.368 \\ 1.4_\wedge \overline{)0.5_\wedge 152} \\ \underline{4\,2} \ \ \\ 95 \\ \underline{84} \\ 112 \\ \underline{112} \\ 0 \end{array}$$

13. $\dfrac{36 \text{ tiles}}{9 \text{ square feet}} = \dfrac{9 \times 4}{9} = 4 \text{ tiles/square foot}$

14.
$$\dfrac{20}{25} \overset{?}{=} \dfrac{300}{375}$$
$$20 \times 375 \overset{?}{=} 25 \times 300$$
$$7500 = 7500 \quad \text{True}$$
Yes, this is a proportion.

15.
$$\dfrac{8}{2.5} = \dfrac{n}{7.5}$$
$$8 \times 75 = 2.5 \times n$$
$$\dfrac{60}{2.5} = \dfrac{2.5 \times n}{2.5}$$
$$n = 24$$

16.
$$\dfrac{3 \text{ faculty}}{19 \text{ students}} = \dfrac{n \text{ faculty}}{4263 \text{ students}}$$
$$3 \times 4263 = 19 \times n$$
$$12,789 = 19 \times n$$
$$\dfrac{12,789}{19} = \dfrac{19 \times n}{19}$$
$$673 \approx n$$
There are 673 faculty.

17. $0.355 = 35.5\%$

18. $\dfrac{46.8}{100} = 46.8\%$

19. $1.98 = 198\%$

20.
$$\begin{array}{r} 0.0375 \\ 80\overline{)3.0000} \\ \underline{2\ 40} \\ 600 \\ \underline{560} \\ 400 \\ \underline{400} \\ 0 \end{array}$$

$\dfrac{3}{80} = 0.0375 = 3.75\%$

21. $243\% = 2.43$

22.
$$\begin{array}{r} 0.75 \\ 4\overline{)3.00} \\ \underline{2\ 8} \\ 20 \\ \underline{20} \\ 0 \end{array}$$

$6\dfrac{3}{4}\% = 6.75\% = 0.0675$

23. What percent of 214 is 38?
$$n \times 214 = 38$$
$$\dfrac{n \times 214}{214} = \dfrac{38}{214}$$
$$n \approx 0.1776$$
$$n = 17.76\%$$

24. $n = 1.7\% \times 6740$
$n = 0.017 \times 6740$
$n = 114.58$

25. 40 is 25% of what number?
$$40 = 25\% \times n$$
$$40 = 0.25 \times n$$
$$\dfrac{40}{0.25} = \dfrac{0.25 \times n}{0.25}$$
$$n = 160$$

26. 95% of 200 is what number?
$n = 95\% \times 200$
$n = 0.95 \times 200$
$n = 190$

27. Decrease $= 20\% \times 680 = 0.2 \times 680 = 136$
Price $= 680 - 136 = 544$
She will pay \$544.

28.
$$58 = 25\% \times n$$
$$58 = 0.25n$$
$$\dfrac{58}{0.25} = \dfrac{0.25n}{0.25}$$
$$n = 232$$
232 vehicles sold last year.

29. $8.86 - 7.96 = 0.9$
$$7.96 \times n = 0.9$$
$$\dfrac{7.96 \times n}{7.96} = \dfrac{0.9}{7.96}$$
$$n \approx 0.1131$$
This was an 11.31% increase.

30. $I = P \times R \times T = 3400 \times 0.09 \times 2 = 612$
\$612 is the interest he paid.

Chapter 6

6.1 Exercises

2. We know that each day has 24 hours. Each hour has 60 minutes. Therefore, we know that each day has $24 \times 60 = 1440$ minutes. The unit fraction we want is $\dfrac{1440 \text{ minutes}}{1 \text{ day}}$. So we multiply $27 \text{ days} \times \dfrac{1440 \text{ minutes}}{1 \text{ day}}$. The day units divide out. We obtain 38,800 minutes. Thus, 27 days = 38,880 minutes.

4. 5280 feet = 1 mile

6. 1 pound = 16 ounces

8. 2 cups = 1 pint

10. 60 minutes = 1 hour

12. $63 \text{ feet} \times \dfrac{1 \text{ yard}}{3 \text{ feet}} = 21 \text{ yards}$

14. $180 \text{ inches} \times \dfrac{1 \text{ foot}}{12 \text{ inches}} = 15 \text{ feet}$

16. $11 \text{ feet} \times \dfrac{12 \text{ inches}}{1 \text{ foot}} = 132 \text{ inches}$

18. $5 \text{ miles} \times \dfrac{5280 \text{ feet}}{\text{mile}} = 26,400 \text{ feet}$

20. $21,120 \text{ feet} \times \dfrac{1 \text{ mile}}{5280 \text{ feet}} = 4 \text{ miles}$

22. $15 \text{ gallons} \times \dfrac{4 \text{ quarts}}{1 \text{ gallon}} = 60 \text{ quarts}$

24. $24 \text{ pints} \times \dfrac{1 \text{ quart}}{2 \text{ pints}} = 12 \text{ quarts}$

26. $40 \text{ fluid ounces} \times \dfrac{1 \text{ cup}}{8 \text{ fluid ounces}} = 5 \text{ cups}$

28. $6\dfrac{1}{2} \text{ gallons} \times \dfrac{8 \text{ pints}}{1 \text{ gallon}} = 52 \text{ pints}$

30. $56 \text{ days} \times \dfrac{1 \text{ week}}{7 \text{ days}} = 8 \text{ weeks}$

32. $1500 \text{ seconds} \times \dfrac{1 \text{ minute}}{60 \text{ seconds}} = 25 \text{ minutes}$

34. $12 \text{ ounces} \times \dfrac{1 \text{ pound}}{16 \text{ ounces}} = 0.75 \text{ pound}$

36. $4\dfrac{3}{4} \text{ tons} = \dfrac{19}{4} \text{ tons}$

$\dfrac{19}{4} \text{ tons} \times \dfrac{2000 \text{ pounds}}{\text{ton}} = 9500 \text{ pounds}$

38. $23 \text{ pints} \times \dfrac{2 \text{ cups}}{1 \text{ pint}} = 46 \text{ cups}$

40. $4.25 \text{ pounds} \times \dfrac{16 \text{ ounces}}{1 \text{ pound}} = 68 \text{ ounces}$

42. $90 \text{ inches} \times \dfrac{1 \text{ foot}}{12 \text{ inches}} = 7.5 \text{ feet}$

44. $2 \text{ hours} \times \dfrac{3600 \text{ seconds}}{1 \text{ hour}} = 7200 \text{ seconds}$

$4 \text{ minutes} \times \dfrac{60 \text{ seconds}}{1 \text{ minute}} = 240 \text{ seconds}$

$$\begin{array}{r} 7200 \\ 240 \\ +\ \ 55 \\ \hline 7495 \end{array}$$

A time of 2:04:55 is equivalent to 7495 seconds.

46. $36\dfrac{1}{4} \text{ feet} \times \dfrac{12 \text{ inches}}{1 \text{ foot}} = \dfrac{145}{4} \times \dfrac{12}{1} \text{ inches}$
$= 435 \text{ inches}$

She threw a distance of 435 inches.

48. $40 \text{ ounces} \times \dfrac{1 \text{ pound}}{16 \text{ ounces}} \times \dfrac{\$6.00}{1 \text{ pound}} = \$15.00$

He pays $15.00.

50. a. $7 \text{ yards} \times \dfrac{3 \text{ feet}}{1 \text{ yard}} = 21 \text{ feet}$

So, 7 yards 2 feet = 21 + 2 = 23 feet

$12 \text{ yards} \times \dfrac{3 \text{ feet}}{1 \text{ yard}} = 35 \text{ feet}$

So, 12 yards 1 foot = 36 + 1 = 37 feet

perimeter $= 2(23) + 2(27)$

$= 46 + 74$

$= 120 \text{ feet}$

The perimeter is 120 feet.

b. cost $= \$1.75 \times 120 = \$210$

It will cost $210.

52. $7 \text{ years} \times \dfrac{365 \text{ days}}{1 \text{ year}} \times \dfrac{24 \text{ hours}}{1 \text{ day}} = 61,320 \text{ hours}$

It grew for 61,320 hours.

54. 618 rounds to 600.

$600 \text{ days} \times \dfrac{1 \text{ month}}{30 \text{ days}} \approx 20 \text{ months}$

The plant is about 20 months old.

56. 3170 rounds to 3000.

640 rounds to 600.

$\dfrac{3000 \text{ miles}}{600 \text{ miles/hour}} \approx 5 \text{ hours}$

$318 \text{ minutes} \times \dfrac{1 \text{ hour}}{60 \text{ minutes}} = 5{:}18$

Our estimate was very close. It was only 18 minutes less than the pilot's prediction.

Cumulative Review

57. $560 - 515 = \$45$ per month

$\$45 \times 12 \times 20 = \$10,800$

They will save a total of $10,800.

58. part used $= 3(123) + 2(69) = 369 + 138 = 507$ MB

part not used $= 650 - 507 = 143$ MB

percent $= \dfrac{143}{650} = 0.22 = 22\%$

22% of his disk is still free for storage.

59. $\dfrac{n}{115} = \dfrac{7}{5}$

$n \times 5 = 7 \times 115$

$\dfrac{n \times 5}{5} = \dfrac{805}{5}$

$n = 161$ miles

They are likely to cover 161 miles.

60. $\dfrac{n}{1300} = \dfrac{12}{150}$

$n \times 150 = 1300 \times 12$

$\dfrac{n \times 150}{150} = \dfrac{15,600}{150}$

$n = 104$

104 students dropped the course during the first two weeks of the semester.

Classroom Quiz 6.1

1. $27 \text{ feet} \times \dfrac{12 \text{ inches}}{1 \text{ foot}} = 324 \text{ inches}$

2. $35 \text{ gallons} \times \dfrac{4 \text{ quarts}}{1 \text{ gallon}} = 140 \text{ quarts}$

3. $250 \text{ seconds} \times \dfrac{1 \text{ minute}}{60 \text{ seconds}} \approx 4.17 \text{ minutes}$

6.2 Exercises

2. centi-

4. milli-

6. deka-

8. 79 centimeters = 790 millimeters

10. 8.3 kilometers = 8300 meters

12. 10,600 millimeters = 10.6 meters

14. 9.14 centimeters = 0.0914 meters

16. 7 kilometers = 700,000 centimeters

18. 840 millimeters = 0.00084 kilometer

20. 6300 mm = 630 cm = 6.3 m

22. 6.8 km = 6800 m = 680,000 cm

24. (b), 20 cm would be the most reasonable measurement.

26. (a), 1.4 km would be the most reasonable measurement.

28. (c), 8 mm would be the most reasonable measurement.

30. (b), 32 cm would be the most reasonable measurement.

32. (c), 320 m would be the most reasonable measurement.

34. 270 decimeters = 27 meters

36. 530 dekameters = 5300 meters

38. 435 hectometers = 43.5 kilometers

40. 845 m + 5.79 km + 701 m
= 845 m + 5790 m + 701 m
= 7336 m

42. 305 mm + 45.4 cm + 318 cm
= 30.5 cm + 45.4 cm + 318 cm
= 393.9 cm

44. 8 dm + 21 mm + 38 cm
= 80 cm + 2.1 cm + 38 cm
= 120.1 cm

46. 2.2 cm + 3.42 mm + 2.7 cm
= 2.2 cm + 0.342 cm + 2.7 cm
= 5.242 cm or 52.42 mm
The wall is 5.242 cm or 52.42 mm thick.

48. 82 m + 471 cm + 0.32 km
= 82 m + 4.71 m + 320 m
= 406.71 m

50. 56.3 centimeters = 0.563 meter

52. True

54. True

56. True

58. False; a mile is longer than a mile.

60. a. 94,380,000 centimeters = 943,800 meters
The run is 943,800 meters.

  b. 94,380,000 centimeters = 943.8 kilometers
The run is 943.8 kilometers.

62. a. 335 meters = 0.335 kilometer
The height of the dam is 0.335 km.

  b. 335 meters = 33,500 centimeters
The height of the dam is 33,500 cm.

64.   278,000
        $- \underline{211,000}$
          67,000 m
The subway system in Seoul is 67,000 meters longer than that of Paris.

66. 371,000 m = 0.371 megameter

68. 415 km × 0.62 = 257.3 miles
London's subway system is about 257.3 miles long.

Cumulative Review

70. 57% of what number is 2850?
$$\frac{57}{100} = \frac{2850}{n}$$
$$57 \times n = 100 \times 2850$$
$$\frac{57 \times n}{57} = \frac{285,000}{57}$$
$$n = 5000$$

71. $n = 0.03\% \times 5900$
$n = 0.0003 \times 5900$
$n = 1.77$

72. 13 is 25% of what number?
$$13 = 25\% \times n$$
$$13 = 0.25n$$
$$\frac{13}{0.25} = \frac{0.25n}{0.25}$$
$$52 = n$$

73. $n = 75\% \times 20$
$n = 0.75 \times 20$
$n = 15$

Classroom Quiz 6.2

1. 9.5 kilometers = 9500 meters

2. 5.23 centimeters = 0.0523 meter

3. 82 millimeters = 8.2 centimeters

6.3 Exercises

2. 1 mL

4. 1 kg

6. 1 L

8. 5 kL = 5000 L

10. 25 L = 25,000 mL

12. 31.5 mL = 0.0315 L

14. 368 L = 0.368 kL

16. 14.3 kL = 14,300,000 mL

18. 152 mL = 152 cm^3

20. 8835 mL = 0.008835 kL

22. 122 L = 122,000 mL = 122,000 cm^3

24. 2940 g = 2.94 kg

26. 13 mg = 0.013 g

28. 986 mg = 0.986 g

30. 14.6 kg = 14,600 g

32. 9500 kg = 9.5 t

34. 18 mL = 0.018 L = 0.000018 kL

36. 0.315 kL = 315 L = 315,000 cm^3

38. 0.098 kg = 98 kg = 98,000 mg

40. 7183 g = 7.183 kg = 0.007183 t

42. (c), 4 mL would be the most reasonable measurement.

44. (b), 0.49 kg would be the most reasonable measurement.

46. 152 L + 473 mL + 77.3 L
= 152 L + 0.473 L + 77.3 L
= 229.773 L or 229,773 mL

48. 2 kg + 42 mg + 120 g
= 2000 g + 0.042 g + 120 g
= 2120.042 g or 2,120,042 mg

50. False; 1 metric ton = 1,000,000 grams

52. False; small amounts of medicine are often measured in mL or cc.

54. True

56. True

58. $\dfrac{n}{56 \text{ kg}} = \dfrac{\$6.80}{4 \text{ kg}}$

$n = \dfrac{56 \text{ kg} \times \$6.80}{4 \text{ kg}}$

$n = \$95.20$

He will pay $95.20 for the sauce.

60. $1 \text{ kg} \times \dfrac{1000 \text{ g}}{1 \text{ kg}} \times \dfrac{\$21.06}{1 \text{ g}} = \$21,060$

The price for a kilogram would be $21,060.

62. 9,100,000,000
$\underline{-\ 6,200,000,000}$
   2,900,000,000 metric tons

It increased by 2,900,000,000 metric tons.

64. 15,600,000,000 metric tons
= 15,600,000,000,000 kilograms
It is estimated that emissions will be
15,600,000,000,000 kg.

66. Increase = 11.4 − 9.1 = 2.3 billion metric tons

Percent of increase $= \dfrac{2.3}{9.1} = \dfrac{p}{100}$

$= 9.1p \times 230$

$= \dfrac{9.1p}{9.1} \times \dfrac{230}{9.1}$

$p \approx 25.27\%$

17.2 × 25.27% ≈ 4.35 billion metric tons
17.2 + 4.35 = 21.55 billion metric tons
The emissions will be 21,550,000,000 metric tons.

Cumulative Review

67. percent $= \dfrac{14}{70} = 0.20 = 20\%$

68. n = 23% of 250
$n = 0.23 \times 250$
$n = 57.5$

69. n = 10% of 4800
$n = 0.1 \times 4800$
$n = 480$
Price = 4800 − 480 = 4320
$n = 105\% \times 4320$
$n = 1.05 \times 4320$
$n = 4536$
Marilyn paid $4536.

70. Commission $= 8\% \times 8960$
$$= 0.08 \times 8960$$
$$= 716.80$$
She earned a commission of $716.80.

Classroom Quiz 6.3

1. 52 liters = 0.052 kiloliters

2. 492.3 milligrams = 0.4923 gram

3. 35.8 grams = 35,800 milligrams

How Am I Doing? Sections 6.1–6.3

1. $48 \text{ feet} \times \dfrac{1 \text{ yard}}{3 \text{ feet}} = 16 \text{ yards}$

2. $24 \text{ quarts} \times \dfrac{1 \text{ gallon}}{4 \text{ quarts}} = 6 \text{ gallons}$

3. $3 \text{ miles} \times \dfrac{1760 \text{ yards}}{\text{miles}} = 5280 \text{ yards}$

4. $6400 \text{ pounds} \times \dfrac{1 \text{ ton}}{2000 \text{ pounds}} = 3.2 \text{ tons}$

5. $22 \text{ minutes} \times \dfrac{60 \text{ seconds}}{1 \text{ minute}} = 1320 \text{ seconds}$

6. $5 \text{ gallons} \times \dfrac{8 \text{ pints}}{1 \text{ gallon}} = 40 \text{ pints}$

7. 2 pounds = 32 ounces
$32 + 4 = 36$ ounces
$36 \text{ ounces} \times \dfrac{1 \text{ pound}}{16 \text{ ounces}} = 2.25 \text{ pounds}$
$2.25 \text{ pounds} \times \dfrac{\$6.80}{1 \text{ pound}} = \$15.30$
Isabel spent $15.30.

8. 6.75 km = 6750 m

9. 73.9 m = 7390 cm

10. 34 cm = 340 mm

11. 27 mm = 0.027 m

12. 5296 mm = 529.6 cm

13. 482 m = 0.482 km

14. 1.2 km = 1200 m
$$\begin{array}{r} 1200 \text{ m} \\ 192 \text{ m} \\ + \ \ 984 \text{ m} \\ \hline 2376 \text{ m} \end{array}$$

15. 305 cm + 82.5 m + 6150 mm
$= 3.05 \text{ m} + 82.5 \text{ m} + 6.150 \text{ m}$
$= 91.7 \text{ m}$

16. $\begin{array}{r} 78 \text{ cm} = 0.78 \text{ m} \\ + 128 \text{ cm} = 1.28 \text{ m} \\ \hline 2.06 \text{ m} \end{array}$
$$\begin{array}{r} 3.40 \\ -2.06 \\ \hline 1.34 \text{ m or } 134 \text{ cm} \end{array}$$
The length that has single insulation is 1.34 m or 134 cm.

17. 5.66 L = 5660 mL

18. 535 g = 0.535 kg

19. 56.3 kg = 0.0563 t

20. 4.8 kL = 4800 L

21. 568 mg = 0.568 g

22. $8.9 \text{ L} = 8900 \text{ cm}^3$

23. 75 kg = 75,000 g
$$\dfrac{x}{75,000} = \dfrac{7.75}{5000}$$
$$5000x = 7.75(75,000)$$
$$\dfrac{5000x}{5000} = \dfrac{581,250}{5000}$$
$$x = 116.25$$
The mission will spend $116.25.

24. 35 kg = 35,000 g
$$\dfrac{x}{35,000} = \dfrac{32.50}{5000}$$
$$5000x = 32.50(35,000)$$
$$\dfrac{5000x}{5000} = \dfrac{1,137,500}{5000}$$
$$x = 227.5$$
It will cost $227.50.

25. 200 mL = 0.2 L
$0.2 \text{ L} \times \dfrac{36}{1 \text{ L}} = \$7.20$
They paid $7.20.

26. $0.5 \text{ kg} = 500 \text{ g}$

$500 \text{ g} \times \dfrac{\$11.20}{1 \text{ g}} = \$5600$

He paid $5600.

6.4 Exercises

2. The liter is approximately the same volume as a quart. The liter is slightly larger.

4. The kilogram is approximately double a pound.

6. $11 \text{ ft} \times \dfrac{0.305 \text{ m}}{1 \text{ ft}} \approx 3.36 \text{ m}$

8. $13 \text{ in.} \times \dfrac{2.54 \text{ cm}}{1 \text{ in.}} \approx 33.02 \text{ cm}$

10. $115 \text{ m} \times \dfrac{1.09 \text{ yd}}{1 \text{ m}} \approx 125.35 \text{ yd}$

12. $42.5 \text{ yd} \times \dfrac{0.914 \text{ m}}{1 \text{ yd}} \approx 38.85 \text{ m}$

14. $68 \text{ mi} \times \dfrac{1.61 \text{ km}}{1 \text{ m}} \approx 109.48 \text{ km}$

16. $12.75 \text{ m} \times \dfrac{1.09 \text{ yd}}{1 \text{ m}} \approx 13.90 \text{ yd}$

18. $19.6 \text{ cm} \times \dfrac{0.394 \text{ in.}}{1 \text{ cm}} \approx 7.72 \text{ in.}$

20. $400 \text{ m} \times \dfrac{3.28 \text{ ft}}{1 \text{ m}} = 1312 \text{ ft}$

22. $16 \text{ km} \times \dfrac{0.62 \text{ mi}}{1 \text{ km}} = 9.92 \text{ mi}$

24. $63 \text{ gal} \times \dfrac{3.79 \text{ L}}{1 \text{ gal}} = 238.77 \text{ L}$

26. $28 \text{ qt} \times \dfrac{0.946 \text{ L}}{1 \text{ qt}} \approx 26.49 \text{ L}$

28. $15 \text{ L} \times \dfrac{0.264 \text{ gal}}{1 \text{ L}} \approx 3.96 \text{ gal}$

30. $6.5 \text{ L} \times \dfrac{1.06 \text{ qt}}{1 \text{ L}} = 6.89 \text{ qt}$

32. $45 \text{ kg} \times \dfrac{2.2 \text{ lb}}{1 \text{ kg}} \approx 99 \text{ lb}$

34. $155 \text{ lb} \times \dfrac{0.454 \text{ kg}}{1 \text{ lb}} = 70.37 \text{ kg}$

36. $34 \text{ oz} \times \dfrac{28.35 \text{ g}}{1 \text{ oz}} = 963.9 \text{ g}$

38. $188 \text{ kg} \times \dfrac{2.2 \text{ lb}}{\text{kg}} = 413.6 \text{ lb}$

40. $105 \text{ g} \times \dfrac{0.0353 \text{ oz}}{1 \text{ g}} \approx 3.71 \text{ oz}$

42. $14 \text{ ft} \times \dfrac{12 \text{ in.}}{1 \text{ ft}} \times \dfrac{2.54 \text{ cm}}{1 \text{ in.}} = 426.72 \text{ cm}$

44. $\dfrac{120 \text{ km}}{\text{hr}} \times \dfrac{0.62 \text{ mi}}{1 \text{ km}} = 74.4 \text{ mi/hr}$

46. $\dfrac{300 \text{ ft}}{1 \text{ sec}} \times \dfrac{3600 \text{ sec}}{1 \text{ hr}} \times \dfrac{1 \text{ mi}}{5280 \text{ ft}} \approx 205 \text{ mi/hr}$

48. $7 \text{ mm} \times \dfrac{1 \text{ cm}}{10 \text{ mm}} \times \dfrac{0.394 \text{ in.}}{1 \text{ cm}} \approx 0.28 \text{ in.}$

50. $F = 1.8 \times C + 32 = 1.8 \times 105 + 32 = 221$
$221°F$

52. $F = 1.8 \times C + 32 = 1.8 \times 21 + 32 = 69.8$
$69.8°F$

54. $C = \dfrac{5 \times F - 160}{9} = \dfrac{5 \times 131 - 160}{9} = \dfrac{495}{9} = 55$
$55°C$

56. $C = \dfrac{5 \times F - 160}{9} = \dfrac{5 \times 88 - 160}{9} = \dfrac{280}{9} \approx 31.11$
$31.11°C$

58. $75 + 83 + 78 = 236 \text{ km}$
$236 \text{ km} \times \dfrac{0.62 \text{ mi}}{1 \text{ km}} = 146.32 \text{ mi}$
John and Sandy traveled 146.32 miles.

60. $6 \text{ L} \times \dfrac{0.264 \text{ gal}}{1 \text{ L}} = 1.584 \text{ gal}$
No; six liters of water is only 1.584 gallons. This is less than 2 gallons.

62. $22.2 \text{ kg} \times \dfrac{2.2 \text{ lb}}{1 \text{ kg}} = 48.84 \text{ lb}$

The weight is 48.84 pounds.

64. $2.31 \text{ m} \times \dfrac{3.28 \text{ ft}}{1 \text{ m}} \approx 7.58 \text{ ft}$

Her height is 7.58 feet.

66. $F = 1.8 \times C + 32 = 1.8 \times 15 + 32 = 59$
$F = 1.8 \times C + 32 = 1.8 \times 30 + 32 = 86$
It should be stored between 59°F and 86°F.

68. $40,325 \text{ km} \times \dfrac{0.62 \text{ mi}}{1 \text{ km}} = 25,001.5 \text{ mi}$

This is equivalent to 25,001.5 miles.

70. $36 \times 1.09 \times 1.09 = 42.7716 \text{ sq yd}$

72. American: $7 \times 5 \times 24 = \$840$

French: $7 \text{ yd} \times \dfrac{0.914 \text{ m}}{1 \text{ yd}} = 6.398$

$5 \text{ yd} \times \dfrac{0.914 \text{ m}}{1 \text{ yd}} = 4.57$

$6.398 \times 4.57 \times 26 \approx \$760$

French carpet is cheaper by $840 - 760 = \$80$.

Cumulative Review

73. $3^4 \times 2 - 5 + 12 = 81 \times 2 - 5 + 12$
$ = 162 - 5 + 12$
$ = 169$

74. $96 + 24 \div 4 \times 3 = 96 + 6 \times 3 = 96 + 18 = 114$

75. $\dfrac{1}{2} \cdot \dfrac{3}{4} - \dfrac{1}{5}\left(\dfrac{1}{2}\right)^2 = \dfrac{1}{2} \cdot \dfrac{3}{4} - \dfrac{1}{5}\left(\dfrac{1}{4}\right)$

$\phantom{\dfrac{1}{2} \cdot \dfrac{3}{4} - \dfrac{1}{5}\left(\dfrac{1}{2}\right)^2} = \dfrac{3}{8} - \dfrac{1}{20}$

$\phantom{\dfrac{1}{2} \cdot \dfrac{3}{4} - \dfrac{1}{5}\left(\dfrac{1}{2}\right)^2} = \dfrac{15}{40} - \dfrac{2}{40}$

$\phantom{\dfrac{1}{2} \cdot \dfrac{3}{4} - \dfrac{1}{5}\left(\dfrac{1}{2}\right)^2} = \dfrac{13}{40}$

76. $\dfrac{5}{6} - \dfrac{1}{2}\left(\dfrac{5}{6} - \dfrac{1}{3}\right) = \dfrac{5}{6} - \dfrac{1}{2}\left(\dfrac{5}{6} - \dfrac{2}{6}\right)$

$\phantom{\dfrac{5}{6} - \dfrac{1}{2}\left(\dfrac{5}{6} - \dfrac{1}{3}\right)} = \dfrac{5}{6} - \dfrac{1}{2}\left(\dfrac{3}{6}\right)$

$\phantom{\dfrac{5}{6} - \dfrac{1}{2}\left(\dfrac{5}{6} - \dfrac{1}{3}\right)} = \dfrac{5}{6} - \dfrac{3}{12}$

$\phantom{\dfrac{5}{6} - \dfrac{1}{2}\left(\dfrac{5}{6} - \dfrac{1}{3}\right)} = \dfrac{10}{12} - \dfrac{3}{12}$

$\phantom{\dfrac{5}{6} - \dfrac{1}{2}\left(\dfrac{5}{6} - \dfrac{1}{3}\right)} = \dfrac{7}{12}$

Classroom Quiz 6.4

1. $38 \text{ mi} \times \dfrac{0.62 \text{ mi}}{1 \text{ km}} = 23.56 \text{ miles}$

2. $4.25 \text{ yd} \times \dfrac{0.914 \text{ m}}{14 \text{ yd}} = 3.88 \text{ meters}$

3. $14 \text{ gal} \times \dfrac{3.79 \text{ L}}{1 \text{ gal}} = 53.06 \text{ liters}$

6.5 Exercises

2. $27\dfrac{3}{4} + 22\dfrac{1}{4} + 10 = 60 \text{ in.}$

$60 \text{ in.} \times \dfrac{1 \text{ ft}}{12 \text{ in.}} = 5 \text{ ft}$
The perimeter is 5 feet.

4. $85 + 70 = 155$

$630 \text{ feet} \times \dfrac{1 \text{ yd}}{3 \text{ ft}} = 210 \text{ yd}$

$\begin{array}{r} 210 \\ -\ 155 \\ \hline 55 \end{array}$

55 yards will be let for the third side.

6. $\begin{aligned} \text{Perimeter} &= 2 \times 87 + 2 \times 152 \\ &= 174 \times 304 \\ &= 478 \text{ cm} \\ &= 4.78 \text{ m} \end{aligned}$

$\text{Cost} = 4.78 \text{ m} \times \dfrac{\$7.00}{1 \text{ m}} = \$33.46$

It will cost \$33.46 to insulate the window.

8. $1.24 \text{ m} = 1240 \text{ cm}$

$\dfrac{1240}{4} = 310$

The length will be 310 cm/piece.

10. $18.5 \text{ ft} \times \dfrac{0.305 \text{ m}}{1 \text{ ft}} \approx 5.64 \text{ meters}$

The longest hair is about 5.64 meters.

12. $\dfrac{\$0.39}{1 \text{ lb}} \times \dfrac{2.2 \text{ lb}}{1 \text{ kg}} \approx \$0.86/\text{kg}$

Bananas are more expensive in Texas.

14. $F = 1.8 \times C + 32 = 1.8 \times 39 + 32 = 102.2$
$102.2 - 95 = 7.2$
The difference is 7.2°F. The temperature last year was 7.2°F less than today's temperature.

16. $C = \dfrac{5 \times F - 160}{9}$

$\quad = \dfrac{5 \times 111 - 160}{9}$

$\quad = \dfrac{555 - 160}{9}$

$\quad = \dfrac{395}{9}$

$\quad \approx 43.89$

$\quad \begin{array}{r} 43.89 \\ -14.0 \\ \hline 29.89 \end{array}$

An Indian would report the temperature as 43.89°C; Oslo was cooler by 29.89°C.

18. a. $\dfrac{600 \text{ km}}{1 \text{ hr}} \times \dfrac{0.62 \text{ mi}}{1 \text{ km}} \approx 372 \text{ mi/hr}$
The jet's speed was 372 mi/hr.

b. Yes; $372 > 350$

20. $\dfrac{1 \text{ qt}}{1 \text{ day}} \times \dfrac{1 \text{ gal}}{4 \text{ qt}} \times \dfrac{31 \text{ day}}{1 \text{ mo}} = 7\dfrac{3}{4} \text{ gal}$

A total of $7\dfrac{3}{4}$ gallons will have dripped out.

22. $3.4 \text{ tons} \times \dfrac{2000 \text{ lb}}{1 \text{ ton}} \times \dfrac{\$0.015}{1 \text{ lb}} = \$102$
The tax was \$102.

24. $16 \text{ oz} - 5 \text{ oz} = 11 \text{ oz}$

$11 \text{ oz} \times \dfrac{28.35 \text{ g}}{1 \text{ oz}} \approx 311.85 \text{ g}$

There was \$311.85 grams of fruit.

26. a. $12 \text{ L} \times \dfrac{1.06 \text{ qt}}{1 \text{ L}} \approx 12.72 \text{ qt}$
$18 - 12.72 = 5.28 \text{ qt}$
She bought 5 qt extra.

b. $5 \times 2.75 = \$13.75$
It cost an extra \$!3.75.

28. a. $275 \text{ km} \times \dfrac{0.62 \text{ mi}}{1 \text{ km}} \approx 170.5 \text{ mi}$

$170.5 \text{ mi} \times \dfrac{1 \text{ gal}}{20 \text{ mi}} \times \dfrac{\$3.50}{1 \text{ gal}} \approx \$29.84$

The fuel cost him \$29.84.

b. $\dfrac{20 \text{ mi}}{1 \text{ gal}} \times \dfrac{1.61 \text{ km}}{1 \text{ mi}} \times \dfrac{0.264 \text{ gal}}{1 \text{ L}} \approx 8.50 \text{ km/L}$

He gets approximately 8.50 km/L.

30. $\dfrac{36,000 \text{ gal}}{1 \text{ hr}} \times \dfrac{8 \text{ pt}}{1 \text{ gal}} \times \dfrac{1 \text{ hr}}{3,600 \text{ sec}} = 80 \text{ pt/sec}$

Yes; 36,000 gal/hr is exactly equivalent to 80 pt/sec.

Cumulative Review

31. $6 \text{ in.} \times \dfrac{7.75 \text{ mi}}{3 \text{ in.}} = 15.5 \text{ mi}$
The train must go 15.5 miles.

32. $\dfrac{2}{7.5} = \dfrac{11}{n}$

$2 \times n = 7.5 \times 11$

$\dfrac{2 \times n}{2} = \dfrac{82.5}{2}$

$\quad n = 41.25 \text{ yards}$

The famous fishing schooner is 41.25 yards.

Classroom Quiz 6.5

1. $F = 1.8 \times C + 32$
$\quad = 1.8 \times 36 + 32$
$\quad = 64.8 + 32$
$\quad = 96.8$
$96.8 - 94 = 2.8$
Actual temperature was 2.8°F hotter than predicted.

2. $\dfrac{20.5 \text{ qt}}{1 \text{ min}} \times \dfrac{1 \text{ gal}}{4 \text{ qt}} \times \dfrac{60 \text{ min}}{1 \text{ hr}} = \dfrac{1230}{4} = 307.5$

It can pump 307.5 gallons per hour.

3. perimeter $= 2(4 \text{ km}) + 2(9 \text{ km})$
$$= 8 \text{ km} + 18 \text{ km}$$
$$= 26 \text{ km}$$

$$26 \text{ km} \times \frac{0.62 \text{ mi}}{1 \text{ km}} = 16.1 \text{ miles}$$

The perimeter of this park is 16.1 miles.

Putting Your Skills to Work

1.   200.00
    150.50
    120.25
     50.00
  + 25.00
    545.75

The total amount of her deposits is $545.75.

2.   238.50
     75.00
    200.00
     28.56
  + 36.00
    578.06

The total amount of her checks is $578.06.

3. Since $578.06 > $545.75, she spent more than she deposited, but the $300.50 would help her to cover her expenses.

4. $(300.50 + 200.00 + 150.50 + 120.25 + 50)$
$$- (238.5 + 75.00 + 200.00)$$
$$= 821.25 - 513.5$$
$$= 307.75$$
Her balance on May 25 was $307.75.

5. $300.50 + 545.75 - 578.06 = 268.19$
Assume her balance is $268.19.

6. Eventually she will be in debt.

Chapter 6 Review Problems

1. $33 \text{ ft} \times \dfrac{1 \text{ yd}}{3 \text{ ft}} = 11 \text{ yd}$

2. $27 \text{ ft} \times \dfrac{1 \text{ yd}}{3 \text{ ft}} = 9 \text{ yd}$

3. $5 \text{ mi} \times \dfrac{1760 \text{ yd}}{1 \text{ mi}} = 8800 \text{ yd}$

4. $6 \text{ mi} \times \dfrac{1760 \text{ yd}}{1 \text{ mi}} = 10,560 \text{ yd}$

5. $126 \text{ in.} \times \dfrac{1 \text{ ft}}{12 \text{ in.}} = 10.5 \text{ ft}$

6. $150 \text{ in.} \times \dfrac{1 \text{ ft}}{12 \text{ in.}} = 12.5 \text{ ft}$

7. $2.5 \text{ mi} \times \dfrac{5280 \text{ ft}}{1 \text{ mi}} = 13,200 \text{ ft}$

8. $4 \text{ mi} \times \dfrac{5280 \text{ ft}}{1 \text{ mi}} = 21,120 \text{ ft}$

9. $7 \text{ tons} \times \dfrac{2000 \text{ lb}}{1 \text{ ton}} = 14,000 \text{ lb}$

10. $4 \text{ tons} \times \dfrac{2000 \text{ lb}}{1 \text{ ton}} = 8000 \text{ lb}$

11. $8 \text{ oz} \times \dfrac{1 \text{ lb}}{16 \text{ oz}} = 0.5 \text{ lb}$

12. $12 \text{ oz} \times \dfrac{1 \text{ lb}}{16 \text{ oz}} = 0.75 \text{ lb}$

13. $15 \text{ gal} \times \dfrac{4 \text{ qt}}{1 \text{ gal}} = 60 \text{ qt}$

14. $21 \text{ gal} \times \dfrac{4 \text{ qt}}{1 \text{ gal}} = 84 \text{ qt}$

15. $31 \text{ pt} \times \dfrac{1 \text{ qt}}{2 \text{ pt}} = 15.5 \text{ qt}$

16. $27 \text{ pt} \times \dfrac{1 \text{ qt}}{2 \text{ pt}} = 13.5 \text{ qt}$

17. $56 \text{ cm} = 560 \text{ mm}$

18. $29 \text{ cm} = 290 \text{ mm}$

19. $1763 \text{ mm} = 176.3 \text{ cm}$

20. $2598 \text{ mm} = 259.8 \text{ cm}$

21. $13.25 \text{ m} = 1325 \text{ cm}$

22. $16.75 \text{ m} = 1675 \text{ cm}$

23. $10,000 \text{ m} = 10 \text{ km}$

24. $8200 \text{ m} = 8.2 \text{ km}$

25. $6.2 \text{ m} + 121 \text{ cm} + 0.52 \text{ m}$
$= 6.2 \text{ m} + 1.21 \text{ m} + 0.52 \text{ m}$
$= 7.93 \text{ m}$

26. $9.8 \text{ m} + 673 \text{ cm} + 0.48 \text{ m}$
$= 9.8 \text{ m} + 6.73 \text{ m} + 0.48 \text{ m}$
$= 17.01 \text{ m}$

27. $0.024 \text{ km} + 1.8 \text{ m} + 983 \text{ cm}$
$= 24 \text{ m} + 1.8 \text{ m} + 9.83 \text{ m}$
$= 35.63 \text{ m}$

28. $0.078 \text{ km} + 5.5 \text{ m} + 609 \text{ cm}$
$= 78 \text{ m} + 5.5 \text{ m} + 6.09 \text{ m}$
$= 89.59 \text{ m}$

29. $17 \text{ kL} = 17{,}000 \text{ L}$

30. $23 \text{ kL} = 23{,}000 \text{ L}$

31. $196 \text{ kg} = 196{,}000 \text{ g}$

32. $721 \text{ kg} = 721{,}000 \text{ g}$

33. $95 \text{ mg} = 0.095 \text{ g}$

34. $78 \text{ mg} = 0.078 \text{ g}$

35. $3500 \text{ g} = 3.5 \text{ kg}$

36. $12{,}750 \text{ g} = 12.75 \text{ kg}$

37. $765 \text{ cc} = 765 \text{ mL}$

38. $423 \text{ cm}^3 = 423 \text{ mL}$

39. $0.256 \text{ L} = 256 \text{ mL} = 256 \text{ cm}^3$

40. $0.922 \text{ L} = 922 \text{ mL} = 922 \text{ cc}$

41. $42 \text{ kg} \times \dfrac{2.2 \text{ lb}}{1 \text{ kg}} \approx 92.4 \text{ lb}$

42. $9 \text{ ft} \times \dfrac{0.305 \text{ m}}{1 \text{ ft}} \approx 2.75 \text{ m}$

43. $45 \text{ mi} \times \dfrac{1.61 \text{ km}}{1 \text{ mi}} = 72.45 \text{ km}$

44. $88 \text{ mi} \times \dfrac{1.61 \text{ km}}{1 \text{ mi}} = 141.68 \text{ km}$

45. $14 \text{ cm} \times \dfrac{0.394 \text{ in.}}{1 \text{ cm}} \approx 5.52 \text{ in.}$

46. $18 \text{ cm} \times \dfrac{0.394 \text{ in.}}{1 \text{ cm}} \approx 7.09 \text{ in.}$

47. $20 \text{ lb} \times \dfrac{0.454 \text{ kg}}{1 \text{ lb}} \approx 9.08 \text{ kg}$

48. $30 \text{ lb} \times \dfrac{0.454 \text{ kg}}{1 \text{ lb}} \approx 13.62 \text{ kg}$

49. $50 \text{ yd} \times \dfrac{0.914 \text{ m}}{1 \text{ yd}} = 45.7 \text{ m}$

50. $100 \text{ yd} \times \dfrac{0.914 \text{ m}}{1 \text{ yd}} = 91.4 \text{ m}$

51. $\dfrac{80 \text{ km}}{1 \text{ hr}} \times \dfrac{0.62 \text{ mi}}{1 \text{ km}} = 49.6 \text{ mi/hr}$

52. $\dfrac{70 \text{ km}}{1 \text{ hr}} \times \dfrac{0.62 \text{ mi}}{1 \text{ km}} = 43.4 \text{ mi/hr}$

53. $F = 1.8 \times C + 32$
$= 1.8 \times 12 + 32$
$= 21.6 + 32$
$= 53.6°\text{F}$

54. $F = 1.8 \times 32 + 32 = 57.6 + 32 = 89.6°\text{F}$

55. $C = \dfrac{5 \times F - 160}{9} = \dfrac{5 \times 221 - 160}{9} = 105$
$105°\text{C}$

56. $C = \dfrac{5 \times F - 160}{9} = \dfrac{5 \times 185 - 160}{9} = 85$
$85°\text{C}$

57. $C = \dfrac{5 \times F - 160}{9} = \dfrac{5 \times 32 - 160}{9} = 0$
$0°\text{C}$

58. $C = \dfrac{5 \times F - 160}{9}$
$= \dfrac{5 \times 212 - 160}{9}$
$= \dfrac{1060 - 160}{9}$
$= \dfrac{900}{9}$
$= 100°\text{C}$

59. $13 \text{ L} \times \dfrac{0.264 \text{ gal}}{1 \text{ L}} \approx 3.43 \text{ gal}$

60. $27 \text{ qt} \times \dfrac{0.946 \text{ L}}{1 \text{ qt}} \approx 25.54 \text{ L}$

61. $5 \text{ yd} \times \dfrac{3 \text{ ft}}{\text{yd}} = 15 \text{ ft}$

$A = lw$
$A = (18)(15)$
$A = 270 \text{ sq ft}$

$270 \text{ sq ft} \times \dfrac{1 \text{ sq yd}}{9 \text{ sq ft}} = 30 \text{ sq yd}$

The area is 270 square feet or 30 square yards.

62. a. $7\dfrac{2}{3} \text{ ft} \times 4\dfrac{1}{3} \text{ ft} + 5 \text{ ft} = 16\dfrac{3}{3} \text{ ft} = 17 \text{ feet}$
The perimeter is 17 feet.

b. $17 \text{ feet} \times \dfrac{12 \text{ in.}}{1 \text{ foot}} = 204 \text{ in.}$
The perimeter is 204 inches.

63. a. $16 \text{ m} + 84 \text{ m} + 16 \text{ m} + 84 \text{ m} = 200 \text{ m}$
The perimeter is 200 meters.

b. $200 \text{ m} = 0.2 \text{ km}$
The perimeter is 0.2 kilometer.

64. $510 \text{ g} \times \dfrac{0.0353 \text{ oz}}{1 \text{ g}} \approx 18 \text{ oz}$

$\dfrac{\$0.16}{1 \text{ oz}} \times 18 \text{ oz} \approx \$2.88$
The cereal costs $2.88.

65. $15 \text{ meters} \times \dfrac{3.28 \text{ feet}}{1 \text{ meter}} = 49.2 \text{ feet}$
$49.2 - 45 = 4.2$
No; they are 4.2 feet short.

66. $70 \dfrac{\text{mi}}{\text{hr}} \times \dfrac{1.61 \text{ km}}{1 \text{ mi}} = 112.7 \dfrac{\text{km}}{\text{hr}}$
Yes; she was driving 112.7 km/hr.

67. $F = 1.8 \times C + 32 = 1.8 \times 185 + 32 = 365°$
$390° - 365° = 25°\text{F too hot}$

68. $19 \text{ m} = 1900 \text{ cm}$

Bottom part $= 1900 \times \dfrac{1}{5} = 380 \text{ cm}$

The length of the pole that has the water seal is 380 cm.

69. $\dfrac{1 \text{ mi}}{91.41 \text{ sec}} \times \dfrac{60 \text{ min}}{1 \text{ hr}} \times \dfrac{60 \text{ sec}}{1 \text{ min}} = \dfrac{3600}{91.41}$
$\approx 39.38 \text{ mi/hr}$
The horse's speed was 39.38 mi/hr.

70. $\dfrac{2 \text{ mi}}{198 \text{ sec}} \times \dfrac{60 \text{ min}}{1 \text{ hr}} \times \dfrac{60 \text{ sec}}{1 \text{ min}} = \dfrac{7200}{198}$
$\approx 36.36 \text{ mi/hr}$
The horse's speed was 36.36 mi/hr.

71. $2.2 + 1.4 + 3.8 = 7.4 \text{ kg}$

$7.4 \text{ kg} \times \dfrac{2.2 \text{ lb}}{1 \text{ kg}} \approx 16.28 \text{ lb}$

They are carrying 6.28 pounds; they are slightly over the weight limit.

72. $\dfrac{\$1.05}{1 \text{ L}} \times \dfrac{1 \text{ L}}{0.264 \text{ gal}} \approx \$3.98/\text{gal}$
The gas costs $3.98/gal.

73. $1.88 \text{ m} \times \dfrac{3.28 \text{ ft}}{1 \text{ m}} \approx 6.1664 \text{ ft}$

Now, $6 \text{ ft } 2 \text{ in.} = 6 \text{ ft } \dfrac{2}{12} \text{ ft} = 6\dfrac{1}{6} \text{ ft} \approx 6.1667 \text{ ft}$

The person would be comfortable in the car.

74. $4 \text{ m} \times \dfrac{3.28 \text{ ft}}{1 \text{ m}} = 13.12 \text{ ft}$

$12 \text{ m} \times \dfrac{3.28 \text{ ft}}{1 \text{ m}} = 39.36 \text{ ft}$

Area $= 13.12 \times 39.36 \approx 516.4 \text{ sq ft}$
He needs approximately 516.4 square feet of sealer.

75. $4 \text{ lb} \times \dfrac{\$1.23}{1 \text{ kg}} \times \dfrac{0.454 \text{ kg}}{1 \text{ lb}} \approx \$2.23$
The cost is about $2.23.

How Am I Doing? Chapter 6 Test

1. $1.6 \text{ tons} \times \dfrac{2000 \text{ lb}}{1 \text{ ton}} = 3200 \text{ lb}$

2. $19 \text{ ft} \times \dfrac{12 \text{ in.}}{1 \text{ ft}} = 228 \text{ in.}$

3. $21 \text{ gal} \times \dfrac{4 \text{ qt}}{1 \text{ gal}} = 84 \text{ qt}$

4. $36,960 \text{ ft} \times \dfrac{1 \text{ mi}}{5280 \text{ ft}} = 7 \text{ mi}$

5. $1800 \text{ sec} \times \dfrac{1 \text{ min}}{60 \text{ sec}} = 30 \text{ min}$

6. $3 \text{ cups} \times \dfrac{1 \text{ qt}}{4 \text{ cups}} = 0.75 \text{ qt}$

7. $8 \text{ oz} \times \dfrac{1 \text{ lb}}{16 \text{ oz}} = 0.5 \text{ lb}$

8. $5.5 \text{ yd} \times \dfrac{3 \text{ ft}}{1 \text{ yd}} = 16.5 \text{ ft}$

9. $9.2 \text{ km} = 9200 \text{ m}$

10. $9.88 \text{ cm} = 0.0988 \text{ m}$

11. $46 \text{ mm} = 4.6 \text{ cm}$

12. $12.7 \text{ m} = 1270 \text{ cm}$

13. $0.936 \text{ cm} = 9.36 \text{ mm}$

14. $46 \text{ L} = 0.046 \text{ kL}$

15. $28.9 \text{ mg} = 0.0289 \text{ g}$

16. $983 \text{ g} = 0.983 \text{ kg}$

17. $0.92 \text{ L} = 920 \text{ mL}$

18. $9.42 \text{ g} = 9420 \text{ mg}$

19. $42 \text{ mi} \times \dfrac{1.61 \text{ km}}{1 \text{ mi}} = 67.62 \text{ km}$

20. $1.78 \text{ yd} \times \dfrac{0.914 \text{ m}}{1 \text{ yd}} \approx 1.63 \text{ m}$

21. $9 \text{ cm} \times \dfrac{0.394 \text{ in.}}{1 \text{ cm}} \approx 3.55 \text{ in.}$

22. $30 \text{ km} \times \dfrac{0.62 \text{ mi}}{1 \text{ km}} = 18.6 \text{ mi}$

23. $7.3 \text{ kg} \times \dfrac{2.2 \text{ lb}}{1 \text{ kg}} = 16.06 \text{ lb}$

24. $3 \text{ oz} \times \dfrac{28.35 \text{ g}}{1 \text{ oz}} = 85.05 \text{ g}$

25. $15 \text{ gal} \times \dfrac{3.79 \text{ L}}{1 \text{ gal}} = 56.85 \text{ L}$

26. $3 \text{ L} \times \dfrac{1.06 \text{ qt}}{1 \text{ L}} = 3.18 \text{ qt}$

27. a. $3 \text{ m} + 7 \text{ m} + 3 \text{ m} + 7 \text{ m} = 20 \text{ m}$
   The perimeter is 20 meters.

b. $20 \text{ m} \times \dfrac{1.09 \text{ yd}}{1 \text{ m}} = 21.8 \text{ yd}$
   The perimeter is 21.8 yards.

28. a. $F = 1.8 \times C + 32 = 1.8 \times 35 + 32 = 95$
   $95°F - 80°F = 15°F$
   There are 15°F between the two
   temperatures.

b. Yes; $80°F < 95°F$

29. $\dfrac{5.5 \text{ qt}}{1 \text{ min}} \times \dfrac{1 \text{ gal}}{4 \text{ qt}} \times \dfrac{60 \text{ min}}{1 \text{ hr}} = 82.5 \text{ gal/hr}$
   The pump is running at 82.5 gal/hr.

30. a. $100 \times 3 = 300 \text{ km}$
   He can travel 300 km.

b. $300 \text{ km} \times \dfrac{0.62 \text{ mi}}{1 \text{ km}} = 186 \text{ mi}$
   $200 - 186 = 14 \text{ mi farther}$
   He will need to travel 14 miles farther.

31. $1\dfrac{6}{16} + 2\dfrac{2}{16} + 1\dfrac{12}{16} = 4\dfrac{20}{16} = 5\dfrac{4}{16} = 5\dfrac{1}{4} \text{ lb}$

   He bought a total of $5\dfrac{1}{4}$ pounds of fruit.

32. $F = 1.8 \times C + 32 = 1.8 \times 40 + 32 = 104$
   The temperature was 104°F.

Cumulative Test for Chapters 1–6

1. $\begin{array}{r} 9824 \\ -\ 3796 \\ \hline 6028 \end{array}$

2. $\begin{array}{r} 608 \\ \times\quad 305 \\ \hline 3\ 040 \\ 182\ 40 \\ \hline 185,440 \end{array}$

3.

$$
\begin{array}{r}
270 \\
32\overline{)8645} \\
\underline{64} \\
224 \\
\underline{224} \\
05
\end{array}
$$

270 R 5

4. $\dfrac{9}{14} + \dfrac{5}{7} + \dfrac{4}{21} = \dfrac{27}{42} + \dfrac{30}{42} + \dfrac{8}{42}$

$$= \dfrac{27 + 30 + 8}{42}$$

$$= \dfrac{65}{42}$$

$$= 1\dfrac{23}{42}$$

5.

$$
\begin{array}{r}
3\dfrac{1}{8} \\
-1\dfrac{3}{4} \\
\hline
\end{array}
\qquad
\begin{array}{r}
2\dfrac{9}{8} \\
-1\dfrac{6}{8} \\
\hline
1\dfrac{3}{8}
\end{array}
$$

6. $0.2 \times (10 - 5)^2 \div \dfrac{1}{3} = 0.2 \times 5^2 \div \dfrac{1}{3}$

$$= 0.2 \times 25 \div \dfrac{1}{3}$$

$$= 5 \div \dfrac{1}{3}$$

$$= 5 \times \dfrac{3}{1}$$

$$= 15$$

7. $\dfrac{14}{20} \overset{?}{=} \dfrac{3}{4}$

$14 \times 4 \overset{?}{=} 20 \times 3$

$56 \neq 60$

no

8. $\dfrac{0.4}{n} = \dfrac{2}{30}$

$0.4 \times 30 = n \times 2$

$\dfrac{12}{2} = \dfrac{n \times 2}{2}$

$n = 6$

9. $\dfrac{6.5 \text{ cm}}{68 \text{ g}} = \dfrac{20 \text{ cm}}{n \text{ g}}$

$6.5 \times n = 68 \times 20$

$6.5 \times n = 1360$

$\dfrac{6.5 \times n}{6.5} = \dfrac{1360}{6.5}$

$n \approx 209.23 \text{ g}$

The 20-cm wire will weigh 209.23 g.

10. What percent of 74 is 148?

$n \times 74 = 148$

$\dfrac{n \times 74}{74} = \dfrac{148}{74}$

$n = 2 = 200\%$

11. $n = 15\% \times 800$

$n = 0.15 \times 800$

$n = 120$

12. 0.5% of what number is 100?

$0.5\% \times n = 100$

$\dfrac{0.005 \times n}{0.005} = \dfrac{100}{0.005}$

$n = 20{,}000$

13. $38 \text{ qt} \times \dfrac{1 \text{ gal}}{4 \text{ qt}} = 9.5 \text{ gal}$

14. $2.5 \text{ tons} \times \dfrac{2000 \text{ lb}}{1 \text{ ton}} = 5000 \text{ lb}$

15. $7 \text{ pt} \times \dfrac{1 \text{ qt}}{2 \text{ pt}} = 3.5 \text{ qt}$

16. $25 \text{ ft} \times \dfrac{12 \text{ in.}}{1 \text{ ft}} = 300 \text{ in.}$

17. $3.7 \text{ km} = 3700 \text{ m}$

18. $62.8 \text{ g} = 0.0628 \text{ kg}$

19. $9.2 \text{ L} = 9200 \text{ mL}$

20. $5 \text{ cm} = 0.05 \text{ m}$

21. $42 \text{ lb} \times \dfrac{16 \text{ oz}}{1 \text{ lb}} = 672 \text{ oz}$

22. $C = \dfrac{5 \times F - 160}{9}$

$\quad = \dfrac{5 \times 50 - 160}{9}$

$\quad = \dfrac{250 - 160}{9}$

$\quad = \dfrac{90}{9}$

$\quad = 10^{\circ}C$

23. $28 \text{ gal} \times \dfrac{3.79 \text{ L}}{1 \text{ gal}} = 106.12 \text{ L}$

24. $48 \text{ kg} \times \dfrac{2.2 \text{ lb}}{1 \text{ kg}} = 105.6 \text{ lb}$

25. $30 \text{ in.} \times \dfrac{2.54 \text{ cm}}{1 \text{ in.}} = 76.2 \text{ cm}$

26. $9 \text{ mi} \times \dfrac{1.61 \text{ km}}{1 \text{ m}} = 14.49 \text{ km}$

27. $6 \text{ yd} + 4 \text{ yd} + 3 \text{ yd} = 13 \text{ yd}$

$13 \text{ yd} \times \dfrac{0.914 \text{ m}}{1 \text{ yd}} \approx 11.88 \text{ m}$

The perimeter is 11.88 meters.

28. $F = 1.8 \times C + 32 = 1.8 \times 15 + 32 = 59^{\circ}F$

$59^{\circ} - 15^{\circ} = 44^{\circ}F$

The difference is $44^{\circ}F$; the $15^{\circ}C$ temperature is higher.

29. $\dfrac{100 \text{ km}}{1 \text{ hr}} \times 1\dfrac{1}{2} \text{ hr} = 150 \text{ km}$

$150 \text{ km} \times \dfrac{0.62 \text{ mi}}{1 \text{ km}} = 93 \text{ mi}$

$100 - 93 = 7$

He needs to travel 7 miles farther.

30. $2.5 \times 80 = 200 \text{ ft}$

$200 \text{ ft} \times \dfrac{1 \text{ yd}}{3 \text{ ft}} = 66.\overline{6} \text{ yd or} \approx 66.7 \text{ yd}$

Technically, she needs $66\dfrac{2}{3}$ yards, but in real life she should buy 67 yards.

Chapter 7

Exercise Set 7.1

2. An obtuse angle is an angle whose measure is between 90° and 180°.

4. Supplementary angles are two angles whose measures have a sum of 180°.

6. Two angles that are formed by intersecting lines and have a common side and a common vertex are called adjacent angles.

8. If a transversal intersects two lines, the two angles that are on opposite sides of the transversal and are between the other two lines and called alternate interior angles.

10. $\angle DBC$, $\angle ABE$

12. $\angle ABD$ and $\angle DBC$
$\angle ABE$ and $\angle CBE$

14. $\angle DBA$, $\angle CBE$

16. $\angle NOL = 65°$

18. $\angle NOM = 65° + 20° = 85°$

20. $\angle MOK = 90° - 20° = 70°$

22. $\angle KOJ = 180°$

24. $90° - 5° = 85°$

26. $180° - 18° = 162°$

28. $\angle a = 90° - 74° = 16°$

30. $\angle a = 87° - 43° = 44°$

32. $\angle a = 115° - 44° - 26° = 45°$

34. $\angle a = 43°$
$\angle b = \angle c = 180° - 43° = 137°$

36. $\angle b = 119°$
$\angle a = \angle c = 180° - 119° = 61°$

38. $\angle a = 116°$
$\angle b = \angle c = 180° - 116° = 64°$

40. $\angle c = \angle d = \angle g = 26°$
$\angle a = \angle b = \angle e = \angle f = 180° - 26° = 154°$

42. $\angle x = 180° - 121° = 59°$
The angle of inclination is 59°.

44. New angle is $72° - 9° = 63°$ north of west.

Cumulative Review

45. $159.5 + 229.5 + 182.5 + 178.5 = 750$ km
$750 \text{ km} \times \dfrac{0.62 \text{ mi}}{1 \text{ km}} = 465$ mi
The total distance is 750 km or 465 mi.

46. $34 \text{ km} \times \dfrac{0.62 \text{ mi}}{1 \text{ km}} \approx 21.1$ mi
He needs to drive about 21.1 miles farther.

47. Percent miles = $100 + 5 = 105\%$
Miles = 105% of $24 = 1.05 \times 24 = 25.2$ miles
He should jog at most 25.2 miles.

48. Increase = $27 - 24 = 3$
3 is what percent of 24?
$p \times 24 = 3$
$p = \dfrac{3}{24}$
$p = 0.125$
12.5% is the percent of increase.

Classroom Quiz 7.1

1. $\angle a = \angle c = 137°$

2. $\angle b = 180° - 137° = 43°$

3. $\angle f = \angle c = 137°$

7.2 Exercises

2. To find the perimeter of a figure, we <u>add</u> the lengths of all of the sides.

4. All area is measured in <u>square</u> units.

6. $P = 2l + 2w$
$= 2(9 \text{ cm}) + 2(1.5 \text{ cm})$
$= 18 \text{ cm} + 3 \text{ cm}$
$= 21$ cm

8. $P = 2l + 2w$
$= 2(11.3 \text{ ft}) + 2(8.7 \text{ ft})$
$= 22.6 \text{ ft} + 17.4 \text{ ft}$
$= 40$ ft

10. $P = 4s = 4(15.6 \text{ ft}) = 62.4 \text{ ft}$

12. $P = 2l + 2w$
$= 2(9.4 \text{ m}) + 2(4.3 \text{ m})$
$= 18.8 \text{ m} + 8.6 \text{ m}$
$= 27.4 \text{ m}$

14. $P = 4s = 4(9.63 \text{ cm}) = 38.52 \text{ cm}$

16. $8.5 \text{ ft} \times \dfrac{12 \text{ in.}}{1 \text{ ft}} = 102 \text{ in.}$
$P = 2l + 2w$
$= 2(102 \text{ in.}) + 2(30 \text{ in.})$
$= 204 \text{ in.} + 60 \text{ in.}$
$= 264 \text{ in.}$
or
$30 \text{ in.} \times \dfrac{1 \text{ ft}}{12 \text{ in.}} = 2.5 \text{ ft}$
$P = 2l + 2w$
$= 2(8.5 \text{ ft}) + 2(2.5 \text{ ft})$
$= 17 \text{ ft} + 5 \text{ ft}$
$= 22 \text{ ft}$

18. $P = 4s = 4(0.097 \text{ mm}) = 0.388 \text{ mm}$

20. $P = 4s = 4\left(5\dfrac{3}{4} \text{ cm}\right) = 4\left(\dfrac{23}{4} \text{ cm}\right) = 23 \text{ m}$

22.

$\begin{aligned} & 3\dfrac{1}{2} \text{ cm} \\ & 7 \text{ cm} \\ & 12 \text{ cm} \\ & 6 \text{ cm} \\ & 8\dfrac{1}{2} \text{ cm} \\ &\underline{+\ \ \ 1 \text{cm}} \\ &P = 38 \text{ cm} \end{aligned}$

24.

$\begin{aligned} & 10 \text{ m} \\ & 10 \text{ m} \\ & 10 \text{ m} \\ & 2 \text{ m} \\ & 6 \text{ m} \\ & 2 \text{ m} \\ & 6 \text{ m} \\ & 2 \text{ m} \\ & 6 \text{ m} \\ & 2 \text{ m} \\ & 6 \text{ m} \\ &\underline{+\ \ 2 \text{ m}} \\ & 64 \text{ m} \\ &P = 64 \text{ m} \end{aligned}$

26. $A = lw = (5.1 \text{ m})(5.1 \text{ m}) = 26.01 \text{ m}^2$

28. $A = lw = 12.4 \text{ mi} \times 8 \text{ mi} = 99.2 \text{ mi}^2$

30. $57 \text{ yd} \times \dfrac{3 \text{ ft}}{1 \text{ yd}} = 171 \text{ ft}$
$A = lw = (171 \text{ ft})(15 \text{ ft}) = 2565 \text{ ft}^2$
or
$15 \text{ ft} \times \dfrac{1 \text{ yd}}{3 \text{ ft}} = 5 \text{ yd}$
$A = lw = 57 \text{ yd} \times 5 \text{ yd} = 285 \text{ yd}^2$

32. a. $A = 21 \text{ m} \times 10 \text{ m} + 8 \text{ m} \times 7 \text{ m} + 3 \text{ m} \times 15 \text{ m}$
$= 210 \text{ m}^2 + 56 \text{ m}^2 + 45 \text{ m}^2$
$= 311 \text{ m}^2$
The area is 311 m^2.

b.

$\begin{aligned} & 21 \text{ m} \\ & 10 \text{ m} \\ & 6 \text{ m} \\ & 3 \text{ m} \\ & 8 \text{ m} \\ & 8 \text{ m} \\ & 7 \text{ m} \\ &\underline{+\ 21 \text{ m}} \\ & 84 \text{ m} \end{aligned}$

The perimeter is 84 meters.

34. $P = 2(80 \text{ yd}) + 2(120 \text{ yd})$
$= 160 \text{ yd} + 240 \text{ yd}$
$= 400 \text{ yd}$
$4(400 \text{ yd}) = 1600 \text{ yd}$
They ran 1600 yards.
$1760 \text{ yd} - 1600 \text{ yd} = 160 \text{ yd}$
Another 160 yards would be a mile.

36. $P = 2(5.4 \text{ ft}) + 2(8.1 \text{ ft})$
   $= 10.8 \text{ ft} + 16.2 \text{ ft}$
   $= 27 \text{ ft}$

   $\text{Cost} = 27 \text{ ft} \times \dfrac{\$32.50}{\text{ft}} = \$877.50$
   The frame will cost $877.50.

38. a. $1 \times 8, 2 \times 7, 3 \times 6, 4 \times 5$
   There are four possible shapes.

   b. $A = 1 \times 8 = 8 \text{ sq ft}$
   $A = 2 \times 7 = 14 \text{ sq ft}$
   $A = 3 \times 6 = 18 \text{ sq ft}$
   $A = 4 \times 5 = 20 \text{ sq ft}$

   c. The 4 ft × 5 ft garden has the largest area.

40. $A = lw + lw$
   $= (21 \text{ ft})(13 \text{ ft}) - (7 \text{ ft})(6 \text{ ft})$
   $= 273 \text{ ft}^2 + 42 \text{ ft}^2$
   $= 231 \text{ ft}^2$

   $\text{Cost of carpet} = 231 \text{ ft}^2 \times \dfrac{\$14.50}{\text{yd}^2} \times \dfrac{1 \text{ yd}^2}{9 \text{ ft}^2}$
   $\approx \$372.17$
   $P = 13 \text{ ft} + 21 \text{ ft} + 13 \text{ ft} + 4 \text{ ft} + 6 \text{ ft} + 7 \text{ ft}$
   $\quad + 6 \text{ ft} + 10 \text{ ft}$
   $= 80 \text{ ft}$

   $\text{Cost of binding} = 80 \text{ ft} \times \dfrac{\$1.50}{\text{yd}} \times \dfrac{1 \text{ yd}}{3 \text{ ft}} = \$40$
   Total cost = $372.17 + $40 = $412.17

Cumulative Review

41.
```
  156.8
   27.2
+  39.3
------
  223.3
```

42.
```
  200.57
- 193.39
-------
    7.18
```

43.
```
    1076
 ×  20.3
-------
   322 8
 21 520
-------
 21,842.8
```

44.
```
        1.57593
12.3.)19.3.84000
       12 3
       ----
        7 0 8
        6 1 5
        -----
          9 34
          8 61
          ----
           730
           615
           ---
          1150
          1107
          ----
           430
           369
           ---
```
   ≈ 1.5759

Classroom Quiz 7.2

1. $P = 2l + 2w$
   $= 2(4 \text{ mi}) + 2(7 \text{ mi})$
   $= 8 \text{ mi} + 14 \text{ mi}$
   $= 22 \text{ mi}$

2. $A = s^2 = (1.5 \text{ m})^2 = 2.25 \text{ m}^2$

3. $A = lw = (9 \text{ ft})(14 \text{ ft}) = 126 \text{ ft}^2$

   $\text{Cost} = \dfrac{126 \text{ ft}^2}{1} \cdot \dfrac{\$8}{1 \text{ ft}^2} = \$1008$

7.3 Exercises

2. To find the area of a parallelogram, multiply the base times the <u>height</u>.

4. The area of a trapezoid is one-half the height times the <u>sum</u> of the bases.

6. $P = 2(14.7 \text{ m}) + 2(21.5 \text{ m})$
   $= 29.4 \text{ m} + 43 \text{ m}$
   $= 72.4 \text{ m}$

8. $P = 2(12.3 \text{ in.}) + 2(2.6 \text{ in.})$
   $= 24.6 \text{ in.} + 5.2 \text{ in.}$
   $= 29.8 \text{ in.}$

10. $A = bh = (9.5 \text{ m})(24.8 \text{ m}) = 235.6 \text{ m}^2$

12. $A = bh = (126 \text{ yd})(28 \text{ yd}) = 3528 \text{ yd}^2$

14. $P = 4(14 \text{ yd}) = 56 \text{ yd}$

$A = bh = (14 \text{ yd})(9 \text{ yd}) = 126 \text{ yd}^2$

16. $P = 4(25 \text{ ft}) = 100 \text{ ft}$

$A = bh = (25 \text{ ft})(17 \text{ ft}) = 425 \text{ ft}^2$

18. $P = 17 \text{ yd} + 24 \text{ yd} + 17 \text{ yd} + 35 \text{ yd} = 93 \text{ yd}$

20. $P = 18.5 \text{ m} + 23 \text{ m} + 43.5 \text{ m} + 48 \text{ m} = 133 \text{ m}$

22. $A = \dfrac{h(b+B)}{2}$

$= \dfrac{(15 \text{ cm})(9.8 \text{ cm} + 18.3 \text{ cm})}{2}$

$= \dfrac{(15 \text{ cm})(28.1 \text{ cm})}{2}$

$= 210.75 \text{ cm}^2$

24. $A = \dfrac{h(b+B)}{2}$

$= \dfrac{(20 \text{ km})(24 \text{ km} + 31 \text{ km})}{2}$

$= \dfrac{(20 \text{ km})(55 \text{ km})}{2}$

$= 550 \text{ km}^2$

26. a. Top area $= lw = (22 \text{ m})(31 \text{ m}) = 682 \text{ m}^2$

Bottom area $= \dfrac{h(b+B)}{2}$

$= \dfrac{(8 \text{ m})(22 \text{ m} + 27 \text{ m})}{2}$

$= \dfrac{(8 \text{ m})(49 \text{ m})}{2}$

$= 196 \text{ m}^2$

Total area $= 682 \text{ m}^2 + 196 \text{ m}^2 = 878 \text{ m}^2$

b. The orange object is a rectangle.

c. The yellow object is a trapezoid.

28. a. Top area $= bh = (9 \text{ ft})(25 \text{ ft}) = 225 \text{ ft}^2$

Bottom area $= \dfrac{h(b+B)}{2}$

$= \dfrac{(14 \text{ ft})(9 \text{ ft} + 17 \text{ ft})}{2}$

$= \dfrac{(14 \text{ ft})(26 \text{ ft})}{2}$

$= 182 \text{ ft}^2$

Total area $= 225 \text{ ft}^2 + 182 \text{ ft}^2 = 407 \text{ ft}^2$

b. The orange object is a parallelogram.

c. The yellow object is a trapezoid.

30. Top area $= lw = (50 \text{ yd})(72 \text{ yd}) = 3600 \text{ yd}^2$

Bottom area $= \dfrac{h(b+B)}{2}$

$= \dfrac{(24 \text{ yd})(50 \text{ yd} + 68 \text{ yd})}{2}$

$= \dfrac{(24 \text{ yd})(118 \text{ yd})}{2}$

$= 1416 \text{ yd}^2$

Total area $= 3600 \text{ yd}^2 + 1416 \text{ yd}^2 = 5016 \text{ yd}^2$

Cost $= 5016 \text{ yd}^2 \times \dfrac{\$22}{\text{yd}^2} = \$110,352$

The carpet will cost a total of $110,532.

Cumulative Review

31. $40 \text{ qt} \times \dfrac{1 \text{ gal}}{4 \text{ qt}} = 10 \text{ gal}$

32. $500 \text{ cm} = 5 \text{ m}$

33. $4 \text{ yd} \times \dfrac{36 \text{ in.}}{1 \text{ yd}} = 144 \text{ in.}$

34. $8.2 \text{ kg} = 8200 \text{ g}$

Classroom Quiz 7.3

1. $P = 2(23 \text{ in.}) + 2(18 \text{ in.}) = 46 \text{ in.} + 36 \text{ in.} = 82 \text{ in.}$

2. $A = bh = (20 \text{ ft})(12.5 \text{ ft}) = 250 \text{ ft}^2$

3. $A = \dfrac{h(b+B)}{2}$

$= \dfrac{8 \text{ cm}(12 \text{ cm} + 18 \text{ cm})}{2}$

$= \dfrac{8 \text{ cm}(30 \text{ cm})}{2}$

$= 120 \text{ cm}^2$

7.4 Exercises

2. The sum of the angle measures of a triangle is 180°.

4. You could conclude that two of the sides of the triangle are equal.

6. The area of the triangle is the base times the height divided by two.

8. False; a right triangle has one angle of 90°.

10. False; two sides of an isosceles triangle are of equal length.

12. False; a scalene triangle has no two sides of equal lengths.

14. True

16. $180° - (23° + 95°) = 180° - 118° = 62°$

18. $180° - (94.5° + 68.2°) = 180° - 162.7° = 17.3°$

20. $P = 27 \text{ m} + 44 \text{ m} + 23 \text{ m} = 94 \text{ m}$

22. $P = 36.2 \text{ in.} + 47.65 \text{ in.} + 47.65 \text{ in.} = 131.5 \text{ in.}$

24. $P = 3\left(12\frac{2}{3}\right) = 3\left(\frac{38}{3}\right) = 38 \text{ feet}$

26. $A = \dfrac{bh}{2} = \dfrac{(4.5)(7)}{2} = 15.75 \text{ in.}^2$

28. $A = \dfrac{bh}{2} = \dfrac{(3.6 \text{ cm})(11.2 \text{ cm})}{2} = 20.16 \text{ cm}^2$

30. $A = \dfrac{1}{2}bh$

$= \dfrac{1}{2}\left(11\frac{1}{4} \text{ ft}\right)\left(4\frac{2}{3} \text{ ft}\right)$

$= \dfrac{1}{2}\left(\frac{45}{4} \text{ ft}\right)\left(\frac{14}{3} \text{ ft}\right)$

$= \dfrac{105}{4} \text{ ft}^2$

$= 26\frac{1}{4} \text{ ft}^2$

32. Large triangle area $= \dfrac{bh}{2} = \dfrac{(9 \text{ ft})(12 \text{ ft})}{2} = 54 \text{ ft}^2$

Small triangle area $= \dfrac{bh}{2} = \dfrac{(3 \text{ ft})(5 \text{ ft})}{2} = 7.5 \text{ ft}$

Shaded area $= 54 \text{ ft}^2 - 7.5 \text{ ft}^2 = 46.5 \text{ ft}^2$

34. Area of rectangle $= lw$

$= (25 \text{ yd})(20 \text{ yd})$

$= 500 \text{ yd}^2$

Area of triangle $= \dfrac{bh}{2} = \dfrac{(25 \text{ yd})(8 \text{ yd})}{2} = 100 \text{ yd}^2$

Shaded area $= 500 \text{ yd}^2 - 100 \text{ yd}^2 = 400 \text{ yd}^2$

36. Area of side $= lw = (45 \text{ ft})(20 \text{ ft}) = 900 \text{ ft}^2$
Area of front (or back)

$= lw + \dfrac{bh}{2}$

$= (35 \text{ ft})(20 \text{ ft}) + \dfrac{(35 \text{ ft})(5 \text{ ft})}{2}$

$= 700 \text{ ft}^2 + 87.5 \text{ ft}^2$

$= 787.5 \text{ ft}^2$

Area of 4 sides (total area)

$= 2(900 \text{ ft}^2) + 2(787.5 \text{ ft}^2)$

$= 1800 \text{ ft}^2 + 1575 \text{ ft}^2$

$= 3375 \text{ ft}^2$

The total area of all four vertical sides of the building is 3375 ft^2.

38. Draw a vertical line through the middle of the wing to produce two identical triangles. For each triangle, $b = 22 \text{ yd}$ and $h = \dfrac{29 \text{ yd}}{2} = 14.5 \text{ yd}$.

$A = \dfrac{bh}{2} = \dfrac{(22 \text{ yd})(14.5 \text{ yd})}{2} = 159.5 \text{ yd}^2$

Total area $= 2(159.5 \text{ yd}^2) = 319 \text{ yd}^2$

$\text{Cost} = 319 \text{ yd}^2 \times \dfrac{\$90}{\text{yd}^2} = \$28,710$

The total cost is $28,710.

40. $\text{percentage} = \dfrac{5 + 5 + 5}{20 + 20 + 20} = \dfrac{15}{60} = \dfrac{1}{4} = 0.25$

The smallest triangle perimeter is 25% of the largest triangle perimeter.

Cumulative Review

41. $\dfrac{5}{n} = \dfrac{7.5}{18}$

$5 \times 18 = 7.5 \times n$

$\dfrac{90}{7.5} = \dfrac{7.5n}{7.5}$

$12 = n$

42.
$$\frac{n}{\frac{3}{4}} = \frac{7}{\frac{1}{8}}$$
$$\frac{1}{8} \times n = \frac{3}{4} \times 7$$
$$\frac{1}{8}n = \frac{21}{4}$$
$$\frac{1}{8} \times \frac{8}{1}n = \frac{21}{4} \times \frac{8}{1}$$
$$n = 21 \times 2 = 42$$

43.
$$\frac{2800}{124} = \frac{3500}{n}$$
$$2800 \times n = 124 \times 3500$$
$$\frac{2800n}{2800} = \frac{434,000}{2800}$$
$$n = 155 \text{ tons}$$
155 tons of trash could be collected.

$$\frac{124}{122} = \frac{155}{n}$$
$$124 \times n = 122 \times 155$$
$$\frac{124n}{124} = \frac{18,910}{124}$$
$$n = 152.5 \text{ miles}$$
152.5 miles of coastline could be cleaned up.

44.
$$\frac{n}{425} = \frac{68}{300}$$
$$300 \times n = 425 \times 68$$
$$\frac{300 \times n}{300} = \frac{28,900}{300}$$
$$n = 96.\overline{3}$$
$$n \approx 96$$
About 96 magazines would be taken.

Classroom Quiz 7.4

1. $P = 13.8 \text{ m} + 45.2 \text{ m} + 38.5 \text{ m} = 97.5 \text{ meters}$

2. $A = \dfrac{bh}{2} = \dfrac{(12 \text{ ft})(9 \text{ ft})}{2} = 54 \text{ ft}^2$

3. $180° - (45.6° + 58.2°) = 180° - 103.8° = 76.2°$

7.5 Exercises

2. $\sqrt{49}$ is "the <u>square root</u> of 49."

4. 32 is not a perfect square because no whole number when multiplied by itself equals 32.

6. $\sqrt{0.04} = 0.2$ since $(0.2)(0.2) = 0.04$.

8. $\sqrt{16} = 4$

10. $\sqrt{81} = 9$

12. $\sqrt{196} = 14$

14. $\sqrt{225} = 15$

16. $\sqrt{121} = 11$

18. $\sqrt{324} = 18$

20. $\sqrt{25} + \sqrt{64} = 5 + 8 = 13$

22. $\sqrt{0} + \sqrt{121} = 0 + 11 = 11$

24. $\sqrt{169} - \sqrt{64} = 13 - 8 = 5$

26. $\sqrt{196} + \sqrt{36} - \sqrt{16} = 14 + 6 - 4 = 20 - 4 = 16$

28. $\sqrt{225} \times \sqrt{9} = 15 \times 3 = 45$

30. a. Yes, because $17 \times 17 = 289$.

    b. $\sqrt{289} = 17$

32. $\sqrt{45} \approx 6.708$

34. $\sqrt{82} \approx 9.055$

36. $\sqrt{194} \approx 13.928$

38. $\sqrt{62 \text{ m}^2} \approx 7.874 \text{ m}$

40. $\sqrt{250 \text{ m}^2} \approx 15.811 \text{ m}$

42. $\sqrt{20} + \sqrt{81} \approx 4.472 + 9 = 13.472$

44. $\sqrt{154} - \sqrt{36} \approx 12.410 - 6 = 6.410$

46. $\sqrt{8164} \text{ ft} \approx 90.4 \text{ ft}$
The diagonal measures about 90.4 ft.

48. $\sqrt{3589} \text{ in.} \approx 60 \text{ in.}$
The diagonal measures about 60 in.

50. $\sqrt{578} + \sqrt{984} \approx 24.0416 + 31.3688$
$$= 55.4104 \text{ which rounds to } 55.410$$

Cumulative Review

51. $A = lw = (60 \text{ in.})(80 \text{ in.}) = 4800 \text{ sq in.}$
The area is 4800 sq in.

52. 80.5 km = 80,500 meters
He "joggled" 80,500 meters.

53. $30 \text{ km} \times \dfrac{1 \text{ mi}}{1.61 \text{ km}} \approx 18.6 \text{ mi}$
The race is about 18.6 miles.

54. $17 \text{ cm} = \dfrac{0.394 \text{ in.}}{1 \text{ cm}} \approx 6.7 \text{ in.}$
It can reach a length of about 6.7 in.

Classroom Quiz 7.5

1. $\sqrt{81} = 9$

2. $\sqrt{25} + \sqrt{121} = 5 + 11 = 16$

3.
$$A = s^2$$
$$169 \text{ m}^2 = s^2$$
$$\sqrt{169 \text{ m}^2} = \sqrt{s^2}$$
$$13 \text{ m} = s$$

How Am I Doing? Sections 7.1–7.5

1. $90° - 72° = 18°$

2. $180° - 63° = 117°$

3. $\angle a = 180° - 136° = 44°$
$\angle b = 136°$
$\angle a = \angle c = 44°$

4. $P = 2(6.5 \text{ m}) + 2(2.5 \text{ m}) = 13 \text{ m} + 5 \text{ m} = 18 \text{ m}$

5. $P = 4(3.5 \text{ m}) = 14 \text{ m}$

6. $A = (4.8 \text{ cm})^2 = 23.04 \text{ cm}^2$

7. $A = 5.8 \text{ yd} \times 3.9 \text{ yd} = 22.62 \text{ yd}^2$

8. $P = 2(9.2 \text{ yd}) + 2(3.6 \text{ yd})$
$\quad = 18.4 \text{ yd} + 7.2 \text{ yd}$
$\quad = 25.6 \text{ yd}$

9. $P = 17 \text{ ft} + 15 \text{ ft} + 25\dfrac{1}{2} \text{ ft} + 21\dfrac{1}{2} \text{ ft} = 79 \text{ ft}$

10. $A = 27 \text{ in.} \times 13 \text{ in.} = 351 \text{ in.}^2$

11.
$$A = \frac{1}{2}h(b+B)$$
$$= \frac{1}{2}(9 \text{ in.})(16 \text{ in.} + 22 \text{ in.})$$
$$= \frac{1}{2}(9 \text{ in.})(38 \text{ in.})$$
$$= 171 \text{ in.}^2$$

12.
$$A = 7 \text{ m} \times 9 \text{ m} + \frac{1}{2}(10 \text{ m} + 7 \text{ m})(4 \text{ m})$$
$$= 63 \text{ m}^2 + \frac{1}{2}(17 \text{ m})(4 \text{ m})$$
$$= 97 \text{ m}^2$$

13. $180° - (43° + 81°) = 180° - 124° = 56°$

14.
$$P = 9\frac{1}{2} \text{ in.} + 4 \text{ in.} + 6\frac{1}{2} \text{ in.}$$
$$= 13\frac{1}{2} \text{ in.} + 6\frac{1}{2} \text{ in.}$$
$$= 20 \text{ in.}$$

15. $A = \dfrac{1}{2}(16 \text{ m})(9 \text{ m}) = 72 \text{ m}^2$

16. a.
$$A = \frac{1}{2}(44 \text{ ft} + 30 \text{ ft})(16 \text{ ft})$$
$$= \frac{1}{2}(74 \text{ ft})(16 \text{ ft})$$
$$= 592 \text{ ft}^2$$
592 ft^2 of paint is needed for the sign.

b. $P = 20 \text{ ft} + 30 \text{ ft} + 20 \text{ ft} + 44 \text{ ft} = 114 \text{ ft}$
114 ft of trim is needed for the sign.

17. $\sqrt{64} = 8$

18. $\sqrt{225} + \sqrt{16} = 15 + 4 = 19$

19. $\sqrt{169} = 13$

20. $\sqrt{256} = 16$

21. $\sqrt{46} \approx 6.782$

7.6 Exercises

2. Square the length of the hypotenuse and square the length of the leg. Subtract the value of the leg squared from the value of the hypotenuse squared. Take the square root of the result.

4. $h = \sqrt{16^2 + 12^2} = \sqrt{256 + 144} = \sqrt{400} = 20$ yd

6. $\text{leg} = \sqrt{21^2 - 7^2}$
$= \sqrt{441 - 49}$
$= \sqrt{392}$
≈ 19.799 ft

8. $h = \sqrt{8^2 + 2^2} = \sqrt{64 + 4} = \sqrt{68} = 8.246$ m

10. $h = \sqrt{7^2 + 7^2} = \sqrt{49 + 49} = \sqrt{98} \approx 9.899$ m

12. $\text{leg} = \sqrt{13^2 - 11^2}$
$= \sqrt{169 - 121}$
$= \sqrt{48} \approx 6.928$ yd

14. $\text{leg} = \sqrt{20^2 - 14^2}$
$= \sqrt{400 - 196}$
$= \sqrt{204} \approx 14.283$ ft

16. $h = \sqrt{6^2 + 8^2} = \sqrt{36 + 64} = \sqrt{100} = 10$ m

18. $\text{leg} = \sqrt{23^2 - 9^2}$
$= \sqrt{529 - 81}$
$= \sqrt{448} \approx 21.166$ ft

20. $\text{hypotenuse} = \sqrt{15^2 + 18^2}$
$= \sqrt{225 + 64}$
$= \sqrt{289}$
$= 17$ ft
The guy wire is 17 ft.

22. $\text{hypotenuse} = \sqrt{4^2 + 3^2} = \sqrt{16 + 9} = \sqrt{25} = 5$ mi
He is 5 miles from this starting point.

24. $\text{leg} = \sqrt{20^2 - 18^2} = \sqrt{400 - 324} = \sqrt{76} \approx 8.7$ ft
The distance is 8.7 feet.

26. Side opposite $30° = \frac{1}{2}(10.6) = 5.3$ ft

The other leg $= \sqrt{10.6^2 - 5.3^2}$
$= \sqrt{112.36 - 28.09}$
$= \sqrt{84.27}$
≈ 9.2 ft

28. The other leg = 5 m
hypotenuse $= \sqrt{2} \times \text{leg}$
$= \sqrt{2} \times 5$
$\approx 1.414 \times 5$
≈ 7.1 m

30. The other leg = 3 cm
hypotenuse $= \sqrt{2} \times \text{leg}$
$= \sqrt{2} \times 3$
$\approx 1.414 \times 3$
≈ 4.2 cm

32. hypotenuse $= \sqrt{8^2 + 6^2}$
$= \sqrt{64 + 36}$
$= \sqrt{100}$
$= 10$ m
The antenna support is 10 meters long.

34. hypotenuse $= \sqrt{7^2 + 9^2}$
$= \sqrt{49 + 81}$
$= \sqrt{130}$
≈ 11.40 in.
The length of the diagonal is 11.40 inches.

36. $\text{leg} = \sqrt{45^2 - 43^2}$
$= \sqrt{2025 - 1849}$
$= \sqrt{176}$
≈ 13.266 yd

Cumulative Review

37. $A = \dfrac{bh}{2} = \dfrac{(31 \text{ m})(22 \text{ m})}{2} = 341 \text{ m}^2$
The area of the land is 341 m^2.

38. $A = lw = (20.5 \text{ ft})(14.5 \text{ ft}) = 297.25 \text{ ft}^2$
The area of the garden is 297.25 ft^2.

39. $A = s^2 = (21 \text{ in.})^2 = 441 \text{ in.}^2$

The area of the window is 441 in.^2.

40. $A = bh = (88 \text{ yd})(48 \text{ yd}) = 4224 \text{ yd}^2$

The area of the roof is 4224 yd^2.

Classroom Quiz 7.6

1. $h = \sqrt{9^2 + 7^2} = \sqrt{81 + 49} = \sqrt{130} \approx 11.40$ feet

2. $\text{leg} = \sqrt{15^2 - 12^2}$
$= \sqrt{225 - 144}$
$= \sqrt{81}$
$= 9$ centimeters

3. $\text{leg} = \sqrt{22^2 - 18^2}$
$= \sqrt{484 - 324}$
$= \sqrt{160}$
≈ 12.65 meters
The distance is 12.65 meters.

7.7 Exercises

2. The radius is a line segment from the <u>center</u> to a point on the circle.

4. Divide the diameter by 2. Square the result, then multiply this by 3.

6. You need to find the area of the circle with the given radius, then divide by 2.

8. $d = 2r = 2(33 \text{ in.}) = 66 \text{ in.}$

10. $d = 2r$
$= 2\left(12\dfrac{3}{8}\right)$
$= 2\left(\dfrac{99}{8}\right)$
$= \dfrac{99}{4}$
$= 24\dfrac{3}{4}$ or 24.75 yd

12. $r = \dfrac{d}{2} = \dfrac{65 \text{ yd}}{2} = 32.5 \text{ yd}$

14. $r = \dfrac{d}{2} = \dfrac{27.06 \text{ cm}}{2} = 13.53 \text{ cm}$

16. $C = \pi d = 3.14(17 \text{ cm}) = 53.38 \text{ cm}$

18. $C = 2\pi r = 2(3.14)(24.5 \text{ in.}) = 153.86 \text{ in.}$

20. $C = \pi d = (3.14)(24 \text{ in.}) = 75.36 \text{ in.}$

Distance $= (75.36 \text{ in.})(5 \text{ rev}) \times \dfrac{1 \text{ ft}}{12 \text{ in.}} = 31.4 \text{ ft}$

22. $A = \pi r^2$
$= 3.14(7 \text{ yd})^2$
$= 3.14(49 \text{ yd})^2$
$= 153.86 \text{ yd}^2$

24. $A = \pi r^2$
$= 3.14(12.5)^2$
$= 3.14(156.25)$
$\approx 490.63 \text{ in.}^2$

26. $r = \dfrac{d}{2} = \dfrac{52 \text{ cm}}{2} = 26 \text{ cm}$
$A = \pi r^2$
$= 3.14(26 \text{ cm})^2$
$= 3.14(676 \text{ cm}^2)$
$= 2122.64 \text{ cm}^2$

28. $A = \pi r^2$
$= 3.14(8 \text{ ft})^2$
$= 3.14(64 \text{ ft}^2)$
$= 200.96 \text{ ft}^2$

30. $r = \dfrac{120 \text{ mi}}{2} = 60 \text{ mi}$
$A = \pi r^2$
$= 3.14(60 \text{ mi})^2$
$= 3.14(3600 \text{ mi}^2)$
$= 11,304 \text{ mi}^2$

32. $A = \pi r^2 - \pi r^2$
$= 3.14(13 \text{ m})^2 - 3.14(9 \text{ m})^2$
$= 3.14(169 \text{ m}^2) - 3.14(81 \text{ m}^2)$
$= 530.66 \text{ m}^2 - 254.34 \text{ m}^2$
$= 276.32 \text{ m}^2$

34. $A = lw - \dfrac{1}{2}\pi r^2$

$= (14 \text{ m})(7 \text{ m}) - \dfrac{1}{2}(3.14)(7 \text{ m})^2$

$= 98 \text{ m}^2 - \dfrac{1}{2}(3.14)(49 \text{ m}^2)$

$= 98 \text{ m}^2 - 76.93 \text{ m}^3$

$= 21.07 \text{ m}^2$

36. $r = \dfrac{d}{2} = \dfrac{18 \text{ m}}{2} = 9 \text{ m}$

$A = \dfrac{1}{2}\pi r^2 + lw$

$= \dfrac{1}{2}(3.14)(9 \text{ m})^2 + (20 \text{ m})(18 \text{ m})$

$= \dfrac{1}{2}(3.14)(81 \text{ m}^2) + 360 \text{ m}^2$

$= 127.17 \text{ m}^2 + 360 \text{ m}^2$

$= 487.17 \text{ m}^2$

38. $r = \dfrac{d}{2} = \dfrac{50 \text{ yd}}{2} = 25 \text{ yd}$

$A = \pi r^2 + lw$

$= (3.14)(25 \text{ yd})^2 + (110 \text{ yd})(50 \text{ yd})$

$= 1962.5 \text{ yd}^2 + 5500 \text{ yd}^2$

$= 7462.5 \text{ yd}^2$

$\text{Cost} = 7462.5 \text{ yd}^2 \times \dfrac{\$0.20}{\text{yd}^2} = \$1492.50$

40. $C = \pi d = 3.14(2 \text{ ft}) = 6.28 \text{ ft}$
The length of the strip is 6.28 feet.

42. $C = 2\pi r = 2(3.14)(14 \text{ in.}) \approx 87.92 \text{ in.}$

$\text{Distance} = 35(87.92 \text{ in.}) \times \dfrac{1 \text{ ft}}{12 \text{ in.}} \approx 256.43 \text{ ft}$

The car travels 256.43 feet.

44. $1 \text{ mi} = 5280 \text{ ft} \times \dfrac{12 \text{ in.}}{1 \text{ ft}} = 63,360 \text{ in.}$

$C = 2\pi r = 2(3.14)(15 \text{ in.}) = 94.2 \text{ in.}$

$\text{rev} = \dfrac{63,360 \text{ in.}}{94.2 \text{ in.}} \approx 672.61$

His wheels make 672.61 revolutions.

46. a. $A = \pi r^2$

$= 3.14(1.5)^2$

$= 3.14(2.25)$

$= 7.07 \text{ mi}^2$

The delivery area is 7.07 mi^2.

b. $\dfrac{C}{2} = \dfrac{2\pi r}{2} = \pi r = 3.14(1.5) = 4.71 \text{ mi}$
He will drive 4.71 miles.

48. $A = \pi r^2$

$= 3.14(300)^2$

$= 3.14(90,000)$

$= 282,600 \text{ mi}^2$

The area is $282,600 \text{ mi}^2$.

50. a. $\text{Cost} = \dfrac{10}{8} = 1.25 = \$1.25$

$r = \dfrac{d}{2} = \dfrac{14 \text{ in.}}{2} = 7 \text{ in.}$

$\dfrac{A}{8} = \dfrac{\pi r^2}{8} = \dfrac{3.14(7 \text{ in.})^2}{8} = 19.2 \text{ in}^2$

The cost is $1.25 per slice and the area is 19.2 in.^2.

b. $\text{Cost} = \dfrac{12}{9} \approx 1.33 = \$1.33$

$\dfrac{A}{9} = \dfrac{s^2}{9} = \dfrac{(12.5 \text{ in.})^2}{9} \approx 17.4 \text{ in}^2$

The cost is $1.33 per slice and the area is 17.4 in.^2.

c. For the 14-in.-diameter pizza, it is about $\dfrac{\$1.25}{19.2 \text{ in.}^2} \approx \$0.065$ per in.^{2}; for the square pizza, it is about $\dfrac{\$1.33}{17.4 \text{ in.}^2} \approx \$0.076$ per in.^{2}; the 14-inch round pizza is a better value.

Cumulative Review

51. $n = 25\% \times 120$
$n = 0.25 \times 120$
$n = 30$

52. $n = 0.5\% \times 60$
$\quad n = 0.005 \times 60$
$\quad n = 0.3$

53. $10\% \times n = 7$
$\quad 0.10n = 7$
$\quad \dfrac{0.10n}{0.10} = \dfrac{7}{0.10}$
$\qquad n = 70$

54. $19\% \times n = 570$
$\quad 0.19n = 570$
$\quad \dfrac{0.19n}{l0.19} = \dfrac{570}{0.19}$
$\qquad n = 3000$

Classroom Quiz 7.7

1. $C = \pi d \approx 3.14(12 \text{ in.}) = 37.68 \text{ in.}$

2. $A = \pi r^2 \approx 3.14(7)^2 = 153.86 \text{ m}^2$

3. rectangle $A = 500 \text{ ft} \times 400 \text{ ft} = 200{,}000 \text{ ft}^2$
circle $A = \pi r^2 \approx 3.14(150 \text{ ft})^2 = 70{,}650 \text{ ft}^2$
Area not watered $= 200{,}000 \text{ ft}^2 - 70{,}650 \text{ ft}^2$
$\qquad\qquad\qquad\quad = 129{,}350 \text{ ft}^2$

7.8 Exercises

2. a. pyramid

  b. $V = \dfrac{Bh}{3}$

4. a. box or rectangular solid

  b. $V = lwh$

6. a. cube

  b. $V = s^3$

8. $V = lwh$
$\quad = (20 \text{ mm})(14 \text{ mm})(2.5 \text{ mm})$
$\quad = 700 \text{ mm}^3$

10. $V = \pi r^2 h$
$\quad = 3.14(2 \text{ m})^2(7 \text{ m})$
$\quad = 3.14(4 \text{ m}^2)(7 \text{ m})$
$\quad = 87.92 \text{ m}^3$
$\quad \approx 87.9 \text{ m}^3$

12. $r = \dfrac{d}{2} = \dfrac{30 \text{ m}}{2} = 15 \text{ m}$
$V = \pi r^2 h$
$\quad = 3.14(15 \text{ m})^2(9 \text{ m})$
$\quad = 3.14(225 \text{ m}^2)(9 \text{ m})$
$\quad = 6358.5 \text{ m}^3$

14. $V = \dfrac{4\pi r^3}{3}$
$\quad = \dfrac{4(3.14)(12 \text{ yd})^3}{3}$
$\quad = \dfrac{4(3.14)(1728 \text{ yd}^3)}{3}$
$\quad \approx 7234.6 \text{ yd}^3$

16. $V = \dfrac{Bh}{3} = \dfrac{24(55)}{3} = 440 \text{ ft}^3$

18. $V = s^3 = (0.8)^3 = 0.512 \text{ cm}^3$

20. $V = \dfrac{\pi r^2 h}{3}$
$\quad = \dfrac{3.14(6)^2(4)}{3}$
$\quad = \dfrac{3.14(36)(4)}{3}$
$\quad = 150.72 \text{ yd}^3$

22. $V = \dfrac{1}{2} \times \dfrac{4\pi r^3}{3}$
$\quad = \dfrac{1}{2} \times \dfrac{4(3.14)(6 \text{ m})^3}{3}$
$\quad = \dfrac{1}{2} \times \dfrac{4(3.14)(216 \text{ m}^3)}{3}$
$\quad = \dfrac{1}{2} \times 904.32 \text{ m}^3$
$\quad \approx 452.2 \text{ m}^3$

24. $V = \dfrac{\pi r^2 h}{3}$

$= \dfrac{3.14(9 \text{ cm})^2(12 \text{ cm})}{3}$

$= \dfrac{3.14(81 \text{ cm}^2)(12 \text{ cm})}{3}$

$\approx 1017.4 \text{ cm}^3$

26. $V = \dfrac{\pi r^2 h}{3}$

$= \dfrac{3.14(9 \text{ ft})^2(14.2 \text{ ft})}{3}$

$= \dfrac{3.14(81 \text{ ft}^2)(14.2 \text{ ft})}{3}$

$\approx 1203.9 \text{ ft}^3$

28. $B = (3 \text{ m})(3 \text{ m}) = 9 \text{ m}^2$

$V = \dfrac{Bh}{3} = \dfrac{(9 \text{ m}^2)(7 \text{ m})}{3} = 21 \text{ m}^3$

30. $B = (6 \text{ m})(12 \text{ m}) = 72 \text{ m}^2$

$V = \dfrac{Bh}{3} = \dfrac{(72 \text{ m}^2)(5 \text{ m})}{3} = 120 \text{ m}^3$

32. $4 \text{ in.} \times \dfrac{1 \text{ ft}}{12 \text{ in.}} \times \dfrac{1 \text{ yd}}{3 \text{ ft}} = \dfrac{1}{9} \text{ yd}$

$V = lwh$

$= (120 \text{ yd})(7 \text{ yd})\left(\dfrac{1}{9} \text{ yd}\right)$

$= (840 \text{ yd}^2)\left(\dfrac{1}{9} \text{ yd}\right)$

$\approx 93.3 \text{ yd}^3$

He will need 93.3 yd^3 of stone.

34. Outer $= \pi r^2 h$

$= 3.14(6 \text{ in.})^2(25 \text{ in.})$

$= 3.14(36 \text{ in.}^2)(25 \text{ in.})$

$= 2826 \text{ in.}^3$

Inner $= \pi r^2 h$

$= 3.14(4 \text{ in.})^2(25 \text{ in.})$

$= 3.14(16 \text{ in.}^2)(25 \text{ in.})$

$= 1256 \text{ in.}^3$

Difference $= 2826 \text{ in.}^3 - 1256 \text{ in.}^3 = 1570 \text{ in.}^3$

The volume is 1570 in.^3.

36. Softball:

$r = \dfrac{d}{2} = \dfrac{3.8 \text{ in.}}{2} = 1.9 \text{ in.}$

$V = \dfrac{4\pi r^3}{3}$

$= \dfrac{4(3.14)(1.9 \text{ in.})^3}{3}$

$= \dfrac{4(3.14)(6.859 \text{ in.}^3)}{3}$

$\approx 28.7 \text{ in.}^3$

Baseball:

$r = \dfrac{d}{2} = \dfrac{1.7 \text{ in.}}{2} = 0.85 \text{ in.}$

$V = \dfrac{4\pi r^3}{3}$

$= \dfrac{4(3.14)(0.85 \text{ in.})^3}{3}$

$= \dfrac{4(3.14)(0.614125)}{3}$

$\approx 2.6 \text{ in.}^3$

Difference $= 28.7 \text{ in.}^3 - 2.6 \text{ in.}^3 \approx 26.1 \text{ in.}^3$

38. $V = lwh = (8 \text{ in.})(3 \text{ in.})(14 \text{ in.}) = 336 \text{ in.}^3$

Cereal area $= \dfrac{3}{4} \cdot 336 \text{ in.}^3 = 252 \text{ in.}^3$

There are 252 in.^3 of cereal in the box.

40. $V = \dfrac{\pi r^2 h}{3}$

$= \dfrac{3.14(5 \text{ cm})^2(9 \text{ cm})}{3}$

$= \dfrac{3.14(25 \text{ cm}^2)(9 \text{ cm})}{3}$

$= 235.5 \text{ cm}^3$

Cost $= 235.5 \text{ cm}^3 \times \dfrac{\$4.00}{1 \text{ cm}^3} = \$942$

The total cost is $942.

42. $V = \pi r^2 h = 3.14\left(\dfrac{20 \text{ ft}}{2}\right)^2(9 \text{ ft}) = 2826 \text{ ft}^3$

The volume is 2826 ft^3.

44. $V = 263,900 \text{ yd}^2$

Weight $= 263,900 \text{ yd}^2 \times \dfrac{422 \text{ lb}}{1 \text{ yd}^2}$

$= 111,365,800 \text{ lb}$

Weight $= 111,365,800 \text{ lb} \times \dfrac{1 \text{ ton}}{2000 \text{ lb}}$

$= 55,682.9 \text{ tons}$

The pyramid weighs 111,365,800 lb or 55,682.9 tons.

Cumulative Review

1. $V = \dfrac{4\pi r^3}{3} = \dfrac{4(3.14)(4 \text{ cm})^3}{3} \approx 267.95 \text{ cm}^3$

2. $V = \dfrac{Bh}{3} = \dfrac{(7 \text{ yd} \times 6 \text{ yd})(8 \text{ yd})}{3} = 112 \text{ yd}^3$

3. $V = \pi r^2 h = 3.14(3 \text{ m})^2 (13 \text{ m}) = 367.38 \text{ m}^3$

4. Answers may vary. Possible solution:

The volume is larger by $\dfrac{4^2}{3^2} = \dfrac{16}{9}$.

Classroom Quiz 7.8

1. $V = \dfrac{4\pi r^3}{3} = \dfrac{4(3.14)(3 \text{ cm})^3}{3} = 113.04 \text{ cm}^3$

2. $V = \dfrac{Bh}{3} = \dfrac{(8 \text{ yd})^2 (10 \text{ yd})}{3} \approx 213.33 \text{ yd}^3$

3. $V = \pi r^2 h = 3.14(2 \text{ m})^2 (12 \text{ m}) = 150.72 \text{ m}^3$

7.9 Exercises

2. The corresponding sides of similar triangles have the same <u>ratio</u>.

4. Set up a proportion of the perimeter of the larger triangle to the perimeter of the smaller triangle equal to the side of the large triangle to the corresponding side of the small triangle. Use p for the perimeter of the smaller triangle. Substitute the numbers for the other quantities. Solve the proportion for p.

6. $\dfrac{n}{3} = \dfrac{24}{8}$

$8n = (3)(24)$

$8n = 72$

$\dfrac{8n}{89} = \dfrac{72}{8}$

$n = 9$

9 m

8. $\dfrac{n}{15} = \dfrac{7}{16}$

$16n = (15)(7)$

$16n = 105$

$\dfrac{16n}{16} = \dfrac{105}{16}$

$n \approx 6.6$

6.6 ft

10. $\dfrac{n}{9} = \dfrac{20}{12.5}$

$12.5n = 9(20)$

$\dfrac{12.5n}{12.5} = \dfrac{180}{12.5}$

$n = 14.4 \text{ ft}$

12. a corresponds to d.
b corresponds to f.
c corresponds to e.

14. $\dfrac{n}{5} = \dfrac{30}{9}$

$9n = (5)(30)$

$9n = 150$

$\dfrac{9n}{9} = \dfrac{150}{9}$

$n \approx 16.7$

The shortest side of the actual lobby will be 16.7 m.

16. $\dfrac{2}{5} = \dfrac{n}{18}$

$2(18) = 5(n)$

$36 = 5n$

$7.2 \text{ ft} = n$

The width of the porch is 7.2 feet.

18.

$$\frac{n}{\frac{1}{4}} = \frac{36}{\frac{3}{4}}$$

$$\frac{3}{4}n = \left(\frac{1}{4}\right)(36)$$

$$\frac{3}{4}n = 9$$

$$\frac{3}{4} \times \frac{4}{3}n = 9 \times \frac{4}{3}$$

$$n = 12$$

The wall will be 12 ft tall.

20.

$$\frac{n}{8} = \frac{35}{7}$$

$$7n = (8)(35)$$

$$7n = 280$$

$$\frac{7n}{7} = \frac{280}{7}$$

$$n = 40$$

The flagpole is 40 ft.

22.

$$\frac{n}{610} = \frac{6}{8}$$

$$8n = (610)(6)$$

$$8n = 3660$$

$$\frac{8n}{8} = \frac{3660}{8}$$

$$n = 457.5$$

The rock is 457.5 ft tall.

24.

$$\frac{n}{7} = \frac{20}{11}$$

$$11n = (7)(20)$$

$$11n = 140$$

$$\frac{11n}{11} = \frac{140}{11}$$

$$n \approx 12.7 \text{ ft}$$

26.

$$\frac{n}{10} = \frac{30}{22}$$

$$22n = 10(30)$$

$$\frac{22n}{22} = \frac{300}{22}$$

$$n \approx 13.6 \text{ cm}$$

Cumulative Review

27.

$$2 \times 3^2 + 4 - 2 \times 5 = 2 \times 9 + 4 - 2 \times 5$$
$$= 18 + 4 - 10$$
$$= 22 - 10$$
$$= 12$$

28.

$$100 \div (8-3)^2 \times 2^3 = 100 \div (5^2)(2^3)$$
$$= 100 \div (25)(8)$$
$$= 4 \times 8$$
$$= 32$$

29. $\dfrac{4}{5} \times \dfrac{5}{3} - \dfrac{1}{3} = \dfrac{4}{3} - \dfrac{1}{3} = \dfrac{3}{3} = 1$

30. $\dfrac{8}{5} \div 3 - \dfrac{1}{3} = \dfrac{8}{5} \cdot \dfrac{1}{3} - \dfrac{1}{3} = \dfrac{8}{15} - \dfrac{1}{3} = \dfrac{8}{15} - \dfrac{5}{15} = \dfrac{3}{15} = \dfrac{1}{5}$

Classroom Quiz 7.9

1.

$$\frac{20}{12} = \frac{7}{n}$$

$$20n = 12(7)$$

$$\frac{20n}{20} = \frac{84}{20}$$

$$n = 4.2 \text{ in.}$$

2.

$$\frac{13}{2} = \frac{14}{n}$$

$$13n = 2(14)$$

$$13n = 28$$

$$n \approx 2.15 \text{ m}$$

3.

$$\frac{6}{5} = \frac{4}{n}$$

$$6n = 5(4)$$

$$6n = 20$$

$$\frac{6n}{6} = \frac{20}{6}$$

$$n \approx 3.33 \text{ ft}$$

7.10 Exercises

2. a. Trip = 22 km + 20 km = 42 km

$$\text{Speed} = \frac{42 \text{ km}}{0.6 \text{ hr}} = 70 \text{ km/hr}$$

b. Trip = 10 km + 20 km = 30 km

$$\text{Speed} = \frac{30 \text{ km}}{0.5 \text{ hr}} = 60 \text{ km/hr}$$

c. Trip via the supermarket has the higher speed.

4. $A = (16 \text{ ft})(7 \text{ ft}) = 112 \text{ ft}^2$

$A = (14 \text{ ft})(7 \text{ ft}) = 98 \text{ ft}^2$

$A = (12 \text{ ft})(7 \text{ ft}) = 84 \text{ ft}^2$

Total $A = 112 \text{ ft}^2 + 98 \text{ ft}^2 + 2 \times 84 \text{ ft}^2 = 378 \text{ ft}^2$

$\text{Time} = 378 \text{ ft}^2 \times \dfrac{25 \text{ min}}{80 \text{ ft}^2} \approx 118 \text{ min}$

It will take them 118 min or 1 hr 58 min.

6. $A = lw = 19 \times \dfrac{3}{4}(8) = 114 \text{ ft}^2$

$\text{Cost} = 4(114) = \$456$
The tile will cost \$456.

8. $A = \dfrac{bh}{2} + lw - lw$

$= \dfrac{(24 \text{ ft})(6 \text{ ft})}{2} + (15 \text{ ft})(24 \text{ ft}) - (3 \text{ ft})(6 \text{ ft})$

$= 72 \text{ ft}^2 + 360 \text{ ft}^2 - 18 \text{ ft}^2$

$= 414 \text{ ft}^2$

$\text{Cost} = 414 \text{ ft}^2 \times \dfrac{1 \text{ yd}^2}{9 \text{ ft}^2} \times \dfrac{\$18}{\text{yd}^2} = \$828$

\$828 is the cost to put siding on this side of the barn.

10. $V = lwh - Bh$

$V = 3 \times 4 \times 7 \times (1 \text{ m})^3 - 3.14 \times (1 \text{ m})^2 + 7 \text{ m}$

$V = 84 \text{ m}^3 - 21.98 \text{ m}^3$

$V \approx 62.02 \text{ m}^3$

$\text{Cost} = 62.02 \text{ mm}^3 \times \dfrac{\$1.20}{\text{m}^3} \approx \$74.42$

The concrete will cost \$74.42.

12. a. $P = \text{square side} + \text{square side}$

$\quad + \dfrac{1}{4} \text{ circle circumference}$

$= 140 \text{ m} + 140 \text{ m} + \dfrac{1}{4}(2 \times 3.14 \times 140 \text{ m})$

$= 499.8 \text{ m}$

The perimeter is 499.8 meters.

b. $\text{Cost} = 499.8 \text{ m} \times \dfrac{\$15}{\text{m}} = \$7497$

It will cost \$7497 to put the fence around the park.

14. $V = 2(lwh)$

$= 2\left(15 \text{ ft} \times 11 \text{ ft} \times \dfrac{2}{12} \text{ ft}\right)$

$= 55 \text{ ft}^3$

Yes, the volume of wood chips he needs is 55 cubic feet.

Cumulative Review

15.

$$
\begin{array}{r}
128 \\
16\overline{)2048} \\
\underline{16} \\
44 \\
\underline{32} \\
128 \\
\underline{128} \\
0
\end{array}
$$

16.

$$
\begin{array}{r}
308 \\
42\overline{)12{,}936} \\
\underline{12\ 6} \\
336 \\
\underline{336} \\
0
\end{array}
$$

17.

$$
\begin{array}{r}
0.25 \\
1.3_\wedge\overline{)0.3_\wedge 25} \\
\underline{2\ 6} \\
65 \\
\underline{65} \\
0
\end{array}
$$

18.

$$
\begin{array}{r}
4.87 \\
0.52_\wedge\overline{)2.53_\wedge 24} \\
\underline{2\ 08} \\
45\ 2 \\
\underline{41\ 6} \\
3\ 64 \\
\underline{3\ 64} \\
0
\end{array}
$$

Classroom Quiz 7.10

1. $A = \text{rectangle area} + \text{circle area (2 halves)}$

$= lw + \pi r^2$

$= (120 \text{ yd})(30 \text{ yd}) + 3.14(15 \text{ yd})^2$

$= 4306.5 \text{ yd}^2$

The area of the new field is 4306.5 yd^2.

2. A = rectangle area -8(window area)

$= (20 \text{ ft})(36 \text{ ft}) - 8(3 \text{ ft})(2 \text{ ft})$

$= 672 \text{ ft}^2$

He needs to cover 672 ft^2 with paint.

3. Total Cost

$= (\text{Cost per m}^2)(\text{Area of triangle in m}^2)$

$= \$30/\text{m}^2\left(\dfrac{1}{2} \times 20 \text{ m} \times 13 \text{ m}\right)$

$= \$3900$

The carpeting will cost \$3900.

Putting Your Skills to Work

1. $16 \text{ ft} \times 18 \text{ ft} = 288 \text{ ft}^2$

$12 \text{ ft} \times 11 \text{ ft} = 132 \text{ ft}^2$

$12 \text{ ft} \times 12 \text{ ft} = 144 \text{ ft}^2$

2. $288 \text{ ft}^2 \times \dfrac{1 \text{ yd}^2}{9 \text{ ft}^2} = 32 \text{ yd}^2$

$132 \text{ ft}^2 \times \dfrac{1 \text{ yd}^2}{9 \text{ ft}^2} = 14\dfrac{2}{3} \text{ yd}^2$

$144 \text{ ft}^2 \times \dfrac{1 \text{ yd}^2}{9 \text{ ft}^2} = 16 \text{ yd}^2$

The total is $32 + 14\dfrac{2}{3} + 16 = 62\dfrac{2}{3} \text{ yd}^2$.

3. Store A: $62\dfrac{2}{3} \text{ yd}^2 \times \dfrac{\$15}{\text{yd}^2} + \$99 = \$1039$

Store B: $62\dfrac{2}{3} \text{ yd}^2 \times \dfrac{\$16.50}{\text{yd}^2} = \$1034$

Store C: $62\dfrac{2}{3} \text{ yd}^2 \times \dfrac{\$18.00}{\text{yd}^2} - \$25 = \$1103$

Store B is least expensive.

4. Answers will vary.

5. Answers will vary.

Chapter 7 Review Problems

1. $90° - 76° = 14°$

2. $180° - 76° = 104°$

3. $\angle b = 146°$

$\angle a = \angle c = 180° - 146° = 34°$

4. $\angle t = \angle x = \angle y = 65°$

$\angle s = \angle u = \angle w = \angle z = 180° - 65° = 115°$

5. $P = 2(9.5 \text{ m}) + 2(2.3 \text{ m})$

$= 19 \text{ m} + 4.6 \text{ m}$

$= 23.6 \text{ m}$

6. $P = 4s = 4(12.7 \text{ yd}) = 50.8 \text{ yd}$

7. $A = (5.9 \text{ cm})(2.8 \text{ cm}) = 16.52 \text{ cm}^2 \approx 16.5 \text{ cm}^2$

8. $A = s^2 = (7.2 \text{ in.})^2 = 51.84 \text{ in.}^2 \approx 51.8 \text{ in.}^2$

9. $P = 3(8 \text{ ft}) + 2(2 \text{ ft}) + 4 \text{ ft} + 2(3 \text{ ft})$

$= 24 \text{ ft} + 4 \text{ ft} + 4 \text{ ft} + 6 \text{ ft}$

$= 38 \text{ ft}$

10. $P = 3(11 \text{ ft}) + 2(7 \text{ ft}) + 2(3.5 \text{ ft}) + 4 \text{ ft}$

$= 33 \text{ ft} + 14 \text{ ft} + 7 \text{ ft} + 4 \text{ ft}$

$= 58 \text{ ft}$

11. $A = (14 \text{ m})(5 \text{ m}) - (1 \text{ m})^2$

$= 70 \text{ m}^2 - 2 \text{ m}^2$

$= 68 \text{ m}^2$

12. $A = (9 \text{ m})^2 - (2.7 \text{ m})(6.5 \text{ m})$

$= 81 \text{ m}^2 - 17.55 \text{ m}^2$

$= 63.45 \text{ m}^2$

$\approx 63.5 \text{ m}^2$

13. $P = 2(38.5 \text{ m}) + 2(14 \text{ m})$

$= 77 \text{ m} + 28 \text{ m}$

$= 105 \text{ m}$

14. $P = 5 \text{ mi} + 22 \text{ mi} + 5 \text{ mi} + 30 \text{ mi} = 62 \text{ mi}$

15. $A = (70 \text{ ft})(50 \text{ ft}) = 3500 \text{ ft}^2$

16. $A = \dfrac{18 \text{ yd}(21 \text{ yd} + 19 \text{ yd})}{2}$

$= \dfrac{18 \text{ yd}(40 \text{ yd})}{2}$

$= 360 \text{ yd}^2$

17. $A = \dfrac{(8 \text{ cm})(13 \text{ cm} + 20 \text{ cm})}{2}$

    $\qquad + \dfrac{(20 \text{ cm})(9 \text{ cm} + 20 \text{ cm})}{2}$

    $\quad = \dfrac{(8 \text{ cm})(33 \text{ cm})}{2} + \dfrac{(20 \text{ cm})(29 \text{ cm})}{2}$

    $\quad = 132 \text{ cm}^2 + 290 \text{ cm}^2$

    $\quad = 422 \text{ cm}^2$

18. $A = (15 \text{ m})(17 \text{ m}) + (17 \text{ m})(6 \text{ m})$

    $\quad = 255 \text{ m}^2 + 102 \text{ m}^2$

    $\quad = 357 \text{ m}^2$

19. $P = 18 + 21 + 21 = 60$ ft

20. $P = 15.5 + 15.5 + 15.5 = 46.5$ ft

21. $180° - (28° + 45°) = 180° - 73° = 107°$

22. $180° - (90° + 35°) = 180° - 125° = 55°$

23. $A = \dfrac{(8.5 \text{ m})(12.3 \text{ m})}{2}$

    $\quad = \dfrac{104.55 \text{ m}^2}{2}$

    $\quad = 52.275 \text{ m}^2$

    $\quad \approx 52.3 \text{ m}^2$

24. $A = \dfrac{(12.5 \text{ m})(9.5 \text{ m})}{2}$

    $\quad = \dfrac{118.75 \text{ m}^2}{2}$

    $\quad = 59.375 \text{ m}^2$

    $\quad \approx 59.4 \text{ m}^2$

25. $A = (18 \text{ m})(22 \text{ m}) + \dfrac{(18 \text{ m})(6 \text{ m})}{2}$

    $\quad = 396 \text{ m}^2 + 54 \text{ m}^2$

    $\quad = 450 \text{ m}^2$

26. $A = (12 \text{ m})(6 \text{ m}) + \dfrac{(6 \text{ m})(3 \text{ m})}{2} + \dfrac{(6 \text{ m})(2 \text{ m})}{2}$

    $\quad = 72 \text{ m}^2 + 9 \text{ m}^2 + 6 \text{ m}^2$

    $\quad = 87 \text{ m}^2$

27. $\sqrt{81} = 9$

28. $\sqrt{64} = 8$

29. $\sqrt{121} = 11$

30. $\sqrt{144} + \sqrt{16} = 12 + 4 = 16$

31. $\sqrt{100} - \sqrt{36} + \sqrt{196} = 10 - 6 + 14 = 18$

32. $\sqrt{45} \approx 6.708$

33. $\sqrt{62} \approx 7.874$

34. $\sqrt{165} \approx 12.845$

35. $\sqrt{180} \approx 13.416$

36. hypotenuse $= \sqrt{3^2 + 4^2} = \sqrt{9 + 16} = \sqrt{25} = 5$ km

37. hypotenuse $= \sqrt{13^2 - 12^2}$

    $\qquad\qquad = \sqrt{169 - 144}$

    $\qquad\qquad = \sqrt{25}$

    $\qquad\qquad = 5$ yd

38. leg $= \sqrt{20^2 - 18^2}$

    $\qquad = \sqrt{400 - 324}$

    $\qquad = \sqrt{76}$

    $\qquad \approx 8.72$ cm

39. $h = \sqrt{6^2 + 7^2} = \sqrt{36 + 49} = \sqrt{85} \approx 9.22$ m

40. hypotenuse $= \sqrt{5^2 + 4^2}$

    $\qquad\qquad = \sqrt{25 + 16}$

    $\qquad\qquad = \sqrt{41}$

    $\qquad\qquad \approx 6.4$ cm

    The distance is about 6.4 cm.

41. hypotenuse $= \sqrt{18^2 + 1.5^2}$

    $\qquad\qquad = \sqrt{324 + 2.25}$

    $\qquad\qquad = \sqrt{326.25}$

    $\qquad\qquad \approx 18.1$ ft

    The ramp is 18.1 feet.

42. leg $= \sqrt{11^2 - 9^2} = \sqrt{121 - 81} = \sqrt{40} \approx 6.3$ ft

    The distance is 6.3 feet.

43. leg $= \sqrt{7^2 - 6^2} = \sqrt{49 - 36} = \sqrt{13} \approx 3.6$ ft

    The width is 3.6 feet.

44. $d = 2r = 2(53 \text{ cm}) = 106 \text{ cm}$

45. $r = \dfrac{d}{2} = \dfrac{126 \text{ cm}}{2} = 63 \text{ cm}$

46. $C = \pi d = 3.14(20 \text{ m}) = 62.8 \text{ m}$

47. $C = 2\pi r = 2(3.14)(9 \text{ in.}) = 56.52 \text{ in.} \approx 56.5 \text{ in.}$

48. $A = \pi r^2$
$= 3.14(9 \text{ m})^2$
$= 3.14(81 \text{ m})^2$
$= 254.34 \text{ m}^2$
$\approx 254.3 \text{ m}^2$

49. $r = \dfrac{d}{2} = \dfrac{8.6 \text{ ft}}{2} = 4.3 \text{ ft}$
$A = \pi r^2$
$= 3.14(4.3 \text{ ft})^2$
$= 3.14(18.49 \text{ ft})^2$
$\approx 58.06 \text{ ft}^2$

50. $A = \pi r^2 - \pi r^2$
$= 3.14(11 \text{ in.})^2 - 3.14(7 \text{ in.})^2$
$= 3.14(121 \text{ in.}^2) - 3.14(49 \text{ in.}^2)$
$= 379.94 \text{ in.}^2 - 153.86 \text{ in.}^2$
$= 226.08 \text{ in.}^2$
$\approx 226.1 \text{ in.}^2$

51. $A = \pi r^2 - \pi r^2$
$= 3.14(10 \text{ m})^2 - 3.14(6 \text{ m})^2$
$= 3.14(100 \text{ m}^2) - 3.14(36 \text{ m}^2)$
$= 314 \text{ m}^2 - 113.04 \text{ m}^2$
$= 200.96 \text{ m}^2$
$\approx 201.0 \text{ m}^2$

52. $A = lw + \pi r^2$
$= (24 \text{ ft})(10 \text{ ft}) + 3.14(5 \text{ ft})^2$
$= 240 \text{ ft}^2 + 78.5 \text{ ft}^2$
$= 318.5 \text{ ft}^2$

53. $A = lw - \pi r^2$
$= (20 \text{ m})(14 \text{ m}) - 3.14(7 \text{ m})^2$
$= 280 \text{ m}^2 - 153.86 \text{ m}^2$
$= 126.14 \text{ m}^2$
$\approx 126.1 \text{ m}^2$

54. $A = bh - \pi r^2$
$= (12 \text{ ft})(10 \text{ ft}) - 3.14(2 \text{ ft})^2$
$= 120 \text{ ft}^2 - 12.56 \text{ ft}^2$
$= 107.44 \text{ ft}^2$
$\approx 107.4 \text{ ft}^2$

55. $A = \dfrac{h(b + B)}{2} + \dfrac{1}{2} \times \pi r^2$
$= \dfrac{5 \text{ m}(8 \text{ m} + 14 \text{ m})}{2} + \dfrac{1}{2} \times (3.14)(4 \text{ m})^2$
$= \dfrac{5 \text{ m}(22 \text{ m})}{2} + \dfrac{1}{2} \times (3.14)(16 \text{ m}^2)$
$= 55 \text{ m} + 25.12 \text{ m}^2$
$= 80.12 \text{ m}^2$
$\approx 80.1 \text{ m}^2$

56. $V = lwh = (20.8)(7.5)(8.1) = 1263.6 \text{ ft}^3$
The storage area has a volume of 1263.6 ft^3.

57. $V = \dfrac{4\pi r^3}{3}$
$= \dfrac{4(3.14)(4.5)^3}{3}$
$= \dfrac{4(3.14)(91.125)}{3}$
$\approx 381.5 \text{ in.}^3$
The volume of the ball is 381.5 in.^3.

58. $V = \pi r^2 h$
$= 3.14(1.5 \text{ ft})^2(3 \text{ ft})$
$= 3.14(2.25 \text{ ft}^2)(3 \text{ ft})$
$\approx 21.2 \text{ ft}^3$
The volume of the can is 21.2 ft^3.

59. $V = \pi r^2 h$

$\quad = 3.14(1.5 \text{ in.})^2 (5 \text{ in.})$

$\quad = 3.14(2.25 \text{ in.}^2)(5 \text{ in.})$

$\quad \approx 35.3 \text{ in.}^3$

The volume of the coffee is 35.3 in.^3.

60. $B = (7 \text{ m})(7 \text{ m}) = 49 \text{ m}^2$

$V = \dfrac{Bh}{3} = \dfrac{(49 \text{ m}^2)(15 \text{ m})}{3} = 245 \text{ m}^3$

The volume of the sculpture is 245 m^3.

61. $V = \dfrac{\pi r^2 h}{3}$

$\quad = \dfrac{3.14(20 \text{ ft})^2 (9 \text{ ft})}{3}$

$\quad = \dfrac{3.14(400 \text{ ft}^2)(9 \text{ ft})}{3}$

$\quad = 3768 \text{ ft}^3$

The volume of the cone is 3768 ft^3.

62. $V = \dfrac{\pi r^2 h}{3}$

$\quad = \dfrac{3.14(17 \text{ yd})^2 (30 \text{ yd})}{3}$

$\quad = \dfrac{3.14(289 \text{ yd}^2)(30 \text{ yd})}{3}$

$\quad = \dfrac{27{,}223.8 \text{ yd}^3}{3}$

$\quad = 9074.6 \text{ yd}^3$

The volume of the polluted ground was 9074.6 yd^3.

63. $\dfrac{n}{2} = \dfrac{45}{3}$

$3n = (2)(45)$

$3n = 90$

$\dfrac{3n}{3} = \dfrac{90}{3}$

$n = 30$

30 m

64. $\dfrac{n}{20} = \dfrac{6}{36}$

$36n = (20)(6)$

$36n = 120$

$\dfrac{36n}{36} = \dfrac{120}{36}$

$n \approx 3.3 \text{ m}$

65. Small figure: $P = 7 + 18 + 7 + 26 = 58 \text{ cm}$

$\dfrac{n}{58} = \dfrac{108}{18}$

$18n = 108(58)$

$\dfrac{18n}{18} = \dfrac{6264}{18}$

$n = 348$

348 cm

66. Small figure: $P = 13 + 19 + 12 + 26 = 70 \text{ ft}$

$\dfrac{n}{70} = \dfrac{32.5}{13}$

$13n = 70(32.5)$

$\dfrac{13n}{13} = \dfrac{2275}{13}$

$n = 175$

175 ft

67. $3\dfrac{1}{2} \times 3\dfrac{1}{2} = \dfrac{7}{2} \times \dfrac{7}{2} = \dfrac{49}{4}$

$\dfrac{n}{\frac{49}{4}} = \dfrac{12}{1}$

$n = \left(\dfrac{49}{4}\right)(12) = 147$

The finished banner needs 147 yd^2 of fabric.

68. $V = \dfrac{\pi r^2 h}{3}$

$\quad = \dfrac{3.14(9 \text{ in.})^2 (24 \text{ in.})}{3}$

$\quad = \dfrac{3.14(81 \text{ in.}^2)(24 \text{ in.})}{3}$

$\quad \approx 2034.7 \text{ in.}^3$

$W = 2034.7 \text{ in.}^3 \times \dfrac{16 \text{ g}}{1 \text{ in.}^3} = 32{,}555.2 \text{ g}$

The tank holds 2034.7 in.^3 and the weight of the acid is $32{,}555 \text{ g}$.

69. $A = lw - lw$

$\quad = (14 \text{ yd})(8 \text{ yd}) - (4 \text{ yd})(5 \text{ yd})$

$\quad = 112 \text{ yd}^2 - 20 \text{ yd}^2$

$\quad = 92 \text{ yd}^2$

$\text{Cost} = 92 \text{ yd}^2 \times \dfrac{\$8}{\text{yd}^2} = \$736$

The carpeting will cost $736.

70. a. Trip = 32 km + 18 km = 50 km

$\text{Speed} = \dfrac{50 \text{ km}}{0.5 \text{ hr}} = 100 \text{ km/hr}$

b. Trip = 26 km + 14 km + 16 km = 56 km

$\text{Speed} = \dfrac{56 \text{ km}}{0.8 \text{ hr}} = 70 \text{ km/hr}$

c. The more rapid rate is through Ipswich.

71. a. $V = \pi r^2 h + \dfrac{1}{2} \times \dfrac{4\pi r^3}{3}$

$\quad = 3.14(9 \text{ ft})^2 (80 \text{ ft}) + \dfrac{1}{2} \times \dfrac{4(3.14)(9 \text{ ft})^3}{3}$

$\quad = 3.14(81 \text{ ft}^2)(80 \text{ ft}) + \dfrac{1}{2} \times \dfrac{4(3.14)(729 \text{ ft}^3)}{3}$

$\quad = 20{,}347.2 \text{ ft}^3 + \dfrac{1}{2} \times 3052.08 \text{ ft}^3$

$\quad = 21{,}873.24 \text{ ft}^3$

The volume is $\approx 21{,}873.2 \text{ ft}^3$.

b. $B = 21{,}873.2 \text{ ft}^3 \times \dfrac{0.8 \text{ bushel}}{1 \text{ ft}^3}$

It will hold $\approx 17{,}498.6$ bushels.

72. 2.757 billion × 1.244 $\text{ft}^3 = 3.429708 \text{ ft}^3$

$\qquad\qquad\qquad = 3{,}429{,}708{,}000 \text{ ft}^3$

$3{,}429{,}708{,}000 \text{ ft}^3$ of storage was needed.

73. $h = \dfrac{V}{lw}$

$\quad = \dfrac{3{,}429{,}108{,}000 \text{ ft}^3}{(10{,}000 \text{ ft})(20{,}000 \text{ ft})}$

$\quad = \dfrac{3{,}429{,}108{,}000 \text{ ft}^3}{200{,}000{,}000 \text{ ft}^2}$

$\quad \approx 17.1 \text{ ft}$

The bin would need to be 17.1 feet high.

74. $V = lwh = (2.25)(4)(2) = 18 \text{ ft}^3$

$18 \text{ ft}^3 \times \dfrac{62 \text{ lb}}{\text{ft}^3} = 1116 \text{ lb}$

$1116 \text{ lb} \times \dfrac{1 \text{ gal}}{8.6 \text{ lb}} \approx 130 \text{ gal}$

The aquarium holds 1116 lb of water or 130 gallons.

75. $2 \text{ ft} \times \dfrac{12 \text{ in.}}{1 \text{ ft}} = 24 \text{ in.}$

$4 \text{ ft} \times \dfrac{12 \text{ in.}}{1 \text{ ft}} = 48 \text{ in.}$

$V = lwh = 24(48)(1.5) = 1728 \text{ in}^3$

1728 in.^3 of gravel are needed.

76. $C = 2\pi r = 2(3.14)(30 \text{ ft}) = 188.4 \text{ ft}$

$5(188.4) = 942 \text{ ft}$

The pony walks 942 ft for each ride.

77. $r = \dfrac{d}{2} = \dfrac{18 \text{ yd}}{2} = 9 \text{ yd}$

$P = 2l + 2\pi r$

$\quad = 2(25 \text{ yd}) + 2(3.14)(9 \text{ yd})$

$\quad \approx 106.5 \text{ yd}$

The perimeter is 106.5 yards.

78. $\text{Cost} = 106.5 \text{ yd} \times \dfrac{3 \text{ ft}}{1 \text{ yd}} \cdot \dfrac{1 \text{ spool}}{150 \text{ ft}}$

$\qquad\quad = 2.13 \text{ or order 3 spools}$

They need to order 3 spools.

79. $\text{leg} = \sqrt{33^2 - 30^2}$

$\qquad = \sqrt{1089 - 900}$

$\qquad = \sqrt{189}$

$\qquad \approx 13.7 \text{ ft}$

The person is about 13.7 feet from the edge of the pond.

80. $r = \dfrac{d}{2} = \dfrac{90 \text{ m}}{2} = 45 \text{ m}$

$$V = \dfrac{4\pi r^2}{3}$$

$$= \dfrac{4(3.14)(45 \text{ m})^3}{2}$$

$$= \dfrac{4(3.14)(91,125 \text{ m}^3)}{3}$$

$$= 381,510 \text{ m}^3$$

The volume is 381,510 cubic meters.

81. $18 \text{ in.} \times \dfrac{1 \text{ ft}}{12 \text{ in.}} = \dfrac{3}{2}$

$$r = \dfrac{d}{2} = \dfrac{\frac{3}{2}}{2} = \dfrac{3}{4} \text{ ft} = 0.75 \text{ ft}$$

$$V = \pi r^2 h$$

$$= 3.14(0.75 \text{ ft})^2 (5 \text{ ft})$$

$$= 3.14(0.5625 \text{ ft}^2)(5 \text{ ft})$$

$$= 8.83125 \text{ ft}^3$$

$$\approx 8.8 \text{ ft}^3$$

The tank holds approximately 8.8 cubic feet.

82. $V \approx 8.8 \text{ ft}^3$

$$\text{gallons} = 8.8 \text{ ft}^3 \times \dfrac{7.5 \text{ gal}}{1 \text{ ft}^3} = 66 \text{ gal}$$

The tank holds approximately 66 gallons.

83. $A = \dfrac{(35 \text{ ft})(45 \text{ ft} + 50 \text{ ft})}{2}$

$$= \dfrac{(35 \text{ ft})(95 \text{ ft})}{2}$$

$$= \dfrac{3325 \text{ ft}^2}{2}$$

$$= 1662.5 \text{ ft}^2$$

The area of the front lawn is 1662.5 square feet.

84. $A = 1662.5 \text{ ft}^2$

$$\text{Cost} = 1662.5 \text{ ft}^2 \times \dfrac{\$0.50}{1 \text{ ft}^2} \times 3 \text{ times/yr}$$

$$= \$2493.75$$

The total cost is \$2493.75.

How Am I Doing? Chapter 7 Test

1. $\angle b = \angle a = 52°$
$\angle c = 180° - 52° = 128°$
$\angle e = \angle c = 128°$

2. $P = 2(9 \text{ yd}) + 2(11 \text{ yd}) = 18 \text{ yd} + 22 \text{ yd} = 40 \text{ yd}$

3. $P = 4(6.3 \text{ ft}) = 25.2 \text{ ft}$

4. $P = 2(6.5 \text{ m}) + 2(3.5 \text{ m})$
$= 13 \text{ m} + 7 \text{ m}$
$= 20 \text{ m}$

5. $P = 2(13 \text{ m}) + 22 \text{ m} + 32 \text{ m}$
$= 26 \text{ m} + 22 \text{ m} + 32 \text{ m}$
$= 80 \text{ m}$

6. $P = 58.6 \text{ m} + 32.9 \text{ m} + 45.5 \text{ m} = 137 \text{ m}$

7. $A = (10 \text{ yd})(18 \text{ yd}) = 180 \text{ yd}^2$

8. $A = (10.2 \text{ m})^2 = 104.04 \text{ m}^2 \approx 104.0 \text{ m}^2$

9. $A = (13 \text{ m})(6 \text{ m}) = 78 \text{ m}^2$

10. $A = \dfrac{(9 \text{ m})(7 \text{ m} + 25 \text{ m})}{2}$

$$= \dfrac{(9 \text{ m})(32 \text{ m})}{2}$$

$$= \dfrac{288 \text{ m}^2}{2}$$

$$= 144 \text{ m}^2$$

11. $A = \dfrac{(4 \text{ cm})(6 \text{ cm})}{2} = \dfrac{24 \text{ cm}^2}{2} = 12 \text{ cm}^2$

12. $\sqrt{144} = 12$

13. $\sqrt{169} = 13$

14. $90° - 63° = 27°$

15. $180° - 107° = 73°$

16. $180° - (12.5° + 83.5°) = 180° - 96° = 84°$

17. $\sqrt{54} \approx 7.348$

18. $\sqrt{135} \approx 11.619$

19. $\text{hypotenuse} = \sqrt{7^2 + 5^2}$
$= \sqrt{49 + 25}$
$= \sqrt{74}$
$= 8.602$

20. $\text{leg} = \sqrt{26^2 - 24^2} = \sqrt{676 - 576} = \sqrt{100} = 10$

21. $\text{hypotenuse} = \sqrt{5^2 + 3^2}$
$$= \sqrt{25 + 9}$$
$$= \sqrt{34}$$
$$\approx 5.83 \text{ cm}$$
The distance between the holes in 5.83 cm.

22. $\text{hypotenuse} = \sqrt{15^2 - 12^2}$
$$= \sqrt{225 - 144}$$
$$= \sqrt{81}$$
$$= 9 \text{ ft}$$
The ladder is 9 ft from the house.

23. $r = \dfrac{d}{2} = \dfrac{18}{2} = 9 \text{ ft}$
$C = 2\pi r = 2(3.14)(9) \approx 56.52 \text{ ft}$

24. $r = \dfrac{d}{2} = \dfrac{12}{2} = 6 \text{ ft}$
$A = \pi r^2 = 3.14(6)^2 = 3.14(36) = 113.04 \text{ ft}^2$

25. $A = bh - \pi r^2$
$$= (15 \text{ in.})(8 \text{ in.}) - (3.14)(2 \text{ in.})^2$$
$$= 120 \text{ in.}^2 - 12.56 \text{ in.}^2$$
$$= 107.44 \text{ in.}^2$$
$$\approx 107.4 \text{ in.}^2$$

26. $A = \dfrac{h(b+B)}{2} + \dfrac{1}{2} \times \pi r^2$
$$= \dfrac{(7 \text{ in.})(10 \text{ in.} + 20 \text{ in.})}{2} + \dfrac{1}{2} \times (3.14)(5 \text{ in.})^2$$
$$= \dfrac{(7 \text{ in.})(30 \text{ in.})}{2} + \dfrac{1}{2} \times (3.14)(25 \text{ in.}^2)$$
$$= 105 \text{ in.}^2 + 39.25 \text{ in.}^2$$
$$= 144.25 \text{ in.}^2$$
$$\approx 144.3 \text{ in.}^2$$

27. $V = lwh = 3.5(20)(10) = 700 \text{ m}^3$

28. $V = \dfrac{\pi r^2 h}{3}$
$$= \dfrac{3.14(8 \text{ m})^2 (12 \text{ m})}{3}$$
$$= \dfrac{3.14(64 \text{ m}^2)(12 \text{ m})}{3}$$
$$= 803.84 \text{ m}^3$$
$$\approx 803.8 \text{ m}^3$$

29. $V = \dfrac{4\pi r^3}{3}$
$$= \dfrac{4(3.14)(3 \text{ m})^3}{3}$$
$$= \dfrac{4(3.14)(27 \text{ m}^3)}{3}$$
$$= 113.04 \text{ m}^3$$
$$\approx 113.0 \text{ m}^3$$

30. $V = \pi r^2 h$
$$= 3.14(9 \text{ ft})^2 (2 \text{ ft})$$
$$= 3.14(81 \text{ ft}^2)(2 \text{ ft})$$
$$= 508.68 \text{ ft}^3$$
$$\approx 508.7 \text{ ft}^3$$

31. $B = (4 \text{ m})(3 \text{ m}) = 12 \text{ m}^2$
$$V = \dfrac{Bh}{3} = \dfrac{(12 \text{ m}^2)(14 \text{ m})}{3} = 56 \text{ m}^3$$

32. $\dfrac{n}{18} = \dfrac{13}{5}$
$$5n = 18(13)$$
$$\dfrac{5n}{5} = \dfrac{234}{5}$$
$$n = 46.8 \text{ m}$$

33. $\dfrac{n}{7} = \dfrac{60}{10}$
$$10n = 7(60)$$
$$\dfrac{10n}{10} = \dfrac{420}{10}$$
$$n = 42 \text{ ft}$$

34. $r = \dfrac{d}{2} = 20$ yd

$\begin{aligned}
A &= lw - \pi r^2 \\
&= (130 \text{ yd})(40 \text{ yd}) + 3.14(20 \text{ yd})^2 \\
&= 5200 \text{ yd}^2 + 1256 \text{ yd}^2 \\
&= 6456 \text{ yd}^2
\end{aligned}$

The area of the field is 6456 yd^2.

35. $A = 6456 \text{ yd}^2$

$\text{Cost} = 6456 \text{ yd}^2 \times \dfrac{\$0.40}{1 \text{ yd}^2} = \$2582.40$

It will cost \$2582.40 to fertilize the field.

Cumulative Test for Chapters 1–7

1. $\begin{array}{r} 126,350 \\ 278,120 \\ + \ 531,290 \\ \hline 935,760 \end{array}$

2. $\begin{array}{r} 163 \\ \times \ 205 \\ \hline 815 \\ 32 \ 60 \\ \hline 33,415 \end{array}$

3. $\dfrac{17}{18} - \dfrac{11}{12} = \dfrac{34}{36} - \dfrac{33}{36} = \dfrac{1}{36}$

4. $\dfrac{3}{7} \div 2\dfrac{1}{4} = \dfrac{3}{7} \div \dfrac{9}{4} = \dfrac{3}{7} \times \dfrac{4}{9} = \dfrac{4}{21}$

5. $56.1279 \approx 56.13$

6. $\begin{array}{r} 9.034 \\ \times \ \ \ 0.8 \\ \hline 7.2272 \end{array}$

7. $2.634 \times 10^2 = 2.634 \times 100 = 263.4$

8. $\begin{array}{r} 83 \ \ \ \ \\ 0.021_\wedge \overline{)1.743_\wedge} \\ \underline{1\ 68} \ \ \ \\ 63 \\ \underline{63} \\ 0 \end{array}$

9. $\dfrac{3}{n} = \dfrac{2}{18}$

$\begin{aligned}
3 \times 18 &= n \times 2 \\
54 &= n \times 2 \\
\dfrac{52}{2} &= \dfrac{n \times 2}{2} \\
27 &= n
\end{aligned}$

10. $\dfrac{10}{5.9} = \dfrac{2500}{n}$

$\begin{aligned}
10 \times n &= 5.9 \times 2500 \\
\dfrac{10n}{10} &= \dfrac{14,750}{10} \\
n &= 1475 \text{ copies}
\end{aligned}$

There were 1475 copies sold.

11. $\dfrac{18}{24} = 0.75 = 75\%$

75% of the shots went into the basket.

12. 0.8% of what number is 16?

$\begin{aligned}
0.8\% \times n &= 16 \\
\dfrac{0.008 \times n}{0.008} &= \dfrac{16}{0.008} \\
n &= 2000
\end{aligned}$

13. What is 15% of 120?

$n = 15\% \times 120 = 0.15 \times 20 = 18$

14. $586 \text{ cm} \times \dfrac{1 \text{ m}}{100 \text{ cm}} = 5.86 \text{ m}$

15. $42 \text{ yd} \times \dfrac{36 \text{ in.}}{1 \text{ yd}} = 1512 \text{ in.}$

16. $88 \text{ km} \times \dfrac{0.62 \text{ mi}}{1 \text{ km}} = 54.56 \text{ mi}$

17. $P = 2(15 \text{ m}) + 2(10.5 \text{ m}) = 30 \text{ m} + 21 \text{ m} = 51 \text{ m}$

18. $P = 24 \text{ cm} + 9 \text{ cm} + 31 \text{ cm} + 9 \text{ cm} = 73 \text{ cm}$

19. $C = \pi d = 3.14(18 \text{ yd}) = 56.52 \text{ yd} \approx 56.5 \text{ yd}$

20. $A = \dfrac{bh}{2}$

$\quad = \dfrac{(1.3 \text{ cm})(2.4 \text{ cm})}{2}$

$\quad = \dfrac{2.88 \text{ cm}^2}{2}$

$\quad = 1.44 \text{ cm}^2$

$\quad \approx 1.4 \text{ cm}^2$

21. $A = \dfrac{h(b+B)}{2}$

$\quad = \dfrac{(18 \text{ m})(26 \text{ m} + 34 \text{ m})}{2}$

$\quad = \dfrac{(18 \text{ m})(60 \text{ m})}{2}$

$\quad = 540 \text{ m}^2$

22. $A = lw + bh$

$\quad = (12 \text{ m})(12 \text{ m}) + (12 \text{ m})(4 \text{ m})$

$\quad = 144 \text{ m}^2 + 48 \text{ m}^2$

$\quad = 192 \text{ m}^2$

23. $A = lw - lw$

$\quad = (35 \text{ yd})(20 \text{ yd}) - (6 \text{ yd})(6 \text{ yd})$

$\quad = 700 \text{ yd}^2 - 36 \text{ yd}^2$

$\quad = 664 \text{ yd}^2$

24. $A = \pi r^2$

$\quad = 3.14(4 \text{ m})^2$

$\quad = 3.14(16 \text{ m})^2$

$\quad = 50.24 \text{ m}^2$

$\quad \approx 50.2 \text{ m}^2$

25. $V = \pi r^2 h = (3.14)(1.5)^2 (6) \approx 42.4 \text{ in.}^3$

26. $r = \dfrac{d}{2} = \dfrac{12}{2} = 6 \text{ in.}$

$\quad V = \dfrac{4\pi r^3}{3}$

$\quad = \dfrac{4(3.14)(6)^3}{3}$

$\quad = \dfrac{4(3.14)(216)}{3}$

$\quad \approx 904.3 \text{ in.}^3$

27. $B = (14 \text{ cm})(21 \text{ cm}) = 294 \text{ cm}^2$

$\quad V = \dfrac{Bh}{3} = \dfrac{(294 \text{ cm}^2)(32 \text{ m})}{3} = 3136 \text{ cm}^3$

28. $V = \dfrac{\pi r^2 h}{3}$

$\quad = \dfrac{3.14(8 \text{ m})^2 (15.2 \text{ m})}{3}$

$\quad = \dfrac{3.14(64 \text{ m}^2)(15.2 \text{ m})}{3}$

$\quad \approx 1018.2 \text{ m}^3$

29. $\dfrac{n}{9} = \dfrac{30}{7}$

$\quad 7n = 9(30)$

$\quad \dfrac{7n}{7} = \dfrac{270}{7}$

$\quad n = 38.6 \text{ m}$

30. $\dfrac{n}{11} = \dfrac{1.5}{4}$

$\quad 4n = (11)(1.5)$

$\quad 4n = 16.5$

$\quad \dfrac{4n}{4} = \dfrac{16.5}{4}$

$\quad n = 4.125$

$\quad n \approx 4.1$

$\quad 4.1 \text{ ft}$

31. a. $A = (14 \text{ yd})(6 \text{ yd}) + (5 \text{ yd})(5 \text{ yd}) + \dfrac{(5 \text{ yd})(6 \text{ yd})}{2}$

$\qquad = 84 \text{ yd}^2 + 25 \text{ yd}^2 + 15 \text{ yd}^2$

$\qquad = 124 \text{ yd}^2$

$\qquad$ The area is 124 yd^2.

b. $\text{Cost} = 124 \text{ yd}^2 \times \dfrac{\$8}{1 \text{ yd}^2} = \$992$

$\qquad$ The cost is \$992.00.

32. $\sqrt{144} + \sqrt{81} = 12 + 9 = 21$

33. $\sqrt{57} \approx 7.550$

34. $\text{hypotenuse} = \sqrt{10^2 + 3^2}$

$\qquad\qquad\qquad = \sqrt{100 + 9}$

$\qquad\qquad\qquad = \sqrt{109}$

$\qquad\qquad\qquad \approx 10.440 \text{ in.}$

35. $\text{leg} = \sqrt{7^2 - 5^2} = \sqrt{49 - 25} = \sqrt{24} \approx 4.899$ m

36. $\begin{aligned} \text{hypotenuse} &= \sqrt{32^2 + 10^2} \\ &= \sqrt{1024 + 100} \\ &= \sqrt{1124} \\ &\approx 33.53 \text{ mi} \end{aligned}$

The ocean liner is approximately 33.53 miles from its starting point.

37. $20 \text{ ft} \times \dfrac{12 \text{ in.}}{1 \text{ ft}} = 240 \text{ in.}$

$\begin{aligned} \text{Number needed} &= 240 \div 7\frac{1}{2} \\ &= 240 \div \frac{15}{2} \\ &= 240 \times \frac{2}{15} \\ &= 32 \text{ paintbrushes} \end{aligned}$

You would need 32 paint brushes.

Chapter 8

8.1 Exercises

2. Multiply $45\% \times 4000$, which is
$0.45 \times 4000 = 1800$ students.

4. Subtract the total from answers 1 and 2 from the 4000.
$4000 - 2800 = 1200$
The answer would be 1200.

6. Choose the two smallest sectors; charitable contributions and utilities.

8. Transportation is labeled $650.

10. $300 + \$1000 = \$1300$
$1300 is allotted for food or rent.

12. $\dfrac{\$1000}{\$400} = \dfrac{1000 \div 200}{400 \div 200} = \dfrac{5}{2}$

14. $\dfrac{\$300}{\$2700} = \dfrac{300 \div 300}{2700 \div 300} = \dfrac{1}{9}$

16. Choose the largest sector; 40 years or older, but younger than 60.

18. 20 years old or older but younger than 40 is labeled 83 million or 83,000,000 people.

20. $(84 + 39 + 11)$ million $= 134$ million or 134,000,000 people

22. $\dfrac{(83+84+39+11)\text{ million}}{82\text{ million}} = \dfrac{217}{82}$

24. $\dfrac{11\text{ million}}{299\text{ million}} = \dfrac{11}{299}$

26. $100\% - 56\% = 44\%$

28. $22\% + 8\% = 30\%$
$n = 30\% \times 1010 = 0.3 \times 1010 = 303$ people
303 people responded that quick service or reasonable prices was most important.

30. $11\% - 8\% = 3\%$
$n = 3\% \times 1010 = 0.03 \times 1010 = 30$ people
About 30 people felt that atmosphere was more important than quick service.

32. United States is labeled 24.8%.
Find 24.8% of 45,600,000.
$0.248 \times 45{,}600{,}000 = 11{,}308{,}800$
11,308,800 vehicles were produced in the United States.

34. China (15.9%), Japan (25.2%), South Korea (8.3%)
$15.9\% + 25.2\% + 8.3\% = 49.4\%$
49.4% were produced in Asia.

36. $100\% - 49.4\% = 50.6\%$
50.6% were not produced in Asia.

38. Europe = France + Spain + Germany
$\quad = 7.0\% + 6.1\% + 12.7\%$
$\quad = 25.8\%$
$25.8\% - 24.8\% = 1\%$
1% of $45{,}600{,}000 = 0.01 \times 45{,}600{,}000$
$\qquad\qquad\qquad\qquad = 456{,}000$
456,000 more vehicles were produced in Europe than in the United States.

Cumulative Review

39. $A = \dfrac{bh}{2} = \dfrac{12 \times 20}{2} = 120 \text{ ft}^2$

40. $A = bh = (17 \text{ in.})(12 \text{ in.}) = 204 \text{ in.}^2$

41. $A = 2lw + 2lw$
$\quad = 2(7 \text{ yd})(12 \text{ yd}) + 2(7 \text{ yd})(20 \text{ yd})$
$\quad = 2(84 \text{ yd}^2) + 2(140 \text{ yd}^2)$
$\quad = 168 \text{ yd}^2 + 280 \text{ yd}^2$
$\quad = 448 \text{ yd}^2$

$448 \text{ yd}^2 \times \dfrac{1 \text{ gal}}{28 \text{ yd}^2} = 16 \text{ gal}$

It will take 16 gallons of paint to cover the barn.

42. $A = \pi r^2$
$\quad = 3.14(8 \text{ cm})^2$
$\quad = 3.14(64 \text{ cm}^2)$
$\quad = 200.96 \text{ cm}^2$

$200.96 \text{ cm}^2 \times \dfrac{1 \text{ g}}{64 \text{ cm}^2} = 3.14 \text{ g} \approx 3 \text{ g}$

It will take about 3 grams of silver.

Classroom Quiz 8.1

1. $4\% + 43\% = 47\%$
   47% of the vehicles sold will be station wagons or four-door sedans.

2. $(29\% + 8\%)$ of $890,000 = 37\%$ of $890,000$
   $$= 0.37 \times 890,000$$
   $$= 329,300 \text{ vehicles}$$
   329,300 vehicles sold will be SUVs or two-door coupes.

3. $(100\% - 16\%)$ of $890,000 = 84\%$ of $890,000$
   $$= 0.84 \times 890,000$$
   $$= 747,600 \text{ vehicles}$$
   747,600 vehicles will not be minivans.

8.2 Exercises

2. The bar rises to 42, which represents an approximate population of 42 million or 42,000,000 people.

4. The bar rises to 34, which represents an approximate population of 34 million or 34,000,000 people.

6. 2000 to 2020: $42 - 34 = 8$ million
   $42 + 8 = 50$ million or 50,000,000 people
   The population is expected to be 50,000,000 people in 2040.

8. The bar rises to 107, which represents an average cost of $10,700.

10. $60 - 107 = -47$
    The cost is $4700 less.

12. 2000–01: $87 - 48 = 39$
    2001–02: $92 - 51 = 41$
    2002–03: $98 - 56 = 42$
    2003–04: $107 - 60 = 47$
    2004–05: $114 - 63 = 51$
    The greatest difference is in the academic year 2004–2005.

14. $107 - 98 = 9$
    The cost increased by $900.

16. 2-year: $60 + 63 = 123$
    4-year: $107 + 114 = 221$
    $221 - 123 = 98$
    The savings is $9800.

18. $\dfrac{114 - 87}{87} \approx 0.31$ or about 31%
    The percent increase in cost was about 31%.

20. The dot for 2005 is at 2.5, which represents $2.5 million or $2,500,000.

22. The line from 1999 to 2001 goes upward at the steepest angle. This represents the largest increase.

24. 2003: 2.4
    2005: 2.5
    $2.5 - 2.4 = 0.1$
    $2.5 + 5(0.1) = 3.0$
    The average salary in 2015 would be $3 million or $3,000,000.

26. The dot for October, 2006 is about halfway between 2 and 3. This represents 2.5 inches.

28. The line that represents 2007 is above the line that represents 2006 for the months July, August, and September.

30. $1.5 - 0.5 = 1$ in.
    1 more inch of rain fell in September 2006 than in August 2006.

Cumulative Review

31. $(5+6)^2 - 18 \div 9 \times 3 = 11^2 - 18 \div 9 \times 3$
    $$= 121 - 18 \div 9 \times 3$$
    $$= 121 - 2 \times 3$$
    $$= 121 - 6$$
    $$= 115$$

32. $\dfrac{1}{5} \times \left(\dfrac{1}{5} - \dfrac{1}{6} \right) \times \dfrac{2}{3} = \dfrac{1}{5} + \left(\dfrac{6}{30} - \dfrac{5}{30} \right) \times \dfrac{2}{3}$
    $$= \dfrac{1}{5} + \dfrac{1}{30} \times \dfrac{2}{3}$$
    $$= \dfrac{1}{5} + \dfrac{1}{45}$$
    $$= \dfrac{9}{45} + \dfrac{1}{45}$$
    $$= \dfrac{10}{45}$$
    $$= \dfrac{2}{9}$$

33. 22.4% of 39,307,000 = 0.224 × 39,307,000
$$= 8,804,768 \text{ people}$$
8,804,768 people in this age group had bachelor's degrees.

34. 27% of $n = 2174$
$$0.27n = 2174$$
$$n = \frac{2174}{0.27}$$
$$n \approx 8052 \text{ miles}$$
There are about 8052 miles of national scenic trails in the United States.

Classroom Quiz 8.2

1. The dot for homes in 1995 is at 1050.

2. Subtract the number of homes from the number of condominiums in 2005.
$$1500 - 300 = 1200$$

3. Find the year where the point on the line for homes is 600 more than the point on the line for condominiums; 1990.

How Am I Doing? Sections 8.1–8.2

1. The sector labeled Yosemite is labeled 13%.

2. Great Smoky Mountain National Park (the largest sector) is the park where the greatest number of visitors go.

3. 12% + 11% = 23%
23% of the visitors went to Olympic or Yellowstone National Park.

4. $n = 17\%(25,700,000)$
$n = 0.17(25,700,000)$
$n \approx 4,369,000$ visitors
About 4,369,000 visitors went to Grand Canyon National Park.

5. 13% + 11% = 24%
$n = 24\%(25,700,000)$
$= 0.24(25,700,000)$
$\approx 6,168,000$ visitors
About 6,168,000 visitors went to Yosemite or Yellowstone National Park.

6. The bar rises to 450. Therefore, there were 450 housing starts in Springfield in the first quarter of 2006.

7. The bar rises to 550. Therefore, there were 550 housing starts in the second quarter of 2007.

8. The shortest bar represents the 4th quarter of 2006. Therefore, the smallest number of housing starts were during the fourth quarter of 2006.

9. The tallest bar represents the 3rd quarter of 2007. Therefore, the greatest number of housing starts were during the third quarter of 2007.

10. 600 − 350 = 250 more starts
There were 250 more housing starts in the third quarter of 2007 than in the third quarter of 2006.

11. 450 − 300 = 150 fewer starts
There were 150 fewer housing starts in the first quarter of 2007 than in the first quarter of 2006.

12. Look for the lowest dots on the line representing production of television sets. During August and December the production of television sets was the lowest.

13. Look for the highest dot on the line representing the sales of television sets. During December the sales of television sets was the highest.

14. The first month where the line for sales crosses and is higher than the line for production occurs in November. Therefore, November is the first month in which the production was lower than sales.

15. **a.** The dot for sales in August is at 20 which represents 20,000 television sets sold in August.

    b. The dot for sales in November is halfway between 30 and 40 which is 35 or 35,000 television sets sold in November.

8.3 Exercises

2. You want the intervals to be of equal class width. The range from 22 to 66 is 44. Dividing 44 by 3 you get 15 to the nearest whole number. So you make each interval of width 15. Thus, a good choice would be class widths of 22–37, 38–53, 54–69.

4. In the intervals that Jason made the number 400 would be counted twice. Similarly, 500 and 600 would be counted twice. He should rather use 300–399, 400–499, 500–599, and 600–699.

6. The bar for 200,000–499,999 rises to 60, so the number of U.S. cities that have a population of 200,000–499,999 is 60 cities.

8. The bar for 75,000–99,999 rises to 120, so the number of U.S. cities that have a population of 75,000–99,999 is 120 cities.

10. Add the heights of all the bars.
$120 + 150 + 60 + 20 + 10 = 360$ cities

12. Add the heights of the three bars representing 100,000–199,999 (150), 200,000–499,999 (60) and 500,000–999,999 (20).
$150 + 60 + 20 = 230$ cities

14. The bar for $25 or more rises to 7000, so 7000 books are priced at $25.00 or more.

16. The shortest bar represents less than $3.00, so the bookstore sold the least amount of books costing less than $3.00.

18. Add the heights of the bars representing $10.00 to $14.99 (12,000), $15.00 + $24.99 (13,000) and $25 or more (7000).
$12{,}000 + 13{,}000 + 7000 = 32{,}000$ books

20. Add the heights of the bars representing $3.00 to $4.99 (8000), $5.00 to $7.99 (17,000) and $5.00 to $7.99 (10,000).
$8000 + 17{,}000 + 10{,}000 = 35{,}000$ books

22.
$$\begin{array}{r} 3{,}000 \\ 8{,}000 \\ + \ 17{,}000 \\ \hline 28{,}000 \text{ books} \end{array}$$
$$\frac{28{,}000}{70{,}000} = \frac{2}{5} = 0.40 = 40\%$$
40% of the 70,000 books sold were under $8.00.

24. Tally: |||| |||
Frequency: 8

26. Tally: ||
Frequency: 2

28. Tally: |||
Frequency: 3

30. Tally: |
Frequency: 1

32. Add the frequencies for 37°–41° (3), 42°–46° (2) and 47°–51° (1).
$3 + 2 + 1 = 6$ days

Cumulative Review

34.
$$\frac{182}{m} = \frac{25}{19}$$
$$182 \times 19 = m \times 25$$
$$3458 = 25m$$
$$\frac{3458}{25} = \frac{25m}{25}$$
$$138.32 = m$$

35.
$$\frac{n}{18} = \frac{3.5}{9}$$
$$9n = 18 \times 3.5$$
$$9n = 63$$
$$\frac{9n}{9} = \frac{63}{9}$$
$$n = 7$$

36.
$$\frac{375 \text{ mi}}{7.5 \text{ gal}} = \frac{n}{12.3 \text{ gal}}$$
$$375 \times 12.3 = 7.5 \times n$$
$$4612.5 = 7.5n$$
$$\frac{4612.5}{7.5} = \frac{7.5n}{7.5}$$
$$615 \text{ miles} = n$$
He can drive 615 miles on a full tank.

37.
$$\frac{\text{snow}}{\text{water}} : \frac{23 \text{ in.}}{2 \text{ in.}} = \frac{150 \text{ in.}}{n \text{ in.}}$$
$$23 \times n = 2 \times 150$$
$$23 \times n = 300$$
$$\frac{23 \times n}{23} = \frac{300}{23}$$
$$n \approx 13.0$$
This corresponds to 13.0 in. of water.

Classroom Quiz 8.3

1. The bar for 5–8 rises to 600, which represents 600 people.

2. Add the heights of the bars for 13–16, 17–20, and 21–24.
$900 + 300 + 150 = 1350$ people

3. $300 - 150 = 150$ people

8.4 Exercises

2. The mode of a set of data is the number or numbers that occur most often. Some sets of data, like 5, 6, 6, 7 clearly have one mode. It is 6. Other sets of data, like 5, 5, 6, 7, 7, have two

values that occur most often. There are two modes—5 and 7. Some sets of data, like 4, 5, 6, 7, 8, do not have any value that occurs more often than any other value. This set does not have a mode.

4. Mean $= \dfrac{28+17+18+21+24+30+30}{7}$

$= \dfrac{168}{7}$

$= 24$

The mean is 24 pizzas.

6. Mean $= \dfrac{91+90+87+78+68+60}{6}$

$= \dfrac{474}{6}$

$= 79°F$

The mean temperature is 79°F.

8. Mean $= \dfrac{541+561+840+422}{3+3+4+2}$

$= \dfrac{2364}{12}$

$= 197$ pins

Her bowling average is 197 pins.

10. $\begin{array}{r} 63,000 \\ 98,000 \\ 104,000 \\ 109,000 \\ +\,108,000 \\ \hline 482,000 \end{array}$

Mean $= \dfrac{482,000}{5} = 96,400$ people

The mean population is 96,400 people.

12. Mean $= \dfrac{260+375+408+416}{10+15+17+16} = \dfrac{1459}{58} \approx 25.2$

The average is 25.2 mi/gal.

14. 512, 539, 548, 554, 560
Median = 548

16. 7.5, 7.8, 7.9, 8.1, 8.2, 8.8

Median $= \dfrac{7.9+8.1}{2} = 8.0$

18. $18,000, $24,000, $29,000, $32,000, $35,000, $60,000

Median $= \dfrac{\$29,000+\$32,000}{2} = \$30,500$

The median annual income is $30,500.

20. 35, 40, 45, 45, 50, 60, 80
Median = 45 minutes
The median swimming time is 45 minutes.

22. $5.99, $7.99, $9.99, $10.99, $11.99, $12.99, $13.99, $14.99, $15.99
Median = $11.99
The median price is $11.99.

24. 1.2, 1.5, 1.6, 1.7, 2.0, 2.3, 2.4, 2.5

Median $= \dfrac{1.7+2.0}{2} = 1.85$ pounds

The median amount purchased was 1.85 pounds.

26. mean for total points

$= \dfrac{2430+2132+2105+2070}{4}$

$= \dfrac{8737}{4}$

$= 2184.25$ points

mean points per game

$= \dfrac{31.6+27.3+28.4+25.2}{4}$

$= \dfrac{112.5}{4}$

$= 28.125$ points

28. $\begin{array}{r} \$5679 \\ 6902 \\ 1530 \\ 2738 \\ 2999 \\ 4105 \\ 3655 \\ 5980 \\ +\;\;\; 4430 \\ \hline \$38,018 \end{array}$

Mean $= \dfrac{\$38,018}{9} \approx \$4224.22$

The mean price is $4224.22.

30. 14.77, 15.276, 18.90, 19.02, 21.375, 29.2

Median $= \dfrac{18.9+19.02}{2} = \dfrac{37.92}{2} = 18.96$

32. $\text{Mean} = \dfrac{1381 + 1405 + 1405 + 1520 + 1592}{5}$

    $= \$1460.60$

    1381, 1405, 1405, 1520, 1592
    Median = \$1405
    The mean amount is \$1460.60 and the median amount is \$1405.

34. The mode is 84 which occurs twice.

36. The modes are 141 and 144 which both occur twice.

38. 315, 430, 315, 330, 430, 315, 460
    Mode = \$315 which occurs three times.

40. $\text{Mean} = \dfrac{568 + 388 + 588 + 688 + 750 + 900 + 388}{7}$

    $= \dfrac{4270}{7}$

    $= 610$ passengers

    388, 388, 568, 588, 688, 750, 900
    Median = 588 passengers
    Mode = 388 passengers since it occurs twice.

42. **a.** $\text{Mean} = \dfrac{11.7 + 11.6 + 12.0 + 12.1 + 11.9 + 18 + 11.5 + 12.4}{8}$

    $= \dfrac{101.2}{8}$

    $= 12.65$ seconds
    The mean time is 12.65 seconds.

    b. 11.5, 11.6, 11.7, 11.9, 12.0, 12.1, 12.4, 18
    $\text{Median} = \dfrac{11.9 + 12.0}{2} = 11.95$ seconds
    The median time is 11.95 seconds.

    c. There is no mode.

    d. The median, because the log time of 18 seconds affects the mean.

44. **a.** $\text{Mean} = \dfrac{3 + 7 + 8 + 6 + 9 + 28 + 3}{7}$

    ≈ 9.1 nights
    The mean is 9.1 nights.

    b. 3, 3, 6, 7, 8, 9, 28
    Median = 7 nights
    The median is 7 nights.

    c. Mode = 3 nights
    The mode is 3 nights since it occurs twice.

d. The median is the most representative. For three months he travels more than this. For three months he travels less than this. In one month he was away from home exactly 7 nights. The mean is distorted because of the very high value of 28 in June. The mode is artificially low because he is overnight for travel 3 nights in January and July. This is not representative of what usually happens.

Cumulative Review

45. $A = \dfrac{bh}{2}$

$= \dfrac{(7 \text{ in.})(5.5 \text{ in.})}{2}$

$= \dfrac{38.5 \text{ in.}^2}{2}$

$= 19.25 \text{ in.}^2$

$\approx 19.3 \text{ in.}^2$

The area is 19.3 in.^2.

46. $A = \pi r^2$

$= 3.14(40 \text{ ft}^2)$

$= 3.14(1600 \text{ ft})^2$

$= 5024 \text{ ft}^2$

$\text{water} = 2 \times 5024 \text{ ft} \times \dfrac{2 \text{ gal}}{1 \text{ ft}^2}$

$= 20{,}096 \text{ gallons per hour}$

$20{,}096$ gallons per hour are needed to water the fields.

47. $A = bh = (5 \text{ ft})(4 \text{ ft}) = 20 \text{ ft}^2$

$\text{Cost} = 20 \text{ ft}^2 \times \dfrac{\$16.50}{1 \text{ ft}^2} = \$330$

The cost to make the sign is $330.

48. $V = \pi r^2 h$

$= 3.14(1.5)^2(7)$

$= 3.14(2.25)(7)$

$= 49.455$

$\text{Cost} = \dfrac{\$1.98}{49.455 \text{ in.}^2} \approx \$0.04/\text{in.}^3$

The cost is about $0.04 per in.^{3}.

Classroom Quiz 8.4

1. 1, 3, 5, 5, 7, 9, 16, 17, 24, 32

$\text{median} = \dfrac{7+9}{2} = \dfrac{16}{2} = 8 \text{ times}$

The median is 8 times.

2. $\text{mean} = \dfrac{24+3+1+32+5+17+7+5+9+16}{10}$

$= \dfrac{119}{10}$

$= 11.9 \text{ times}$

The mean is 11.9 times.

3. mode = 5 times because it occurs twice.

Putting Your Skills to Work

1. $72° - 68° = 4°$

$4 \times 0.02 \times 205 = 16.4$

They could expect to save $16.40 per month.

2. $84° - 78° = 6°$

$6 \times 0.02 \times 205 = 24.6$

They could expect to save $24.60 per month.

3. $\dfrac{5°}{1 \text{ mo}} \times \dfrac{12 \text{ mo}}{1} \times \dfrac{\$205}{1 \text{ mo}} \times \dfrac{0.02}{1°} = \$246$

They could expect to save $246 per year.

4. Answers will vary.

5. Answers will vary.

6. $\$2.95 \times 100 = \$295$

$\$4.45 \times 100 = \$445$

$\$445 - \$295 = \$150$

The difference in cost is $150.

7. $\$4.45 \times 100 \times 5 = \$2225$

He can expect to pay $2225.

8. 4° lower: $\dfrac{4}{72} = 0.08$ or 8% savings

8% of 2225 = $0.08 \times 2225 = 178$

He will save $178.

9. 8° lower: $\dfrac{8}{72} = 0.16$ or 16% savings

16% of 2225 = $0.16 \times 2225 = 356$

He will save $356.

10. $445 = $ what percent of 2225?

$\dfrac{445}{2225} = 20\%; \ 10°$ lower

He needs to get it at $72° - 10° = 62°$.

Chapter 8 Review Problems

1. 13 computers were manufactured by IBM.

2. 32 computers were manufactured by Apple.

3. $43 + 25 = 68$ computers were manufactured by Dell or Compaq.

4. $21 + 6 = 27$ computers were manufactured by Gateway or Acer.

5. $\dfrac{13}{21}$ is the ratio of IBM to Gateway.

6. $\dfrac{43}{32}$ is the ratio of Dell to Apple.

7. $\dfrac{25}{140} \approx 0.179 = 17.9\%$

   Approximately 17.9% of the computers are manufactured by Compaq.

8. $\dfrac{32}{140} \approx \dfrac{32}{140} \approx 0.229 = 22.9\%$

   Approximately 22.9% of the computers are manufactured by Apple.

9. $23\% + 25\% = 48\%$
   48% of the students are majoring in business or social sciences.

10. $100\% - 23\% = 77\%$
    77% of the students are majoring in an area other than business.

11. Art is the smallest sector.

12. Business is the second to largest sector.

13. $8\% + 1\% = 20\% = \dfrac{1}{5}$

    Art and education together make up one-fifth of the graph.

14. $n = 15\%(8000) = 0.15(8000) = 1200$ students
    1200 students are majoring in language arts.

15. $n = 42\%(8000) = 0.42(8000) = 3360$ students
    3360 students are majoring in a science.

16. $23\% - 12\% = 11\%$
    $n = 11\%(8000) = 0.11(8000) = 880$ students
    880 more students are majoring in business than education.

17. The height of the bar for prescription drugs in 2000 is 121, which represents $121 billion or $121,000,000,000.

18. The height of the bar for physician/clinical services in 2010 is 611, which represents $611 billion or $611,000,000,000.

19. $611 - 430 = 181$
    $181 billion or $181,000,000,000 is the expected increase.

20. $204 - 121 = 83$
    $83 billion or $83,000,000,000 is the expected increase.

21. The greatest difference in bar heights for any 5-year period for prescription drugs is from 2005 to 2010.

22. The greatest difference in bar heights for any 5-year period for physician/clinical services is from 2005 to 2010.

23. $\dfrac{430}{204} = \dfrac{215}{102}$ is the ratio.

24. $\dfrac{299}{611} = \dfrac{23}{47}$ is the ratio.

25. The height of the bar is 9.3, which represents 9.3 million or 9,300,000 tons.

26. The height of the bar is 2.1, which represents 2.1 million or 2,100,000 tons.

27. The greatest difference in bar heights for grapefruit for any two consecutive years is between 2004 and 2005.

28. The greatest difference in bar heights for oranges for any two consecutive years is between 2004 and 2005.

29. $12.9 + 2.2 = 15.1$ million or 15,100,000 tons of citrus fruit was produced in 2004.

30. $7.6 + 1.6 = 9.2$ million or 9,200,000 tons of citrus fruit is estimated in 2007.

31. The greatest difference in bar heights for any one year is 2004.

32. The smallest difference in bar heights for any one year is 2007.

33. $\text{mean} = \dfrac{11.5 + 12.9 + 9.3 + 9.0 + 7.6}{5}$

$= \dfrac{50.3}{5}$

$= 10.06$ million or 10,060,000 tons

The average orange production is 10,060,000 tons.

34. $\text{mean} = \dfrac{2.1 + 2.2 + 1.0 + 1.2 + 1.6}{5}$

$= \dfrac{8.1}{5}$

$= 1.62$ million or 1,620,000 tons

The average grapefruit production is 1,620,000 tons.

35. $1.6 - 1.2 = 0.4$

$1.6 + 0.4 = 2$ million or 2,000,000 tons

The estimated production of grapefruits in 2008 is 2,000,000 tons.

36. $12.9 - 7.6 = 5.3$

$7.6 - 5.3 = 2.3$ million or 2,300,000 tons

The estimated production of oranges in 2010 is 2,300,000 tons.

37. The dot for 2004 is at 4, which represents 400 students.

38. The dot for 2006 is about halfway between 3 and 4, which represents 350 students.

39. $7 - 2 = 5$ or 500 more students graduated in 2007 than in 2002.

40. $3.5 - 5.5 = -2.0$ or 200 fewer students graduated in 2006 than in 2005.

41. The line between any two consecutive points that is the most gradual is between 2002 and 2003.

42. The line goes down from left to right between 2005 and 2006.

43. $\text{mean} = \dfrac{2 + 2.5 + 4 + 5.5 + 3.5 + 7}{6}$

$= \dfrac{24.5}{6}$

≈ 4.08 or about 408 students

The average is about 408 students.

44. $\dfrac{5.5 - 4}{4} = \dfrac{1.5}{4} = 0.375$ or 37.5%

The percentage of increase is 37.5%.

45. The dot on the graph is at 45, which represents 45,000 cones.

46. The dot on the graph is at 30, which represents 30,000 cones.

47. $20,000 - 10,000 = 10,000$ more cones were purchased in May 2006 than May 2007.

48. $60,000 - 30,000 = 30,000$ more cones were purchased in August 2007 than August 2006

49. $20 + 30 + 55 + 30 = 135$ or 135,000 cones were purchased between May and August of 2006.

50. $20 + 45 + 60 + 40 = 165$ or 165,000 cones were purchased between June and September of 2007.

51. The sharp drop in the number of ice cream cones purchased from July 2006 to August 2006 is probably directly related to the weather. Since August was cold and rainy, significantly fewer people wanted ice cream during August.

52. The sharp increase in the number of ice cream cones purchased from June 2007 to July 2007 is probably directly related to the weather. Since June was cold and rainy and July was warm and sunny, significantly more people wanted ice cream during July.

53. The dot on the graph is at 37, which represents 3700 degrees.

54. The dot on the graph is at 34, which represents 3400 degrees.

55. $36 - 33 = 3$ or 300 more degrees were awarded in 2005.

56. $36 - 37 = -1$ or 100 fewer degrees were awarded in 1999.

57. The line representing psychology is above the line representing physical sciences for the years 1999 and 2001.

58. The line representing physical sciences is above the line representing psychology for the years 1997 and 2005.

59. The lines cross at year 2003.

60. The line decreases the most between years 1999 to 2001.

61. The line increases the most between years 2003 to 2005.

62. Between 1999 to 2001, the number of doctorates in both fields decreased by 300; from 2003 to 2005, physical science doctorates increased by 300.

63. $36 - 33 = 3$
$36 + 3 = 39$ or 3900 degrees is the expected number of degrees in 2007.

64. $33 - 34 = -1$
$33 + (-1) = 32$ or 3200 degrees is the expected number of degrees in 2009.

65. The bar rises to 65, which represents 65 pairs.

66. The bar rises to 10, which represents 10 pairs.

67. $55 + 65 + 25 = 145$ pairs sold between size 7 and size 9.5.

68. Sold $= 5 + 20 + 55 + 65 + 25 + 10 = 180$ pairs
$p = \dfrac{180}{200} = 0.9 = 90\%$ of the shoes sold during the grand opening.

69. Difference $= 65 - 20 = 45$ pairs
45 more pairs of size 8–8.5 sold than of size 6–6.5.

70. $\dfrac{25}{180} = \dfrac{5}{36}$ or 5 to 36 is the ratio of size 9–9.5 to the total pairs sold.

71. Tally: ||||| |||||
Frequency: 10

72. Tally: ||||| |||
Frequency: 8

73. Tally: |||
Frequency: 3

74. Tally: |||||
Frequency: 5

75. Tally: ||
Frequency: 2

76.

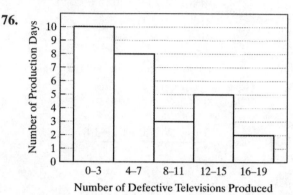

Number of Defective Televisions Produced

77. $10 + 8 = 18$ times, there were between 0 and 7 defective television sets.

78. Mean $= \dfrac{86 + 83 + 88 + 95 + 97 + 100 + 81}{7}$
$= \dfrac{630}{7}$
$= 90$
$= 90°F$
The mean temperature is 90°F.

79. Mean $= \dfrac{145 + 162 + 95 + 67 + 43 + 26}{6} = \$89.67$
The mean gas bill is $89.67.

80. Mean
$= \dfrac{12,000 + 17,000 + 24,000 + 29,000 + 19,000}{5}$
$= 20,200$ people
The mean number of people is 20,200.

81. Mean $= \dfrac{882 + 913 + 1017 + 1592 + 1778 + 1936}{6}$
$= \dfrac{8118}{6}$
$= 1353$ employees
The mean number of employees is 1353.

82. $21,690, $28,500, $29,300, $35,000, $37,000, $38,600, $43,600, $45,300

$$\text{Median} = \frac{\$35,000 + \$37,000}{2} = \$36,000$$

The median cost is $36,000.

83. $98,000, $120,000, $126,000, $135,000, $139,000, $144,000, $150,000, $154,000, $156,000, $170,000

$$\text{Median} = \frac{\$139,000 + \$144,000}{2} = \$141,500$$

The median cost is $141,500.

84. 4, 7, 8, 10, 15, 28, 28, 30, 31, 34, 35, 38, 43, 54, 77, 79

$$\text{Median} = \frac{30 + 31}{2} = 30.5 \text{ years}$$

Mode = 28 years

85. 3, 9, 13, 14, 15, 15, 16, 18, 19, 21, 24, 25, 26, 28, 31, 36

$$\text{Medan} = \frac{18 + 19}{2} = 18.5 \text{ deliveries}$$

Mode = 15 deliveries

86. The median, because of one low score, 31

87. The median is better because the mean is skewed by one high data item, 39.

88. a. $\text{Mean} = \dfrac{2 + 3 + 2 + 4 + 7 + 12 + 5}{7} = 5 \text{ hours}$

The mean is 5 hours.

b. 2, 2, 3, 4, 5, 7, 12
Median = 4 hours
The median is 4 hours.

c. Mode = 2 hours since it occurs twice.
The mode is 2 hours.

d. The median is the most representative. On three days she uses the computer more than 4 hours and on three days she uses the computer less than 4 hours. One day she used it exactly 7 hours. The mean is distorted a little because of the very large number of hours on Friday. The mode is artificially low because she happened to use the computers only two hours on Sunday and Tuesday. All other days it was more than this.

How Am I Doing? Chapter 8 Test

1. 37% is the sector marked Passed inspections.

2. 21% is the sector marked 2 violations.

3. Add the percents from the three sectors, 3 violations, 4 violations, and more than 4 violations.
6% + 2% + 4% = 12%

4. $30\% \times 300,000 = 0.30 \times 300,000$
$= 90,000$ automobiles
had one safety violation.

5. $21\% + 6\% = 27\%$
$27\% \times 300,000 = 0.27 \times 300,000$
81,000 automobiles had 2 or 3 violations.

6. The bar representing private in 1991–1992 rises to 12, which is $12,000.

7. The bar representing public in 1996–1997 rises to 3, which is $3000.

8. 20,000 − 12,000 = $8000
The increase was $8000.

9. 5000 − 3000 = $2000
The increase was $2000.

10. 14,000 − 3000 = $11,000
The difference in cost was $11,000.

11. 20,000 − 5000 = $15,000
The difference in cost was $15,000.

12. The dot on the graph is at 20, or 20 years.

13. The dot on the graph is at 26, or 26 years.

14. 48 − 36 = 12 years
He is expected to live 12 years longer.

15. The difference between the two graphs is the greatest at age 35.

16. The difference between the two graphs is the least at age 65.

17. The bar rises to 60, which represents 60,000 televisions.

18. The bar rises to 25, which represents 25,000 televisions.

19. Add the heights of the bars for 12–14 and 15–17.
15,000 + 5000 = 20,000 televisions last more than 11 years.

20. Add the heights of the bars for 9–11 and 12–14.
45,000 + 15,000 = 60,000 televisions last 9–14 years.

21. 10 + 16 + 15 + 12 + 18 + 17 + 14 + 10 + 13 + 20
= 145

Mean $= \dfrac{145}{10} = 14.5$

The mean quiz score is 14.5.

22. 10, 10, 12, 13, 14, 15, 16, 17, 18, 20

Median $= \dfrac{14+15}{2} = 14.5$

The median quiz score is 14.5.

23. Mode = 10 since it occurs twice.

24. Mean or median because they are the same and representative of the typical score.

Cumulative Test for Chapters 1–8

1.
$$\begin{array}{r} 1,376 \\ 2,804 \\ 9,003 \\ +\ 7,642 \\ \hline 20,825 \end{array}$$

2.
$$\begin{array}{r} 2008 \\ \times\ \ 37 \\ \hline 14\ 056 \\ 60\ 24\ \ \\ \hline 74,296 \end{array}$$

3. $\quad 7\dfrac{1}{5} \qquad\qquad 7\dfrac{8}{40} \qquad 6\dfrac{48}{40}$

$\quad -3\dfrac{3}{8} \qquad\quad -3\dfrac{15}{40} \quad -3\dfrac{15}{40}$

$\qquad\qquad\qquad\qquad\qquad\qquad 3\dfrac{33}{40}$

4. $10\dfrac{3}{4} \div \dfrac{3}{8} = \dfrac{43}{4} \times \dfrac{8}{3} = \dfrac{86}{3}$ or $28\dfrac{2}{3}$

5. 1796.4289 rounds to 1796.43.

6.
$$\begin{array}{r} 200.58 \\ -\ 127.93 \\ \hline 72.65 \end{array}$$

7.
$$0.72_{\wedge}\overline{)52.00_{\wedge}56}$$
$$\begin{array}{r} 72.23 \\ \underline{50\ 4\ \ \ \ } \\ 1\ 60 \\ \underline{1\ 44} \\ 16\ 5 \\ \underline{14\ 4} \\ 2\ 16 \\ \underline{2\ 16} \\ 0 \end{array}$$

8. $\dfrac{7}{n} = \dfrac{35}{3}$

$7 \times 3 = n \times 35$

$\dfrac{21}{35} = \dfrac{n \times 35}{35}$

$0.6 = n$

9. $\dfrac{n}{26,390} = \dfrac{3}{2030}$

$2030n = 3 \times 26,390$

$\dfrac{2030n}{2030} = \dfrac{79,170}{2030}$

$n = 39$ defects

Approximately 39 cars had major engine defects.

10. $n = 1.3\% \times 25$
$n = 0.013 \times 25$
$n = 0.325$

11. $20\% \times n = 12$

$0.2n = 12$

$\dfrac{0.2n}{0.2} = \dfrac{12}{0.2}$

$n = 60$

12. 198 cm = 1.98 m (move decimal 2 places left)

13. $18 \text{ yd} \times \dfrac{3 \text{ ft}}{1 \text{ yd}} = 54 \text{ ft}$

14. $A = \pi r^2 = 3.14(3 \text{ in.})^2 = 3.14(9 \text{ in.}^2) \approx 28.3 \text{ in.}^2$

15. $P = 4s = 4(15) = 60 \text{ ft}$
$A = s^2 = (15)^2 = 225 \text{ ft}^2$

16. 40% of 38.5 = 0.4 × 38.5 = 15.4 or $15.4 billion or $15,400,000,000 was spent on food.

17. 24% − 7% = 17%
17% of 38.5 = 0.17 × 38.5 = 6.545
$6.545 billion or $6,545,000,000 more was spent on vet care than on grooming and boarding.

18. 636 − 597 = 39 million or 39,000,000 is the expected increase.

19. The greatest difference between the heights of the bars for one year is 2006.
644 − 415 = 229 million or 229,000,000

20. 4.0 − 2.5 = 1.5 inches
Jacksonville gets 1.5 more inches of rain.

21. The line representing Miami is above the line representing Jacksonville for the months April, May, and June.

22. The bar rises to 8, which represents 8 students.

23.   4 students ages 17–19
7 students ages 20–22
+ 5 students ages 23–25
16 students less than 26 years of age

24.   Mean $= \dfrac{\$5.00 + \$4.50 + \$3.95 + \$4.90 + \$7.00 + \$12.15 + \$4.50 + \$6.00}{2}$

$= \dfrac{\$48.00}{8}$

$= \$6.00$

The mean hourly wage is $6.00.

25. $3.95, $4.50, $4.50, $4.90, $5.00, $6.00, $7.00, $12.15

Median $= \dfrac{\$4.90 + \$5.00}{2} = \$4.95$

The median hourly wage is $4.95.

26. Mode = $4.50 since it occurs twice.

Chapter 9

9.1 Exercises

2. Find the absolute value of each number. Then subtract those two absolute values. Use the sign of the number with the larger absolute value.

4. Since −8 lies to the left of 6, −8 < 6.

6. Since −7 lies to the right of −14, −7 > −14.

8. Since 6 lies to the right of −3, 6 > −3.

10. Since −15 lies to the left of −13, −15 < −13.

12. $|6| = 6$

14. $|-18| = 18$

16. $-5 + (-13) = -18$

18. $-8.3 + (-3.7) = -12$

20. $12.5 + 7.8 = 20.3$

22. $\dfrac{5}{6} + \dfrac{1}{4} = \dfrac{10}{12} + \dfrac{3}{12} = \dfrac{13}{12}$ or $1\dfrac{1}{12}$

24. $-5\dfrac{1}{4} + \left(-\dfrac{3}{4}\right) = -6$

26. $15 + (-6) = 9$

28. $-21 + 15 = -6$

30. $-42 + 57 = 15$

32. $-7.2 + 4.04 = -3.16$

34. $\dfrac{7}{20} + \left(-\dfrac{19}{20}\right) = -\dfrac{12}{20} = -\dfrac{3}{5}$

36. $\dfrac{5}{12} + \left(-\dfrac{7}{12}\right) = -\dfrac{2}{12} = -\dfrac{1}{6}$

38. $-34 + (-2) = -36$

40. $3.72 + (-4.1) = -0.38$

42. $-514 + (-176) = -690$

44. $-18 + 7 = -11$

46. $-5\dfrac{3}{8} + \left(-3\dfrac{5}{8}\right) = -8\dfrac{8}{8} = -9$

48. $-6.89 + 15.9 = 9.01$

50. $\dfrac{5}{6} + (-3) = \dfrac{5}{6} + \left(-\dfrac{18}{6}\right) = -\dfrac{13}{6}$ or $-2\dfrac{1}{6}$

52. $-10.8 + (-14.3) + 12.7 = -25.1 + 12.7 = -12.4$

54. $-13 + 8 + (-12) + 17 = -5 + (-12) + 17$
$$= -17 + 17$$
$$= 0$$

56. $3 + (-9) + 10 + (-3) + (-15) + 8$
$$= [-9 + (-3) + (-15)] + (3 + 10 + 8)$$
$$= -27 + 21$$
$$= -6$$

58. $\left(-\dfrac{1}{7}\right) + \left(-\dfrac{5}{21}\right) + \left(\dfrac{3}{14}\right)$
$$= \left(-\dfrac{6}{42}\right) + \left(-\dfrac{10}{42}\right) + \left(\dfrac{9}{42}\right)$$
$$= -\dfrac{16}{42} + \dfrac{9}{42}$$
$$= -\dfrac{7}{42}$$
$$= -\dfrac{1}{6}$$

60. $-\$16,000 + (-\$25,000) = -\$41,000$
The report is a total loss of $41,000.

62. $-\$11,000 + \$8400 = -\$2600$
The report is a total loss of $2600.

64. $\$15,700 + (-\$20,400) + \$9000 = -\$4700 + 9000$
$$= \$4300$$
The report is a total profit of $4300.

66. $-9° + 15° = 6°F$
The afternoon temperature was 6°F.

68. $-7° + (-15°) = -22°F$
The new temperature was −22°F.

70. $-0.15 + 0.91 + (-0.12) + 0.32 + 0.01$
$= -0.27 + 1.24$
$= 0.97$
The net gain was 0.97.

72. $20 + (-13) + 5 = 7 + 5 = +12$ yards
The total was a gain of 12 yards.

74. $\$97.40 + (-\$95.00) + (-\$4.50)$
$= \$2.40 + (-\$4.50)$
$= -\$2.10$
The actual balance is $-\$2.10$.

Cumulative Review

75. $V = \dfrac{4\pi r^3}{3} = \dfrac{4(3.14)(6 \text{ ft})^3}{3} \approx 904.3 \text{ ft}^3$
The volume is 904.3 ft^3.

76. $B = 9 \times 7 = 63$
$V = \dfrac{Bh}{3} = \dfrac{(63)(10)}{3} = 210$ cubic meters
The volume is 210 m^3.

77. $57, 59, 60, 60, 61, 62$
$\text{Median} = \dfrac{60 + 60}{2} = 60$

78. $\text{Mean} = \dfrac{36 + 42 + 39 + 39 + 41 + 43}{6} = \dfrac{240}{6} = \$40$

Classroom Quiz 9.1

1. $22 + (-8) + 18 + (-15) = 14 + 18 + (-15)$
$= 32 + (-15)$
$= 17$

2. $7.6 + (-5.8) = 1.8$

3. $-6\dfrac{1}{4} + 3\dfrac{3}{4} = -5\dfrac{5}{4} + 3\dfrac{3}{4} = -2\dfrac{2}{4} = -2\dfrac{1}{2}$

9.2 Exercises

2. $-7 - (5) = -7 + 5 = -2$

4. $-10 - (-2) = -10 + 2 = -8$

6. $5 - 12 = 5 + (-12) = -7$

8. $-6 - 18 = -6 + (-18) = -24$

10. $-12 - (-20) = -12 + 20 = 8$

12. $53 - (-28) = 53 + 28 = 81$

14. $10 - 14 = 10 + (-14) = -4$

16. $-17 - (-30) = -17 + 30 = 13$

18. $500 - 150 = 500 + (-150) = 350$

20. $420 - (-300) = 420 + 300 = 720$

22. $-4.1 - 3.9 = -4.1 + (-3.9) = -8$

24. $8.5 - 19.2 = 8.5 + (-19.2) = -10.7$

26. $-6.8 - (-2.9) = -6.8 + 2.9 = -3.9$

28. $13.92 - (-14.86) = 13.92 + 14.86 = 28.78$

30. $\dfrac{5}{7} - \left(-\dfrac{6}{7}\right) = \dfrac{5}{7} + \dfrac{6}{7} = \dfrac{11}{7}$ or $1\dfrac{4}{7}$

32. $-\dfrac{2}{8} - \dfrac{1}{4} = -\dfrac{2}{8} + \left(-\dfrac{1}{4}\right) = -\dfrac{2}{8} + \left(-\dfrac{2}{8}\right) = -\dfrac{4}{8} = -\dfrac{1}{2}$

34. $-7\dfrac{5}{8} - \left(-12\dfrac{2}{3}\right) = -7\dfrac{5}{8} + 12\dfrac{2}{3}$
$= -7\dfrac{15}{24} + 12\dfrac{16}{24}$
$= 5\dfrac{1}{24}$

36. $\dfrac{3}{5} - \dfrac{11}{12} = \dfrac{3}{5} + \left(-\dfrac{11}{12}\right) = \dfrac{36}{60} + \left(-\dfrac{55}{60}\right) = -\dfrac{19}{60}$

38. $7 - (-3) + 9 = 7 + 3 + 9 = 10 + 9 = 19$

40. $-8 - 5 - (-17) = -8 + (-5) + 17 = -13 + 17 = 4$

42. $32 - (-12) - (-18) = 32 + 12 + 18 = 62$

44. $-13 - (-4) - 15 = -13 + 4 + (-15)$
$= -9 + (-15)$
$= -24$

46. $12 - 5 - 4 - 8 = 12 + (-5) + (-4) + (-8)$
$= 7 + (-4) + (-8)$
$= 3 + (-8)$
$= -5$

48. $-2.5 + 3.2 - 6.3 - (-5.4)$
$= -2.5 + 3.2 + (-6.3) + 5.4$
$= 0.7 + (-6.3) + 5.4$
$= -5.6 + 5.4$
$= -0.2$

50. $19,340 - (-502) = 19,340 + 502 = 19,842$ ft
Mount Kilimanjaro is 19,842 feet above Lake Asal.

52. $27° - (-33°) = 27° + 33° = 60°$F
The difference in temperature is 60°F.

54. $642 - (-57) = 642 + 57 = 699$ ft
The difference in height is 699 feet.

56. $-6,300 + (-34,700) = -\$41,000$
The change in status is –\$41,000.

58. $18,700 + (-34,700) + (-6,300) + 43,600$
$\quad + (-12,400)$
$= 62,300 + (-53,400)$
$= \$8900$
The change in status is +\$8900.

60. $32\frac{1}{4} + 3\frac{1}{4} + \left(-3\frac{3}{4}\right) + 2\frac{3}{4} = 35\frac{2}{4} + \left(-3\frac{3}{4}\right) + 2\frac{3}{4}$
$\qquad\qquad = 31\frac{3}{4} + 2\frac{3}{4}$
$\qquad\qquad = \$34\frac{1}{2}$ or \$34.50

The value of one share is $\$34\frac{1}{2}$ or \$34.50.

Cumulative Review

61. $20 \times 2 \div 10 + 4 - 3 = 40 \div 10 + 4 - 3$
$\qquad\qquad\qquad = 4 + 4 - 3$
$\qquad\qquad\qquad = 8 - 3$
$\qquad\qquad\qquad = 8 + (-3)$
$\qquad\qquad\qquad = 5$

62. $2 + 3 \times (5 + 7) \div 9 = 2 + 3 \times 12 \div 9$
$\qquad\qquad\qquad = 2 + 36 \div 9$
$\qquad\qquad\qquad = 2 + 4$
$\qquad\qquad\qquad = 6$

Classroom Quiz 9.2

1. $-\frac{5}{11} - \left(-\frac{7}{22}\right) = -\frac{5}{11} + \frac{7}{22} = -\frac{10}{22} + \frac{7}{22} = -\frac{3}{22}$

2. $9.6 - (-4.8) = 9.6 + 4.8 = 14.4$

3. $-18 - 56 = -18 + (-56) = -74$

9.3 Exercises

2. To multiply two numbers with different signs, multiply the absolute values. The sign of the result is negative.

4. $(15)(5) = 75$

6. $(-30)(-6) = 180$

8. $(-15)(12) = -180$

10. $4(-34) = -136$

12. $(8.5)(-0.3) = -2.55$

14. $(-7.35)(-10.5) = 77.175$

16. $\left(-\frac{5}{12}\right)\left(-\frac{2}{3}\right) = \frac{5}{18}$

18. $\left(-\frac{9}{4}\right)\left(-\frac{10}{27}\right) = \frac{90}{108} = \frac{5}{6}$

20. $-63 \div 7 = -9$

22. $\frac{52}{-13} = -4$

24. $\frac{-180}{-45} = 4$

26. $-36 \div (-4) = 9$

28. $-\frac{3}{20} \div \left(-\frac{6}{5}\right) = -\frac{3}{20}\left(-\frac{5}{6}\right) = \frac{1}{8}$

30. $\dfrac{-\frac{26}{15}}{-\frac{13}{7}} = -\frac{26}{15} \div \left(-\frac{13}{7}\right) = -\frac{26}{15} \times \left(-\frac{7}{13}\right) = \frac{14}{15}$

32. $30.45 \div (-5) = -6.09$

34. $\frac{66.6}{-9} = -7.4$

36. $\frac{-320,000}{-8000} = 40$

38. $6(-11) = -66$

40. $(-10)(-7) = 70$

42. $\dfrac{36}{-2} = -18$

44. $-50 \div -5 = 10$

46. $(-1.6)(3) = -4.8$

48. $0.069 \div (-2.3) = -0.03$

50. $\left(-\dfrac{4}{9}\right)\left(-\dfrac{9}{13}\right) = \dfrac{4}{13}$

52. $\dfrac{11}{4} \div \left(-\dfrac{33}{6}\right) = \dfrac{11}{4} \cdot \left(-\dfrac{6}{33}\right) = -\dfrac{1}{2}$

54. $5(-4)(-6) = -20(-6) = 120$

56. $(-3)(2)(-9) = -6(-9) = 54$

58. $7(-2)(-5)\left(\dfrac{1}{7}\right) = -14(-5)\left(\dfrac{1}{7}\right) = 70\left(\dfrac{1}{7}\right) = 10$

60. $(5)(-40)(-20)(-8) = (-200)(-20)(-8)$
$\qquad = (4000)(-8)$
$\qquad = -32{,}000$

62. $9(-6)(-4)(-3)(0) = -54(-4)(-3)(0)$
$\qquad = 216(-3)(0)$
$\qquad = -648(0)$
$\qquad = 0$

64. $\left(-\dfrac{2}{3}\right) \div \left(-\dfrac{2}{3}\right)\left(\dfrac{3}{5}\right) = \left(-\dfrac{2}{3}\right) \times \left(-\dfrac{3}{2}\right)\left(\dfrac{3}{5}\right)$
$\qquad\qquad\qquad\qquad = 1\left(\dfrac{3}{5}\right)$
$\qquad\qquad\qquad\qquad = \dfrac{3}{5}$

66. $120(0.80) + 85(-2.20) = 96 + (-187) = -91$
She lost \$91.

68. $\dfrac{-8° + (-5°) + (-18°) + (-22°) + (-6°) + 3° + 7°}{7}$
$= -\dfrac{49°}{7}$
$= -7°\text{F}$
The average temperature was $-7°$F.

70. $5(-\$1.5) = -\$7.5$ million
There was a loss of \$7.5 million or \$7,500,000.

72. $9(-3) = -27$

74. $10(-2) + 12(+1) = -20 + 12 = -8$

76. $-6(-2) = 12$
Change is $+12$.

78. $3(-1) + 2(1) + 1(2) = -3 + 2 + 2 = -1 + 2 = 1$
She is one point above par.

Cumulative Review

79. $A = bh = (15 \text{ in.})(6 \text{ in.}) = 90$ square inches
The area is 90 in.^2.

80. $A = \dfrac{h(b + B)}{2}$
$\quad = \dfrac{(12 \text{ m})(18 \text{ m} + 26 \text{ m})}{2}$
$\quad = \dfrac{(12 \text{ m})(44 \text{ m})}{2}$
$\quad = \dfrac{528 \text{ m}^2}{2}$
$\quad = 264$ square meters
The area is 264 m^2.

Classroom Quiz 9.3

1. $7(-12) = -84$

2. $(3)(-5)(-2)(-3)(-2) = -15(-2)(-3)(-2)$
$\qquad\qquad\qquad\qquad = 30(-3)(-2)$
$\qquad\qquad\qquad\qquad = -90(-2)$
$\qquad\qquad\qquad\qquad = 180$

3. $-168 \div 12 = -14$

How Am I Doing? Sections 9.1–9.3

1. $-7 + (-12) = -19$

2. $-23 + 19 = -4$

3. $7.6 + (-3.1) = 4.5$

4. $8 + (-5) + 6 + (-9) = 14 + (-14) = 0$

5. $\dfrac{8}{9} + \left(-\dfrac{2}{3}\right) = \dfrac{8}{9} + \left(-\dfrac{6}{9}\right) = \dfrac{2}{9}$

6. $-\dfrac{5}{6} + \left(-\dfrac{1}{3}\right) = -\dfrac{5}{6} + \left(-\dfrac{2}{6}\right) = -\dfrac{7}{6}$ or $-1\dfrac{1}{6}$

7. $-2.8 + (-4.2) = -7$

8. $-3.7 + 5.4 = 1.7$

9. $13 - 21 = 13 + (-21) = -8$

10. $-26 - 15 = -26 + (-15) = -41$

11. $\dfrac{5}{17} - \left(-\dfrac{9}{17}\right) = \dfrac{5}{17} + \dfrac{9}{17} = \dfrac{14}{17}$

12. $-19 - (-7) = -19 + 7 = -12$

13. $-12.5 - 3.8 = -12.5 + (-3.8) = -16.3$

14. $2.8 - 5.6 = 2.8 + (-5.6) = -2.8$

15. $21 - (-21) = 21 + 21 = 42$

16. $\dfrac{2}{3} - \left(-\dfrac{3}{5}\right) = \dfrac{2}{3} + \dfrac{3}{5} = \dfrac{10}{15} + \dfrac{9}{15} = \dfrac{19}{15}$ or $1\dfrac{4}{15}$

17. $(-3)(-8) = 24$

18. $-48 \div (-12) = 4$

19. $-72 \div 9 = -8$

20. $(5)(-4)(2)(-1)\left(-\dfrac{1}{4}\right) = -20(2)(-1)\left(-\dfrac{1}{4}\right)$
$$= -40(-1)\left(-\dfrac{1}{4}\right)$$
$$= 40\left(-\dfrac{1}{4}\right)$$
$$= -10$$

21. $\dfrac{72}{-3} = -24$

22. $\dfrac{-\frac{3}{4}}{-\frac{4}{5}} = -\dfrac{3}{4} \div \left(-\dfrac{4}{5}\right) = -\dfrac{3}{4}\left(-\dfrac{5}{4}\right) = \dfrac{15}{16}$

23. $(-8)(-2)(-4) = 16(-4) = -64$

24. $120 \div (-12) = -10$

25. $18 - (-6) = 18 + 6 = 24$

26. $-7(-3) = 21$

27. $-15 \div 10 = -1.5$

28. $1.6 + (-1.8) + (-3.4) = -0.2 + (-3.4) = -3.6$

29. $2.9 - 3.5 = 2.9 + (-3.5) = -0.6$

30. $\left(-\dfrac{1}{3}\right) + \left(-\dfrac{2}{5}\right) = \left(-\dfrac{5}{15}\right) + \left(-\dfrac{6}{15}\right) = -\dfrac{11}{15}$

31. $\left(-\dfrac{7}{10}\right)\left(-\dfrac{2}{7}\right) = \dfrac{1}{5}$

32. $2\dfrac{1}{3} \div \left(-\dfrac{2}{3}\right) = \dfrac{7}{3} \cdot \left(-\dfrac{3}{2}\right) = -\dfrac{7}{2} = -3\dfrac{1}{2}$

33. Average $= \dfrac{2 + (-6) + (-10) + (-8) + (-3) + 4}{6}$
$$= \dfrac{-21}{6}$$
$$= -3.5°\text{F}$$
The average temperature was $-3.5°$F.

9.4 Exercises

2. $-20 \div (-5)(6) = 4(6) = 24$

4. $60 \div (-20)(5) = (-3)(5) = -15$

6. $15 - (-18) \div 3 = 15 - (-6) = 15 + 6 = 21$

8. $(-56) \div (-7) + 30 \div (-15) = 8 + (-2) = 6$

10. $6(-3) + 8(-1) - (-2) = -18 + (-8) + 2$
$$= -26 + 2$$
$$= -24$$

12. $-10(2.6 - 1.9) = -10(0.7) = -7$

14. $8 - 70 \div 5 = 8 - 14 = 8 + (-14) = -6$

16. $9(-6) + 6 = -54 + 6 = -48$

18. $-6(7) + 8(-3) + 5 = -42 + (-24) + 5$
$$= -66 + 5$$
$$= -61$$

20. $10(-5) - 4(12) = -50 + (-48) = -98$

22. $20 - 3(-2) + (-20) \div (-5) = 20 + 6 + 4$
$$= 26 + 4$$
$$= 30$$

24. $\dfrac{11 - 3 - 2}{-9 - 5 + 8} = \dfrac{6}{-6} = -1$

26. $\dfrac{12-4+10}{5(-3)+9} = \dfrac{18}{-15+9} = \dfrac{18}{-6} = -3$

28. $\dfrac{-25 \div 5 + (-3)(-4) - 7}{8 - (18 \div 3)} = \dfrac{-5 + 12 - 7}{8 - 6} = \dfrac{0}{2} = 0$

30. $\dfrac{6(-3) \div (-2) + 5}{32 \div (-8)} = \dfrac{-18 \div (-2) + 5}{-4}$

$\qquad = \dfrac{9 + 5}{-4}$

$\qquad = \dfrac{14}{-4}$

$\qquad = -\dfrac{7}{2}$

$\qquad = -3\dfrac{1}{2}$

32. $\dfrac{8(-4) - 4}{(-42) \div (-6) + (12 - 10)} = \dfrac{8(-4) - 4}{(-42) \div (-6) + 2}$

$\qquad = \dfrac{-32 - 4}{7 + 2}$

$\qquad = \dfrac{-36}{9}$

$\qquad = -4$

34. $-5(8 - 3) + 6^2 = -5(5) + 6^2$

$\qquad = -5(5) + 36$

$\qquad = -25 + 36$

$\qquad = 11$

36. $-20 \div 2 + (6 - 3)^4 = -20 \div 2 + 3^4$

$\qquad = -20 \div 2 + 81$

$\qquad = -10 + 81$

$\qquad -71$

38. $(6)\left(-2\dfrac{1}{2}\right) + 2\dfrac{1}{3} \div \dfrac{1}{3} = (6)\left(-\dfrac{5}{2}\right) + \dfrac{7}{3} \times \dfrac{3}{1}$

$\qquad = -15 + 7$

$\qquad = -8$

40. $\left(\dfrac{5}{8} - \dfrac{1}{8}\right)^2 - \left(-\dfrac{5}{6}\right)\left(\dfrac{8}{5}\right) = \left(\dfrac{1}{2}\right)^2 - \left(-\dfrac{5}{6}\right)\left(\dfrac{8}{5}\right)$

$\qquad = \dfrac{1}{4} - \left(-\dfrac{5}{6}\right)\left(\dfrac{8}{5}\right)$

$\qquad = \dfrac{1}{4} - \left(-\dfrac{4}{3}\right)$

$\qquad = \dfrac{3}{12} + \dfrac{16}{12}$

$\qquad = \dfrac{19}{12}$

$\qquad = 1\dfrac{7}{12}$

42. $(0.6)^2 - 5.2(-3.4) = 0.36 - 5.2(-3.4)$

$\qquad = 0.36 + 17.68$

$\qquad = 18.04$

44. $\dfrac{(-9°) + (-13°) + (-11°)}{3} = \dfrac{-33}{3} = -11°\text{F}$

The average high temperature is $-11°\text{F}$.

46. $\dfrac{21 + (-1) + (-9) + (-13) + (-11) + 0}{6} = \dfrac{-13}{6}$

$\qquad\qquad\qquad\qquad\qquad\qquad \approx -2.2°\text{F}$

The average high temperature is $-2.2°\text{F}$.

48. $[-27 + (-21) + (-14) + (-3) + 17 + 38 + 49$
$\qquad\quad + 46 + 35 + 12 + (-10) + (-18)] \div 12$

$\quad = \dfrac{104}{12}$

$\quad \approx 8.7°\text{F}$

The average yearly low temperature is $8.7°\text{F}$.

Cumulative Review

49. $3840 \text{ m} = \dfrac{3840}{1000} \text{ km} = 3.84 \text{ km}$

The telephone wire is 3.84 km long.

50. $36.8 \text{ grams} = 36.8 \times 1000 \text{ milligrams}$
$\qquad\qquad\qquad = 36{,}800 \text{ milligrams}$

It contains 36,800 mg of protein.

Classroom Quiz 9.4

1. $(-3)(-5) - 3(7 - 5)^3 = (-3)(-5) - 3(2)^3$

$\qquad = (-3)(-5) - 3(8)$

$\qquad = 15 - 24$

$\qquad = 15 + (-24)$

$\qquad = -9$

2. $-7.6+9.4-(-6.5)-3(1.2)$
$=-7.6+9.4+6.5+(-3.6)$
$=1.8+6.5+(-3.6)$
$=8.3+(-3.6)$
$=4.7$

3. $\dfrac{5+(-22)\div 2}{3(-4)-5(-2)}=\dfrac{5+(-11)}{-12+10}=\dfrac{-6}{-2}=3$

9.5 Exercises

2. We need to move the decimal point one place to the right. This means we will need a negative exponent for 10. Since we moved the decimal point one place we will use 10^{-1}. Thus, $0.787=7.87\times10^{-1}$.

4. The value of a must be a number greater than or equal to 1 but smaller than 10.

6. $340=3.4\times10^2$

8. $5200=5.2\times10^3$

10. $78,100=7.81\times10^4$

12. $238,000=2.38\times10^5$

14. $100,000=1\times10^5$

16. $28,000,000=2.8\times10^7$

18. $0.0242=2.42\times10^{-2}$

20. $0.00613=6.13\times10^{-3}$

22. $0.17=1.7\times10^{-1}$

24. $0.00079=7.9\times10^{-4}$

26. $0.00000198=1.98\times10^{-6}$

28. $0.00000007=7\times10^{-8}$

30. $2.19\times10^4=21,900$

32. $8.1215\times10^4=81,215$

34. $3.8\times10^{11}=380,000,000,000$

36. $3.5\times10^{-2}=0.035$

38. $7.12\times10^{-1}=0.712$

40. $2\times10^{12}=2,000,000,000,000$

42. $8.139\times10^{-9}=0.000000008139$

44. $76,371=7.6371\times10^4$

46. $5.7\times10^{-2}=0.057$

48. $0.0000134=1.34\times10^{-5}$

50. $3.49\times10^6=3,490,000$

52. $2,700,000,000=2.7\times10^9$ acres
The world's forests total 2.7×10^9 acres of wooded area.

54. $0.000000005=5\times10^{-9}$ m
The radius is 5×10^{-9} meter.

56. $10^{-15}=0.000000000000001$ second
A femtosecond is 0.000000000000001 sec.

58. $3.16\times10^{-10}=0.000000000316$ meter
The diameter is 0.000000000316 m.

60. $8.795\times10^{12}=\$8,795,000,000,000$
The debt is $\$8,795,000,000,000$.

62. $\begin{aligned}&8.17\times10^9\\+\;&2.76\times10^9\\\hline&10.93\times10^9=1.093\times10^{10}\text{ atoms}\end{aligned}$

64. $\begin{aligned}&6.34\times10^{20}\\&1.76\times10^{20}\\+\;&3.21\times10^{20}\\\hline&11.31\times10^{20}=1.131\times10^{21}\text{ tons}\end{aligned}$

66. $\begin{aligned}&9.00\times10^{10}\\-\;&1.26\times10^9\end{aligned}$ $\begin{aligned}&9.000\times10^{10}\\-\;&0.126\times10^{10}\\\hline&8.874\times10^{10}\text{ meters}\end{aligned}$

68. $1.39\times10^8 + 5.747\times10^7$

$= 1.39\times10^8 + 0.5747\times10^8$

$= 1.9647\times10^8$ square miles

The total area is 1.9647×10^8 mi^2.

70. $41(5.88 \text{ trillion}) = 241.08 \text{ trillion miles}$

$= 241.08\times10^{12}$ miles

$= 2.4108\times10^{14}$ miles

It is 2.4108×10^{14} miles from Earth.

Cumulative Review

71.
$$\begin{array}{r} 12.5 \\ \times\ 0.21 \\ \hline 125 \\ 2\ 50 \\ \hline 2.625 \end{array}$$

72.
$$\begin{array}{r} 0.258 \\ 0.53_\wedge\overline{)0.13_\wedge674} \\ \underline{10\ 6} \\ 3\ 07 \\ \underline{2\ 65} \\ 424 \\ \underline{424} \\ 0 \end{array}$$

73. $\text{Cost} = 4(2\times9 + 2\times13)$

$= 4(18 + 26)$

$= 4(44)$

$= \$176$

It will cost $176.

74. $\dfrac{70}{95} = \dfrac{x}{800}$

$70\times800 = 95x$

$\dfrac{56,000}{95} = \dfrac{95x}{95}$

$589 \approx x$

The cliff is about 589 feet tall.

Classroom Quiz 9.5

1. $0.00863 = 8.63\times10^{-3}$

2. $12,987,000 = 1.2987\times10^7$

3. $7.83\times10^{-5} = 0.0000783$

Putting Your Skills to Work

1. $4\times\dfrac{2}{3} = \dfrac{4}{1}\times\dfrac{2}{5} = \dfrac{8}{3}$

Clarice prepares $\dfrac{8}{3}$ cups of rice each week.

2. $\dfrac{21 \text{ ounces}}{1 \text{ cup}}\times\dfrac{8}{3}$ cups $= 56$ ounces

Clarice's family consumes 56 ounces of rice each week.

3. $\dfrac{1 \text{ lb}}{16 \text{ oz}}\times56$ oz $= \dfrac{7}{2}$ or $3\dfrac{1}{2}$ lb

Clarice's family eats $3\dfrac{1}{2}$ pounds each week.

4. a. $15.73 - 9.25 = 6.48$

$\dfrac{6.48}{25} \approx 0.26$

It increased by $0.26/lb.

b. $\dfrac{9.25}{25} = 0.37; \dfrac{0.26}{0.37} \approx 0.70$

It is a 70% increase.

5. $\dfrac{15.73}{25} = 0.6292; \ 0.6292(3.5) \approx 2.20$

The cost in today's prices is $2.20 per week.

6. Answers will vary.

7. Answers will vary.

Chapter 9 Review Problems

1. $-20 + 5 = -15$

2. $-18 + 4 = -14$

3. $-3.6 + (-5.2) = -8.8$

4. $10.4 + (-7.8) = 2.6$

5. $-\dfrac{1}{5} + \left(-\dfrac{1}{3}\right) = -\dfrac{3}{15} + \left(-\dfrac{5}{15}\right) = -\dfrac{8}{15}$

6. $\dfrac{9}{10} + \left(-\dfrac{5}{2}\right) = \dfrac{9}{10} + \left(-\dfrac{25}{10}\right) = -\dfrac{16}{10} = -\dfrac{8}{5}$

7. $20 + (-14) = 6$

8. $-95 + 45 = -50$

9. $(-82) + 50 + 35 + (-18) = -100 + 85 = -15$

10. $12 + (-7) + (-8) + 3 = 15 + (-15) = 0$

11. $25 - 36 = 25 + (-36) = -11$

12. $12 - 40 = 12 + (-40) = -28$

13. $14.5 - (-6) = 14.5 + 6 = 20.5$

14. $16 - (-2.2) = 16 + 2.2 = 18.2$

15. $-11.4 - 5.8 = -11.4 + (-5.8) = -17.2$

16. $-5.2 - 7.1 = -5.2 + (-7.1) = -12.3$

17. $-\dfrac{2}{5} - \left(-\dfrac{1}{3}\right) = -\dfrac{2}{5} + \dfrac{1}{3} = -\dfrac{6}{15} + \dfrac{5}{15} = -\dfrac{1}{15}$

18. $3\dfrac{1}{4} - \left(-5\dfrac{2}{3}\right) = 3\dfrac{3}{12} + 5\dfrac{8}{12} = 8\dfrac{11}{12}$

19. $5 - (-2) - (-6) = 5 + 2 + 6 = 7 + 6 = 13$

20. $-15 - (-3) + 9 = -15 + 3 + 9 = -12 + 9 = -3$

21. $9 - 8 - 6 - 4 = 9 + (-8) + (-6) + (-4)$
$$= 1 + (-6) + (-4)$$
$$= -5 + (-4)$$
$$= -9$$

22. $-7 - 8 - (-3) = -7 + (-8) + 3 = -15 + 3 = -12$

23. $\left(-\dfrac{2}{7}\right)\left(-\dfrac{1}{5}\right) = \dfrac{2}{35}$

24. $\left(-\dfrac{6}{15}\right)\left(\dfrac{5}{12}\right) = -\dfrac{1}{6}$

25. $(5.2)(-1.5) = -7.8$

26. $(-3.6)(-1.2) = 4.32$

27. $-60 \div (-20) = 3$

28. $-18 \div (-3) = 6$

29. $\dfrac{-36}{4} = -9$

30. $\dfrac{70}{-14} = -5$

31. $\dfrac{-13.2}{-2.2} = 6$

32. $\dfrac{48}{-3.2} = -15$

33. $\dfrac{-\frac{3}{4}}{\frac{1}{6}} = -\dfrac{3}{4} \div \dfrac{1}{6} = -\dfrac{3}{4} \times \dfrac{6}{1} = -\dfrac{9}{2}$ or $-4\dfrac{1}{2}$

34. $\dfrac{-\frac{1}{3}}{-\frac{7}{9}} = -\dfrac{1}{3} \div \left(-\dfrac{7}{9}\right) = -\dfrac{1}{3} \times \left(-\dfrac{9}{7}\right) = \dfrac{3}{7}$

35. $3(-5)(-2) = -15(-2) = 30$

36. $(-2)(3)(-6)(-1) = -6(-6)(-1) = 36(-1) = -36$

37. $10 + 40 \div (-4) = 10 + (-10) = 0$

38. $21 - (-9) \div 3 = 21 - (-3) = 21 + 3 = 24$

39. $2(-6) + 3(-4) - (-13) = -12 + (-12) + 13$
$$= -24 + 13$$
$$= -11$$

40. $-49 \div (-7) + 3(-2) = 7 + (-6) = 1$

41. $36 \div (-12) + 50 \div (-25) = -3 + (-2) = -5$

42. $21 - (-30) \div 15 = 21 - (-2) = 21 + 2 = 23$

43. $50 \div 25(-4) = 2(-4) = -8$

44. $-3.5 \div (-5) - 1.2 = 0.7 - 1.2 = -0.5$

45. $2.5(-2) + 3.8 = -5 + 3.8 = -1.2$

46. $\dfrac{8 - 17 + 1}{6 - 10} = \dfrac{-8}{-4} = 2$

47. $\dfrac{9 - 3 + 4(-3)}{2 - (-6)} = \dfrac{9 + (-3) + (-12)}{2 + 6} = \dfrac{-6}{8} = -\dfrac{3}{4}$

48. $\dfrac{20 \div (-5) - (-6)}{(2)(-2)(-5)} = \dfrac{-4 + 6}{20} = \dfrac{2}{20} = \dfrac{1}{10}$

49. $\dfrac{(22 - 4) \div (-2)}{-12 - 3(-5)} = \dfrac{18 \div (-2)}{-12 + 15} = \dfrac{-9}{3} = -3$

50. $-3+4(2-6)^2 \div (-2) = -3+4(-4)^2 \div (-2)$
$$= -3+4(16) \div (-2)$$
$$= -3+64 \div (-2)$$
$$= -3+(-32)$$
$$= -35$$

51. $2(7-11)^2 - 4^3 = 2(-4)^2 - 4^3$
$$= 2(16) - 64$$
$$= 32 + (-64)$$
$$= -32$$

52. $-50 \div (-10) + (5-3)^4 = -50 \div (-10) + 2^4$
$$= -50 \div (-10) + 16$$
$$= 5 + 16$$
$$= 21$$

53. $\dfrac{2}{3} - \dfrac{2}{5} \div \left(\dfrac{1}{3}\right)\left(-\dfrac{3}{4}\right) = \dfrac{2}{3} - \dfrac{2}{5}\left(\dfrac{3}{1}\right)\left(-\dfrac{3}{4}\right)$
$$= \dfrac{2}{3} - \dfrac{6}{5}\left(-\dfrac{3}{4}\right)$$
$$= \dfrac{2}{3} + \dfrac{18}{20}$$
$$= \dfrac{40}{60} + \dfrac{54}{60}$$
$$= \dfrac{94}{60}$$
$$= \dfrac{47}{30} \text{ or } 1\dfrac{17}{30}$$

54. $\left(\dfrac{2}{3}\right)^2 - \dfrac{3}{8}\left(\dfrac{8}{5}\right) = \dfrac{4}{9} - \dfrac{3}{8}\left(\dfrac{8}{5}\right)$
$$= \dfrac{4}{9} - \dfrac{3}{5}$$
$$= \dfrac{20}{45} - \dfrac{27}{45}$$
$$= -\dfrac{7}{45}$$

55. $(1.2)^2 + (2.8)(-0.5) = 1.44 + (2.8)(-0.5)$
$$= 1.44 + (-1.4)$$
$$= 0.04$$

56. $1.4(4.7-4.9) - 12.8 \div (-0.2)$
$$= 1.4(-0.2) - 12.8 \div (-0.2)$$
$$= -0.28 + 64$$
$$= 63.72$$

57. $4160 = 4.16 \times 10^3$

58. $3,700,000 = 3.7 \times 10^6$

59. $200,000 = 2 \times 10^5$

60. $0.007 = 7.0 \times 10^{-3}$

61. $0.0000218 = 2.18 \times 10^{-5}$

62. $0.00000763 = 7.63 \times 10^{-6}$

63. $1.89 \times 10^4 = 18,900$

64. $3.76 \times 10^3 = 3760$

65. $7.52 \times 10^{-2} = 0.0752$

66. $6.61 \times 10^{-3} = 0.00661$

67. $9 \times 10^{-7} = 0.0000009$

68. $8 \times 10^{-8} = 0.00000008$

69. $3.14 \times 10^5 = 314,000$

70. $4.89 \times 10^4 = 48,900$

71.
$$\begin{array}{r} 2.42 \times 10^7 \\ +\ 5.76 \times 10^7 \\ \hline 8.18 \times 10^7 \end{array}$$

72.
$$\begin{array}{r} 6.11 \times 10^{10} \\ +\ 3.87 \times 10^{10} \\ \hline 9.98 \times 10^{10} \end{array}$$

73.
$$\begin{array}{r} 3.42 \times 10^{14} \\ -\ 1.98 \times 10^{14} \\ \hline 1.44 \times 10^{14} \end{array}$$

74.
$$\begin{array}{r} 1.76 \times 10^{26} \\ -\ 1.08 \times 10^{26} \\ \hline 0.68 \times 10^{26} = 6.8 \times 10^{25} \end{array}$$

75. $123,120,000,000,000 = 1.2312 \times 10^{14}$ drops
This is equivalent to 1.2312×10^{14} drops.

76. This is equivalent to 5.983×10^{24} kilograms.

77. $93,000,000 = 9.3 \times 10^7$

$9.3 \times 10^7 \text{ miles} \times \dfrac{5.28 \times 10^3 \text{ feet}}{1 \text{ mi}}$

$= 49.104 \times 10^{10} \text{ ft}$

$= 4.9104 \times 10^{11} \text{ feet}$

The distance is 4.9104×10^{11} feet.

78. $280,000 \times 93,000,000 = (2.8 \times 10^5) \times (9.3 \times 10^7)$

$\qquad\qquad\qquad\qquad = 2.604 \times 10^{13} \text{ miles}$

The distance is 2.604×10^{13} miles.

79. $1.67 \text{ yg} = 1.67 \times 10^{-24} \text{ grams}$

$0.00091 \text{ yg} = 9.1 \times 10^{-28} \text{ grams}$

80. $2.5 \times 10^8 = 250,000,000 \text{ meters}$

The diameter is 250,000,000 m.

81. $384.4 \times 10^6 = 384,400,000 \text{ meters}$

The distance is 384,400,000 m.

82. $-5 + 6 + (-7) = 1 + (-7) = -6 \text{ yards}$

The total loss was 6 yards.

83. Top of Fred's head: $-282 + 6 = -276 \text{ ft}$

Distance to plane:

$2400 - (-276) = 2400 + 276 = 2676 \text{ ft}$

The distance is 2676 feet.

84. $-\$18 + (-\$20) + \$40 = -\$38 + \$40 = \$2$

The balance is \$2.

85. $\dfrac{-16° + (-18°) + (-5°) + 3° + (-12°)}{5} = \dfrac{-48°}{5}$

$\qquad\qquad\qquad\qquad\qquad\qquad = -9.6°\text{F}$

The average temperature was $-9.6°$F.

86. $2(-1) + (-2) + 4(1) + 2 = -2 + (-2) + 4 + 2$

$\qquad\qquad\qquad\qquad\quad = -4 + 4 + 2$

$\qquad\qquad\qquad\qquad\quad = 0 + 2$

$\qquad\qquad\qquad\qquad\quad = 2$

Frank was 2 points above par.

How Am I Doing? Chapter 9 Test

1. $-26 + 15 = -11$

2. $-31 + (-12) = -43$

3. $12.8 + (-8.9) = 3.9$

4. $-3 + (-6) + 7 + (-4) = -9 + 7 + (-4)$

$\qquad\qquad\qquad\qquad\quad = -2 + (-4)$

$\qquad\qquad\qquad\qquad\quad = -6$

5. $-5\dfrac{3}{4} + 2\dfrac{1}{4} = -3\dfrac{2}{4} = -3\dfrac{1}{2}$

6. $-\dfrac{1}{4} + \left(-\dfrac{5}{8}\right) = -\dfrac{2}{8} + \left(-\dfrac{5}{8}\right) = -\dfrac{7}{8}$

7. $-32 - 6 = -32 + (-6) = -38$

8. $23 - 18 = 23 + (-18) = 5$

9. $\dfrac{4}{5} - \left(-\dfrac{1}{3}\right) = \dfrac{4}{5} + \dfrac{1}{3} = \dfrac{12}{15} + \dfrac{5}{15} = \dfrac{17}{15} \text{ or } 1\dfrac{2}{15}$

10. $-50 - (-7) = -50 + 7 = -43$

11. $-2.5 - (-6.5) = -2.5 + 6.5 = 4$

12. $-8.5 - 2.8 = -8.5 + (-2.8) = -11.3$

13. $\dfrac{1}{12} - \left(-\dfrac{5}{6}\right) = \dfrac{1}{12} + \dfrac{5}{6} = \dfrac{1}{12} + \dfrac{10}{12} = \dfrac{11}{12}$

14. $-15 - (-15) = -15 + 15 = 0$

15. $(-20)(-6) = 120$

16. $27 \div \left(-\dfrac{3}{4}\right) = 27 \times \left(-\dfrac{4}{3}\right) = -36$

17. $-40 \div (-4) = 10$

18. $(-9)(-1)(-2)(4)\left(\dfrac{1}{4}\right) = 9(-2)(4)\left(\dfrac{1}{4}\right)$

$\qquad\qquad\qquad\qquad\qquad = -18(4)\left(\dfrac{1}{4}\right)$

$\qquad\qquad\qquad\qquad\qquad = -72\left(\dfrac{1}{4}\right)$

$\qquad\qquad\qquad\qquad\qquad = -18$

19. $\dfrac{-39}{-13} = 3$

20. $\dfrac{-\dfrac{3}{5}}{\dfrac{6}{7}} = -\dfrac{3}{5} \div \dfrac{6}{7} = -\dfrac{3}{5} \times \dfrac{7}{6} = \dfrac{7}{10}$

21. $(-12)(0.5)(-3) = (-6)(-3) = 18$

22. $96 \div (-3) = -32$

23. $7 - 2(-5) = 7 + 10 = 17$

24. $-2.5 - 1.2 \div (-0.4) = -2.5 - (-3) = -2.5 + 3 = 0.5$

25. $18 \div (-3) + 24 \div (-12) = -6 + (-2) = -8$

26. $-6(-3) - 4(3-7)^2 = -6(-3) - 4(-4)^2$
$$= -6(-3) - 4(16)$$
$$= 18 - 64$$
$$= -46$$

27. $1.3 - 9.5 - (-2.5) + 3(-0.5)$
$$= 1.3 + (-9.5) + 2.5 + (-1.5)$$
$$= -8.2 + 2.5 + (-1.5)$$
$$= -5.7 + (-1.5)$$
$$= -7.2$$

28. $-48 \div (-6) - 7(-2)^2 = -48 \div (-6) - 7(4)$
$$= 8 + (-28)$$
$$= -20$$

29. $\dfrac{3+8-5}{(-4)(6)+(-6)(3)} = \dfrac{3+8-5}{-24+(-18)} = \dfrac{6}{-42} = -\dfrac{1}{7}$

30. $\dfrac{5+28 \div (-4)}{7-(-5)} = \dfrac{5+(-7)}{7+5} = \dfrac{-2}{12} = -\dfrac{1}{6}$

31. $80,540 = 8.054 \times 10^4$

32. $0.000007 = 7 \times 10^{-6}$

33. $9.36 \times 10^{-5} = 0.0000936$

34. $7.2 \times 10^4 = 72,000$

35. $\dfrac{-14° + (-8°) + (-5°) + 7° + (-11°)}{5} = -\dfrac{-31°}{5}$
$$= -6.2°F$$
The average temperature is $-6.2°F$.

36. $2 \times 5.8 \times 10^{-5}$
$\underline{+\ 2 \times 7.8 \times 10^{-5}}$

11.6×10^{-5}
$\underline{+\ 15.6 \times 10^{-5}}$
27.2×10^{-5} or 2.72×10^{-4} meter

The perimeter is 2.72×10^{-4} m.

37. $58.3 - (-128.6) = 58.3 + 128.6 = 186.9°F$
The difference in temperatures is $186.9°F$.

Cumulative Test for Chapters 1–9

1. $28,981$
$\underline{-\ 16,598}$
$12,383$

2.
$$\begin{array}{r} 127 \\ 36\overline{)4572} \\ 36 \\ \hline 97 \\ 72 \\ \hline 252 \\ 252 \\ \hline 0 \end{array}$$

3. $3\dfrac{1}{4}$ $3\dfrac{3}{12}$
$\underline{+\ 8\dfrac{2}{3}}$ $\underline{+\ 8\dfrac{8}{12}}$
$11\dfrac{11}{12}$

4. $1\dfrac{5}{6} \times 2\dfrac{1}{2} = \dfrac{11}{6} \times \dfrac{5}{2} = \dfrac{55}{12}$ or $4\dfrac{7}{12}$

5. 9.812456 rounds to 9.812.

6. 16.030
9.100
3.510
$\underline{+\ 0.025}$
28.665

7. 12.89
$\underline{\times\ 5.12}$
2578
$1\ 289$
$\underline{64\ 45}$
65.9968

8.　$\dfrac{n}{8} = \dfrac{56}{7}$

　　$n \times 7 = 8 \times 56$

　　$n \times 7 = 448$

　　$\dfrac{n \times 7}{7} = \dfrac{448}{7}$

　　$n = 64$

9.　$\dfrac{n \text{ defects}}{2808 \text{ parts}} = \dfrac{7 \text{ defects}}{156 \text{ parts}}$

　　$156 \times n = 7 \times 2808$

　　$\dfrac{156 \times n}{156} = \dfrac{19,656}{156}$

　　$n = 126 \text{ defects}$

　　You would expect 126 defects.

10.　$n = 0.8\% \times 38$

　　$n = 0.008 \times 38$

　　$n = 0.304$

11.　10% of what is 12?

　　$\dfrac{10}{100} = \dfrac{12}{b}$

　　$10b = 100 \times 12$

　　$\dfrac{10b}{10} = \dfrac{1200}{10}$

　　$b = 120$

12.　94 km = 94,000 m (move decimal 3 places right)

13.　$50 \text{ ft} \times \dfrac{1 \text{ yd}}{3 \text{ ft}} = 16\dfrac{2}{3} \text{ yd}$

14.　$P = 2(12.5) + 2(10) = 25 + 20 = 45$ feet
　　The perimeter is 45 feet.

15.　$A = \pi r^2 = (3.14)(5)^2 = 78.5$
　　The area is 78.5 square meters.

16.　a.　There are 300 students age 23–25.

　　b.　　　　500 students age 20–22
　　　　　　300 students age 23–25
　　　　　　200 students age 26–28
　　　　　　<u>100 students age 29–31</u>
　　　There are 1100 students over age 19.

　　c.　　　　400 age 17–19
　　　　　　200 age 26–28
　　　　　　<u>100 age 29–31</u>
　　　There are 700 students less than 20 or older than 25 years.

17.　$\sqrt{169} + \sqrt{81} = 13 + 9 = 22$

18.　$-10.9 + (-3.5) = -14.4$

19.　$-\dfrac{1}{4} + \dfrac{2}{3} = -\dfrac{3}{12} + \dfrac{8}{12} = \dfrac{5}{12}$

20.　$7 - 18 = 7 + (-18) = -11$

21.　$-12 - (-7) = -12 + 7 = -5$

22.　$5(-3)(-1)(-2)(2) = -15(-1)(-2)(2)$
　　　　　　　　　　　$= 15(-2)(2)$
　　　　　　　　　　　$= -30(2)$
　　　　　　　　　　　$= -60$

23.　$\dfrac{-\frac{4}{5}}{-\frac{21}{35}} = -\dfrac{4}{5} \div \left(-\dfrac{21}{35}\right) = -\dfrac{4}{5}\left(-\dfrac{35}{21}\right) = \dfrac{4}{3} \text{ or } 1\dfrac{1}{3}$

24.　$6 - 3(-4) = 6 - (-12) = 6 + 12 = 18$

25.　$(-45) \div (15 - 20) = (-45) \div (-5) = 9$

26.　$\dfrac{(-2)(-1) + (-4)(-3)}{1 + (-4)(2)} = \dfrac{2 + 12}{1 + (-8)} = \dfrac{14}{-7} = -2$

27.　$\dfrac{(-11)(-8) \div 22}{1 - 7(-2)} = \dfrac{88 \div 22}{1 + 14} = \dfrac{4}{15}$

28.　$28,940 = 2.894 \times 10^4$

29.　$0.0000549 = 5.49 \times 10^{-5}$

30.　$3.85 \times 10^7 = 38,500,000$

31.　$7 \times 10^{-5} = 0.00007$

Chapter 10

10.1 Exercises

2. Like terms are terms that have identical variables and identical exponents.

4. All the variables must be the same. The first term has two variables x and y. The second term has only the variable x. In order to have like terms the same exact variables must appear in each term.

6. $S = 3\pi r^3$: variables are S, r

8. $p = \dfrac{7ab}{4}$: variables are p, a, b

10. $p = 2 \times w + 2 \times l$
$p = 2w + 2l$

12. $A = \dfrac{a \times b + a \times c}{3}$
$A = \dfrac{ab + ac}{3}$

14. $-12x + 40x = 28x$

16. $4x - 10x + 3x = -6x + 3x = -3x$

18. $\dfrac{2}{5}x - \dfrac{2}{3}x + \dfrac{7}{15}x = \dfrac{6}{15}x - \dfrac{10}{15}x + \dfrac{7}{15}x = \dfrac{3}{15}x = \dfrac{1}{5}x$

20. $x + 12x + 11 + 7 = 13x + 18$

22. $3.8x + 2 - 1.9x - 3.5 = 3.8x - 1.9x + 2 - 3.5$
$\qquad = 1.9x - 1.5$

24. $22x - 13y - 23 - 8x = 22x - 8x - 13y - 23$
$\qquad = 14x - 13y - 23$

26. $19 - \left(4\dfrac{1}{4}\right)x + \left(2\dfrac{3}{8}\right)x - 8$

$= 19 - 8 - \left(4\dfrac{1}{4}\right)x + \left(2\dfrac{3}{8}\right)x$

$= 11 + \left(-\dfrac{17}{4} + \dfrac{19}{8}\right)x$

$= 11 + \left(-\dfrac{34}{8} + \dfrac{19}{8}\right)x$

$= 11 - \dfrac{15}{8}x$ or $11 - \left(1\dfrac{7}{8}\right)x$

28. $10b + 3a - 8b - 5c + a = 3a + a + 10b - 8b - 5c$
$\qquad = 4a + 2b - 5c$

30. $\dfrac{1}{4}x + \dfrac{1}{3}y - \dfrac{7}{12}x - \dfrac{1}{2}y = \dfrac{1}{4}x - \dfrac{7}{12}x + \dfrac{1}{3}y - \dfrac{1}{2}y$

$= \dfrac{3}{12}x - \dfrac{7}{12}x + \dfrac{2}{6}y - \dfrac{3}{6}y$

$= -\dfrac{4}{12}x - \dfrac{1}{6}y$

$= -\dfrac{1}{3}x - \dfrac{1}{6}y$

32. $3.1x + 2.9x - 8 - 12.8x - 3.2x + 3$
$= 3.1x + 2.9x - 12.8x - 3.2x - 8 + 3$
$= -10x - 5$

34. $4.5n - 5.9m + 3.9 - 7.2n + 9m$
$= 4.5n - 7.2n - 5.9m + 9m + 3.9$
$= -2.7n + 3.1m + 3.9$

36. a. Perimeter
$= 2x - 4 + x + 9 + 2x + 6 + x + 5$
$= 2x + 2x + x + x - 4 + 9 + 6 + 5$
$= 6x + 16$

b. Perimeter $= 6x + 16 + 6x + 16$
$\qquad = 6x + 6x + 16 + 16$
$\qquad = 12x + 32$
It is doubled.

Cumulative Review

37. $3 \times n = 36$
$\dfrac{3 \times n}{3} = \dfrac{36}{3}$
$n = 12$

38. $8 \times n = 64$
$\dfrac{8 \times n}{8} = \dfrac{64}{8}$
$n = 8$

39. $\dfrac{n}{6} = \dfrac{12}{15}$
$n \times 15 = 6 \times 12$
$\dfrac{n \times 15}{15} = \dfrac{72}{15}$
$n = 4.8$

40. $\dfrac{n}{9} = \dfrac{36}{40}$

$n \times 40 = 9 \times 36$

$n \times 40 = 324$

$\dfrac{n \times 40}{40} = \dfrac{324}{40}$

$n = 8.1$

41. 10% of 80 = $0.10 \times 80 = 8$

42. 50% of 80 = $0.50 \times 80 = 40$

Classroom Quiz 10.1

1. $-7a - 3b + 8a - 13b = -7a + 8a - 3b - 13b$
$\qquad\qquad\qquad\qquad\quad = a - 16b$

2. $\dfrac{1}{6}x - \dfrac{5}{18}y - \dfrac{7}{12}x - \dfrac{8}{9}y$

$= \dfrac{1}{6}x - \dfrac{7}{12}x - \dfrac{5}{18}y - \dfrac{8}{9}y$

$= \left(\dfrac{2}{12} - \dfrac{7}{12} \right)x + \left(-\dfrac{5}{18} - \dfrac{16}{18} \right)y$

$= -\dfrac{5}{12}x - \dfrac{21}{18}y$

$= -\dfrac{5}{12}x - \dfrac{7}{6}y$

3. $-8x + 34y + 21 - 13x - 9y - 43$
$= -8x - 13x + 34y - 9y + 21 - 43$
$= -21x + 25y - 22$

10.2 Exercises

2. The variable in the expression $5x + 9$ is x.

4. The distribution property takes the multiplication of a number times the sum and distributes it to a multiplication by each value that was added.
$3(x + 2y) = 3x + 3(2y) = 3x + 6y$

6. $8(4x - 5) = 8(4x) - 8(5) = 32x - 40$

8. $(-5)(x + y) = (-5)(x) + (-5)(y) = -5x - 5y$

10. $-5(6.2x - 7y) = -5(6.2x) - 5(-7y) = -31x + 35y$

12. $(-2x + 8y)(-12) = (-2x)(-12) + (8y)(-12)$
$\qquad\qquad\qquad\qquad = 24x - 96y$

14. $(7a - 11b)(6) = 7a(6) - 11b(6) = 42a - 66b$

16. $(-4 - 9z)(-7) = (-4y)(-7) + (-9z)(-7)$
$\qquad\qquad\qquad = 28y + 63z$

18. $6(2p - 7q + 11) = 6(2p) + 6(-7q) + 6(11)$
$\qquad\qquad\qquad\quad = 12p - 42q + 66$

20. $4\left(\dfrac{2}{3}x + \dfrac{1}{4}y - \dfrac{3}{8} \right) = 4\left(\dfrac{2}{3}x \right) + 4\left(\dfrac{1}{4}y \right) + 4\left(-\dfrac{3}{8} \right)$
$\qquad\qquad\qquad\qquad\qquad = \dfrac{8}{3}x + y - \dfrac{3}{2}$

22. $-14(-5a + 1.4b - 2.5)$
$= (-14)(-5a) + (-14)(1.4b) + (-14)(-2.5)$
$= 70a - 19.6b + 35$

24. $(-7a + 11b - 10c - 9)(7)$
$= (-7a)(7) + (11b)(7) + (-10c)(7) + (-9)(7)$
$= -49a + 77b - 70c - 63$

26. $(-3)(1.4x - 7.6y - 9z - 4)$
$= (-3)(1.4x) + (-3)(-7.6y) + (-3)(-9z)$
$\qquad + (-3)(-4)$
$= -4.2x + 22.8y + 27z + 12$

28. $\dfrac{1}{3}\left(-3x + \dfrac{1}{2}y + 2z - 3 \right)$

$= \dfrac{1}{3}(-3x) + \dfrac{1}{3}\left(\dfrac{1}{2}y \right) + \dfrac{1}{3}(2z) + \dfrac{1}{3}(-3)$

$= -x + \dfrac{1}{6}y + \dfrac{2}{3}z - 1$

30. $-\dfrac{1}{6}(-18s + 6t - 24)$

$= -\dfrac{1}{6}(-18s) - \dfrac{1}{6}(6t) - \dfrac{1}{6}(-24)$

$= 3s - t + 4$

32. $S = 2(lw + lh + wh) = 2lw + 2lh + 2wh$

34. $S = 2\pi r(h + r) = 2\pi r(h) + 2\pi r(r) = 2\pi rh + 2\pi r^2$

36. $8(4x + 3) + 2(x - 15)$
$= 8(4x) + 8(3) + 2(x) + 2(-15)$
$= 32x + 24 + 2x - 30$
$= 34x - 6$

38. $11(2a - 3b) - 2(a + 5b)$
$= 11(2a) + 11(-3b) - 2(a) - 2(5b)$
$= 22a - 33b - 2a - 10b$
$= 20a - 43b$

40. $2.4(x + 3.5y) + 2(1.4x + 1.9y)$
$= 2.4x + 8.4y + 2.8x + 3.8y$
$= 5.2x + 12.2y$

42. $3(-4a + c + 4b) - 4(2c + b - 6a)$
$= -12a + 3c + 12b - 8c - 4b + 24a$
$= 12a + 8b - 5c$

44. $A = ab - ac$
$A = a(b - c)$
Hence, $a(b - c) = ab - ac$.

Cumulative Review

45. $P = 2l + 2w$
$= 2(7.5 \text{ ft}) + 2(4 \text{ ft})$
$= 15 \text{ ft} + 8 \text{ ft}$
$= 23 \text{ ft}$
The perimeter is 23 feet.

46. $A = \dfrac{1}{2}bh = \dfrac{1}{2}(8.5 \text{ in.})(15 \text{ in.}) = 63.75 \text{ in}^2$
The area is 63.75 square inches.

Classroom Quiz 10.2

1. $8\left(-\dfrac{11}{12}x - \dfrac{5}{4}y\right) = 8\left(-\dfrac{11}{12}x\right) + 8\left(-\dfrac{5}{4}y\right)$
$\qquad = -\dfrac{88}{12}x - \dfrac{40}{4}y$
$\qquad = -\dfrac{22}{3}x - 10y$

2. $-2.5(-4x + 5y + z - 6)$
$= -2.5(-4x) - 2.5(5y) - 2.5(z) - 2.5(-6)$
$= 10x - 12.5y - 2.5z + 15$

3. $5(3x + 8y) - 2(-3x + 4y)$
$= 5(3x) + 5(8y) - 2(-3x) - 2(4y)$
$= 15x + 40y + 6x - 8y$
$= 21x + 32y$

10.3 Exercises

2. The <u>solution</u> of an equation is that number which makes the equation true.

4. To use the addition property to solve the equation $x - 8 = 9$, we add <u>+8</u> to both sides of the equation.

6. $\qquad y - 14 = 27$
$y - 14 + 14 = 27 + 14$
$\qquad\qquad y = 41$

8. $\qquad x + 8 = 12$
$x + 8 + (-8) = 12 + (-8)$
$\qquad\qquad x = 4$

10. $\qquad y + 12 = -8$
$y + 12 + (-12) = -8 + (-12)$
$\qquad\qquad y = -20$

12. $\qquad 10 + y = -9$
$10 + (-10) + y = -9 + (-10)$
$\qquad\qquad y = -19$

14. $\qquad -20 + y = 10$
$-20 + 20 + y = 10 + 20$
$\qquad\qquad y = 30$

16. $\qquad 3.1 = y - 5.4$
$3.1 + 5.4 = y - 5.4 + 5.4$
$\qquad 8.5 = y$

18. $\qquad x + 7.5 = -9.3$
$x + 7.5 + (-7.5) = -9.3 + (-7.5)$
$\qquad\qquad x = -16.8$

20. $\qquad y - 29.8 = -15$
$y - 29.8 + 29.8 = -15 + 29.8$
$\qquad\qquad y = 14.8$

22. $\qquad \dfrac{7}{10} = x + \dfrac{1}{10}$
$\dfrac{7}{10} + \left(-\dfrac{1}{10}\right) = x + \dfrac{1}{10} + \left(-\dfrac{1}{10}\right)$
$\qquad \dfrac{6}{10} = x$
$\qquad \dfrac{3}{5} = x$

24. $\qquad y - \dfrac{2}{7} = \dfrac{6}{7}$
$y - \dfrac{2}{7} + \dfrac{2}{7} = \dfrac{6}{7} + \dfrac{2}{7}$
$\qquad\qquad y = \dfrac{8}{7} \text{ or } 1\dfrac{1}{7}$

26.
$$y + \frac{1}{2} = -\frac{3}{4}$$
$$y + \frac{1}{2} + \left(-\frac{1}{2}\right) = -\frac{3}{4} + \left(-\frac{1}{2}\right)$$
$$y = -\frac{3}{4} + \left(-\frac{2}{4}\right)$$
$$= -\frac{5}{4}$$
$$= -1\frac{1}{4}$$

28.
$$\frac{1}{3} + y = 4\frac{7}{12}$$
$$-\frac{1}{3} + \frac{1}{3} + y = -\frac{1}{3} + 4\frac{7}{12}$$
$$y = -\frac{4}{12} + 4\frac{7}{12}$$
$$y = 4\frac{3}{12}$$
$$y = 4\frac{1}{4} \text{ or } \frac{17}{4}$$

30.
$$5x + 1 = 4x - 3$$
$$5x + (-4x) + 1 = 4x + (-4x) - 3$$
$$x + 1 = -3$$
$$x + 1 + (-1) = -3 + (-1)$$
$$x = -4$$

32.
$$8x - 3 = 7x - 12$$
$$8x - 3 + 3 = 7x - 12 + 3$$
$$8x = 7x - 9$$
$$8x - 7x = 7x - 7x - 9$$
$$x = -9$$

34.
$$10x + 3 = 9x + 11$$
$$10x + (-9x) + 3 = 9x + (-9x) + 11$$
$$x + 3 = 11$$
$$x + 3 - 3 = 11 - 3$$
$$x = 8$$

36.
$$14x - 8 = 13x - 10$$
$$14x + (-13x) - 8 = 13x + (-13x) - 10$$
$$x - 8 = -10$$
$$x - 8 + 8 = -10 + 8$$
$$x = -2$$

38.
$$x + 1.2 = -3.8$$
$$x + 1.2 + (-1.2) = -3.8 + (-1.2)$$
$$x = -5$$

40.
$$-15 = -6 + x$$
$$-15 + 6 = -6 + 6 + x$$
$$-9 = x$$

42.
$$z + \frac{2}{3} = \frac{7}{12}$$
$$x + \frac{2}{3} + \left(-\frac{2}{3}\right) = \frac{7}{12} + \left(-\frac{2}{3}\right)$$
$$= \frac{7}{12} + \left(-\frac{8}{12}\right)$$
$$= -\frac{1}{12}$$

44.
$$3x - 8 = 2x - 15$$
$$3x + (-2x) - 8 = 2x + (-2x) - 15$$
$$x - 8 = -15$$
$$x - 8 + 8 = -15 + 8$$
$$x = -7$$

46.
$$5.4y + 3 = 4.4y - 1$$
$$5.4y + 3 + (-3) = 4.4y - 1 + (-3)$$
$$5.4y = 4.4y - 4$$
$$5.4y - 4.4y = 4.4y - 4.4y - 4$$
$$y = -4$$

48.
$$9x + 6 = 10x - 9$$
$$-9x + 9x + 6 = -9x + 10x - 9$$
$$6 = x - 9$$
$$6 + 9 = x - 9 + 9$$
$$15 = x$$

50. To solve the equation $4x = -12$, divide both sides of the equation by 4 so that x stands alone on one side of the equation.

Cumulative Review

51. $5x - y + 3 - 2x + 4y = 5x - 2x - y + 4y + 3$
$$= 3x + 3y + 3$$

52. $7(2x + 3y) - 3(5x - 1)$
$$= 7(2x) + 7(3y) + (-3)(5x) + (-3)(-1)$$
$$= 14x + 21y - 15x + 3$$
$$= 14x - 15x + 21y + 3$$
$$= -x + 21y + 3$$

53. $\text{mean} = \dfrac{85 + 78 + 92 + 83 + 72}{5} = \dfrac{410}{5} = 82$

The mean is $82.

54. List in order: 80, 84, 85, 86, 90, 93, 98
median = 86

Classroom Quiz 10.3

1. $$x - 24.3 = -20.5$$
$$x - 24.3 + 24.3 = -20.5 + 24.3$$
$$x = 3.8$$

2. $$7x + 14 = 6x - 32$$
$$7x + (-6x) + 14 = 6x + (-6x) - 32$$
$$x + 14 = -32$$
$$x + 14 + (-14) = -32 + (-14)$$
$$x = -46$$

3. $$5x - 5 = -12 + 4x$$
$$5x + (-4x) - 5 = -12 + 4x + (-4x)$$
$$x - 5 = -12$$
$$x - 5 + 5 = -12 + 5$$
$$x = -7$$

10.4 Exercises

2. The division property states that we may divide each side of an equation by <u>the same nonzero number</u> to obtain an equivalent equation.

4. The coefficient of the variable is $1\frac{3}{5} = \frac{8}{5}$. We multiply both sides of the equation by $\frac{5}{8}$ because $\frac{8}{5} \times \frac{5}{8} = 1$.

6. $$8x = 56$$
$$\frac{8x}{8} = \frac{56}{8}$$
$$x = 7$$

8. $$5y = -45$$
$$\frac{5y}{5} = \frac{-45}{5}$$
$$y = -9$$

10. $$-7y = 22$$
$$\frac{-7y}{-7} = \frac{22}{-7}$$
$$y = -\frac{22}{7}$$

12. $$-11y = -121$$
$$\frac{-11y}{-11} = \frac{-121}{-11}$$
$$y = 11$$

14. $$-88 = -8m$$
$$\frac{-88}{-8} = \frac{-8m}{-8}$$
$$11 = m$$

16. $$0.5y = 50$$
$$\frac{0.5y}{0.5} = \frac{50}{0.5}$$
$$y = 100$$

18. $$21.6 = 2.4n$$
$$\frac{21.6}{2.4} = \frac{2.4n}{2.4}$$
$$9 = n$$

20. $$-0.4y = 6.88$$
$$\frac{-0.4y}{-0.4} = \frac{6.88}{-0.4}$$
$$y = -17.2$$

22. $$\frac{3}{4}x = 3$$
$$\frac{4}{3} \cdot \frac{3}{4}x = \frac{4}{3} \cdot \frac{3}{1}$$
$$x = 4$$

24. $$\frac{5}{6}y = 10$$
$$\frac{6}{5} \cdot \frac{5}{6}y = \frac{6}{5} \cdot \frac{10}{1}$$
$$y = 12$$

26. $$\frac{2}{3}z = \frac{1}{3}$$
$$\frac{3}{2} \cdot \frac{2}{3}z = \frac{3}{2} \cdot \frac{1}{3}$$
$$z = \frac{1}{2}$$

28. $$-\frac{5}{4}x = \frac{10}{3}$$
$$-\frac{4}{5} \cdot \left(-\frac{5}{4}\right)x = -\frac{4}{5} \cdot \frac{10}{3}$$
$$x = -\frac{8}{3} \text{ or } -2\frac{2}{3}$$

30.
$$\frac{3}{4}y = -3\frac{3}{8}$$
$$\frac{4}{3} \cdot \frac{3}{4}y = -3\frac{3}{8} \cdot \frac{4}{3}$$
$$y = -\frac{27}{8} \cdot \frac{4}{3} = -\frac{9}{2} \text{ or } -4\frac{1}{2}$$

32.
$$\left(-2\frac{1}{5}\right)z = -33$$
$$-\frac{11}{5}z = -33$$
$$-\frac{5}{11} \cdot \left(-\frac{11}{5}\right)z = -\frac{5}{11} \times (-33)$$
$$z = 15$$

34.
$$-75 = -15x$$
$$\frac{-75}{-15} = \frac{-15x}{-15}$$
$$5 = x$$

36.
$$\frac{4}{5}x = -8$$
$$\left(\frac{5}{4}\right)\left(\frac{4}{5}x\right) = \left(\frac{5}{4}\right)(-8)$$
$$x = -10$$

38.
$$1.6x = 0.064$$
$$\frac{1.6x}{1.6} = \frac{0.064}{1.6}$$
$$x = 0.04$$

40.
$$20 = -\frac{5}{6}x$$
$$\left(-\frac{6}{5}\right)(20) = \left(-\frac{6}{5}\right)\left(-\frac{5}{6}x\right)$$
$$-24 = x$$

Cumulative Review

41. $6 - 3x + 5y + 7x - 12y$
$$= -3x + 7x + 5y - 12y + 6$$
$$= 4x - 7y + 6$$

42. $-2(3a - 5b + c) + 5(-a + 2b - 5c)$
$$= (-2)(3a) + (-2)(-5b) + (-2)(c) + 5(-a) + 5(2b)$$
$$\quad + 5(-5c)$$
$$= -6a + 10b - 2c - 5a + 10b - 25c$$
$$= -6a - 5a + 10b + 10b - 2c - 25c$$
$$= -11a + 20b - 27c$$

43. decrease $= \$7.34 - \$5.50 = \$1.84$
$$\text{percent} = \frac{1.84}{7.34} \approx 0.251 = 25.1\%$$
The percentage of decrease was 25.1%.

44. percent covered: $\dfrac{1,755,637}{2,166,086} \approx 0.811$ or 81.1%

percent not covered: $100\% - 81.1\% = 18.9\%$

Classroom Quiz 10.4

1. $-7x = -21$
$$\frac{-7x}{-7} = \frac{-21}{-7}$$
$$x = 3$$

2. $-10.5 = 1.5x$
$$\frac{-10.5}{1.5} = \frac{1.5x}{1.5}$$
$$-7 = x$$

3.
$$-\frac{5}{8}x = \frac{3}{4}$$
$$-\frac{8}{5} \cdot \left(-\frac{5}{8}x\right) = -\frac{8}{5} \cdot \frac{3}{4}$$
$$x = -\frac{6}{5} \text{ or } -1.2 \text{ or } -1\frac{1}{5}$$

10.5 Exercises

2. You want to obtain all the *x*-terms on the left side of the equation. So you want to remove the $4x$ from the right hand side of the equation. This means you would add $-4x$ to each side.

4. $5 - 3x = -4x + 1$
$$5 - 3(6) \stackrel{?}{=} -4(6) + 1$$
$$5 - 18 \stackrel{?}{=} -24 + 1$$
$$-13 \neq -23$$
No

6. $12x - 7 = 3 - 18x$
$$12\left(\frac{1}{3}\right) - 7 \stackrel{?}{=} 3 - 18\left(\frac{1}{3}\right)$$
$$4 - 7 \stackrel{?}{=} 3 - 6$$
$$-3 = -3 \text{ Yes}$$

8.
$$12x - 30 = 6$$
$$12x - 30 + 30 = 6 + 30$$
$$12x = 36$$
$$\frac{12x}{12} = \frac{36}{12}$$
$$x = 3$$

10.
$$9x - 3 = -7$$
$$9x - 3 + 3 = -7 + 3$$
$$9x = -4$$
$$\frac{9x}{9} = \frac{-4}{9}$$
$$x = -\frac{4}{9}$$

12.
$$-3x = 7x + 14$$
$$-3x + (-7x) = 7x + (-7x) + 14$$
$$-10x = 14$$
$$\frac{-10x}{-10} = \frac{14}{-10}$$
$$x = -\frac{14}{10} = -\frac{7}{5} \text{ or } -1\frac{2}{5}$$

14.
$$11x + 12 = -21$$
$$11x + 12 + (-12) = -21 + (-12)$$
$$11x = -33$$
$$\frac{11x}{11} = \frac{-33}{11}$$
$$x = -3$$

16.
$$0.78 = 3x - 0.12$$
$$0.78 + 0.12 = 3x - 0.12 + 0.12$$
$$0.90 = 3x$$
$$\frac{0.9}{3} = \frac{3x}{3}$$
$$0.3 = x$$

18.
$$\frac{3}{4}x + 2 = -10$$
$$\frac{3}{4}x + 2 + (-2) = -10 + (-2)$$
$$\frac{3}{4}x = -12$$
$$\frac{4}{3} \cdot \frac{3}{4}x = -12 \cdot \frac{4}{3}$$
$$x = -16$$

20.
$$3x + 4 = 7x - 12$$
$$3x + (-3x) + 4 = 7x + (-3x) - 12$$
$$4 = 4x - 12$$
$$4 + 12 = 4x - 12 + 12$$
$$16 = 4x$$
$$\frac{16}{4} = \frac{4x}{4}$$
$$4 = x$$

22.
$$8 + x = 3x - 6$$
$$8 + x + (-x) = 3x + (-x) - 6$$
$$8 = 2x - 6$$
$$8 + 6 = 2x - 6 + 6$$
$$14 = 2x$$
$$\frac{14}{2} = \frac{2x}{2}$$
$$7 = x$$

24.
$$2x + 11 = 7x - 4$$
$$2x + (-7x) + 11 = 7x + (-7x) - 4$$
$$-5x + 11 = -4$$
$$-5x + 11 + (-11) = -4 + (-11)$$
$$-5x = -15$$
$$\frac{-5x}{-5} = \frac{-15}{-5}$$
$$x = 3$$

26.
$$1.2 + 0.5y = -0.8 - 0.3y$$
$$1.2 + (-1.2) + 0.5y = -0.8 + (-1.2) - 0.3y$$
$$0.5y = -2 - 0.3y$$
$$0.5y + 0.3y = -2 - 0.3y + 0.3y$$
$$0.8y = -2$$
$$\frac{0.8y}{0.8} = \frac{-2}{0.8}$$
$$y = -2.5$$

28.
$$0.4x + 0.5 = -1.9 - 0.8x$$
$$10(0.4x + 0.5) = 10(-1.9 - 0.8x)$$
$$4x + 5 = -19 - 8x$$
$$4x + 8x + 5 = -19 - 8x + 8x$$
$$12x + 5 + (-5) = -19 + (-5)$$
$$12x = -24$$
$$\frac{12x}{12} = \frac{-24}{12}$$
$$x = -2$$

30.
$$6-5x+2=4x+35$$
$$-5x+8=4x+35$$
$$-5x+(-4x)+8=4x+(-4x)+35$$
$$-9x+8=35$$
$$-9x+8+(-8)=35+(-8)$$
$$-9x=27$$
$$\frac{-9x}{-9}=\frac{27}{-9}$$
$$x=-3$$

32.
$$-x-2=-13+3x+8$$
$$-x-2=-5+3x$$
$$-x+(-3x)-2=-5+3x+(-3x)$$
$$-4x-2=-5$$
$$-4x-2+2=-5+2$$
$$-4x=-3$$
$$\frac{-4x}{-4}=\frac{-3}{-4}$$
$$x=\frac{3}{4}$$

34.
$$15-18y-21=15y-22-29y$$
$$-18y-6=-14y-22$$
$$-18y+18y-6=-14y+18y-22$$
$$-6=4y-22$$
$$-6+22=4y-22+22$$
$$16=4y$$
$$\frac{16}{4}=\frac{4y}{4}$$
$$4=y$$

36.
$$4(2x-1)-7x=9$$
$$4(2x)+4(-1)-7x=9$$
$$8x-4-7x=9$$
$$x-4=9$$
$$x-4+4=9+4$$
$$x=13$$

38.
$$13+7(2y-1)=5(y+6)$$
$$13+14y-7=5y+30$$
$$14y+6=5y+30$$
$$14y+(-5y)+6=5y+(-5y)+30$$
$$9y+6=30$$
$$9y+6+(-6)=30+(-6)$$
$$9y=24$$
$$\frac{9y}{9}=\frac{24}{9}$$
$$y=\frac{24}{9}=\frac{8}{3} \text{ or } 2\frac{2}{3}$$

40.
$$10x-3(x-4)=9x-8$$
$$10x-3x+12=9x-8$$
$$7x+12=9x-8$$
$$7x+(-9x)+12=9x+(-9x)-8$$
$$-2x+12=-8$$
$$-2x+12+(-12)=-8+(-12)$$
$$-2x=-20$$
$$\frac{-2x}{-2}=\frac{-20}{-2}$$
$$x=10$$

42.
$$6x+5=\frac{1}{4}(8x-4)$$
$$6x+5=\frac{1}{4}(8x)+\frac{1}{4}(-4)$$
$$6x+5=2x-1$$
$$6x+5+(-5)=2x-1+(-5)$$
$$6x=2x-6$$
$$6x-2x=2x-2x-6$$
$$4x=-6$$
$$\frac{4x}{4}=-\frac{6}{4}$$
$$x=-\frac{3}{2} \text{ or } -1\frac{1}{2}$$

44.
$$-3x-2(x+1)=-4(x-1)$$
$$-3x+(-2)(x)+(-2)(1)=(-4)(x)+(-4)(-1)$$
$$-3x-2x-2=-4x+4$$
$$-5x-2=-4x+4$$
$$-5x-2+2=-4x+4+2$$
$$-5x=-4x+6$$
$$-5x+4x=-4x+4x+6$$
$$-x=6$$
$$\frac{-x}{-1}=\frac{6}{-1}$$
$$x=-6$$

Cumulative Review

45. $V=\dfrac{4\pi r^3}{3}$
$$=\frac{4(3.14)(46 \text{ cm})^3}{3}$$
$$=\frac{4(3.14)(97,336 \text{ cu cm})}{3}$$
$$\approx 407,513.4 \text{ cu cm}$$

The volume is $407,513.4 \text{ cm}^3$.

46. Area = Area of Square − Area of Circle
$$= 6^2 - \pi(2)^2$$
$$= 36 - 3.14(4)$$
$$\approx 23.4$$
The area is 23.4 square inches.

Classroom Quiz 10.5

1.
$$0.6 - 0.8x = 0.7x - 6.9$$
$$0.6 - 0.8x + (-0.7x) = 0.7x + (-0.7x) - 6.9$$
$$0.6 - 1.5x = -6.9$$
$$0.6 + (-0.6) - 1.5x = -6.9 + (-0.6)$$
$$-1.5x = -7.5$$
$$\frac{-1.5x}{-1.5} = \frac{-7.5}{-1.5}$$
$$x = 5$$

2.
$$-3 - 6x + 7 = 23 + 5x + 14$$
$$-6x + 4 = 37 + 5x$$
$$-6x + (-5x) + 4 = 37 + 5x + (-5x)$$
$$-11x + 4 = 37$$
$$-11x + 4 + (-4) = 37 + (-4)$$
$$-11x = 33$$
$$\frac{-11x}{-11} = \frac{33}{-11}$$
$$x = -3$$

3.
$$-4(2x + 8) + 3 = 16 + 2(x - 4)$$
$$-8x - 32 + 3 = 16 + 2x - 8$$
$$-8x - 29 = 8 + 2x$$
$$-8x + (-2x) - 29 = 8 + 2x + (-2x)$$
$$-10x - 29 = 8$$
$$-10x - 29 + 29 = 8 + 29$$
$$-10x = 37$$
$$\frac{-10x}{-10} = \frac{37}{-10}$$
$$x = -\frac{37}{10} \text{ or } -3\frac{7}{10} \text{ or } -3.7$$

How Am I Doing? Sections 10.1–10.5

1. $23x - 40x = -17x$

2. $-8y + 12y - 3y = y$

3. $6a - 5b - 9a + 7b = 6a - 9a - 5b + 7b$
$$= -3a + 2b$$

4. $6y - 8 + 3x - 2 + 4y - 5x$
$$= 3x - 5x + 6y + 4y - 8 - 2$$
$$= -2x + 10y - 10$$

5. $7x - 14 + 5y + 8 - 7y + 9x$
$$= 7x + 9x + 5y - 7y - 14 + 8$$
$$= 16x - 2y - 6$$

6. $4a - 7b + 3c - 5b = 4a - 7b - 5b + 3c$
$$= 4a - 12b + 3c$$

7. $6(7x - 3y) = 6(7x) - 6(3y) = 42x - 18y$

8. $-4\left(\dfrac{1}{2}a - \dfrac{1}{4}b + 3\right) = -4\left(\dfrac{1}{2}a\right) - 4\left(-\dfrac{1}{4}b\right) - 4(3)$
$$= -2a + b - 12$$

9. $-2(1.5a + 3b - 6c - 5)$
$$= (-2)(1.5a) + (-2)(3b) + (-2)(-6c) + (-2)(-5)$$
$$= -3a - 6b + 12c + 10$$

10. $5(2x - y) - 3(3x + y)$
$$= 5(2x) + 5(-y) + (-3)(3x) + (-3)(y)$$
$$= 10x - 5y - 9x - 3y$$
$$= 10x - 9x - 5y - 3y$$
$$= x - 8y$$

11. $(9x + 4y)(-2) = 9x(-2) + 4y(-2) = -18x - 8y$

12. $(7x - 3y)(-3) = 7x(-3) + (-3y)(-3) = -21x + 9y$

13.
$$5 + x = 42$$
$$5 + (-5) + x = 42 + (-5)$$
$$x = 37$$

14.
$$x + 2.5 = 6$$
$$x + 2.5 + (-2.5) = 6 + (-2.5)$$
$$x = 3.5$$

15.
$$y + \frac{4}{5} = -\frac{3}{10}$$
$$y + \frac{4}{5} + \left(-\frac{4}{5}\right) = -\frac{3}{10} + \left(-\frac{4}{5}\right)$$
$$y = -\frac{3}{10} + \left(-\frac{8}{10}\right)$$
$$y = -\frac{11}{10} \text{ or } -1\frac{1}{10}$$

16.
$$-12 = -20 + x$$
$$-12 + 20 = -20 + 20 + x$$
$$8 = x$$

17. $-9y = -72$

$$\frac{-9y}{-9} = \frac{-72}{-9}$$

$$y = 8$$

18. $2.7y = 27$

$$\frac{2.7y}{2.7} = \frac{27}{2.7}$$

$$y = 10$$

19. $\dfrac{3}{5}x = \dfrac{9}{10}$

$$\frac{5}{3}\left(\frac{3}{5}x\right) = \frac{5}{3}\left(\frac{9}{10}\right)$$

$$x = \frac{3}{2} \text{ or } 1\frac{1}{2}$$

20. $84 = -7x$

$$\frac{84}{-7} = \frac{-7x}{-7}$$

$$-12 = x$$

21. $-7 + 6m = 25$

$$-7 + 7 + 6m = 25 + 7$$

$$6m = 32$$

$$\frac{6m}{6} = \frac{32}{6}$$

$$m = \frac{16}{3} \text{ or } 5\frac{1}{3}$$

22. $-11 + 4m = -5m + 7$

$$-11 + 4m + 5m = -5m + 5m + 7$$

$$-11 + 9m = 7$$

$$-11 + 11 + 9m = 7 + 11$$

$$9m = 18$$

$$\frac{9m}{9} = \frac{18}{9}$$

$$m = 2$$

23. $5(x-1) = 7 - 3(x-4)$

$$5x + 5(-1) = 7 + (-3)x + (-3)(-4)$$

$$5x - 5 = 7 - 3x + 12$$

$$5x - 5 = -3x + 19$$

$$5x - 5 + 5 = -3x + 19 + 5$$

$$5x = -3x + 24$$

$$5x + 3x = -3x + 3x + 24$$

$$8x = 24$$

$$\frac{8x}{8} = \frac{24}{8}$$

$$x = 3$$

24. $3x + 7 = 5(5 - x)$

$$3x + 7 = 5(5) + 5(-x)$$

$$3x + 7 = 25 - 5x$$

$$3x + 7 + (-7) = 25 + (-7) - 5x$$

$$3x = 18 - 5x$$

$$3x + 5x = 18 - 5x + 5x$$

$$8x = 18$$

$$\frac{8x}{8} = \frac{18}{8}$$

$$x = \frac{9}{4} \text{ or } 2\frac{1}{4}$$

25. $5x - 18 = 2(x + 3)$

$$5x - 18 = 2x + 2(3)$$

$$5x - 18 = 2x + 6$$

$$5x - 18 + 18 = 2x + 6 + 18$$

$$5x = 2x + 24$$

$$5x - 2x = 2x - 2x + 24$$

$$3x = 24$$

$$\frac{3x}{3} = \frac{24}{3}$$

$$x = 8$$

26. $8x - 5(x + 2) = -3(x - 5)$

$$8x + (-5)x + (-5)(2) = (-3x) + (-3)(-5)$$

$$8x - 5x - 10 = -3x + 15$$

$$3x - 10 = -3x + 15$$

$$3x - 10 + 10 = -3x + 15 + 10$$

$$3x = -3x + 25$$

$$3x + 3x = -3x + 3x + 25$$

$$6x = 25$$

$$\frac{5x}{6} = \frac{25}{6}$$

$$x = \frac{25}{6} \text{ or } 4\frac{1}{6}$$

27. $12 + 4y - 7 = 6y - 9$

$$4y + 5 = 6y - 9$$

$$4y + 5 + 9 = 6y - 9 + 9$$

$$4y + 14 = 6y$$

$$4y - 4y + 14 = 6y - 4y$$

$$14 = 2y$$

$$\frac{14}{2} = \frac{2y}{2}$$

$$7 = y$$

28.
$$0.3x + 0.4 = 0.7x - 1.2$$
$$0.3x + 0.4 + 1.2 = 0.7x - 1.2 + 1.2$$
$$0.3x + 1.6 = 0.7x$$
$$0.3x - 0.3x + 1.6 = 0.7x - 0.3x$$
$$1.6 = 0.4x$$
$$\frac{1.6}{0.4} = \frac{0.4x}{0.4}$$
$$4 = x$$

10.6 Exercises

2. $l = s + 7$

4. $f = s - 42$

6. $q = r - 21$

8. $l = 2w - 8$

10. $l = 2w - 10$

12. $t = 2l + 2$

14. $s - f = 138$

16. $\dfrac{m}{w} = \dfrac{5}{3}$ or $3m = 5w$

18. c = cost of Apple iPod player
$c + 50$ = cost of Microsoft Zune player

20. s = length of the side of the box in centimeters
$s - 38$ = length of the top of the box in
centimeters

22. d = depth of Lake Superior in feet
$d + 1771$ = depth of the Caspian Sea in feet

24. l = Lisa's tips
$l + 12$ = Sam's tips
$l - 6$ = Brenda's tips

26. w = width
$w + 7$ = height
$2w - 1$ = length

28. x = first angle
$3x$ = second angle
$x + 36$ = third angle

Cumulative Review

29. $-6 - (-7)(2) = -6 - (-14) = -6 + 14 = 8$

30. $5 - 5 + 8 - (-4) + 2 - 15$
$$= 5 + (-5) + 8 + 4 + 2 + (-15)$$
$$= 0 + 8 + 4 + 2 + (-15)$$
$$= 12 + 2 + (-15)$$
$$= 14 + (-15)$$
$$= -1$$

31. $-2(3x + 5) + 12 = 8$
$$-6x - 10 + 12 = 8$$
$$-6x + 2 = 8$$
$$-6x + 2 + (-2) = 8 + (-2)$$
$$-6x = 6$$
$$\frac{-6x}{-6} = \frac{6}{-6}$$
$$x = -1$$

32. $3y - 4 - 5y = 10 - y$
$$-4 - 2y = 10 - y$$
$$-4 + 4 - 2y = 10 + 4 - y$$
$$-2y = 14 - y$$
$$-2y + y = 14 - y + y$$
$$-y = 14$$
$$\frac{-y}{-1} = \frac{14}{-1}$$
$$y = -14$$

33. $\dfrac{108}{210} \approx 0.514$

$\dfrac{156}{0.455} \approx 343$

$287 \times 0.446 \approx 128$

Classroom Quiz 10.6

1. The commuting time of Mabel, M, is *triple* the
time of Olivier, O.
$M = 3O$

2. w = width of the rectangle
$2w - 4$ = the length of the rectangle

3. p = the number of students who live with their
parents

$0.5p$ or $\dfrac{p}{2}$ = the number of students who live in
apartments
$p - 1550$ = the number of students who own
their own homes

10.7 Exercises

2. x = length of the shorter piece
$x + 4.5$ = length of longer piece
$$x + x + 4.5 = 20$$
$$2x + 4.5 = 20$$
$$2x + 4.5 + (-4.5) = 20 + (-4.5)$$
$$2x = 15.5$$
$$\frac{2x}{2} = \frac{15.5}{2}$$
$$x = 7.75$$
shorter piece = 7.75 feet
longer piece = 7.75 + 4.5 = 12.25 feet

4. x = number of points scored by Thayer
$x - 27$ = number of points scored by St. Mark's
$$x + x - 27 = 63$$
$$2x - 27 = 63$$
$$2x - 27 + 27 = 63 + 27$$
$$2x = 90$$
$$\frac{2x}{2} = \frac{90}{2}$$
$$x = 45$$
Thayer scored 45 points.
St. Mark's scored 45 − 27 = 18 points.

6. x = number of G tiles
$3x$ = number of A tiles
$2x + 2$ = number of O tiles
$$x + 3x + 2x + 2 = 20$$
$$6x + 2 = 20$$
$$6x + 2 + (-2) = 20 + (-2)$$
$$6x = 18$$
$$\frac{6x}{6} = \frac{18}{6}$$
$$x = 3$$
G tiles = 3
A tiles = 3(3) = 9
O tiles = 2(3) + 2 = 6 + 2 = 8

In problems 8–22, the check is left for the student.

8. x = length of shorter piece
$x + 6.5$ = length of longer piece
$$x + x + 6.5 = 18$$
$$2x + 6.5 = 18$$
$$2x + 6.5 + (-6.5) = 18 + (-6.5)$$
$$2x = 11.5$$
$$\frac{2x}{2} = \frac{11.5}{2}$$
$$x = 5.75$$
shorter piece = 5.75 feet
longer piece = 5.75 + 6.5 = 12.25 feet

10. x = width of room
$2x - 6$ = length of room
$$2x + 2(2x - 6) = 78$$
$$2x + 4x - 12 = 78$$
$$6x - 12 = 78$$
$$6x - 12 + 12 = 78 + 12$$
$$6x = 90$$
$$\frac{6x}{6} = \frac{90}{6}$$
$$x = 15$$
$2x - 6 = 2(15) - 6 = 30 - 6 = 24$
Width is 15 feet; length is 24 feet.

12. x = length of the first side
$2x$ = length of the second side
$x + 15$ = length of the third side
$$x + 2x + x + 15 = 271$$
$$4x + 15 = 271$$
$$4x + 15 + (-15) = 271 + (-15)$$
$$4x = 256$$
$$\frac{4x}{4} = \frac{256}{4}$$
$$x = 64$$
first side = 64 meters
second side = 2(64) = 128 meters
third side = 64 + 15 = 79 meters

14. x = length of the second side
$2x$ = length of the first side
$2x + 3$ = length of the third side
$$x + 2x + 2x + 3 = 63$$
$$5x + 3 = 63$$
$$5x + 3 + (-3) = 63 + (-3)$$
$$5x = 60$$
$$\frac{5x}{5} = \frac{60}{5}$$
$$x = 12$$
second side = 12 inches
first side = 2(12) = 24 inches
third side = 24 + 3 = 27 inches

16. $x - 15$ = number of degrees in angle G
$3x$ = number of degrees in angle H
x = number of degrees in angle I
$$x - 15 + 3x + x = 180$$
$$5x - 15 = 180$$
$$5x - 15 + 15 = 180 + 15$$
$$5x = 195$$
$$\frac{5x}{5} = \frac{195}{5}$$
$$x = 39$$
$3x = 3(39) = 117$

$x - 15 = 39 - 15 = 24$
Angle G measures $24°$; angle H measures $117°$; angle I measures $39°$

18. $x = $ total sales
    $0.06x = $ commission
    $$0.06x + 1000 = 2200$$
    $$0.06x + 1000 + (-1000) = 2200 + (-1000)$$
    $$0.06x = 1200$$
    $$\frac{0.06x}{0.06} = \frac{1200}{0.06}$$
    $$x = 20,000$$

    total sales = $20,000

20. $x = $ yearly rent
    $0.09x = $ commission
    $$0.09x + 50 = 482$$
    $$0.09x + 50 + (-50) = 482 + (-50)$$
    $$0.09x = 432$$
    $$\frac{0.09x}{0.09} = \frac{432}{0.09}$$
    $$x = 4800$$

    yearly rent = $4800

22. $x = $ number of adults
    $x + 67 = $ number of children
    $$x + x + 67 = 321$$
    $$2x + 67 = 321$$
    $$2x + 67 + (-67) = 321 + (-67)$$
    $$2x = 254$$
    $$\frac{2x}{2} = \frac{254}{2}$$
    $$x = 127$$

    Number of adults = 127
    Number of children = 127 + 67 = 194

24. $x = $ days in Korea
    $x = $ days in Japan
    mean = 29.4
    $$29.4 = \frac{42 + 37 + 35 + 34 + 28 + 26 + x + x + 13}{9}$$
    $$29.4 = \frac{215 + 2x}{9}$$
    $$9(29.4) = 9 \cdot \frac{215 + 2x}{9}$$
    $$264.6 = 215 + 2x$$
    $$264.6 + (-215) = 215 + 2x + (-215)$$
    $$49.6 = 2x$$
    $$\frac{49.6}{2} = \frac{2x}{2}$$
    $$24.8 = x$$
    $$25 \approx x$$

    Each country has 25 days.

Cumulative Review

26. What percent of 20 is 12?

$$\frac{n}{100} = \frac{12}{20}$$
$$n \times 20 = 100 \times 12$$
$$\frac{n \times 20}{20} = \frac{1200}{20}$$
$$n = 60 \text{ or } 60\%$$

27. 38% of what number is 190?

$$\frac{38}{100} = \frac{190}{b}$$
$$38 \times b = 100 \times 190$$
$$\frac{38 \times b}{38} = \frac{19,000}{38}$$
$$b = 500$$

28.
$$\frac{x}{12} = \frac{10}{15}$$
$$15x = 12(10)$$
$$\frac{15x}{15} = \frac{120}{15}$$
$$x = 8$$

29. $5 \text{ pounds} \times \left(\dfrac{16 \text{ ounces}}{1 \text{ pound}} \right) = 80 \text{ ounces}$

Classroom Quiz 10.7

1. x = Fred's earnings
$x - 139$ = Robert's earnings
$$x + x - 139 = 567$$
$$2x - 139 = 567$$
$$2x - 139 + 139 = 567 + 139$$
$$2x = 706$$
$$\frac{2x}{2} = \frac{706}{2}$$
$$x = 353$$
$x - 139 = 353 - 139 = 214$
Fred earns $353 per week and Robert earns $214 per week.

2. x = second side length
$2x$ = one side length
$x - 24$ = third side length
$$x + 2x + x - 24 = 138$$
$$4x - 24 = 138$$
$$4x - 24 + 24 = 138 + 24$$
$$4x = 162$$
$$\frac{4x}{4} = \frac{162}{4}$$
$$x = 40.5$$
$2x = 2(40.5) = 81$
$x - 24 = 40.5 - 24 = 16.5$
The second side is 40.5 meters. The first side (one side) is 81 meters. The third side is 16.5 meters.

3. x = width
$2x - 12$ = length
$$P = 2l + 2w$$
$$234 = 2(2x - 12) + 2$$
$$234 = 4x - 24 + 2x$$
$$234 = 6x - 24$$
$$234 + 24 = 6x - 24 + 24$$
$$258 = 6x$$
$$\frac{258}{6} = \frac{6x}{6}$$
$$43 = x$$
$2x - 12 = 2(43) - 12 = 86 - 12 = 74$
The length is 74 feet. The width is 43 feet.

Putting Your Skills to Work

1. Find 5% of $1500 for 1 month.
Then multiply by 12 for one year's savings.
$0.05 \times \$1500 = \$75$
$12 \times \$75 = \$900$
Michael will have saved $900.

2. $\dfrac{\$2500}{12 \text{ mo}} \approx \$209$
Michael needs to save $209 per month.

3. Answers may vary.

4. Answers may vary.

5. Answers may vary.

Chapter 10 Review Problems

1. $-8a + 6 - 5a - 3 = -8a - 5a + 6 - 3 = -13a + 3$

2. $\dfrac{1}{3}x + \dfrac{1}{3} + \dfrac{5}{9} + \dfrac{1}{2}x = \dfrac{1}{3}x + \dfrac{1}{2}x + \dfrac{1}{3} + \dfrac{5}{9}$

$\qquad\qquad\qquad = \dfrac{2}{6}x + \dfrac{3}{6}x + \dfrac{3}{9} + \dfrac{5}{9}$

$\qquad\qquad\qquad = \dfrac{5}{6}x + \dfrac{8}{9}$

3. $5x + 2y - 7x - 9y = 5x - 7x + 2y - 9y$

$\qquad\qquad\qquad\quad = -2x - 7y$

4. $3x - 7y + 8x + 2y = 3x + 8x - 7y + 2y$

$\qquad\qquad\qquad\qquad = 11x - 5y$

5. $5x - 9y - 12 - 6x - 3y + 18$

$\quad = 5x - 6x - 9y - 3y - 12 + 18$

$\quad = -x - 12y + 6$

6. $8a - 11b + 15 - b + 5a - 19$

$\quad = 8a + 5a - 11b - b + 15 - 19$

$\quad = 13a - 12b - 4$

7. $-3(5x + y) = -3(5x) + (-3)(y) = -15x - 3y$

8. $-4(2x + 3y) = -4(2x) + (-4)(3y) = -8x - 12y$

9. $2(x - 3y + 4) = 2(x) + 2(-3y) + 2(4)$

$\qquad\qquad\qquad = 2x - 6y + 8$

10. $5(6a - 8b + 5) = 5(6a) - 5(8b) + 5(5)$

$\qquad\qquad\qquad\quad = 30a - 40b + 25$

11. $10\left(-\dfrac{2}{5}x + \dfrac{1}{2}y - 3\right)$

$\quad = 10\left(-\dfrac{2}{5}x\right) + 10\left(\dfrac{1}{2}y\right) + 10(-3)$

$\quad = -4x + 5y - 30$

12. $-12\left(\dfrac{3}{4}a - \dfrac{1}{6}b - 1\right)$

$\quad = (-12)\left(\dfrac{3}{4}a\right) + (-12)\left(-\dfrac{1}{6}b\right) + (-12)(-1)$

$\quad = -9a + 2b + 12$

13. $5(1.2x + 3y - 5.5) = 5(1.2x) + 5(3y) + 5(-5.5)$

$\qquad\qquad\qquad\qquad = 6x + 15y - 27.5$

14. $6(1.4x - 2y + 3.4) = 6(1.4x) + 6(-2y) + 6(3.4)$

$\qquad\qquad\qquad\qquad = 8.4x - 12y + 20.4$

15. $2(x + 3y) - 4(x - 2y) = 2x + 6y - 4x + 8y$

$\qquad\qquad\qquad\qquad\quad = -2x + 14y$

16. $2(5x - y) - 3(x + 2y) = 10x - 2y - 3x - 6y$

$\qquad\qquad\qquad\qquad\quad = 7x - 8y$

17. $-2(a + b) - 3(2a + 8) = -2a - 2b - 6a - 24$

$\qquad\qquad\qquad\qquad\quad = -8a - 2b - 24$

18. $-4(a - 2b) + 3(5 - a) = -4a + 8b + 15 - 3a$

$\qquad\qquad\qquad\qquad\quad = -7a + 8b + 15y$

19. $\qquad x - 3 = 9$

$\quad x + (-3) + 3 = 9 + 3$

$\qquad\qquad\quad x = 12$

20. $\qquad x + 8.3 = 20$

$\quad x + 8.3 + (-8.3) = 20 + (-8.3)$

$\qquad\qquad\qquad x = 11.7$

21. $\qquad -8 = x - 12$

$\quad -8 + 12 = x - 12 + 12$

$\qquad\quad 4 = x$

22. $\qquad 2.4 = x - 5$

$\quad 2.4 + 5 = x - 5 + 5$

$\qquad 7.4 = x$

23. $\qquad 3.1 + x = -9$

$\quad 3.1 + (-3.1) + x = -9 + (-3.1)$

$\qquad\qquad\qquad x = -12.1$

24. $\qquad 7 + x = 5.8$

$\quad 7 + (-7) + x = 5.8 + (-7)$

$\qquad\qquad\quad x = -1.2$

25. $\qquad x - \dfrac{3}{4} = 2$

$\quad x + \left(-\dfrac{3}{4}\right) + \dfrac{3}{4} = 2 + \dfrac{3}{4}$

$\qquad\qquad x = \dfrac{11}{4}$ or $2\dfrac{3}{4}$

26. $\qquad x + \dfrac{1}{2} = 3\dfrac{3}{4}$

$\quad x + \dfrac{1}{2} + \left(-\dfrac{1}{2}\right) = 3\dfrac{3}{4} + \left(-\dfrac{1}{2}\right)$

$\qquad\qquad x = 3\dfrac{3}{4} + \left(-\dfrac{2}{4}\right)$

$\qquad\qquad x = 3\dfrac{1}{4}$ or $\dfrac{13}{4}$

27.
$$y + \frac{5}{8} = -\frac{1}{8}$$
$$y + \frac{5}{8} + \left(-\frac{5}{8}\right) = -\frac{1}{8} + \left(-\frac{5}{8}\right)$$
$$y = -\frac{6}{8}$$
$$y = -\frac{3}{4}$$

28.
$$x - \frac{5}{6} = \frac{2}{3}$$
$$x - \frac{5}{6} + \frac{5}{6} = \frac{2}{3} + \frac{5}{6}$$
$$x = \frac{4}{6} + \frac{5}{6}$$
$$x = \frac{9}{6} = \frac{3}{2} \text{ or } 1\frac{1}{2}$$

29.
$$2x + 20 = 25 + x$$
$$2x + (-x) + 20 = 25 + x + (-x)$$
$$x + 20 = 25$$
$$x + 20 + (-20) = 25 + (-20)$$
$$x = 5$$

30.
$$7y + 12 = 8y + 3$$
$$7y + 12 + (-7y) = 8y + 3 + (-7y)$$
$$12 = y + 3$$
$$12 + (-3) = y + 3 + (-3)$$
$$9 = y$$

31.
$$8x = -20$$
$$\frac{8x}{8} = \frac{-20}{8}$$
$$x = \frac{-20}{8} = -\frac{5}{2}$$
$$x = -2\frac{1}{2}$$

32.
$$-12y = 60$$
$$\frac{-12y}{-12} = \frac{60}{-12}$$
$$y = -5$$

33.
$$1.5x = 9$$
$$\frac{1.5x}{1.5} = \frac{9}{1.5}$$
$$x = 6$$

34.
$$-1.4y = -12.6$$
$$\frac{-1.4y}{-1.4} = \frac{-12.6}{-1.4}$$
$$y = 9$$

35.
$$-7.2x = 36$$
$$\frac{-7.2x}{-7.2} = \frac{36}{-7.2}$$
$$x = -5$$

36.
$$6x = 1.5$$
$$\frac{6x}{6} = \frac{1.5}{6}$$
$$x = 0.25$$

37.
$$\frac{3}{4}x = 6$$
$$\frac{4}{3} \cdot \frac{3}{4}x = \frac{4}{3} \cdot 6$$
$$x = 8$$

38.
$$\frac{2}{9}x = \frac{5}{18}$$
$$\frac{9}{2} \cdot \frac{2}{9}x = \frac{9}{2} \cdot \frac{5}{18}$$
$$x = \frac{5}{4} \text{ or } 1\frac{1}{4}$$

39.
$$5x - 3 = 27$$
$$5x - 3 + 3 = 27 + 3$$
$$5x = 30$$
$$\frac{5x}{5} = \frac{30}{5}$$
$$x = 6$$

40.
$$8x - 5 = 19$$
$$8x - 5 + 5 = 19 + 5$$
$$8x = 24$$
$$\frac{8x}{8} = \frac{24}{8}$$
$$x = 3$$

41.
$$10 - x = -3x - 6$$
$$10 + (-10) - x = -3x - 6 + (-10)$$
$$-x = -3x - 16$$
$$-x + 3x = -3x + 3x - 16$$
$$2x = \frac{-16}{2}$$
$$x = -8$$

42.
$$7 - 2x = -4x - 11$$
$$7 + (-7) - 2x = -4x - 11 + (-7)$$
$$-2x = -4x - 18$$
$$-2x + 4x = -4x + 4x - 18$$
$$2x = -18$$
$$\frac{2x}{2} = \frac{-18}{2}$$
$$x = -9$$

43.
$$9x - 3x + 18 = 36$$
$$6x + 18 = 36$$
$$6x + 18 + (-18) = 36 + (-18)$$
$$6x = 18$$
$$\frac{6x}{6} = \frac{18}{6}$$
$$x = 3$$

44.
$$4 + 3x - 8 = 12 + 5x + 4$$
$$3x - 4 = 5x + 16$$
$$3x + (-3x) - 4 = 5x + (-3x) + 16$$
$$-4 = 2x + 16$$
$$-4 + (-16) = 2x + 16 + (-16)$$
$$-20 = 2x$$
$$\frac{-20}{2} = \frac{2x}{2}$$
$$-10 = x$$

45.
$$-2(3x + 5) = 4x + 8 - x$$
$$-6x - 10 = 3x + 8$$
$$-6x + (-3x) - 10 = 3x + 8 + (-3x)$$
$$-9x - 10 = 8$$
$$-9x - 10 + 10 = 8 + 10$$
$$-9x = 18$$
$$\frac{-9x}{-9} = \frac{18}{-9}$$
$$x = -2$$

46.
$$2(3x - 4) = 7 - 2x + 5x$$
$$6x - 8 = 7 + 3x$$
$$6x + (-3x) - 8 = 7 + 3x + (-3x)$$
$$3x - 8 = 7$$
$$3x - 8 + 8 = 7 + 8$$
$$3x = 15$$
$$\frac{3x}{3} = \frac{15}{3}$$
$$x = 5$$

47.
$$5 + 2y + 5(y - 3) = 6(y + 1)$$
$$5 + 2y + 5y - 15 = 6y + 6$$
$$7y - 10 = 6y + 6$$
$$7y + (-6y) - 10 = 6y + (-6y) + 6$$
$$y - 10 = 6$$
$$y - 10 + 10 = 6 + 10$$
$$y = 16$$

48.
$$5 - (y + 7) = 10 + 3(y - 4)$$
$$5 - y - 7 = 10 + 3y - 12$$
$$-y - 2 = -2 + 3y$$
$$-y - 2 + (-3y) = -2 + 3y + (-3y)$$
$$-4y - 2 = -2$$
$$-4y - 2 + 2 = -2 + 2$$
$$-4y = 0$$
$$\frac{-4y}{-4} = \frac{0}{4}$$
$$y = 0$$

49. $w = c + 3000$

50. $e = 12 + a$

51. $A = 3B$

52. $l = 2w - 3$

53. r Roberto's salary
$r + 2050 =$ Michael's salary

54. $x =$ length of the first side
$2x =$ length of the second side

55. $d =$ number of days Dennis worked
$2d + 12 =$ number of days Carmen worked

56. $n =$ number of nonfiction books sold
$n + 225 =$ number of fiction books sold

57. $x =$ length of one piece
$x + 6.5 =$ length of other piece
$$x + x + 6.5 = 60$$
$$2x + 6.5 = 60$$
$$2x + 6.5 + (-6.5) = 60 + (-6.5)$$
$$2x = 53.5$$
$$\frac{2x}{2} = \frac{53.5}{2}$$
$$x = 26.75$$
one piece = 26.75 feet
other piece = 26.75 + 6.5 = 33.25 feet

58. x = experienced employee's salary
$x - 28$ = new employee's salary
$$x + x - 28 = 412$$
$$2x - 28 = 412$$
$$2x - 28 + 28 = 412 + 28$$
$$2x = 440$$
$$\frac{2x}{2} = \frac{440}{2}$$
$$x = 220$$
experienced employee = \$220
new employee = 220 − 28 = \$192

59. x = number of customers in February
$2x$ = number of customers in March
$x + 3000$ = number of customers in April
$$x + 2x + x + 3000 = 45,200$$
$$4x + 3000 = 45,200$$
$$4x + 3000 + (-3000) = 45,200 + (-3000)$$
$$4x = 42,200$$
$$\frac{4x}{4} = \frac{42,200}{4}$$
$$x = 10,550$$
February = 10,550
March = 2(10,550) = 21,100
April = 10,550 + 3000 = 13,550

60. x = miles on Friday
$2x$ = miles on Saturday
$x + 30$ = miles on Sunday
$$x + 2x + x + 30 = 670$$
$$4x + 30 = 670$$
$$4x + 30 + (-30) = 670 + (-30)$$
$$4x = 640$$
$$\frac{4x}{4} = \frac{640}{4}$$
$$x = 160$$
$2x = 2(160) = 320$
$x + 30 = 160 + 30 = 190$
Friday = 160 mi; Saturday = 320 mi;
Sunday = 190 mi

61. w = width
$2w - 3$ = length
$$72 = 2w + 2(2w - 3)$$
$$72 = 2w + 4w - 6$$
$$72 = 6w - 6$$
$$72 + 6 = 6w + (-6) + 6$$
$$78 = 6w$$
$$\frac{78}{6} = \frac{6w}{6}$$
$$w = 13$$
width = 13 in.
length = 2(13) − 3 = 23 in.

62. x = width
$3x + 2$ = length
$$2(x) + 2(3x + 2) = 180$$
$$2x + 6x + 4 = 180$$
$$8x + 4 = 180$$
$$8x + 4 + (-4) = 180 + (-4)$$
$$8x = 176$$
$$\frac{8x}{9} = \frac{176}{8}$$
$$x = 22$$
width = 22 m
length = 3(22) + 2 = 68 m

63. x = angle Z
$2x$ = angle Y
$x - 12$ = angle X
$$x + 2x + x - 12 = 180$$
$$4x - 12 = 180$$
$$4x - 12 + 12 = 180 + 12$$
$$4x = 192$$
$$\frac{4x}{4} = \frac{192}{4}$$
$$x = 48$$
Angle Z 48°
Angle Y = 2(48°) = 96°
Angle X = 48° − 12° = 36°

64. $x + 74$ = angle A
x = angle B
$3x$ = angle C
$$x + 74 + x + 3x = 180$$
$$5x + 74 = 180$$
$$5x + 74 + (-74) = 180 + (-74)$$
$$5x = 106$$
$$\frac{5x}{5} = \frac{106}{5}$$
$$x = 21.2$$
angle A = 21.2 + 74 = 95.2°
angle B = 21.2°
angle C = 3(21.2) = 63.6°

65. $p = 2l + 2w$
x = length
$x - 67$ = width
$$346 = 2(x) + 2(x - 67)$$
$$346 = 2x + 2x + 2(-67)$$
$$346 = 4x - 134$$
$$346 + 134 = 4x - 134 + 134$$
$$480 = 4x$$
$$\frac{480}{4} = \frac{4x}{4}$$
$$120 = x$$
Length = 120 yards
Width = 120 − 67 = 53 yards

66. $x = $ length
$x - 44 = $ width
$2(x) + 2(x - 44) = 288$
$\qquad 2x + 2x - 88 = 288$
$\qquad\qquad 4x - 88 = 288$
$\qquad 4x - 88 + 88 = 288 + 88$
$\qquad\qquad\quad 4x = 376$
$\qquad\qquad\quad \dfrac{4x}{4} = \dfrac{376}{4}$
$\qquad\qquad\qquad x = 94$
length $= 94$ feet
width $= 94 - 44 = 50$ feet

67. $x = $ miles an Saturday
$x + 106 = $ miles on Sunday
$\qquad x + x + 106 = 810$
$\qquad\qquad 2x + 106 = 810$
$2x + 106 + (-106) = 810 + (-106)$
$\qquad\qquad\qquad 2x = 704$
$\qquad\qquad\qquad \dfrac{2x}{2} = \dfrac{704}{2}$
$\qquad\qquad\qquad\quad x = 352$
$x + 106 = 352 + 106 = 458$
Saturday $= 352$ mi; Sunday $= 458$ mi

68. $x = $ first week
$x + 156 = $ second week
$x - 142 = $ third week
$\qquad x + x + 156 + x - 142 = 800$
$\qquad\qquad\qquad\quad 3x + 14 = 800$
$\qquad 3x + 14 + (-14) = 800 + (-14)$
$\qquad\qquad\qquad\qquad 3x = 786$
$\qquad\qquad\qquad\qquad \dfrac{3x}{3} = \dfrac{786}{3}$
$\qquad\qquad\qquad\qquad\; x = 262$
first week $= 262$
second week $= 262 + 156 = 418$
third week $= 262 - 142 = 120$

69. Commission $= 600 - 200 = \$400$
4% of what $= 400$
$0.04 \times n = 400$
$\dfrac{0.04n}{0.04} = \dfrac{400}{0.04}$
$\qquad n = 10,000$
The cost of the cars was $10,000.

70. $x = $ cost of the furniture
$0.08x = $ commission
$\qquad 0.08x + 1500 = 3050$
$0.08x + 1500 + (-1500) = 3050 + (-1500)$
$\qquad\qquad\qquad 0.08x = 1550$
$\qquad\qquad\qquad \dfrac{0.08x}{0.08} = \dfrac{1550}{0.08}$
$\qquad\qquad\qquad\qquad x = 19,375$
The cost of the furniture was $19,375.

How Am I Doing? Chapter 10 Test

1. $5a - 11a = -6a$

2. $\dfrac{1}{3}x + \dfrac{5}{8}y - \dfrac{1}{5}x + \dfrac{1}{2}y = \dfrac{1}{3}x - \dfrac{1}{5}x + \dfrac{5}{8}y + \dfrac{1}{2}y$
$\qquad\qquad\qquad\qquad\qquad = \dfrac{5}{15}x - \dfrac{3}{15}x + \dfrac{5}{8}y + \dfrac{4}{8}y$
$\qquad\qquad\qquad\qquad\qquad = \dfrac{2}{15}x + \dfrac{9}{8}y$

3. $\dfrac{1}{4}a - \dfrac{2}{3}b + \dfrac{3}{8}a = \dfrac{2}{8}a + \dfrac{3}{8}a - \dfrac{2}{3}b = \dfrac{5}{8}a - \dfrac{2}{3}b$

4. $6a - 5b - 5a - 3b = 6a - 5a - 5b - 3b = a - 8b$

5. $7x - 8y + 2z - 9z + 8y = 7x - 8y + 8y + 2z - 9z$
$\qquad\qquad\qquad\qquad\qquad\quad = 7x - 7z$

6. $x + 5y - 6 - 5x - 7y + 11$
$\quad = x - 5x + 5y - 7y - 6 + 11$
$\quad = -4x - 2y + 5$

7. $5(12x - 5y) = 5(12x) + 5(-5y) = 60x - 25y$

8. $4\left(\dfrac{1}{2}x - \dfrac{5}{6}y\right) = 4\left(\dfrac{1}{2}x\right) - 4\left(\dfrac{5}{6}y\right) = 2x - \dfrac{10}{3}y$

9. $-1.5(3a - 2b + c - 8)$
$\quad = (-1.5)(3a) + (-1.5)(-2b) + (-1.5)(c)$
$\qquad\qquad + (-1.5)(-8)$
$\quad = -4.5a + 3b - 1.5c + 12$

10. $2(-3a + 2b) - 5(a - 2b) = -6a + 4b - 5a + 10b$
$\qquad\qquad\qquad\qquad\qquad\quad = -11a + 14b$

11. $\qquad -5 - 3x = 19$
$\qquad -5 + 5 - 3x = 19 + 5$
$\qquad\qquad\quad -3x = 24$
$\qquad\qquad\quad \dfrac{-3x}{-3} = \dfrac{24}{-3}$
$\qquad\qquad\qquad x = -8$

12.
$$x - 3.45 = -9.8$$
$$x - 3.45 + 3.45 = -9.8 + 3.45$$
$$x = -6.35$$

13.
$$-5x + 9 = -4x - 6$$
$$-5x + 5x + 9 = -4x + 5x - 6$$
$$9 = x - 6$$
$$9 + 6 = x - 6 + 6$$
$$15 = x$$

14.
$$8x - 2 - x = 3x - 9 - 10x$$
$$7x - 2 = -7x - 9$$
$$7x + 7x - 2 = -7x + 7x - 9$$
$$14x - 2 = -9$$
$$14x - 2 + 2 = -9 + 2$$
$$14x = -7$$
$$\frac{14x}{14} = \frac{-7}{14}$$
$$x = -\frac{1}{2}$$

15.
$$0.5x + 0.6 = 0.2x - 0.9$$
$$0.5x + 0.6 + (-0.6) = 0.2x - 0.9 + (-0.6)$$
$$0.5x = 0.2x - 1.5$$
$$0.5x - 0.2x = 0.2x - 0.2x - 1.5$$
$$0.3x = -1.5$$
$$\frac{0.3x}{0.3} = \frac{-1.5}{0.3}$$
$$x = -5$$

16.
$$-\frac{5}{6}x = \frac{7}{12}$$
$$\left(-\frac{6}{5}\right)\left(-\frac{5}{6}\right)x = \left(-\frac{6}{5}\right)\left(\frac{7}{12}\right)$$
$$x = -\frac{7}{10}$$

17. $s = f + 15$

18. $n = s - 15{,}000$

19. $\frac{1}{2}s$ = measure of the first angle

s = measure of the second angle
$2s$ = measure of the third angle

20. w = width; $2w - 5$ = length

21. x = acres in Prentice farm
$3x$ = acres in Smithfield farm
$$x + 3x = 348$$
$$4x = 348$$
$$\frac{4x}{4} = \frac{348}{4}$$
$$x = 87$$
Prentice farm = 87 acres
Smithfield farm = 3(87) = 261 acres

22. x = Marcia's earnings
$x - 1500$ = Sam's earnings
$$x + x - 1500 = 46{,}500$$
$$2x - 1500 = 46{,}500$$
$$2x - 1500 + 1500 = 46{,}500 + 1500$$
$$2x = 48{,}000$$
$$\frac{2x}{2} = \frac{48{,}000}{2}$$
$$x = 24{,}000$$
Marcia = \$24,000
Sam = 24000 − 1500 = \$22,500

23. x = number of afternoon students
$x - 24$ = number of morning students
$x + 12$ = number of evening students
$$x + x - 24 + x + 12 = 183$$
$$3x - 12 = 183$$
$$3x - 12 + 12 = 183 + 12$$
$$3x = 195$$
$$\frac{3x}{3} = \frac{195}{3}$$
$$x = 65$$
Number of afternoon students = 65
Number of morning students = 65 − 24 = 41
Number of evening students = 65 + 12 = 77

24. x = length
$\frac{1}{2}x + 8$ = width
$$2(x) + 2\left(\frac{1}{2}x + 8\right) = 118$$
$$2x + x + 16 = 118$$
$$3x + 16 = 118$$
$$3x + 16 + (-16) = 118 + (-16)$$
$$3x = 102$$
$$\frac{3x}{3} = \frac{102}{3}$$
$$x = 34$$
length = 34 feet
width = $\frac{1}{2}(34) + 8 = 25$ feet

Cumulative Test for Chapters 1–10

1. $\begin{array}{r} 456 \\ 89 \\ 123 \\ + \ 79 \\ \hline 747 \end{array}$

2. $\begin{array}{r} 309 \\ \times \quad 35 \\ \hline 1\ 545 \\ 9\ 27 \\ \hline 10{,}815 \end{array}$

3. 45,678,934 rounds to 45,678,900.

4. $\dfrac{5}{12} \div \dfrac{1}{6} = \dfrac{5}{12} \times \dfrac{6}{1} = \dfrac{5}{2}$ or $2\dfrac{1}{2}$

5. $3\dfrac{1}{4} \times 2\dfrac{1}{2} = \dfrac{13}{4} \times \dfrac{5}{2} = \dfrac{65}{8}$ or $8\dfrac{1}{8}$

6. $9.3228 \times 10^3 = 9322.8$

7. $\begin{array}{r} 4182.70 \\ - \ 3555.28 \\ \hline 627.42 \end{array}$

8. $\dfrac{n}{36} = \dfrac{35}{52.5}$

    $n \times 52.5 = 36 \times 35$

    $52.5n = 1260$

    $\dfrac{52.5n}{52.5} = \dfrac{1260}{52.5}$

    $n = 24$

9. What is 25% of 180?

    $n = 25\% \times 180$

    $n = 0.25 \times 180$

    $n = 45$

10. 34% of what number is 1870?

    $34\% \times n = 1870$

    $0.34 \times n = 1870$

    $\dfrac{0.34 \times n}{0.34} = \dfrac{1870}{0.34}$

    $n = 5500$

11. 345 mm = 0.345 m

12. $12.5 \ \text{feet} \times \dfrac{12 \ \text{inches}}{1 \ \text{foot}} = 150 \ \text{inches}$

13. $C = \pi d = 3.14(12) \approx 37.7 \ \text{yd}$

14. $A = \dfrac{bh}{2} = \dfrac{(13)(22)}{2} = 143$

    The area is 143 square meters.

15. $\begin{aligned} 4 - 8 + 12 - 32 - 7 &= 4 + (-8) + 12 + (-32) + (-7) \\ &= -4 + 12 + (-32) + (-7) \\ &= 8 + (-32) + (-7) \\ &= -24 + (-7) \\ &= -31 \end{aligned}$

16. $(6)(-3)(-4)(2) = (-18)(-4)(2) = 72(2) = 144$

17. $\begin{aligned} \dfrac{1}{2}a + \dfrac{1}{7}b + \dfrac{1}{4}a - \dfrac{3}{14}b &= \dfrac{1}{2}a + \dfrac{1}{4}a + \dfrac{1}{7}b - \dfrac{3}{14}b \\ &= \dfrac{2}{4}a + \dfrac{1}{4}a + \dfrac{2}{14}b - \dfrac{3}{14}b \\ &= \dfrac{3}{4}a - \dfrac{1}{14}b \end{aligned}$

18. $\begin{aligned} & 3x - 5y - 12 + x - 8y + 20 \\ &= 3x + x - 5y - 8y - 12 + 20 \\ &= 4x - 13y + 8 \end{aligned}$

19. $\begin{aligned} -7(3x - y - 4) &= -7(3x) - 7(-y) - 7(-4) \\ &= -21x + 7y + 28 \end{aligned}$

20. $\begin{aligned} 2(3x - 4y) - 8(x + 2y) &= 6x - 8y - 8x - 16y \\ &= -2x - 24y \end{aligned}$

21. $\begin{aligned} 10y - 3 &= 4y + 21 \\ 10y + (-4y) - 3 &= 4y + (-4y) + 21 \\ 6y - 3 &= 21 \\ 6y - 3 + 3 &= 21 + 3 \\ 6y &= 24 \\ \dfrac{6y}{6} &= \dfrac{24}{6} \\ y &= 4 \end{aligned}$

22.
$$7 - 9y - 12 = 3y + 5 - 8y$$
$$-9y - 5 = -5y + 5$$
$$-9y + 9y - 5 = -5y + 9y + 5$$
$$-5 = 4y + 5$$
$$-5 + (-5) = 4y + 5 + (-5)$$
$$-10 = 4y$$
$$\frac{-10}{4} = \frac{4y}{4}$$
$$-\frac{5}{2} = y \text{ or } y = -2\frac{1}{2}$$

23.
$$x - 2 + 5x + 3 = 183 - x$$
$$6x + 1 = 183 - x$$
$$6x + x + 1 = 183 - x + x$$
$$7x + 1 = 183$$
$$7x + 1 + (-1) = 183 + (-1)$$
$$7x = 182$$
$$\frac{7x}{7} = \frac{182}{7}$$
$$x = 26$$

24.
$$9(2x + 8) = 20 - (x + 5)$$
$$18x + 72 = 20 - x - 5$$
$$18x + 72 = -x + 15$$
$$18x + x + 72 = -x + x + 15$$
$$19x + 72 = 15$$
$$19x + 72 + (-72) = 15 + (-72)$$
$$19x = -57$$
$$\frac{19x}{19} = \frac{-57}{19}$$
$$x = -3$$

25. a = number of adults
$a + 263$ = number of children

26. f = enrollment during fall
$f - 87$ = enrollment during summer

27. x = miles driven on Thursday
$x + 48$ = miles driven on Friday
$x - 95$ = miles driven on Saturday
$$x + x + 48 + x - 95 = 1081$$
$$3x - 47 = 1081$$
$$3x + (-47) + 47 = 1081 + (47)$$
$$3x = 1128$$
$$\frac{3x}{3} = \frac{1128}{3}$$
$$x = 376$$
Thursday = 376 miles
Friday = 376 + 48 = 424 miles
Saturday = 376 − 95 = 281 miles

28. x = width
$2x + 8$ = length
$$2(x) + 2(2x + 8) = 98$$
$$2x + 4x + 16 = 98$$
$$6x + 16 = 98$$
$$6x + 16 + (-16) = 98 + (-16)$$
$$6x = 82$$
$$\frac{6x}{6} = \frac{82}{6}$$
$$x = \frac{41}{3} = 13\frac{2}{3}$$

width $= 13\frac{2}{3}$ feet

length $= 2x + 8$
$$= 2\left(\frac{41}{3}\right) + 8$$
$$= \frac{82}{3} + \frac{24}{3}$$
$$= \frac{106}{3}$$
$$= 35\frac{1}{3} \text{ feet}$$

Practice Final Examination

1. 82,367 = Eighty-two thousand, three hundred sixty-seven

2.
$$\begin{array}{r} 13,428 \\ + 16,905 \\ \hline 30,333 \end{array}$$

3.
$$\begin{array}{r} 19 \\ 23 \\ 16 \\ 45 \\ + 70 \\ \hline 173 \end{array}$$

4.
$$\begin{array}{r} 89,071 \\ - 54,968 \\ \hline 34,103 \end{array}$$

5.
$$\begin{array}{r} 78 \\ \times 54 \\ \hline 312 \\ 390 \\ \hline 4212 \end{array}$$

6.
$$
\begin{array}{r}
2035 \\
\times\ \ 107 \\
\hline
14\ 245 \\
203\ 50\ \ \\
\hline
217,745
\end{array}
$$

7.
$$
\begin{array}{r}
158 \\
7\overline{)1106} \\
\underline{7\ \ \ } \\
40 \\
\underline{35} \\
56 \\
\underline{56} \\
0
\end{array}
$$

8.
$$
\begin{array}{r}
606 \\
26\overline{)15,756} \\
\underline{15\ 6\ \ } \\
156 \\
\underline{156} \\
0
\end{array}
$$

9. $3^4 + 20 \div 4 \times 2 + 5^2 = 81 + 10 + 25 = 116$

10. $512 \div 16 = 32$
The car achieved 32 miles/gallon.

11. $\dfrac{14}{30} = \dfrac{14 \div 2}{30 \div 2} = \dfrac{7}{15}$

12. $3\dfrac{9}{11} = \dfrac{3 \times 11 + 9}{11} = \dfrac{42}{11}$

13. $\dfrac{1}{10} + \dfrac{3}{4} + \dfrac{4}{5} = \dfrac{1}{10} \times \dfrac{2}{2} + \dfrac{3}{4} \times \dfrac{5}{5} + \dfrac{4}{5} \times \dfrac{4}{4}$

$\qquad = \dfrac{2}{20} + \dfrac{15}{20} + \dfrac{16}{20}$

$\qquad = \dfrac{33}{20}$

$\qquad = 1\dfrac{13}{20}$

14. $2\dfrac{1}{3} + 3\dfrac{3}{5} = 2\dfrac{5}{15} + 3\dfrac{9}{15} = 5\dfrac{14}{15}$

15.
$$
\begin{array}{r}
4\dfrac{5}{7} \\
- 2\dfrac{1}{2} \\
\hline
\end{array}
\qquad\qquad
\begin{array}{r}
4\dfrac{10}{14} \\
- 2\dfrac{7}{14} \\
\hline
2\dfrac{3}{14}
\end{array}
$$

16. $1\dfrac{1}{4} \times 3\dfrac{1}{5} = \dfrac{5}{4} \times \dfrac{16}{5} = \dfrac{5 \times 4 \times 4}{4 \times 5} = 4$

17. $\dfrac{7}{9} \div \dfrac{5}{18} = \dfrac{7}{9} \times \dfrac{18}{5} = \dfrac{14}{5}$ or $2\dfrac{4}{5}$

18. $\dfrac{5\frac{1}{2}}{3\frac{1}{4}} = \dfrac{\frac{11}{2}}{\frac{13}{4}} = \dfrac{11}{2} \times \dfrac{4}{13} = \dfrac{22}{13}$ or $1\dfrac{9}{13}$

19. $1\dfrac{1}{2} + 3\dfrac{1}{4} + 2\dfrac{1}{10} = 1\dfrac{10}{20} + 3\dfrac{5}{20} + 2\dfrac{2}{20}$

She jogged $6\dfrac{17}{20}$ miles.

20. $11\dfrac{2}{3} \div 2\dfrac{1}{3} = \dfrac{35}{3} \div \dfrac{7}{3} = \dfrac{35}{3} \times \dfrac{3}{7} = 5$
5 packages can be made.

21. $\dfrac{719}{1000} = 0.719$

22. $0.86 = \dfrac{86}{100} = \dfrac{43}{50}$

23. $0.315 > 0.309$

24. $506.3782 \approx 506.38$

25.
$$
\begin{array}{r}
9.6 \\
3.82 \\
1.05 \\
+ 7.3 \\
\hline
21.77
\end{array}
$$

26.
$$
\begin{array}{r}
3.610 \\
- 2.853 \\
\hline
0.757
\end{array}
$$

27.
$$
\begin{array}{r}
1.23 \\
\times\ 0.4 \\
\hline
0.492
\end{array}
$$

28.

$$
\begin{array}{r}
3.69 \\
0.24_\wedge\overline{)0.88_\wedge 56} \\
\underline{72} \\
16\ 5 \\
\underline{14\ 4} \\
2\ 16 \\
\underline{2\ 16} \\
0
\end{array}
$$

29.

$$
\begin{array}{r}
0.8125 \\
16\overline{)13.0000} \\
\underline{12\ 8} \\
20 \\
\underline{16} \\
40 \\
\underline{32} \\
80 \\
\underline{80} \\
0
\end{array}
$$

$$\frac{13}{16} = 0.8125$$

30. $0.7 + (0.2)^3 - 0.08(0.03) = 0.7 + 0.008 - 0.0024$
$$= 0.708 - 0.0024$$
$$= 0.7056$$

31. $\dfrac{7000}{215} = \dfrac{7000 \div 5}{215 \div 5} = \dfrac{1400 \text{ students}}{43 \text{ faculty}}$

32. $\dfrac{12}{15} = \dfrac{17}{21}$
$$12 \times 21 \overset{?}{=} 15 \times 17$$
$$252 \neq 255 \text{ No}$$

33. $\dfrac{5}{9} = \dfrac{n}{17}$
$$5 \times 17 = 9 \times n$$
$$\frac{85}{9} = \frac{9 \times n}{9}$$
$$n \approx 9.4$$

34. $\dfrac{3}{n} = \dfrac{7}{18}$
$$3 \times 18 = 7 \times n$$
$$\frac{54}{7} = \frac{7 \times n}{7}$$
$$7.7 \approx n$$

35. $\dfrac{n}{12} = \dfrac{5}{4}$
$$n \times 4 = 12 \times 5$$
$$\frac{n \times 4}{4} = \frac{60}{4}$$
$$n = 15$$

36. $\dfrac{n}{7} = \dfrac{36}{28}$
$$n \times 28 = 7 \times 36$$
$$\frac{n \times 28}{28} = \frac{252}{28}$$
$$n = 9$$

37. $\dfrac{2000}{3} = \dfrac{n}{5}$
$$2000 \times 5 = 3 \times n$$
$$\frac{10,000}{3} = \frac{3 \times n}{3}$$
$$n \approx \$3333.33$$
He would earn \$3333.33.

38. $\dfrac{200}{6} = \dfrac{325}{n}$
$$200 \times n = 6 \times 325$$
$$\frac{200 \times n}{200} = \frac{1950}{200}$$
$$n = 9.75$$
They will appear 9.75 inches apart.

39. $\dfrac{68}{5} = \dfrac{4000}{n}$
$$68 \times n = 5 \times 4000$$
$$\frac{68 \times n}{68} = \frac{20,000}{68}$$
$$n \approx \$294.12 \text{ withheld}$$
\$294.12 will be withheld.

40. $\dfrac{18}{1.2} = \dfrac{24}{n}$
$$18 \times n = 1.2 \times 24$$
$$\frac{18 \times n}{18} = \frac{28.8}{18}$$
$$n = 1.6$$
She needs 1.6 lb of butter.

41. $0.0063 = 0.63\%$

42.
$$\frac{17}{80} = \frac{n}{100}$$
$$17 \times 100 = 80 \times n$$
$$\frac{1700}{80} = \frac{80 \times n}{80}$$
$$21.25 = n$$
21.25%

43. $164\% = 1.64 \approx 1.6$

44. $300 \times n = 52$
$$\frac{300 \times n}{300} = \frac{52}{300}$$
$$n \approx 0.173 = 17.3\%$$

45. 6.3% of 4800
$$6.3\% \times 4800 = n$$
$$0.063 \times 4800 = n$$
$$n = 302.4$$

46.
$$\frac{58}{100} = \frac{145}{b}$$
$$58 \times b = 100 \times 145$$
$$\frac{58 \times b}{58} = \frac{14,500}{58}$$
$$b = 250$$

47. 126% of 3400
$$126\% \times 3400 = n$$
$$1.26 \times 3400 = n$$
$$n = 4284$$

48. $11,800 - 0.08(11,800) = 11,800 - 944 = 10,856$
She paid $10,856 for the car.

49.
$$\frac{28}{100} = \frac{1260}{b}$$
$$28 \times b = 100 \times 1260$$
$$\frac{28 \times b}{28} = \frac{126,000}{28}$$
$$b = 4500$$
4500 students are in the student body.

50. Difference = $11.28 - 8.40 = 2.88$
$$\text{percent} = \frac{2.88}{8.40} \approx 0.343 = 34.3\%$$
The percent increase is 34.3%.

51. $17 \text{ qt} \times \dfrac{1 \text{ gallon}}{4 \text{ quarts}} = 4.25 \text{ gallons}$

52. $3.25 \text{ tons} \times \dfrac{2000 \text{ lb}}{1 \text{ ton}} = 6500 \text{ lb}$

53. $16 \text{ ft} \times \dfrac{12 \text{ in.}}{1 \text{ ft}} = 192 \text{ in.}$

54. $5.6 \text{ km} = 5600 \text{ m}$

55. $6.98 \text{ g} = 0.0698 \text{ kg}$

56. $2.48 \text{ ml} = 0.00248 \text{ L}$

57. $12 \text{ mi} \times \dfrac{1.61 \text{ km}}{1 \text{ mi}} = 19.32 \text{ km}$

58. $0.00063182 = 6.3182 \times 10^{-4}$

59. $126,400,000,000 = 1.264 \times 10^{11}$

60. 0.623 cm + 0.74 cm + 0.0428 cm
$= 0.623 \text{ cm} + 0.74 \text{ cm} + 0.00428 \text{ cm}$
$= 1.36728 \text{ cm thick}$

61. $P = 2l + 2w = 2(6) + 2(1.2) = 12 + 2.4 = 14.4 \text{ m}$

62. $P = 82 + 13 + 98 + 13 = 206 \text{ cm}$

63. $A = \dfrac{bh}{2} = \dfrac{6(1.8)}{2} = 5.4 \text{ sq ft}$

64. $A = \dfrac{h(b+B)}{2} = \dfrac{7.5(8+12)}{2} = \dfrac{7.5(20)}{2} = 75 \text{ sq m}$

65. $A = \pi r^2 = 3.14(6)^2 \approx 113.04 \text{ sq m}$

66. $C = 2\pi r$
$$C = 2(3.14)\left(\frac{18}{2}\right) = 56.52 \text{ m}$$

67. $V = \dfrac{\pi r^2 h}{3} = \dfrac{\pi(4)^2(10)}{3} \approx 167.46 \text{ cu cm}$

68. $V = \dfrac{12(19)(2.7)}{3} = 205.2$
205.2 cu ft

69. Total area = Area of square + Area of triangle

$$= s^2 + \frac{bh}{2}$$

$$= (5)^2 + \frac{3(5)}{2}$$

$$= 32.5 \text{ sq m}$$

70.
$$\frac{n}{130} = \frac{30}{120}$$
$$n \times 120 = 30 \times 130$$
$$\frac{n \times 120}{120} = \frac{3900}{120}$$
$$n = 32.5$$

71. There was 8 million dollars in profit.

72. $9 - 8 = 1$
The profits were greater by one million dollars.

73. Find the height of the line at 1980: 50°F

74. The line is the steepest going down from left to right: from 1990 to 2000.

75. Find the height of the bar representing 17–22: 600 students are between 17–22 years old.

76. Add the heights of the bars for 23–28 and 29–34.
$10 + 4 = 14$
1400 students

77. Mean $= \dfrac{8 + 12 + 16 + 17 + 20 + 22}{6} \approx 15.83$

Median $= \dfrac{16 + 17}{2} = 16.5$

78. $\sqrt{49} + \sqrt{81} = 7 + 9 = 16$

79. $\sqrt{123} \approx 11.091$

80. hypotenuse $= \sqrt{9^2 + 12^2}$
$= \sqrt{81 + 144}$
$= \sqrt{225}$
$= 15 \text{ feet}$

81. $-8 + (-2) + (-3) = -10 + (-3) = -13$

82. $-\dfrac{1}{4} + \dfrac{3}{8} = -\dfrac{1}{4} \times \dfrac{2}{2} + \dfrac{3}{8} = -\dfrac{2}{8} + \dfrac{3}{8} = \dfrac{-2+3}{8} = \dfrac{1}{8}$

83. $9 - 12 = 9 + (-12) = -3$

84. $-20 - (-3) = -20 + 3 = -17$

85. $2(-3)(4)(-1) = -6(4)(-1) = -24(-1) = 24$

86. $-\dfrac{2}{3} \div \dfrac{1}{4} = -\dfrac{2}{3} \times \dfrac{4}{1} = -\dfrac{8}{3}$ or $-2\dfrac{2}{3}$

87. $(-16) \div (-2) + (-4) = 8 + (-4) = 4$

88. $12 - 3(-5) = 12 + 15 = 27$

89. $7 - (-3) + 12 \div (-6) = 7 + 3 + (-2) = 10 + (-2) = 8$

90. $\dfrac{(-3)(-1) + (-4)(2)}{(0)(6) + (-5)(2)} = \dfrac{3 + (-8)}{0 + (-10)} = \dfrac{-5}{-10} = \dfrac{1}{2}$ or 0.5

91. $5x - 3y - 8x - 4y = 5x - 8x - 3y - 4y = -3x - 7y$

92. $5 + 2a - 8b - 12 - 6a - 9b$
$= 5 + (-12) + 2a + (-6a) + (-8b) + (-9b)$
$= -7 - 4a - 17b$

93. $-2(x - 3y - 5) = -2(x) + (-2)(-3y) + (-2)(-5)$
$= -2x + 6y + 10$

94. $-2(4x + 2) - 3(x + 3y) = -8x - 4 - 3x - 9y$
$= -11x - 9y - 4$

95.
$$5 - 4x = -3$$
$$5 + (-5) - 4x = -3 + (-5)$$
$$-4x = -8$$
$$\frac{-4x}{-4} = \frac{-8}{-4}$$
$$x = 2$$

96.
$$5 - 2(x - 3) = 15$$
$$5 - 2x + 6 = 15$$
$$-2x + 11 = 15$$
$$-2x + 11 + (-11) = 15 + (-11)$$
$$-2x = 4$$
$$\frac{-2x}{-2} = \frac{4}{-2}$$
$$x = -2$$

97.
$$7 - 2x = 10 + 4x$$
$$7 - 2x + (-4x) = 10 + 4x + (-4x)$$
$$7 - 6x = 10$$
$$7 + (-7) - 6x = 10 + (-7)$$
$$-6x = 3$$
$$\frac{-6x}{-6} = \frac{3}{-6}$$
$$x = -\frac{3}{6}$$
$$x = -\frac{1}{2} \text{ or } x = -0.5$$

98.
$$-3(x + 4) = 2(x - 5)$$
$$-3x - 12 = 2x - 10$$
$$-3x + 3x - 12 = 2x + 3x - 10$$
$$-12 = 5x - 10$$
$$-12 + 10 = 5x - 10 + 10$$
$$-2 = 5x$$
$$\frac{-2}{5} = \frac{5x}{5}$$
$$-\frac{2}{5} = x \text{ or } x = -0.4$$

99. x = number of students taking math
$x + 12$ = number of students taking history
$2x$ = number of students taking psychology
$$x + (x + 12) + 2x = 452$$
$$4x + 12 = 452$$
$$4x + 12 + (-12) = 452 + (-12)$$
$$4x = 440$$
$$\frac{4x}{4} = \frac{440}{4}$$
$$x = 110$$
math = 110
history = 110 + 12 = 122
psychology = 2(110) = 220

100. x = width
$2x + 5$ = length
$$2(x) + 2(2x + 5) = 106$$
$$2x + 4x + 10 = 106$$
$$6x + 10 = 106$$
$$6x + 10 + (-10) = 106 + (-10)$$
$$6x = 96$$
$$\frac{6x}{6} = \frac{96}{6}$$
$$x = 16$$
width = 16 m
length = 2(16) + 5 = 37 m

WITCC